The Crucial Years of Early Anglo-Chinese Relations 1750-1800

by Earl H. Pritchard

1970
OCTAGON BOOKS
New York

Originally published 1936

Reprinted 1970
by special arrangement with Earl H. Pritchard

OCTAGON BOOKS
A DIVISION OF FARRAR, STRAUS & GIROUX, INC.
19 Union Square West
New York, N. Y. 10003

LIBRARY OF CONGRESS CATALOG CARD NUMBER: 78-96191

Printed in U.S.A. by
NOBLE OFFSET PRINTERS, INC.
NEW YORK 3, N. Y.

A la mémoire de
H. B. MORSE,
et de
W. E. SOOTHILL,
mes maîtres regrettés

PREFACE

Most of the material contained in the present study of Anglo-Chinese relations between 1750 and 1800 was originally submitted as a thesis in partial fulfillment of the degree of Doctor of Philosophy at Oxford University in 1933. The study was undertaken as a sequel to a work on Anglo-Chinese relations during the seventeenth and eighteenth centuries and as a forerunner of a study of their relations during the early nineteenth century. The period discussed in the present work has been touched upon to a minor degree by nearly every writer who deals in any way with the foreign or commercial relations of China during the late eighteenth or early nineteenth centuries. Practically all of them, however, give the period no more than a passing glance and need be given only minor consideration when a judgment is formed. A number of works written by contemporaries touch to a greater or lesser degree upon the period, and there are several works upon the Macartney Embassy written by persons who accompanied the mission. These contemporary works, however, must be considered as source materials from which to derive information and not as analytical studies of the period.

James Bromley Eames's *The English in China, 1600-1843* (1909) devotes about fifty pages to the period which is the subject of the present study. Not one word of what he has to say relative to this period is based on manuscript source material, although he constantly refers to a manuscript in the India Office, *Memoir: Intercourse with China*. This memoir was published with some additions in 1834 by Peter Auber, Secretary at the India House, under the title *China, an Outline of its Government, Law, and Policy*, and covers the whole period of Anglo-Chinese relations from 1635 until 1834 in a summary way. In 1908 Helen M. Robbins published a work entitled *Our First Ambassador to China*, which at first glance might seem to be a recent study of the Macartney Embassy. It, however, proves to be a life of Lord Macartney illustrated by letters and papers. The story of the China Embassy is told in the words of his *Journal*, written during the course of the Embassy and first published in John Barrow's *Account of the Public Life and a Selection from the Unpublished Writings of the Earl of Macartney* in 1807. Robbins' edition is an improved and more reliable version than Barrow's and as such is an invaluable source book.

Doctor H. B. Morse covers the period in a summary way in the early chapters of his authoritative and well-known *International Relations of the Chinese Empire.* The early chapters of this work are not based upon manuscript materials, and serve as an introduction to the later part of his work rather than as a final analysis of the period with which I propose to deal. Doctor Morse's *Chronicles of the East India Company Trading to China, 1635-1834* (1926-1929) summarizes, as nearly in the language of the supercargoes as possible, the political and commercial relations of the East India Company with China as contained in over three hundred manuscript volumes at the India Office. The work is a marvellously complete and concise abstract of the documentary and statistical information contained in these volumes, and as such is more of a source book and guide to future students than a finished study of Anglo-Chinese relations during the period.

Since Doctor Morse's last volume was written, some five volumes of *Court Letters* (letters sent from the Court of Directors to the supercargoes in China) covering the years 1784 to 1800 have been added to the India Office, and the greater part of the material contained in the four bulky volumes dealing with the Cathcart and Macartney Embassies was not used by Doctor Morse. In the Wason Collection on China at Cornell University are ten large manuscript volumes of *Macartney Correspondence*—private and heretofore unused papers of Lord Macartney—dealing almost entirely with the Embassy. There are also at Cornell a number of other manuscript materials belonging to the Macartney Collection which are not to be found in the India Office. Because of these unused manuscript sources and because the *Chronicles* are more source material than a final analytical study of Anglo-Chinese relations, there obviously is ample need for a study such as the present one.

In this work I have tried as far as possible not to duplicate the work done by Doctor Morse in the *Chronicles,* and, where our work has overlapped, I have relied implicitly upon the information in the *Chronicles,* so long as their statement was complete enough for my purpose. In the light of these considerations I trust that the present work will find a place as a complete and balanced study of Anglo-Chinese relations during the crucial years from 1750 to 1800. Every primary and secondary published source of information available in English, French, and German, as well as a number of translations from Chinese writers and collections of edicts and state papers has been considered along with the manuscript materials, in the hope of making the present study as complete, well balanced, and authoritative as possible.

With a deep sense of humility and appreciation, I record my debt to the late Doctor H. B. Morse and the late Professor W. E. Soothill, who not only read and constructively criticized the original manuscript but as friends and masters gave stimulation and encouragement. My only regret is that they are unable to see the completed work. To Dr. Cyrus H. Peake of Columbia University, Doctor Arthur W. Hummel of the Library of Congress, and Professor E. L. Woodward of All Souls College, Oxford, all of whom read all or part of the manuscript, I am deeply indebted for many valuable suggestions. It is a pleasure to record my thanks to Mr. W. T. Ottewill, Keeper of the India Office Records, Doctor H. N. Randle, Head of the India Office Library, and their assistants for the facility and courtesy offered me in the use of the India Office records. I wish especially to register my appreciation of the invaluable assistance offered at many times by Miss Gussie Gaskill, Curator of the Wason Collection at Cornell ,and to thank her for a number of translations from the Chinese which she made for me with the assistance of Mr. Chou Ch'eng-yao. Mr. Tai Jen and Mr. J. C. Yang of the Library of Congress have also assisted with a number of translations. For their assistance in reading and correcting the manuscript, I am much indebted to Doctor Paul P. Kies, Editor-in-Chief of *Research Studies of the State College of Washington*, Doctor Harry F. Clements of the State College of Washington, Doctor Calvin S. Brown, a comrade in foreign lands, and to Mae.

Pullman, Washington   E. H. P.
August, 1936

CONTENTS

LIST OF FIGURES

MONEYS, WEIGHTS, AND MEASURES

MONEYS

The tael (T. or Tls.), the basic unit of Chinese currency at Canton, was a hypothetical coin of pure silver weighing 1.208 oz. The only circulating Chinese coin was the copper cash. The basic circulating coin in foreign commerce was the Spanish dollar, with an intrinsic value of 4s. 2d. (4/2), and an exchange value ranging from 5s. 2d. upwards. Between 1619 and 1814 it was invoiced at 5s. in the East India Company's accounts and was packed in chests containing $4,000, or £1,000. The dollar ($) referred to throughout the present work is always the Spanish dollar. The equivalents generally used in the accounts are given below:

10 cash = 1 candareen
10 candareen = 1 mace
10 mace = 1 tael
1 tael = £⅓ or 6s. 8d. or $1.388 or C.R. 3.06 or Pa. 0.83
1 dollar = T. 0.72 or 5s. or C.R. 2.50 or Pa. 0.666
1 pound = T. 3 or $4 or C.R. 10 or Pa. 2.50
1 pagoda = 8s. or $1.50 or T. 1.20
1 current rupee = 2s. or $0.40 or T. 0.326
1 Bombay, Arcot, or sicca rupee = 2s. 3d.

WEIGHTS

1 tael = 1⅓ oz. av. or 579.85 grains or 37.783 grammes
16 taels = 1 catty or 1⅓ lb. av. or 604.53 grammes
100 catties = 1 picul or 133⅓ lbs. av. or 60.453 kilogrammes
1 picul = 133⅓ lbs. or 1⅕ cwt. English or 1⅓ cwt. American
1 long ton = 16.8 piculs
1 short ton = 15 piculs
1 metric ton = 16.54 piculs

MEASURES

1 *ch'ih,* covid, or cubit = 14.1 inches
10 *ch'ih* = 1 *chang* or 141 inches
1 *li* = ⅓ mile or ½ kilometer

LIST OF ABBREVIATIONS OF MANUSCRIPTS

C — Cornell University
IO — India Office
BM — British Museum
PRO — Public Record Office
PP — Parliamentary Papers
CMC — Cornell, *Macartney Correspondence*
CMD — Cornell, *Macartney Documents*
IOC — India Office, *China Factory Records*
IOCCD — India Office, *China: Canton Diaries*
IOCCC — India Office, *China: Canton Consultations*
IOCCE — India Office, *China: Cathcart Embassy*
IOCM — India Office, *China: Macartney Embassy*
WSCPMD — Washington State College, *Pritchard Collection of Macartney Documents on China*

ERRATA

Page 345, footnote 91. Insert *Tsung* after *Kao*.
Page 379, footnote 79. For *Mémoires* read *Mèmoires*.

CHAPTER I

INTRODUCTION

1. *A Point of -View Toward History.*

History may be, as Voltaire with witty satire put it, a pack of lies agreed to; and it must ever be, despite the assurances of the so-called scientific historians, more or less a tangle of falsehoods and misconceptions. The more standardized and "scientific" it becomes, the nearer it approximates the caustic epigram of the eighteenth century wit; but the less cultivated and systematized one finds its fields, the nearer to a tangled web of nonsense it comes. Thus, caught between the upper mill-stone of untruth and the nether mill-stone of incoherence, the would-be writer of history can find relief from his dilemma only through a strategic retreat behind the sheltering cover of a conception which has during the present century taken its place among the permanent dogmas of our society—relativity. If the great field of natural science has at last been forced to accept the relativity of its most basic principles, how much more must history, the twin brother of literature and art, seek its apology and justification in this great conception of the twentieth century.

If "past politics" does not accurately define the nature and scope of history, no more does the meaningless and almost mystical "web of interrelated social, economic, political, and intellectual forces" so commonly used by modern writers in explaining history. It is beyond a doubt inclusive of all these, but it is more. It can never be reduced to the ordered accuracy of the natural sciences; only the individual facts which compose it can be brought after infinite toil and care to this exactness. But history left in this state is chaos, lacking a single distinguishing mark except its own confusion. The larger conception— the framework into which these facts are to be fitted and the arrangement of the facts within it—must forever be the artistic creation of the mind of the writer. Thus, in its final analysis, history can be nothing more than the orderly arrangement of carefully selected and individually unimpeachable facts into a grand design or conception—a picture which to the writer, and to him alone, is the true tableau of the past as he sees it from his point of perspective. It is an art rather than a science.

If, then, the writing of the history of one's own society presents difficulties innumerable, far more thorny is the path of him who aspires to write the story of cultures widely divergent from his own; and he who attempts to study the relations of two cultures is placed in the hopeless position of trying at the same time to interpret his own, which he never fully understands, and to do justice to the foreign culture, which he can never completely assimilate. He may, therefore, ask the indulgence of critical readers if at times he seems to be "walking the night," for he is indeed "wandering between two worlds."

It has become a first principle among certain historians of today to lay the basis of all they say on the "firm" foundation of economic fact in the belief that only in the economic urges of man can one find the true motive forces of group life. If the carrying of this principle to an absurd length is a detriment rather than a help to the interpretation of Western society, it must be used with even more care in dealing with the relations between a Western nation and an Oriental civilization. It must not be overlooked or mitigated in any way, for the more one studies the Chinese merchants and mandarins the more convinced one becomes that they were motivated no less by economic motives than were the Western traders; but one must remember that the ideology of their civilization looked askance upon the commercial motive. This peculiar point of view which made the mandarins speak with one voice on economic matters and yet act in an almost directly opposite way, illustrates the complete difference between the cultural and social institutions, ideas, and points of view of the Oriental and the Occidental, which must be carefully weighed and considered in dealing with the relations between England and China.

2. *Cultural Difficulties Complicating the Relations between China and the West.*

Though a detailed analysis of the cultural difference between England and China is not essential, it seems advisable to point out at the beginning the major points of contrast which complicated the relations between the two peoples. By far the most serious difficulty arose over the idea of equality. This was really caused by the different course of historical evolution through which the two states had gone. England was one of a group of sister states which together made up the relatively new and dynamic Western civilization. Toward the close of the eighteenth century, the Industrial Revolution was infusing into England the energy which was to make her the outstanding representative of Western civilization in the field of commercial and economic expansion. Furthermore, the fact that European states had for centuries lived as a family of nations had led them to build up a system of international law to guide their conduct toward one another. Each nation recognized the other as its theoretical equal in law, and expected its nationals and representatives to be treated as such by outside nations.

In the Orient all was different. China was not one of a group of equal states. She was the Middle Kingdom—a centuries-old civilization which had slowly spread itself over the whole of eastern Asia. Her expansive and creative force had been largely spent in the absorption of the outer peoples who had been either brought within or made tributary to the mother culture. Although a rudimentary conception of the equality of states and of international law had developed in China during the pre-Ch'in period (*Ca.* 1050-221 B. C.), the growth of the Empire caused the disappearance of such ideas.[1] In the eighteenth century China had no conception of equal and independent states and considered outside people as barbarians who should be taught respect for the Middle Kingdom. Against this super-civilized, self-esteeming civilization, ruled by bigoted and self-satisfied mandarins, came a young, virile, and self-confident people who expected to be treated as equals. The advance agents of Western civilization were ambitious and unrefined traders who overstepped barriers and trampled on sacred traditions in their search for commerce. They disregarded dignity, respect for tradition, and quiet, inactive contemplation—things of utmost importance to the scholar-mandarins—and hence were treated with the contemptuous patronage which "immature and uncivilized" peoples deserved.

Out of these circumstances arose the basic conflict over equality. Following out the logic of their thinking, the mandarins at Canton refused to recognize traders and diplomatic officials as their equals and treated them in a most arrogant and cavalier fashion. Communications had to be sent to officials in the form of petitions through the Hong merchants, personal audiences were seldom allowed, haven was refused to foreign ships of war, foreigners were confined to the restricted area of the factories, and new restraints were constantly being heaped upon them. The Imperial government, after a period of vacillation during the late Ming and early Ch'ing periods, finally restricted trade to the

---

[1] Roswell S. Britton, "Chinese Interstate Intercourse before 700 B. C.," *American Journal of International Law*, XXIX (October, 1935), 616-35; E. D. Thomas, *Chinese Political Thought* (New York, 1927), Chap. XV.

single city of Canton, on the outskirts of the Empire, where it was conducted under very onerous conditions. Moreover, it refused to allow foreigners to enter the Empire to study or visit, and treated embassies as tribute missions. This difficulty over equality was apparent from the first, but, as the years passed and the arrogance and abusiveness of the mandarins increased and the value and volume of foreign trade expanded, the Chinese attitude became intolerable to the Westerners.

A second source of trouble arose out of the subjection of the mercantile classes to the ruling classes in China. In England the aristocratic landed interests were balanced against the commercial and industrial bourgeoisie, and the latter were strong enough to bring the government into their service. In China, on the other hand, the scholar-mandarins with their arrogant conservatism and their profound admiration for Chinese culture reigned supreme. The merchants ranked near the bottom of the social scale, and trade was not considered a basic means of improving national welfare.[2] In the eighteenth century the central government disregarded trade as much as possible and left it to be regulated by the provincial mandarins, who, being poorly paid, subject to heavy demands from superior officials, and extremely self-important, loaded it with fees and charges and oppressed the merchants.

Foreign traders were treated with the same contempt and disregard as were the Chinese merchants and when they objected the mandarins were dismayed, irritated, and unable to understand the reason for such unsubmissive behavior. Such action ran counter to the strictly regimented system of Chinese society, in which the mandarins at the top of the pyramid were to be respected and obeyed. Had there existed in China a politically powerful and influential mercantile class which could have resisted official despotism and bureaucratic stagnation, and could this class have asserted its rights to be heard in the council chambers of the nation, one of the major causes of the difficulties between England and China would have been eliminated.

---

[2] Cf. G. F. Hudson, *Europe and China* (London, 1931), pp. 264-66. It should not be assumed that the Chinese government and officials always took an unfavorable attitude toward trade. During the southern Sung and early Ming periods they definitely encouraged foreign trade. See Chang Teh-ch'ang, "Maritime Trade at Canton during the Ming Period," *Chinese Social and Political Science Review,* XVII (July, 1933), 264-82 and J. Kuwabara, "On P'u Shou-keng . . . Superintendent of the Trading Ship's Office . . . towards the end of the Sung Dynasty," *Memoirs of the Research Department of the Tôyô Bunko,* II (1928), 17-79.

A third important cause of trouble was the different attitudes toward justice. Laws in England during the eighteenth century were severe and often barbarous, but in so far as possible they were administered impartially and in such a way that only the guilty should suffer, after having been judged by a jury of their peers.[3] In China, on the other hand, the doctrine of responsibility made it necessary that someone must suffer, whether the guilty person or not, whenever a crime was committed. Their judicial procedure allowed torture to be used in order to extract confessions from suspects or damaging testimony from witnesses, and, in applying their not unreasonable laws to foreigners, they discriminated against the latter.[4] The chief laws with which foreigners came into contact may be briefly summarized:[5]

(1) Premeditated murder or killing by musket fire was punishable by decapitation, the most degrading of all executions.
(2) Killing in an affray, or upon suspicion of theft, or being an accessory to a murder was punishable by strangulation.
(3) Accidental wounding or killing was punishable by fines or types of corporal punishments depending upon the seriousness of the injury.
(4) Killing in lawful self-defense was justifiable and not punishable.

These laws were not unreasonable, but in their application to foreigners the Chinese worked upon the theory that

The barbarians are like beasts, and not to be ruled on the same principles as citizens. Were anyone to attempt controlling them by the great maxims of reason, it would tend to nothing but confusion. The ancient Kings well understood this, and accordingly ruled barbarians by misrule. Therefore to rule barbarians by misrule is the true and best way of ruling them.[6]

In 1743 it was ordered that all future cases between foreigners and natives, where offenders were likely to suffer death by strangulation or beheading, the case was to be tried by the district magistrate and reviewed by the Viceroy, but in minor cases the offenders were to be

---

[3] E. H. Parker, *China Past and Present* (London, 1903), pp. 309-10, 376-87, and *China, her History, Diplomacy, and Commerce* (London, 1917), p. 308; H. B. Morse, *International Relations of the Chinese Empire* (London, 1910), I, 110-17.

[4] Kenneth Scott Latourette, *The Chinese* (New York, 1934), II, 44-47; Hsieh Pao-chao, *The Government of China* (Baltimore, 1925), pp. 215-19; Samuel Wells Williams, *The Middle Kingdom* (New York, 1883), I, 384-93; T. R. Jernigan, *China in Law and Commerce* (New York, 1905), pp. 70-111; G. T. Staunton, *Miscellaneous Notices Relating to China* (Edinburgh, 1822-50), I, 387-402.

[5] G. T. Staunton, *Ta Tsing Leu Lee* (London, 1810), pp. 303-27; Charles Gutzlaff, *China Opened* (London, 1838), II, 78; H. B. Morse, *Chronicles of the East India Company Trading to China* (Oxford, 1926-29), II, 343.

[6] John Francis Davis, *The Chinese* (London, 1836), I, 66.

sent away to be punished by their own countrymen. In 1749 an edict of Ch'ien Lung stated that it was " 'incumbent to have life for life,'—in order to frighten and repress barbarians," for if only native laws were applied to them "the fierce and unruly dispositions of the foreigners [would] cease to be awed." [7] The Chinese adhered to this procedure in dealing with foreigners. The chief dispute arose with the English because the Chinese contended that most homicide cases fell under numbers one and two above, and that, if the guilty party were not produced, some persons connected with the English ship or factory must be held responsible. The English disavowed this personal responsibility for acts of others and generally held that the cases fell under numbers three and four above. After one submission to Chinese justice (the *Lady Hughes* affair, see Chap. V, Sec. 4) in 1784, the English thereafter refused to submit their nationals to the mercies of a Chinese magistrate.

The final disturbing element was the very different mentality of the two peoples as expressed in their civilizations. By this is not meant that one people was inferior to the other mentally, but simply that they thought and acted in a way almost directly opposed to one another. This may have been partially caused by the great difference in the character of their respective languages, but was more largely the result of divergent and separated courses of cultural evolution. They started with different premises in their thinking, their thought patterns were divergent, their objectives were opposite, and their ultimate sense of values was antagonistic. This is seen in their ideas of justice, in their attitudes toward trade and commerce, in their divergent attitude toward new ideas and the use of applied science, in their unrelated ideas of art, beauty, and music, and finally in their different conception of personal responsibility. The whole thing was unwittingly summed up by Sherard Osborn, writing in 1860.[8] He takes the first eleven pages of his book to damn the characteristics of Chinese reasoning which always made them answer "Me no thinke so" to the conclusions of Englishmen.

---

[7] *Ibid.*, I, 414-20; Staunton, *Ta Tsing Leu Lee*, pp. 36, 515-23; Gutzlaff, *China Opened*, II, 78.

[8] Sherard Osborn, *Past and Future of British Relations with China* (Edinburgh, 1860). Besides the works already mentioned, the following are very helpful in forming an idea of Chinese civilization during the eighteenth and early nineteenth centuries: W. H. Medhurst, *China* (London, 1838); Jean Baptiste Du Halde, *Description . . . de l'empire de la Chine* (Paris, 1735); Laurence Binyon's "Introduction" to *Chinese Art*, ed. by Leigh Ashton (London, 1935); Bernhard Karlgren, *Sound and Symbol in Chinese* (London, 1923).

Captain Osborn and his statement represent a perfect example of this different mentality and the difficulties arising from it.

From the foregoing analysis it becomes apparent that the basic institutions, attitudes, and thoughts of the Chinese and English were widely separated and often diametrically opposed. With so few common grounds on which to tread, it is easy to understand why constant misunderstandings and difficulties arose. The desire for trade and the mutual advantages which each nation gained from an introduction of the products of the other was almost their only common link; but the Chinese government's outward contempt for commerce and the vast differences in the economic structures of the two nations rendered smooth co-operation upon even this matter difficult. Viewed from this angle, the early relations between England and China take on primarily the character of contact and conflict between two cultures, and, unless interpreted in this light, they cannot be properly understood. Trade was their common interest; it brought them together and therefore the main difficulties arose over matters pertaining to trade. But deep down beneath the purely commercial element of every dispute—tinging, colouring, directing, even creating it—were fundamentally different attitudes, senses of value, thought processes and objectives—the struggle of culture against culture.

3. *Résumé of the Commercial and Cultural Relations between England and China prior to 1750.*

The people of Elizabethan England probably exhibited more interest in China—or Cathay, as they called it—than did Englishmen of any succeeding period prior to the middle of the eighteenth century.[9] The Renaissance spirit of adventure, internal economic development, the possibilities of the spice trade, and the desire for personal gain and glory combined at this period to create in Englishmen a desire to investigate the strange, almost mythical land of Marco Polo with its fabulous riches. Several unsuccessful expeditions were sent out during the last half of the sixteenth century to discover a northwest or northeast passage to Cathay, and in 1582 and 1596 expeditions at-

---

[9] For a detailed survey of the early relations between England and China, see Morse, *Chronicle*, I, *passim*; E. H. Pritchard, *Anglo-Chinese Relations during the Seventeenth and Eighteenth Centuries* (Urbana, Illinois, 1929), pp. 42-132; Peter Auber, *China* (London, 1834), pp. 130-170; J. B. Eames, *The English in China* (London, 1909), pp. 1-85; A. J. Sargent, *Anglo-Chinese Commerce and Diplomacy* (London, 1907), pp. 1ff.

tempted to reach China by the route around Africa. Interest, however, shifted from Cathay to the East Indies as more definite information of the seaways and the great opportunities of the spice trade reached England through the voyages of Drake, Cavendish, and Lancaster, and the capture of several Portuguese spice ships. The union of the Spanish and Portuguese Crowns (1580) and the defeat of the Armada also opened the colonial empire of Portugal to British attacks, and the exclusion of England and Holland from the Lisbon spice market in 1594 made the question of reaching the East Indies an especially urgent one. The final impetus which brought about England's entrance into the India trade was the raising of the price of pepper from 3/0 (3 shillings) to 6/0 and 8/0 per pound by the Dutch, who had been fast absorbing the spice trade.[10]

In 1599 a group of London merchants, meeting in Founders Hall, organized an association to trade with the East and combat the Dutch, and on the 31st day of December, 1600, they were incorporated as "The Governor and Company of Merchants of London, trading into the East Indies." The Company thus formed consisted of 215 knights, aldermen, and merchants, and was capitalized at £57,543. It was to be managed by a governor and twenty-four committees (persons) and was granted a monopoly for fifteen years of all English trade eastward from the Cape of Good Hope to the Straits of Magellan.[11] The formation of the East India Company brought into existence the institution that was not only to open British trade with China, but to control it until 1833—an institution which guarded zealously its right to the exclusive trade of the regions, served as the representative of the British nation in all matters relating to China, and opposed both public and

---

[10] Cf. John Bruce, *Annals of the East India Company* (London, 1810), I, 1-125; Sir William W. Hunter, *History of British India* (London, 1899), I, 196-235; W. H. Woodward, *The Expansion of the British Empire* (Cambridge, 1919), pp. 9-75; James A. Williamson, *History of British Expansion* (New York, 1922), pp. 12-125; David Macpherson, *History of European Commerce with India* (London, 1812), pp. 72ff.; Sir William Foster, *England's Quest for Eastern Trade* (London, 1933), *passim*; *Calendars of State Papers, Colonial Series: East Indies, 1513-1616*, ed. by W. N. Sainsbury (London, 1862), *passim*.

[11] MSS. India Office, *Court Book*, I. This is printed verbatim in Henry Stevens, *Dawn of the British Trade to the East Indies, 1599-1603* (London, 1886). Manuscript copies of the charter are to be found in the India Office (MSS. *Parchment Records*, No. 2) and the British Museum (MSS. *Harleian*, No. 306, f. 17-25) and the published charter may be found in *Charters Granted to the East India Company* (London, about 1774) and Samuel Purchas, *Purchas His Pilgrimes* (London, 1625), I, 139-47. India Office is hereafter abbreviated IO and British Museum BM.

private interference which would in any way infringe upon its privileges. This fact in large part accounts for the lethargic growth of British public and official interest in matters relating to China.

In 1613 the Company established a factory at Firando (Hirado) in Japan to serve as a base for attempts to open trade with China. But the negotiations which Richard Cox (factor at Firando between 1615 and 1622) carried on with several Chinese merchants for the purpose of opening trade with China came to naught, and after the Amboyna Massacre in 1623 the factory was withdrawn from Japan.[12] The records of the Court of Directors show that the Company maintained a constant hope that China might be opened as a market for English woollens and a purchasing place for silk, and in 1635, after a "Truce and Free Trade to China" had been entered into between the English and Portuguese factories in India, the first British ship (*London*) was sent to Macao from India. Two years later four interloping ships under the direction of Captain Weddell arrived at Macao. After considerable difficulties with the Portuguese and Chinese, they proceeded to Canton, disposed of their cargoes, and obtained an agreement allowing future trade and residence.[13] The financial weakness of the Company, the hostility of the Dutch and Portuguese, the competition of various interloping groups, and the belief that the Chinese were hostile to foreign trade prevented the Company from making any serious efforts to establish a trade with China during the next thirty-five years. Two ships, the *Hinde* in 1644 and the *Surat* in 1664, were sent to Macao from the Company's factories in India without success, and at least five interloping ships are reported as having been at Macao during the period.[14]

---

[12] Ernest M. Satow, *The Voyage of Captain John Saris to Japan, 1613* (London, 1900), *passim*; Richard Cox, *Diary, 1615-22* (London, 1883), *passim*; M. Paske-Smith, *Western Barbarians in Japan and Formosa in Tokugawa Days* (Kobe, 1930), pp. 1-64; Chozo Muto, "A Brief Survey of the History of Anglo-Japanese Relations," *Kaikoku Bunkwa* (Osaka, 1929), pp. 419-55. This last article is in Japanese with many English notes.

[13] *Court Minutes of the East India Company, 1635-39*, ed. by E. B. Sainsbury (Oxford, 1907), I, 118-19, 124-31, 275-76; *The English Factories in India, 1634-36*, ed. by Sir William Foster (Oxford, 1911), V, 211, 226-30; Peter Mundy, *Travels of ...*, ed. by Sir Richard C. Temple (Hakluyt Society Publications, New Series, Nos. 45 and 46, London, 1919), III, Pt. 1, pp. 158-316 and Pt. 2, pp. 429-531; Morse, *Chronicle*, I, 14-30.

[14] *Factories in India, 1642-45*, VII, 179-80, 254; *ibid.*, *1655-60*, X, 49, 60-61, 76-77, 119, 133, 142, 152, 160-61, 196, 203, 206, 312; *ibid.*, *1665-67*, XII, 7; *Court Minutes, 1655-59*, V, 26, 206n; Morse, *Chronicle*, I, 31-35.

With the granting of new charters to the Company in 1657 by Cromwell and in 1661 by Charles II, its fortunes took an upward turn. Interloping activity was suppressed, Dutch competition was weakened by the Navigation Acts and foreign wars, Portuguese hostility was allayed by commercial agreements, and the Indian factories were more firmly established. Under these circumstances the Company began to look toward China as a market and a place of trade. Unfortunately for the continued success of these early attempts, the English chose to establish their factories under the protection of the last remaining adherents of the vanquished Ming Dynasty, who controlled the Island of Formosa and a small bit of territory on the adjacent mainland. A factory was established at Taiwan (on the Island of Formosa) by voyages in 1670 and 1672, and one was opened at Amoy in 1676. The conquest of Formosa by the Manchus led to the abandonment of the Taiwan factory in 1686, despite the edict of Kang Hsi in 1685 opening all Chinese ports to foreign trade. The establishment at Amoy continued a desultory existence, twelve ships going there between 1676 and 1698. In 1672 a factory was also established in Tongking as a base for the indirect silk trade with China.[15]

Unsuccessful attempts were made in 1673, 1683, and 1689 to establish a factory at Canton, which was then under the control of the Manchus. In 1698, however, a new India Company, known as the English Company, was established by act of Parliament, and in 1699 the *Macclesfield,* sent by it, opened a successful factory at Canton. The following year the *Trumball* and the *Eaton,* sent by the new Company, anchored at Chusan and initiated a trade there under the direction of Allen Catchpoole, president of the English Company's supercargoes and His Majesty's Consul-General for the Empire of China. For a few years the London and English Companies carried on a bitter competition, which was, generally speaking, beneficial in stimulating the China trade, and with the agreement for their union in 1702 (completed in 1708), the China trade may be said to have been firmly established. Because of the more favorable possibilities for trade at Canton, the other factories were gradually abandoned (Tongking, 1697; Amoy,

---

[15] IO, *Chinese Factory Records: China Materials,* I, 76-82ff. and II, III, IV, V, *passim,* and *China: Amoy,* XVI, *passim,* and *China: Tonquin and Cochin China,* XVII, *passim*; *Court Minutes, 1671-73,* IX, vii-viii; Morse, *Chronicle,* I, 36-65; Eames, *op. cit.,* pp. 30-40; Paske-Smith, *op. cit.,* pp. 82-122. Hereafter the China manuscripts in the India Office will be abbreviated IOC or as otherwise indicated in the list of abbreviations at the beginning of the Volume.

1707), and with the ending of the factory at Chusan in 1710, Canton remained the only port (except Macao) where foreign trade was carried on.[16]

The first half of the eighteenth century witnessed four important developments in Anglo-Chinese relations. First, the gravitation of all trade to Canton. Second, the gradual expansion of trade, especially that in tea. Third, the development of a number of commercial institutions and practices and the growth of numerous impositions on trade and restrictions on the liberties of the traders which were to dominate the China trade prior to 1842. Fourth, the gradual increase of official hostility and avarice toward foreigners.

British tonnage at Canton increased from 250 in 1699 to about 4,000 in 1751; imports grew from £32,086 in 1699 to £161,092 in 1751, and the value of exports rose from T. 45,928 in 1699 to well over half a million taels (one pound equals three taels) by the middle of the century. The quantity of tea sold at the Company's sales in London increased from 91,183 lbs. in 1700 to 2,710,819 in 1751.[17]

Licensed pilots, linguists or interpreters, and compradores (persons who supplied the ships and factories with provisions) were in evidence from the first, and established factories owned and managed by Hong merchants (merchants licensed to trade with the foreigners), in which the foreign traders resided, were in evidence by 1720. The measurage fee or tonnage duty on vessels, which at first amounted to about three taels per ton, was increased prior to 1722, by a *cumshaw* or present charge amounting to T. 1,950 per ship, to over six taels per ton. The low Imperial import and export duties, which were at first paid directly by the foreign traders to the officials, were greatly increased by numerous impositions of the mandarins. By 1736 the merchants who traded with the foreigners were made responsible for the payment of the import and export duties. In 1703 a three per cent *ad valorem* levy on the value of exports in addition to the regular customs duties was imposed. The next year it was increased to four per cent, and shortly after 1718 it was raised to six per cent, the rate at which it remained until 1842. In 1728 a new ten per cent tax on imports and exports was

---

[16] IOC, IV, 41-90, and V, 602, 647-756, and XIV, *passim*; Morse, *Chronicle,* I, 78-153; 9 and 10 Will. III, cap. 44 for the statute creating the English Company.

[17] Morse, *Chronicle,* I, tables in the back; William Milburn, *Oriental Commerce* (London, 1813), II, 531-4; John Macgregor, *Commercial Statistics* (London, 1844-50), V, 58.

imposed by the Hoppo (Imperial customs officer), and continued to be paid through the Chinese merchants, despite the foreigners' protests, until it was abolished upon the accession of Ch'ien Lung in 1736.[18]

In 1720 the Hong merchants united into a corporate body called the Co-hong, which was abolished the following year because of the united protest of all the foreign traders. The Hong merchants, however, continued to dominate the foreign trade, and in 1728 the foreigners were ordered to confine their business to the respectable Hong merchants and to address the Viceroy only through them. These orders were not strictly enforced, but they constituted the first step in the establishment of the "security merchant" system which gradually shaped itself by 1740. By this system one of the Hong merchants was required to become security for the good behavior of a ship's company and for the prompt payment of the Imperial duties falling due upon the ship and her cargo. The system was disliked by the Chinese merchants because it subjected them to the exactions of the mandarins and by the foreigners because it compelled them to do most of their trading with the merchant who was security for the ship.[19]

In 1718 and again in 1729 the local Chinese officials granted the English virtual extraterritorial rights, but in the various homicide cases during the period the Chinese generally attempted to assert their sovereignty. In 1741 when the H.M.S. *Centurion* reached Canton she was at first refused permission to enter the inner waters, and it was only after a great deal of negotiation that she was allowed facilities for re-fitting.[20]

Prior to the middle of the eighteenth century neither the British nor the Chinese governments took much interest in the affairs of the other, and the public interest in the two nations was even less. The educated public in England showed a certain interest in such works as Le Comte's *Mémoires,* Du Halde's *Description . . . de l'empire*

---

[18] IOC, VII, VIII, *passim*; Morse, *Chronicle,* I, 139-40, 142, 150, 158, 175, 185, 189-92, 249, 259, and tables in the back; Charles Lockyer, *Trade in India* (London, 1711), pp. 98-188; Alexander Hamilton, *A New Account of the East Indies* (Edinburgh, 1727), II, Chaps. 50-52; Peter Osbeck, *Reise nach Ostindien und China* (Rostock, 1765), pp. 300ff.

[19] Henri Cordier, "Les marchands hanistes de Canton," *T'oung Pao,* Ser. II, Vol. III (1902), 37ff; H. B. Morse, *The Gilds of China* (New York, 1909), pp. 58ff; R. Montgomery Martin, *China, Political, Commercial and Social* (London, 1847), II, 10-14.

[20] Richard Walter, *A Voyage Round the World in the Years 1741-44 by George Anson* (London, 1748), I, Chaps. 7-10; G. W. Keeton, *The Development of Extraterritoriality in China* (London, 1928), I, 25-30.

de la Chine, and *Lettres édifiantes et curieuses,* but only about half a dozen works relating to China and written by Englishmen appeared before 1750.[21] The importation of Chinese silks, chinaware, and Chinese lacquer had begun to create a taste in England for Chinese articles, but as yet the Chinese vogue, represented in the rococo style in France, had not spread to England. The use of tea was really the only marked impression upon English life which contact with China had produced. The British government itself had absolutely nothing to do with Chinese affairs and was willing to leave the management of that distant outpost of trade to the East India Company. This state of affairs must be attributed to the great distance which separated the two Empires, the difficulty of obtaining information about China, the relative unimportance of Chinese affairs and trade to England as a whole, and the fact that private traders were excluded from China by the Company's monopoly.

The Chinese public, on the other hand, nursing its contented ignorance, was even more complacent about European affairs, and the self-satisfied Chinese government had no wish to soil its hands by stooping to petty commercial affairs with foreigners. The Peking government, therefore, not only adhered to the traditional policy of provincial autonomy so long as order was maintained, laws enforced, and taxes remitted, but insisted that the local officials should settle barbarian affairs. In turn the provincial officials tried to confine all contact with the Europeans to the Hong merchants and minor mandarins.

4. *A New Epoch in Anglo-Chinese Relations: the Problem of the Present Study.*

About the middle of the eighteenth century, Anglo-Chinese relations entered upon a new and more active era because of certain commercial-diplomatic developments at Canton and because of the spread of the

---

[21] Edmund Scott, *An exact discourse of the Subtilties, Fashons, Pollicies, Religion and Ceremonies of the East Indians, as well Chyneses as Jaudns, there abyding and dweling* (London, 1606) ; John Webb, *An Historical Essay Endeavoring a Probability that the Language of the Empire of China is the Primitive Language* (London, 1669) [this book reappeared in 1678 under the title *The Antiquity of China;* for a full discussion of this work, see Ch'ên Shou-yi, "John Webb: A Forgotten Page in the Early History of Sinology in Europe," *Chinese Social and Political Science Review,* XIX (October, 1935), 295-330] ; Thomas Salmon, *Modern History* (London, 1725), I ; Lockyer and Hamilton referred to in note 18. Lockyer and Hamilton were the only persons who had been to China. It should also be noted that a number of the best contemporary works on China written in French and Spanish were translated into English and circulated among educated people.

rococo influence from Continental Europe to England. So important were the developments at Canton between the years 1750 and 1800, that from our present perspective it is justifiable to call them the crucial years in early Anglo-Chinese relations. During these years the system of trade with China became so stereotyped and the Chinese attitude of arrogant exclusiveness became so evident that the continued commercial expansion of England made inevitable the conflict of later years between the two countries.

Such being the situation, the object of the present study is to review in detail the commercial and semi-diplomatic relations between England and China from the beginning of the new epoch about 1750 to the Macartney Embassy of 1793. The period is characterized by expansion of trade and peaceful efforts to break the rigor of the Canton system and penetrate the wall of Chinese exclusiveness. After the failure of the Macartney Embassy, the British gave up active efforts to produce fundamental changes in their relations with China by the diplomatic route, and life and trade at Canton settled into a fixed routine from which there was no escape except by force. To cover this period adequately, it will be necessary to note the system of trade at Canton as legalized and stereotyped between 1751 and 1761; the growth of British trade with China during the half century following 1750; the struggle between England and other European nations for control of the China trade; the increase of Anglo-Indian trade and relations with China; the influence of British commercial and industrial expansion and of European wars upon English and foreign trade at Canton; the development of commercial, legal, and political disputes between the British and Canton authorities; and the growth of an active governmental interest in Chinese affairs which culminated in the Cathcart and Macartney Embassies.

CHAPTER II

A CRUCIAL TEN YEARS — THE LEGALIZATION AND FIXATION OF THE CANTON SYSTEM (1751-1761)

1. *The Birth of British Cultural Interest in China (1750-1770).*

On the cultural and intellectual side the new era in Anglo-Chinese relations was marked by a brief period in which Chinese design was exceedingly popular and intense interest was shown in the study of Chinese literature and learning. The half century of trade had brought many material objects of Chinese design (porcelain, lacquered cabinets, fire screens, pictures, wallpaper, fans, umbrellas, etc.) to England, and these had encouraged a taste for Chinese things. Then, in the 1740's, the rococo influence, which drew much of its inspiration from China, entered England from France.[1] Although England generally lagged behind the Continent so far as Chinese influences were concerned, she led the way in the development of the Chinese garden, and, with the publication in 1750 of William Halfpenny's *New Designs for Chinese Temples, Triumphal Arches, Garden Seats, Palings, etc.* (enlarged to include inside decorations and garden design in 1751-52), the Chinese vogue may be said to have begun in England.

Both Halfpenny and William Chambers, the chief champion of the Chinese mode in gardening and country house architecture, undoubtedly drew much inspiration from Père Attiret's letter on the Emperor of China's garden at Peking, published in 1749, and first translated into English by Sir H. Beaumont (Joseph Spence) in 1752.[2] The ideas of Chambers, who spent a number of years at Canton studying Chinese architecture and gardening, are best set forth in *Designs of Chinese Buildings* (1757) and *A Dissertation on Oriental Gardening* (1772). In Kew Gardens, which he originally designed, one can still see the Chinese influence.[3] In the field of interior decoration and furni-

---

[1] Hudson, *op. cit.*, pp. 273-90; A. Reichwein, *China and Europe* (New York, 1925), *passim.*

[2] For Attiret's letter, see *Lettres édifiantes*, XXVII (Paris, 1749), 1-38; Spence's translation is in Robert Dodsley's *Fugitive Pieces* (London, 1752). For an excellent discussion of the subject see Ch'ên Shou-yi, "The Chinese Garden in Eighteenth Century England," *T'ien Hsia Monthly*, II (April, 1936), 321-39. See also Myra Reynolds, *The Treatment of Nature in English Poetry* (Chicago, 1909), pp. 271-72.

[3] William Chambers, *Plans . . . of the Gardens and Buildings at Kew in Surrey* (London, 1763).

ture design Thomas Chippendale[4] became the chief proponent of the rococo style, which is best illustrated in his *Gentleman and Cabinet-Maker's Directory,* first published in 1754.

The period also produced a number of compilations on history and travel relating to China written by Englishmen.[5] In the literary field Goldsmith's *Chinese Letters* (1760-61) attracted much attention, and Bishop Thomas Percy displayed considerable interest in China. In 1761 he edited the *Han Kiou Choaan or the Pleasing History,* a romance, the first Chinese translation of any consequence to appear in English. The four-volume edition of this work also included a collection of Chinese proverbs, the story of a Chinese play acted at Canton in 1719, and some fragments of Chinese poetry.[6] A year later Bishop Percy edited a number of *Miscellaneous Pieces Relating to the Chinese,* many of which were translated from the French. They included a new translation of Attiret's letter, Père Premare's translation of "The Little Orphan of the House of Chao" (a tragedy), a dissertation on the Chinese language, a discussion of Chinese drama, "Rules of Conduct by a Chinese Author," and a reprint of part of Chamber's *Designs.*

Members of the Royal Society also showed considerable interest in the possible connections between Chinese and Egyptian writing. In 1764 the Society sent a request to the Jesuits in China for information on this and other subjects and for "two good Dictionaries of the Chinese tongue & Characters with a litteral explanation annexed thereto"

---

[4] Oliver Brackett, *Thomas Chippendale: A Study of His Life, Work and Influence* (London, 1924).

[5] Thomas Astley, *A Description of China,* being Vol. IV, Book I, of *A New Collection of Voyages and Travel* (London, 1745-47); Thomas Salmon, *The Universal Traveler* (London, 1752-53); *The History of China* (London, 1763); John Bell, *Travels from St. Petersburg in Russia to Diverse Parts of Asia* (Glasgow, 1763).

[6] The first three parts of *The Pleasing History* were originally translated into English by James Wilkinson, an Englishman in the service of the Company, before his departure from China in 1719. Wilkinson's translation appears to have been made from a Portuguese manuscript translation from the Chinese. The fourth part remained in the Portuguese translation. The whole manuscript was given to Bishop Percy by a nephew of Wilkinson. Bishop Percy revised and edited the original English translation and rendered the Portuguese of part four into English. The remainder of the pieces in the edition were translated from Du Halde and other Jesuit writers. See Ch'ên Shou-yi, "Thomas Percy and his Chinese Studies," *Chinese Social and Political Science Review,* XX (July, 1936), 202-30.

and books relating to "History civil & natural; Laws; Geography; and the Fundamentals of their Religion." In March, 1765, the supercargoes were able to forward from the missionaries to Doctor Butler and Doctor Morton of the Royal Society answers to their questions and copies of the *Shih Ching,* and *Shuo Wên,* and two dictionaries.[7] Two Englishmen, James Flint and Thomas Bevan, both servants of the Company, also acquired a limited knowledge of the Chinese language during this period.[8]

This sudden outburst of interest in things Chinese had no organic basis and so was short-lived. The commercial connections between England and China were not yet closely knit, and there were no English students or scholars within the Empire to maintain the interest. From the time of the publication of *The Chinese Traveller* in 1775 until the growth of trade and the direct contact obtained through the Macartney Embassy provided the basis for a more fundamental interest in China toward the close of the century, the cultural absorption in the land of Han underwent an eclipse.

At the time when this cultural and intellectual interest in China was at its height in England, events were occurring at Canton in the commercial sphere which were in the end bound to interfere with the *laissez faire* policy of the Chinese and British governments and bring them into direct contact. The steady growth of trade inevitably cemented the connections between the two peoples, but between 1751 and 1761 commercial difficulties at Canton led to the first suggestion of a British embassy to China and caused the Imperial government to confine foreign trade to Canton and to give its sanction to the restraining system of life and trade which custom had established at that port.

2. *Efforts to Abolish the Security Merchant System and the Establishment of the Hongist Monopoly (1751-1755).*

Until the Macartney Embassy reached Peking in 1793 England remained one of the few European nations having extensive intercourse with China which had not sent a mission of some description to the "Dragon Throne." The first European embassy of modern times

---

[7] Morse, *Chronicle,* V, 117-18. The dictionaries were: *Cheng Tzŭ T'ung,* twenty-six volumes, and the *Tzŭ Hui,* fourteen volumes. The *Shuo Wên* was an explanation of the ancient Chinese characters in six volumes, and the *Shih Ching* (Book of Odes) was the classical book of poetry.

[8] Flint was in China from 1736 until his banishment and deportation in 1762, and Bevan was at Canton from 1753 until 1780.

to go to Peking, if we exclude Mediaeval envoys, was a Portuguese sent from Goa under the direction of Thomé Pires. It reached Peking in 1520, but the ambassador was not granted an audience. Of the five later embassies sent by the Portuguese, one was driven from Canton by the Chinese, one was stopped at Malacca by the Portuguese governor, and three reached Peking. About 1575 Legaspi sent from Manila a Spanish mission under two priests, who were well received by the Viceroy of Fukien, but were not allowed to proceed to Peking. The first Russian embassy, under Petlin, reached Peking in 1618, but as he brought no presents (tribute) he was not allowed to see the Emperor. Between this date and the Kropotov mission of 1768, no fewer than eleven Russian envoys or agents were sent to China. Two Dutch embassies reached Peking, one in 1656 and another in 1667, and in 1662 a commercial and diplomatic mission was sent from Batavia to the Viceroy of Fukien. Père Bouvet's mission from the Emperor to the Court of France and its return with a French commercial mission in 1699 established a connection between the French Court and China. Two Papal envoys were also sent to Peking.[9]

The East India Company, drawing wisdom from the experiences of these other embassies—none of which, with the exception of the Russian, obtained any commercial privileges worth mentioning and all of which were compelled to submit to many indignities—refrained from sending embassies to China. The course of events during the 1750's, however, was such that some servants of the Company began to think of an embassy as a possible way of solving their difficulties. Perhaps the earliest suggestion of a mission to the Emperor was made in the spring of 1751 upon the occasion of the celebration of the sixtieth birthday of the Emperor's mother at Nanking. The Canton mer-

---

[9] For accounts of these embassies, see MSS. Cornell, *Macartney Correspondence*, VIII, No. 325 (hereafter abbreviated CMC); IOC, XCI, 413ff; Chang T'ien-tsê, *Sino-Portuguese Trade from 1514 to 1644* (Leyden, 1934), pp. 48-53, 56-61; Andrew Ljungstedt, *An Historical Sketch of the Portuguese Settlement in China* (Boston, 1836), pp. 92-93, 95-96, 99-101, 103-04; John F. Baddely, *Russia, Mongolia, China, 1602-1676* (London, 1919), II, 65-86, 130-46, 167-68, 194-201, 330-60; Gaston Cahen, *Histoire des relations de la Russe avec la Chine sous Pierre le Grand, 1689-1730* (Paris, 1912), pp. 20-22, 35-44, 212; N. Bantysh-Kamenskii, *Diplomatisheskoe sobraine diel mezhdu Bossiiskim i Kitaishim gosudarstvami s 1619 po 1792 god* (Kazan, 1882), *passim*, and 308-16, 324-25; G. Pauthier, *Histoire des relations politiques de la Chine avec la puissances occidentales* (Paris, 1859), pp. 42-46, 73-76, 104, 128-40; *Chinese Repository*, VIII, 422ff.; Williams, *Middle Kingdom* (1883), II, 426-43; Eames *op. cit.*, pp. 103-17; Morse, *International Relations*, I, 41-62; C. Gutzlaff, *A Sketch of Chinese History* (London, 1834), II, 417-45.

chants proposed to John Misenor, the English chief, that Flint (who spoke Chinese) should be sent to Nanking to pay his respects and to solicit commercial privileges, the remittance of the present-charge of 1950 taels, and the reform of other abuses. They offered to pay the expenses of the journey and of the presents, but Misenor refused lest other nations might reap the benefit.[10]

By 1753 the restraints of the security merchant system and the growth of other impositions and restrictions had become so troublesome that the supercargoes began a determined attempt to bring about reform. A petition was drawn up requesting (1) the abolition of the security merchant system because it interfered with trade and was unfair to the Chinese merchant who was appointed security for a ship. It further desired (2) that more efficient service for the unloading of foreign vessels be provided, (3) that linquists and compradores be excused from making presents to the officials, (4) that orders be given to prevent the plundering of foreign goods on the river, (5) that the exactions and rude manners of minor officials in the customs service be stopped, (6) that the posting of placards unfriendly to foreigners which tended to arouse the populace against them be prohibited, and (7) that the British merchants have free access to high officials.[11]

Flint, having had it translated into Chinese, presented it to the Hoppo at the measuring of a ship on August 4. The Hoppo's reply was to uphold the justice and desirability of the existing system and to order the arrest of the person who had translated the petition. Fortune at this juncture threw opportunity into the hands of the supercargoes in the form of Père Hallerstien, a Portuguese missionary and President of the Mathematical Academy at Peking. He had accompanied the Portuguese embassy from Peking to Macao and was now returning to the capital. As a result of his friendly advances, a conference was held between himself and Frederick Pigou, Thomas Fitzhugh, James Flint, and Mason Horner on October 14.

Père Hallerstien indicated his willingness to help the English but held out no prospects of immediate achievements. He was asked what was the proper manner of applying for relief from the grievances under which the foreign trade labored, and whether application should be made to Peking or to the local government. He advised a private audience with the Hoppo in which the grievances were to be explained

[10] Alexander Dalrymple, *Oriental Repertory* (London, 1791-97), II, 313.
[11] Morse, *Chronicle*, V, 9-10.

and their representation to Peking requested. Horner then solicited the missionary's aid in obtaining a friend among the principal mandarins, either by pecuniary or other means, who would support a representation if sent to Peking. Père Hallerstien promised to look for such a friend and to "concert" with him the proper measures to gain the support of the Emperor. He considered it inadvisable for the English to cooperate with the other nations, because money would have to be applied in a secret way and because if any immunities were granted they would then have to be shared with the other nations.[12]

The supercargoes, although feeling that the missionary was wrong in considering the Hoppo rather than the Viceroy the most advisable person to approach, determined to procure for Flint a private audience with the Hoppo. It appears, however, that no attempt was made until the next year, when the first ships of the season were held outside the port until the grievances of the British should be discussed. In July, 1754, Flint went to the Customs House and desired an audience with the Hoppo. As the Hoppo delayed in granting an audience, the supercargoes finally went to the city gate on July 29 and requested an audience with the Viceroy. After some hours, the audience was granted. Their grievances were explained by Flint, and a petition written in Chinese setting forth their complaints was presented. Flint especially represented the difficulties of the security merchant system and asked that it be abolished and the English allowed to pay their duties directly to the officials. The Viceroy promised that their "business would be effectually regulated," and on August 3 the supercargoes were informed that the merchants were to enter into business with them on reasonable terms and that in the future, if the English had complaint to make, they were to have free access to the Viceroy.[13]

The situation was further complicated when in September an English seaman was killed by a Frenchman in one of the chronic affrays between the sailors of the two nations. Upon the insistent demand of the English, the Chinese finally stopped the French trade until the guilty man was given up. He was imprisoned for a time, but was freed by a royal act of grace. During the course of the dispute the Chinese urged the English to settle the matter privately with the French in a friendly manner, thus showing a willingness to surrender their extraterritorial

---

[12] CMC, II, No. 2.

[13] MSS. Cornell, *Macartney Documents*, X, July-August, 1754 (hereafter abbreviated CMD) ; Morse, *Chronicle*, V, 10-14.

jurisdiction when two foreigners were involved. It should be noted that the English, in requesting the Chinese to punish a European for a wrong done to another foreigner, established a precedent which they were later to regret. As a result of these affrays, the French sailors were allotted French Island upon which to exercise, and the English were allowed Danes Island.[14] There can be no doubt that incidents such as this, by confirming the Chinese in the belief that foreigners must be strictly regulated, contributed to the issuance of a series of restrictive decrees in 1755.

In the meantime Frederick Pigou, who returned to England with the ships in the spring of 1754, made a definite proposal for a British embassy to China. It was part of a general plan for the improvement of the Company's position in China and was presented in a long letter— apparently to the Court of Directors.[15] Besides recommending that a resident council of supercargoes with a chief be established at Canton and containing various other intelligent remarks about the conduct of business, the making of purchases, and the size of ships to be sent to China, Pigou proposed that an embassy be sent in 1761, the seventieth anniversary of the Emperor's mother, to solicit privileges and redress of grievances.

> The Ambassador must come in the King's name, but in a Company's Ship, he must never have been in China before; at least not in The Company's Service, or belonging to any Ship, he must be a Man of some rank, or figure, an Officer in the Army would do; he should be a Man of understanding and probity, and not too haughty, he may be attended by Mr. Flint, in quality of one of his Secretarys . . . . The Embassy may be sent, either from Amoy, or from Canton, for to whatever place a Ship comes, carrying a proper flag, which denotes that an Ambassador is on board, the Mandarins are obliged to give notice of it at Court, and to entertain the Ambassador, until he is attended thither by the Persons whom the Emperor sends for that purpose.[16]

He then went on to indicate that the ambassador or one of the secretaries should understand the Latin tongue; that valuable presents should be brought for the Emperor; that because the ambassador's

---

[14] Morse, *Chronicle*, V, 14-19 and *International Relations*, I, 101; Milburn, *op. cit.*, II, 465; Davis, *China* (1857), I, 47-48; Keeton, *op. cit.*, I, 32-33; *Shih Liao Hsün K'an* (Peiping, 1930), Ch. 10, memorial of Yang Ying-chu, dated Ch'ien Lung 20-6-21.

[15] Dalrymple, *op. cit.*, II, 301-316. The letter is undated, but internal evidence proves beyond a doubt that it was written in 1754. The character of the letter suggests that it was a special letter to the Court of Directors, giving them his conclusions and recommendations as a result of his two years' residence in China (1753 and 1754).

[16] *Ibid.*, pp. 311-12.

ship and goods were exempt from duties, the goods should be shipped in the ambassador's name; that, because the French had influence at Peking, it would be advisable to offer to do them some service; that it would be honorable to England if she procured the privileges for other nations as well as for herself, but, if the privileges were to be procured for England alone, it would be advisable to go to Amoy in order not to arouse the opposition of the other nations at Canton. He then suggested that the following things be requested:[17]

(1) That the Company's ships be privileged to trade at any of the Emperor's ports;

(2) That the Company be permitted to maintain a constant resident in China and to build commodious houses and warehouses wherever they chose to trade;

(3) That the Company be permitted to maintain a permanent resident at Peking;

(4) That the existing privileges of the Company be continued and that the 6 per cent and the 1950 taels be remitted;

(5) That the English be allowed the same commercial privileges as the Emperor's subjects, and that they be charged no more than the Emperor's duties;

(6) That the Chinese who serve the Company be not forced to make presents to the mandarins;

(7) That effectual orders be given for the protection of foreigners from insults and for the protection of their goods from being plundered on the river;

(8) That duties be not charged on provisions, liquors, and necessities, and that officers of the customs be prohibited from exacting presents;

(9) That freedom of movement about the city and especially between Canton and Macao be granted, and that the charge for permission to go from Canton to Macao be abolished;

(10) That freedom of access to the mandarins be guaranteed at all times.

While these proposals were being turned over in the minds of the Court of Directors, significant events were transpiring in China. When Pigou returned to China during the autumn of 1755, he found that the net result of the disturbances in 1753 and 1754 had been a series of edicts in May, 1755, issued jointly by the Viceroy and Hoppo, which confirmed the security merchant system, established a strict monopoly of the Hong merchants, made the security merchants and linguists responsible for the acts of the supercargoes and ship officers and the two latter responsible for their men, and in general confirmed and defined in more detail the existing regulations.

---

[17] *Ibid.*, pp. 312-16.

The purport of the edicts was as follows:[18]

(1) In the future, security merchants were to be Hong merchants, a "Hongist Security" was to be answerable for the duties, and trade with the foreigners was to be conducted only by "Hongist Securities."

(2) Shopkeepers were prohibited from engaging in any kind of trade with the Europeans except in the name of a "Hongist Security," and were to be organized into groups of five who were to be mutually responsible for each other.

(3) The interpreters were to obtain the permission of the "Hongist Security" before applying in his name for permission to load goods on foreign ships.

(4) In the future the "Hongist Security" and interpreter were to be responsible for any crimes committed by the supercargoes, captains, officers, and sailors, and the supercargoes and captains were to be responsible for the conduct of the sailors.

Thus the worst fears of the supercargoes had come about, for the edicts threw the "whole business of the place into the hands of a few Merchants [ten], that they [might] levy as a Recompense what prises [*sic.*] they please[d] on the Europeans." The supercargoes protested without success, but the shopkeepers raised such a remonstrance that supplementary decrees allowed them to deal with private foreign traders, "but not in an Goods imported for Account of the Companies." They were allowed to sell such products as chinaware and woven silks, and to retail articles in general except tea or raw silk, which were reserved for the "Hongist Securities." They were especially forbidden from buying "Curiosities of Value, such as Pearl, Coral, Chrystal, True Amber, etc., all which being for the Emperors Use, no Shops [should] presume to interfere." [19]

Besides being aimed at a more effective regulation of the foreigners, the Hongist monopoly was certainly a financial measure on the part of the government and officials. The security merchants had become a convenient tool for extortion from the foreigners. Officials held them responsible for all fees and dues and levied demands upon them until the merchants themselves were opposed to the system. The only way in which the Chinese traders could meet these demands was to charge the foreigners more. The new combination simply increased the efficiency of this tool.[20]

---

[18] CMD, XV, year 1755; Morse, *Chronicle,* V, 21-31, for text of the edicts, pp. 36-44.

[19] Morse, *Chronicle,* V, 30, 41; Eames, *op. cit.,* p. 81; Auber, *op. cit.,* pp. 168-69; Martin, *op. cit.,* II, 14; Milburn, *op. cit.,* II, 46-70.

[20] See Chong-su, *Foreign Trade of China* (New York, 1919), p. 59. See statements in the preamble of the edicts in Morse, *Chronicle,* V, 36-43.

3. *The Confinement of Trade to Canton, the Legalization of the Canton System, and the Establishment of the Co-hong (1756-1761).*

As one means of combating the growing restrictions, the *Earl of Holderness* had been sent to Ningpo and Chusan in 1755 under the direction of Harrison, Fitzhugh, and Flint. She was well received and granted exceptionally favorable privileges. The next year the Company's ship *Griffin* and a Country ship (ship trading between India and China on private account), the *Hardwick*, went to Ningpo and apparently carried on a successful trade. In 1757, however, when the *Onslow* reached Ningpo under the direction of Blount, Flint, and Bevan, she was refused trade. After considerable delay the supercargoes were informed that the Emperor did not wish foreigners to trade at Ningpo. As a result of further prolonged and fruitless negotiations, the ship sailed away with only a partial cargo after being informed that in the future double duties would be charged ships coming to Ningpo.[21]

In the same year Ch'ien Lung issued an edict which, together with supplementary decrees by the Viceroys of Min-Che (Fukien-Chekiang) and Canton, effectively prohibited foreign trade at any Chinese port other than Canton. To insure the confinement of trade to Canton the Emperor ordered that any European ship entering Ningpo or Chusan should surrender its arms, guns, ammunition and sails, and pay double duties. This did not absolutely prohibit trade, but the new Viceroy of Min-Che and the Viceroy of Canton issued edicts prohibiting trade at Ningpo or Chusan and confining it to Canton.[22]

In a sense this act was the culmination of a growing exclusionist sentiment in China. It would probably not have occurred but for the hostility to foreigners; it was the Emperor's way of insuring the least trouble from them in the future, and at the same time reaping financial rewards from their trade. But there were very specific and obvious immediate causes of its issuance. It was the Emperor's and mandarin's reply to the foreigner's attempt to open trade at Ningpo. When British ships began to go to Ningpo, the Cantonese officials and merchants, aroused

---

[21] CMD, XIII, "Extracts of Capt. Math^W. Courts Journal, in the Ship *Earl Holderness*, 1755-56"; *ibid.*, V, letters June 17, 1757-Feb. 11, 1758; Morse, *Chronicle*, V, 49-63; *Shih Liao Hsün K'an*, Ch. 10, memorials dated Ch'ien Lung 20-5-11, 20-5-16, 20-6-9, 20-6-13, 20-6-22, 20-9-19 and 20-10-3.

[22] CMD, V, letter of Jan. 30, 1758, diary entry of Feb. 11, 1758, and memorial dated 22nd year of Ch'ien Lung; Morse, *Chronicle*, V, 53-63; Eames, *op. cit.*, pp. 85-86; Auber, *op. cit.*, pp. 170-171; Milburn, *op. cit.*, II, 461.

by the fear of losing this valuable trade, obtained the support of the Viceroy of Fukien and Chekiang, who had formerly been at Canton, and dispatched a memorial, together with a large sum of money, to Peking requesting that trade be confined to Canton. Ch'ien Lung, fearing the destruction of his newly created engine of revenue, also supported the Canton group. The result was the above-mentioned decrees, which constituted the necessary steps to make the newly created Hongist monopoly completely effective as an organ of official exaction and imperial revenue.[23]

Other factors which probably influenced the Emperor's mind were the troubles with the missionaries, the recent homicide at Canton, numerous brawls among the European sailors, and the memory of the unhappy experience with Commodore Anson. By restricting trade to Canton, he could insure against the occurrence of such trouble at other places within the Empire, and he could also limit the point of entry for missionaries who insisted on violating his exclusion decree. The edicts were, therefore, the result of a combination of private greed, imperial financial need, and public policy looking toward the future tranquility of the Empire.

Although the Court of Directors apparently did not approve Pigou's scheme of an embassy, they determined to make another attempt to break the Canton monopoly and remove the restrictions on trade by direct appeal to Peking if necessary. The supercargoes were directed to renew their protests at Canton, and on December 28, 1758, they presented a petition to the Viceroy setting forth their grievances. On January 4, 1759, a reply was received from the Governor upholding the existing practices. In March the supercargoes returned a spirited reply, which was answered verbally by the Viceroy to the effect that the Governor had already replied to their requests and that if they gave any more trouble he would punish them. On July 6 the Viceroy and Hoppo jointly issued a mandate repeating the regulations issued in 1755, and on July 16 the supercargoes were received in audience by the Hoppo, who heard their complaints and promised to redress some of their minor grievances. Nevertheless, he made no efforts to carry out his promises.[24]

---

[23] The memorial referred to in note 22; Martin, *op. cit.*, II, 14; Morse, *Chronicle*, IV, 318; *ibid.*, V, 49, 53-56; Davis, *Chinese* (1836), I, 48-49; See, *op. cit.*, pp. 57-58, insists that the decree was a revenue measure.

[24] CMD, XV, years 1758-59; Morse, *Chronicle*, V, 76-80.

Driven to despair by these events, the supercargoes resorted to the last expedient recommended by the Court of Directors. They purchased a small seventy-ton snow, the *Success,* and on June 13, 1759, dispatched her to Ningpo under the direction of Flint. At Ningpo, Flint presented a memorial requesting permission to trade, setting forth the grievances under which the Canton trade labored and requesting that they be made known at Peking. Because the mandarins would not receive the memorial, he sailed for Tientsin, where he arrived on July 10. The trading ship *Chesterfield,* which followed Flint to Ningpo, was refused trade and forced to return to Canton. At Tientsin, Flint, after bribing a minor mandarin, was able on July 21 to deliver two copies of his memorial to important officials, who promised to forward it to Peking.

The grievances set forth in the memorial included: (1) the exactions of the minor customs officials, amounting to over T. 355 per ship and the present of T. 1950; (2) the refusal of the officials to allow foreigners to make their complaints in person; (3) the refusal of the officials to settle the debts owed by the Hong merchant Li to the Company; (4) the customs duties charged on provisions imported and exported; (5) the new charges on the passage between Macao and Canton, amounting to about T. 21 each way; (6) the 3 per cent added to customs duties to make up an alleged difference between the Canton and Peking weights, and various other new charges over and above the Imperial duties; and (7) the security merchant system. Flint was required to wait at Tientsin until the Imperial reply was received, and on July 28 he was informed that the Emperor was sending a great mandarin to Canton to investigate and that he was to return overland with the mandarin. The *Success* and her crew were lost at sea on the return voyage to Canton.[25]

A High Commissioner from Peking and the Tartar General from Fukien were sent to investigate conditions at Canton. The latter arrived on August 25, 1759, and the Hoppo was immediately recalled to Peking in disgrace. The High Commissioner arrived on September 10 and a thorough investigation was begun. Many of the complaints were found to be true, and a number of the minor abuses and charges, in-

---

[25] CMD, V, letter of Dec. 29 [1759], and XI, year 1759, for Flint's memorial in French translation; Morse, *Chronicle,* II, 301-05 and V, 75, 80; *Shih Liao Hsün K'an,* Ch. 3, memorial of Yang Ting-chang, dated Ch'ien Lung 24-9-4 and Ch. 9, memorials of the Governor of Chekiang and of the Viceroy of Canton dated Ch'ien Lung 24-8-4 and 24-10-25. Chüan 4, 5, and 6 also contain material on the Flint expedition.

cluding numbers 1, 3, 4, 5 and 6 above, except the 1950 taels, were temporarily removed. The main preoccupation of the officials, however, was the finding out of the name of the Chinese who had translated Flint's memorial. In November the investigating officials left Canton to make their report to Peking. The net result of the whole affair was that the Chinese who had translated the memorial lost his head, and Flint was imprisoned at Macao for three years for having violated the Imperial order not to go to Ningpo and Tientsin. An Imperial edict was sent down in 1760 confirming the principles of the system, as established by long custom and by the edicts of 1755 and 1757, requiring that justice be given to the foreigners, and in general defining and stereotyping the regulations.[26]

The above-mentioned Imperial decree was received in the spring of 1760, and by October the Chinese merchants, with the sanction of the officials, had formed themselves into an association or Co-hong of ten, which was to transact all business with foreigners. When trade opened in 1760, the Hong merchants presented a united front and demanded uniform prices. The English refused to trade with the association and complained to the officials. After considerable discussion the Hoppo informed them that the new procedure had been approved by the Emperor, that acceptance and conformity were imperative, and that the association had been formed to make the merchants jointly responsible for every trouble which the Europeans might make. After some further protest the supercargoes submitted and began making contracts.[27]

Thus at last the spectre of half a century had become a reality, and the foreign trade at Canton was the monopoly of a closed corporation with unlimited control over prices and the support of the officials. The trade regulations and the organization of the Co-hong stereotyped conditions at Canton into a settled policy of restriction. The system thus established retained approximately the same form for eighty years, and it must, therefore, be described in some detail. Before this is done, however, the final effort of the Company to effect a settlement suitable to it should be considered.

The last scene in this long drama was transacted in 1761. In 1760 the Court of Directors determined to send out a special mission to improve the relations between their supercargoes and the Chinese

---

[26] CMD, XV, years 1759-60, and V, years 1759-60; Morse, *Chronicle* V, 81-84, text of edict of 1760, pp. 94-98.

[27] Morse, *Chronicle*, V, 90-93.

officials and to protest against the imprisonment of Flint and against the various impositions between 1755 and 1760. Whether or not this mission was in any way inspired by Pigou's letter of 1754 is uncertain, but it put into use a number of the suggestions which he made. It was under the direction of Captain Nicholas Skottowe, who commanded the Company's ship *Royal George*. He was charged with a letter from the Court of Directors to the Viceroy, and it was to be given out that he was the brother of His Majesty's under-secretary of state. He was to maintain a strictly unbusinesslike character, was never to be seen in any of the shops purchasing articles, was to send for the Chinese merchants when he wanted them, and was never to appear unless in full dress uniform in the streets or at home when receiving visitors.[28]

The mission came too late, because the Imperial edicts of 1757 and 1760 had closed the incident so far as the Chinese were concerned. Captain Skottowe arrived on August 12, 1761, but was not given an audience by the Viceroy. The Court's memorial, however, was trans-lated into Chinese and transmitted to the Viceroy, but his reply had not been received by December 17, when the *Royal George* sailed for Madras. The Court's letter, after expressing their disappointment at being excluded from Ningpo, requested: (1) that Flint be released; (2) that the present of 1950 taels, the 6 per cent charge on exports, and the 2 per cent charged on silver by the Hoppo, be abolished; (3) that the security merchant system be abolished and the supercargoes be allowed to pay the duties directly to the Hoppo; and (4) that the Hoppo consent to hear their complaints, and that direct appeals to the Viceroy be allowed from all decisions of the Hoppo.[29]

The letter was transmitted to Peking, and on January 18, 1762, the reply was received in the form of a mandate to the Chinese merchants. Item four was admitted with certain reservations, but the other three requests were refused. The presents brought by Captain Skottowe, valued at T. 1,101, were refused. After this the Company gave up active attempts to reform the system of trade established by the Chi-nese and turned its attention to the improvement of its trading methods and the strengthening of the bargaining power of its supercargoes in China.

---

[28] CMD, XV, for the season 1760-61; MSS. IO, *China (II): Diaries and Con-sultations, 1760-69,* V, for season 1760-61; Morse, *Chronicle,* V, 104.

[29] Morse, *Chronicle,* V, 104-06; Auber, *op. cit.,* p. 174.

4. The Canton System of Trade after 1760 and Its Significance.

The result of the preceding eight years of conflict was the crystallization of the Canton system through the various Imperial edicts. The establishment of the Hongist monopoly in 1755 was an attempt to bring the foreigners under more effective control, strengthen the Hong merchants, and perfect the security merchant system as a machine for revenue and exaction. The decrees of 1757 were the logical answers to the English attempts to open trade at Ningpo and were necessary to make the newly created Hongist monopoly absolutely effective as a tool of official exaction and imperial revenue. The decree of 1760, which codified and legalized the existing system, was the official answer to the continued British attempts to change the Canton system. With these final flourishes the Imperial government attempted to insure the Empire against foreign penetration and wash its hands forever clean of the troublesome Western traders.

The regulations relating to trade and placing restrictions upon the foreigners, many of which were of long standing and others of which had been established during the past ten years, may be summarized as follows:[30]

(1) All trade except that of a minor sort was confined to the ten to thirteen Hong merchants, organized as a Co-hong, and even minor trading could be done only under license from them (established between 1755 and 1760).

(2) Duties and charges were paid through the Hong merchants, who acted as securities for the foreign ships and who were held responsible for all acts of the foreigners (gradually developed between 1727 and 1760).

(3) All petitions to the officials had to go through the Hong merchants, and direct communication with officials was prohibited (gradually developed into a settled practice by 1760, although it was occasionally departed from at later dates).

(4) The factories where the foreigners lived were under the control of Hong merchants (this was true as early as 1720).

(5) The freedom of movement of foreigners was considerably restricted— the sailors being confined to certain islands, and the traders to Macao during the summer; and even during the trading season the latter were restricted to the regions around their factories at Canton (a gradual development, although more stringently enforced during the 1750's).

---

[30] The most important of these regulations are to be found in the decrees of 1755-60. See Morse, *Chronicle*, V, 29-30, 37-44, 76-80, 89-90, 94-98 and II, 56-57; Morse, *Trade and Administration* (1908), pp. 275-76; J. R. Morrison, *Chinese Commercial Guide* (Canton, 1834), p. 47; Eames, *op. cit.*, pp. 87-90; CMD, XI, a series of edicts and decrees in French translation for the years 1759-60; *Shih Liao Hsün K'an*, Ch. 9, memorial of Li Szu-yao dated Ch'ien Lung 24-10-25.

(6) The firing of guns by foreigners was prohibited, but this was apparently not enforced (an old regulation).

(7) The study of the Chinese language by foreigners was prohibited (1755).[31]

(8) Foreigners were not to have Chinese servants except the "established" linguists and compradores (1755-1760).

(9) Chinese were forbidden to borrow money from foreigners on pain of severe punishment and confiscation of property (1760).

(10) Foreigners were not to employ couriers to carry letters into the interior or to ascertain prices of commodities except with the advice and consent of the officials (1760).

(11) Troops under a mandarin of war were to be charged with the special duty of looking after the European ships and maintaining order (an old regulation but additional troops were added in 1760).

(12) Arms and ammunition were to be deposited before the ship entered the port, but this was not enforced (a regulation going back as far as the beginning of British trade).

(13) Foreign battleships were prohibited from entering the Canton river (an old regulation which was first applied to the British in 1741).

(14) Foreigners who committed crimes were to be punished by the Chinese to the limit of Chinese law (this principle was established by Ch'ien Lung in 1749 but was not rigidly enforced until after 1760).[32]

The charges and impositions upon trade were numerous and showed a considerable increase over those levied early in the century. The first of these charges was the basic measurage charge or port duty paid by all ships. It was one of the few charges on trade paid directly in cash by the foreigners, although even this payment was made to the Hong merchants. The length and breadth of ships were multiplied together and the sum divided by ten to obtain the units of measurage. On the basis of size, ships were divided into three classes. First-rate ships paid dues of T. 7.777 per unit of measurage, second-rate ships paid T. 7.142 per unit and third-rate ships T. 5.000. Practically all of the foreign ships were considered as first-raters. The calculation upon a ship of 758 tons was as follows:[33]

---

[31] Morse, *Chronicle*, V, 27-28; Martin, *op. cit.*, II, 13.

[32] G. T. Staunton, *Ta Tsing Leu Lee*, pp. 36, 515-23; Davis, *The Chinese* (1836), I, 66, 414-20; Morse, *International Relations*, I, 110-17.

[33] IOCCD, LIX, 154, and LXXX, 41; Morse, *Chronicle*, I, 267-68; Milburn, *op. cit.*, II, 492-3; Morrison, *Commercial Guide* (1834), p. 22; H. M. Elmore, *British Mariner's Directory and Guide* (London, 1802), pp. 132-33.

	Tls.
225.4 units x T. 7.777 per unit	1,752.935
Deduct the Emperor's allowance of 20 per cent	350.586
	1,402.349
Add 7 per cent to make it sycee (pure silver)	98.164
	1,500.513
Add 10 per cent for the Hoppo's controller	150.051
Add 2 per cent on the T. 1,402 for the Shupan or Clerks of Hoppo	28.006
Basic measurage fee	1,678.570

To this basic measurage fee had to be added the cumshaw or present, amounting to T. 1,950, which would bring the total charge up to T. 3,629. This present was uniform for all ships of whatever size, except that French ships paid T. 2,050 and Country ships T. 1,850.[34] From these figures and those in footnote 34, it is evident that of a total measurage fee of T. 3,629, the Emperor received T. 3,107, and the Hoppo and his establishment received T. 522 or roughly 15 per cent. In 1762 the basic measurage charge on six ships amounted to T. 8,308 and the present to T. 11,700, a total of T. 20,008.

There were five other direct charges upon each ship. The first was pilotage, a fee which amounted to about T. 100 toward the end of the century, paid to the pilots who had a monopoly of guiding ships in and

---

[34] The present charge was made up as follows (Milburn, *op. cit.*, II, 493; Morse, *Chronicle*, I, 268; Morrison, *Commercial Guide* [1834], pp. 22-23):

	Tls.
To the Emperor on the ship's arrival	1,089.640
To the Emperor on the ship's departure	516.561
To the Liangtao (Grain Commissioner) for the poor	132.000
To the Security Merchant's Dispatchador	12.000
To the Writer (Shupan) on measuring the ship	8.400
To the soldiers attending the measuring	5.560
To the Hoppo's soldiers on arrival of the ship	16.780
To the Fuyuan on arrival of the ship	2.800
To the Kwangchow Fu (Prefect of Canton)	2.800
To the Penyü Hien with jurisdiction over Whampoa	1.700
To the Namhoi Hien with jurisdiction over the factories	1.200
To the Künming Fu (military officer at Macao)	1.200
To the tidewaiters (preventive officers) stationed by the Hoppo on ships during their stay at Whampoa	150.000
To the difference of the Emperor's weights, etc.	9.359
Total	1,950.000

out of the port.[35] A second charge was T. 75 paid to the linguist and his assistant in 1760, but by the end of the century this had risen to over T. 100.[36] The compradore's fees and charges for supplies and provisions constituted a third charge. His fee in 1760 amounted to T. 50, but this was later abolished so far as the Company's ships were concerned. There are no direct figures as to the cost of supplies, but the charter-parties of the Company's ships required the supercargoes to advance each ship £200 a month during its stay at Canton. If a ship stayed four months, this item would be £800, or T. 2400.[37] A fourth charge was about T. 180 paid to the mandarins at Whampoa anchorage for the ship's banksalls (storage sheds on shore) and the privilege of exercising on Danes Island.[38] The fifth charge was the cost of unloading the vessel, which was paid by the owner of the goods and ranged from T. 75 to T. 100. The expense of loading the ship was paid by the linguist out of a piculage fee allowed him by the officials.[39]

Besides the above-mentioned direct charges on trade, there were a number of indirect charges paid by the Hong merchants. These indirect charges, which the foreigners could not calculate but which were levied on the trade in the form of increased prices, were a constant source of annoyance to the traders, because they believed the officials and merchants altered them at will. The official charges that fell under this category were five: (1) *Ching hsiang*, the Imperial customs duty on imports and exports which remained unchanged during the period covered by this study. It amounted to T. 0.150 per picul on cotton, T. 0.300 per picul on lead, T. 0.200 per picul on tea, T. 5.400 per picul on raw silk and T. 0.500 per chang (4 yards) on broadcloth. (2) A surtax of 24 per cent upon the Imperial customs duty, and a

[35] IOC, LXXVIII, 29; Milburn, *op. cit.*, II, 426, 495; Josiah Quincy, *Journal of Major Samuel Shaw* (Boston, 1847), p. 162; W. C. Hunter, *The "Fan Kwae" at Canton* (London, 1882), pp. 11, 28-29; C.L.J. de Guignes, *Voyage à Peking* (Paris, 1808), III, 276-77.

[36] Morse, *Chronicle*, II, 289, and V, 101; Milburn, *op. cit.*, II, 493-95; *Shaw's Journal*, p. 176; De Guignes, *op. cit.*, III, 276; CMC, VII, No. 321.

[37] CMD, XI, Flint's memorial of 1759; CMC, VII, No. 321; *Shaw's Journal*, pp. 174-75; Morse, *Chronicle*, II, 128-29; MSS. Wash. State College (W.S.C.), *Pritchard Collection of Macartney Documents on China*, No. 20, p. 20 for a charter-party of 1792; IO, *Marine Records: Miscellaneous*, CCCCCXXX, Appendix No. 826 for a charter-party in 1784.

[38] *Shaw's Journal*, p. 175; De Guignes, *op. cit.*, III, 276-77; Milburn, *op. cit.*, II, 465; Alfred Spencer, *Memoirs of William Hickey* (London, 1913-23), I, 197.

[39] IOC, LXXX, March 31 and Nov. 14, 1784; CMC, VII, No. 321; Milburn, *op. cit.*, II, 493-95.

further 7 per cent upon the two previous charges to convert them into sycee or pure silver. These two charges seem later to have been combined into a single 30 per cent charge called *chia san* or *chia hao,* part of which went to the Emperor and part of which was appropriated by the Hoppo. (3) *Tan t'ou* or *tan fei,* a piculage or weighing fee amounting about 1760 to T. 0.086 or T. 0.100 per picul on imports and exports. It later rose to T. 0.150 on imports and to T. 0.200 on exports. This fee was divided between the Hoppo, the linguist, the Hong merchants, and various minor mandarins. (4) *Kuei* customs, originally illegal charges or bribes paid to the customs officials which became fixed through usage. (5) The 6 per cent *ad valorem* duty on exports. It was levied upon a fixed rate of valuation for each article. Part of it went to the Emperor, part to the Hoppo, a small part to a hospital for the poor, and a small part to the Hong merchants. This latter represented a tax levied on small shopkeepers for their license to trade with foreigners. Besides these official charges the Hong merchants levied certain indefinite charges, later known as *shih li* or trading arrangements.[40]

The procedure of trade was much the same as earlier in the century. Pilots were taken on outside Macao to guide the ship past the Bogue forts and into the Whampoa anchorage. Linguists and compradores also came aboard at Macao. The ship was measured either at the Bogue or at Whampoa. Here the supercargoes demanded of the "Hoppo a continuance . . . . of all the Privileges that the English Nation [had] enjoyed at this Port, and had his assurances that they would be granted."[41] The traders then proceeded to Canton, where they took up their residence in one of the Hongs or factories provided by the Hong merchants. Their first care was to get an official chop or permit to carry on trade, after which business was begun with the Hong merchants. Contracts were often made a year in advance, and at the end of the trading season all accounts were settled and contracts for the ensuing year entered into. When a ship was loaded, the grand chop or clearance paper had to be obtained before she could depart.

---

[40] CMC, VII, No. 321; IOC, XX, "Rate of duties," near middle of volume and CCLXIV, 102-06; CMD, XV, near end of volume; Morse, *Chronicle,* I, 93, 106, 126, 139, 142-43, and IV, 371 and V, 105; Dalrymple, *op. cit.,* II, 325-32; Lockyer, *op. cit.,* pp. 148-56; Milburn, *op. cit.,* II, 494; Thomas Brooks, *Coins in the East Indies* (London, 1766), pp. 57-72; Morrison, *Commercial Guide* (1834), pp. 31-43.
[41] Morse, *Chronicle,* I, 274.

Figure 1.
Canton River and Factories.

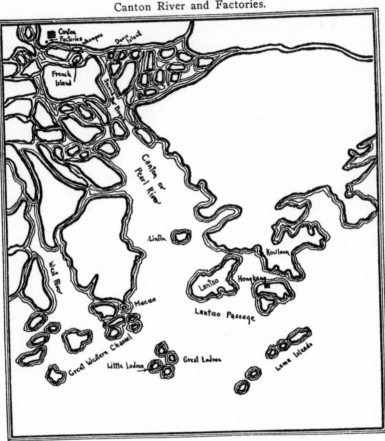

At the end of the trading season in the late spring the supercargoes departed for Macao, where they were compelled to reside until the beginning of the new season in the early fall. The cost of this annual migration to and from Macao amounted in 1760 to about $100. It rose to about $1000 in 1772 and to nearly $10,000 in 1792. The factory charges in 1762 amounted to about T. 20,000.[42] These included table expense and house rent at Canton and Macao, charges of merchandise, the cost of the migration to and from Macao, and the various fees and presents paid to officials and servants. These factory charges plus the

---

[42] CMD, V, letter of Dec. 29 [1759]; Morse, *Chronicle*, V, 88 and II, 208; Appendix VI.

measurage charges made up the Canton charges, which were added to the prime cost of exports to obtain their invoice value.

The system by which the Chinese managed their trade with England having now been noted, a brief comparison between it and the system by which England managed her trade with China may be worthwhile. The basic factor which brought England and China together and which directed the course of their relations during the period covered by this study was commerce. The management of these commercial relations was confined to a dual monopoly, represented on the Chinese side by the Canton Co-hong and on the English side by the East India Company centered in London. This system, which in reality delegated the conduct of all intercourse between the two states to commercial monopolies, had arisen by a trial-and-error process during a long course of evolution, and fairly well represented the two governments' attitude towards one another—namely, the avoidance of official entanglements.

The organization of these two monopolies through which the relations of the two countries were conducted was very different. The East India Company, with its virtual control of all British affairs in Asia, had originated at the beginning of the seventeenth century, when trade to distant parts could be conducted only by powerful commercial monopolies, because the government was both unable and unwilling to afford its protection far beyond the confines of Europe. By the close of the eighteenth century, it still maintained its privileged position despite repeated attacks upon it by commercial and industrial interests outside London, although it was being gradually brought under the control of the government. The East India Company was incorporated on the joint-stock principle, and as such included several thousand British subjects who were able to draw benefit from the monopoly.[43] It was managed by a Court of Directors who controlled and directed its activities as a corporate unit, and its capital and the amount of its dividends were determined by Parliament.

The affairs of the East India Company in China were managed after 1762 by a permanent resident Council of Supercargoes. Prior to 1754 the affairs of each ship had been managed by supercargoes coming and returning on it, who sometimes formed independent Councils for each ship and sometimes combined into several Councils or into a single Council while at Canton. As early as 1753 the policy of leaving

---

[43] Robert Wissett, *Compendium of East India Affairs* (London, 1802), I, section on the "Constitution of the Company."

a resident agent in Canton after the ships had departed was adopted. From 1754 to 1758 several ships were assigned to each of several Councils, one of which held over and maintained a residence in China until the following season. The several Councils generally acted together while at Canton. In 1758 a single Council was appointed to manage all the Company's affairs during the trading season, and continuity was obtained by leaving three resident agents after the ships had departed. The system of competing Councils weakened the bargaining power of the Company, and the constant shift in personnel prevented the most efficient dispatch of business. In the face of the newly created Co-hong the Company was forced to strengthen its supercargoes. From 1762 onward there was a permanent resident Council at Canton presided over by a chief (Thomas Fitzhugh during 1762-67), which was better able to conduct the commercial business and resist in a less offensive way the impositions of the officials and the *démarches* of the Chinese merchants."

The Co-hong, on the other hand, may best be described as a regulated company. Its basis was narrow, inasmuch as it consisted of from ten to thirteen prominent merchants who had a complete monopoly of all foreign trade, although minor merchants could be licensed by them to trade with the foreigners. It had no corporate capital (except the Consoo fund, established about 1779, out of which certain debts were paid, and presents for the Emperor and officials were provided), each merchant trading separately and independently with the foreigners upon his own capital. It had a nominal head, but it did not always unite in a policy of corporate bargaining and uniform price-fixing, despite the fact that an Imperial decree in 1780 directed that it do so." The members of the Co-hong were collectively responsible for the good behavior of the foreigners, the Imperial duties, and the debts of each other. Despite its loose organization, the Co-hong was in a better position to enforce its demands than was the East India Company, because the foreign traders had to come to it.

Thus in a sense the story of Anglo-Chinese relations at this time is but an account of the contact between these two rival organizations as they sparred and angled for advantage. In reality, however, it is more than that and involves economic, political, and even social considera-

"Morse, *Chronicle*, V, preface and pp. 21, 45, 65, 68, 85, 99, 106; Auber, *op. cit.*, p. 174 and note 15 of this chapter.
"IOCCC, LXVIII, 194; Morse, *Chronicle*, II, 57-59.

tions within the two countries which influenced the internal and external policies of both governments and consequently the position taken by their monopolistic representatives. This indirect projection of the home administration into affairs can be seen on the part of the Chinese government in the numerous interferences into the affairs of the Hong merchants by Canton mandarins and even by Peking, and on the part of the British government in such things as the Commutation Act,[46] debates over the monopoly of the China trade, and the embassies sent to China. More important still, the underlying prejudices of each government to a great extent determined and influenced not only the attitudes but also the principles which guided the relations between these two commercial organizations.

Although the establishment of the system described in this section was calculated by the Chinese government to relieve it of future difficulties with the foreigners, it was bound in the end to have exactly the opposite effect. First of all, the legalization of the system made change impossible except through the interposition of government. Furthermore, the system was so troublesome and annoying that the traders were in almost constant conflict with the Chinese, a circumstance which forced both the British and Chinese governments to take notice of affairs at Canton. Finally, the restraining nature of the Hongist monopoly and the confinement of trade to Canton made impossible an indefinite expansion of trade. But trade continued to increase, and after the passage of the Commutation Act in 1784, which reduced the duties on tea imported into England,[47] trade with China grew by leaps and bounds. The inevitable result of these circumstances was the projection of the British government into Chinese affairs in an attempt to reform the Canton system and open new ports to trade by diplomatic methods. The Macartney Embassy aimed to do this, and the first-hand information which it obtained about China and the continued growth of trade provided the basis for a more organic interest in China. The expansion of British power in India and the growing commercial connections between India and China also forced the British government to take a greater interest in Chinese affairs.

[46] *Infra.*, Chap. III, Section 2.

[47] Duties were reduced from an average of 119 per cent to 12½ per cent. 24 Geo. III, cap. 38.

CHAPTER III

THE EAST INDIA COMPANY'S TRADE WITH CHINA
(1760-1800)

1. *General View of British Trade at Canton: Trends during the Period (1764-1800).*

If the abuses in the system of trade at Canton were of great importance in bringing about the first British embassy to China, commercial developments both in England and in the China trade were of even more fundamental importance. This being the situation, it will be necessary in the present chapter to examine generally British trade at Canton and to analyze in detail the Company's trade with China during the third of a century preceding the Embassy. In the succeeding chapter Private, Country, and foreign European trade with China and economic changes within England itself will be considered. British trade at Canton was divided among three distinct groups: the Company, the Private traders, and the Country traders. The Company, with its headquarters in London, had control and supervision over the whole trade. The Private trade was carried on between England and China and between India and China by the commanders and officers of the Company's ships under license of the Company. The Country trade between India and China was conducted by Englishmen resident in India under the license of the Company and by native Indian merchants.

The season 1764-65, the first full trading year after the Seven Years' War, may be taken as the starting point for this survey. During this season the Company had fourteen ships, about 7,000 tons at Canton, and the Country trade had three ships, about 1,500 tons; in 1775-76 the Company had five ships, 3,881 tons at Canton, and the Country trade eight ships, about 4,000 tons; in 1785-86 the Company had nineteen ships, 15,413 tons, the Country trade ten, about 5,000 tons; and in 1795-96 the Company had seventeen ships, 14,766 tons, and the Country trade eighteen ships, 14,850 tons.[1] Appendices IV, VI, XI, and XII and Figures 2 and 5, however, will show more graphically than words the progress of the trade during the thirty-six years from 1764 to 1800.

The most obvious thing is the great increase in the value of both imports and exports over the period. The Company's imports in goods

---

[1] IOCCD, Vols. 58, 81, 83; Morse, *Chronicle*, V, II4, and II, 11, 111, 266, and tables of shipping in the back. Country ships are estimated at 500 tons each, in 1764-65, 1775-76, and 1785-86. A statement of their tonnage in 1795-96 is given in Volume 115 of the *Canton Diaries*.

more than quadrupled, and exports did equally as well. Private trade imports and exports increased materially, and the Country trade imports in goods increased about 10 times, and exports 5 times. A second thing which strikes one's eye is the disparity between the value of imports and exports. In 1765-66 the Company's exports were 202 per cent greater than merchandise imports, in 1775-76 greater by 156 per cent, in 1785-86 greater by 328 per cent, but in 1795-96 greater by only 79 per cent. In the Country trade exactly the opposite was true, merchandise imports in 1775-76 being 18 per cent greater than exports, and in 1795-96, 160 per cent greater. In Private trade the disparity was less marked, but imports always exceeded exports by 10 to 80 per cent.[2] When the totals are examined, however, it appears that on an average imports and exports were more nearly equal. The reason for this situation is that the Company found means for utilizing the residue provided by the Country and Private trades in financing its extensive exports.[3]

It is also important to note that the disparity between the Company's imports and exports showed a tendency to decrease after 1790, whereas the disparity between the Country trade's imports and exports showed a rapid increase after 1785. These facts indicate that the value of British imports in goods showed a greater rate of increase than did exports, and suggest that a genuine demand was developing in China for certain articles brought by the British (Indian cotton, English woollens, opium, metals, and woods). From 1773 onwards the Country trade provided the greater percentage of the imports. In 1775-76 it provided 54 per cent of all merchandise imported; the Company provided but 35 per cent, and Private trade furnished 11 per cent. In 1795-96 the Country trade provided but 49 per cent of the imports, the Company 42 per cent, and Private trade 9 per cent.

The Company, however, furnished the greater percentage of exports. In 1764-65 its exports equalled 70 per cent of the total, in 1785-86, 76 per cent, and in 1795-96, 73 per cent. For the corresponding seasons the Country trade provided but 10, 15, and 18 per cent, respectively; and Private trade provided 20 per cent in 1764-65 and 9 per cent for each of the other two seasons. The total value of the trade (imports and exports), which amounted to T. 2,879,422 in 1764-65, fluctuated about this norm until 1784-85, after which it increased to T. 9,332,803 in 1795-96. Of this total the Company provided 62 per

---

[2] Appendices IV, VI, XI, XII.
[3] *Infra*, Chap. IV, Section 3.

cent, the Country 13 per cent, and Private 25 per cent in 1764-65; whereas in 1795-96 the Company provided 58, the Country 33, and Private 9 per cent.[4]

A final observation of extreme importance is that in 1795-96, perhaps for the first time in the history of the trade, the sales value of goods imported exceeded the actual cost value of goods exported, and in consequence a part of the residue, T. 23,882, was exported to Bengal in the Country trade.[5] Throughout the period the Private trade was usually more than self-supporting (that is, the goods imported were able to finance the goods exported), although it seems certain that small amounts of ready cash were generally brought. Similarly, the Country trade was more than self-supporting in a steadily increasing manner. Bullion was imported in the Country trade during the early part of the period, but by the end it was exported, although small sums for ready cash were still imported. The Company's trade was never self-supporting, and if it could not draw enough money into its treasury from the residue of the Country and Private trade to finance its exports, it had to rely on bullion, bonds, credits from the Hong merchants, or money paid in by Portuguese or other foreign traders in return for bills on London. Taken as a whole, British trade was not self-supporting, during most of the period, but from 1791 onward it hovered on the edge, sometimes rising above, sometimes sinking below the level of self-sufficiency. This achievement of self-sufficiency was caused by the rapid growth of the trade in raw cotton from India and woollens from England, and to a lesser extent by the growth of the opium, metal, and wood trade.

By putting these facts into the most simple generalization, one can say that British trade at Canton increased by 294 per cent over the years between 1764 and 1800; that an ever-increasing majority of the exports were furnished by the Company; that from 1773 onward a majority of imports were furnished by the Country trade; that the ratio of Private trade to the total trade declined from 1764 to 1774, after which it remained relatively the same, providing from 8 to 10 per cent of imports and exports throughout the period; that the Company was dependent upon the Country and Private trade for financing its own; and that until the very end of the period exports in goods exceeded imports in goods, the difference having to be met by imports of bullion,

---

[4] Appendices IV, VI, XI, XII.
[5] IO, *Bengal Commercial Reports: External, 1795-1802,* Range 74, Vol. XIII.

by bonds and credits, and by money paid in by foreigners in return for bills.

The most fundamental fact about the commercial development of the period was that nearly all the enormous increase which took place in the trade occurred after 1784. This is clearly shown in Figure 2. From this Figure it is evident that trade maintained a rather low level prior to 1784, and that it then went up like a sky-rocket, the volume of British exports increasing in three years from T. 2,595,586 to T. 6,099,908, and by 1796 to T. 7,576,269. A corresponding thing occurred, but to a less pronounced degree, in the importation of raw cotton, which remained relatively low at an average of about T. 300,000 per annum until 1784, and then in three years shot up to T. 2,160,217. The close correspondence between the trends of the Company's export trade and the import curve for raw cotton shows how dependent the

Figure 2.

Total British and the Company's Trade at Canton (1760-1800)*.

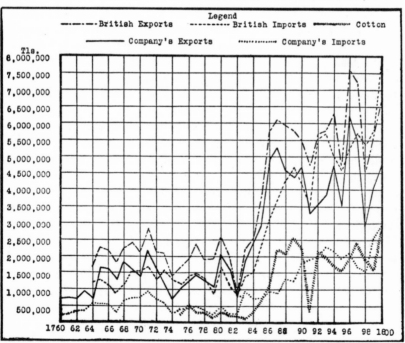

* Based on Appendices, III, IV, VI, XI, XII.

Company was on Indian cotton for financing its exports, and suggests that the amount of raw cotton purchased by the Chinese depended to a certain extent upon how much tea the Company exported.

Considering the phenomenal expansion of trade, one may legitimately ask what caused it. The answer is simple. It was the Commutation Act[6] of 1784 in England—which reduced duties on tea from an average of 119 per cent *ad valorem* to 12½ per cent.[7] Because of the important effect which it had upon the China trade, it seems necessary to turn to a brief consideration of this important measure.

2. *The Commutation Act (August 20, 1784).*

The most important event in the history of Anglo-Chinese relations prior to the abolition of the Company's monopoly of the China trade in 1833 was the Commutation Act. It was passed by the House of Commons on August 16, 1784, and four days later received the Royal assent.[8] Its obstensible object was to safeguard the revenue through the elimination of smuggling by the reduction of duties on tea. This reduction of duties by lowering prices would make smuggling of tea unprofitable, and the reduction of prices would relieve the poor of unnecessary burdens. A secondary and equally important, although less talked of, object was the encouragement of British trade with China at the expense of Continental competitors (France, Sweden, Denmark, Holland, and various interlopers sailing from Ostend under Imperial colors).

The popular demand for tea, together with the ease by which revenue could be collected from it, had caused successive governments throughout the eighteenth century to load it with duties, which between 1768 and 1772 amounted to 64 per cent. For this period the average amount sold by the Company was 8,075,794 lbs. per year. The exigencies of the exchequer, however, caused the government to increase the duties to an average of 106 per cent for the years between 1773 and 1777, with the result that the yearly average of tea sold at the Company's sales declined to 5,559,007 lbs. This alarming decline in the British tea trade led to a temporary reduction of the duties to an average of 100 per cent for the years 1778 and 1779, and under this

---

[6] 24 Geo. III, cap. 38.

[7] Wissett, *Compendium*, II, section on tea; Milburn, *Oriental Commerce*, II, 542.

[8] *Commons Journal, 1784*, XL, 444, 446, 451.

respite the Company's trade showed signs of revival, the average sales between 1778 and 1782 being about 6,000,000 lbs. The closing years of the American War of Independence, however, threw new burdens upon the exchequer, with the result that the duties were raised to 114 per cent in 1783 and to 119 per cent for the first half of the year 1784; consequently the Company's trade suffered a slight decline.[9]

The high duties upon tea had always been an inducement to the smuggler, and numerous harsh and troublesome laws were framed to prevent smuggling. The excessively high duties after 1772 caused the smuggling trade from the Continent to rise by leaps and bounds. As it rose, the Company's trade declined, and the trade of its Continental rivals, which supplied the smugglers with tea, rose. The Company was well aware of the effect of the Government's fiscal policy upon its trade, and the honor of collecting the information and organizing the agitation which finally led to the Commutation Act goes principally to William Richardson,[10] at the time deputy accountant at the India House.

In 1778 Richardson became acquainted with a London wholesale dealer and a Maidstone distiller who were trying to get an Act of Parliament passed to prevent smuggling. From them he obtained information, and he aided them in getting acts passed in 1778 and 1779 which slightly reduced the duties. He also printed a pamphlet against smuggling and organized a number of London tea dealers into an association which met once a week to present information and devise schemes for preventing smuggling. He also organized similar associations in other towns, and the work was helped by the subscription of £500 from the Court of Directors. In 1781 he prepared a plan which would have reduced duties by 16 per cent. It was not favored by the Court of Directors, because they thought the Government would want indemnification for the loss of revenue, and the decrease in duties was not sufficient to eliminate smuggling or the illicit manufacture of adulterated tea in England.

Richardson next evolved the idea of taking off all duties on tea and replacing them by a window tax, which would fall upon the wealthy. He obtained the support of the Earl of Shelburne, who, on July 13, 1782, became Prime Minister. Lord Shelburne had Richardson's plan delivered to the Commissioners of the Customs and Excise for their opinions, and the original of the plan was given to William

[9] Wissett, *Compendium*, II, section on tea; Milburn, *op. cit.*, II, 542.
[10] IO, *Home Miscellaneous*, LXI, 115-19, 151-52.

Pitt (the younger), Chancellor of the Exchequer. Encouraged by ministerial support, Richardson worked out his plan in detail on September 14, 1783. He estimated that between seventeen and eighteen million pounds of tea was consumed annually in England and her dependencies; that between 1772 and 1780 the average annual exportation of tea from China was 18,838,140 lbs., of which 5,639,938 lbs. was brought to England by the Company, 5,500,000 lbs. was consumed upon the Continent, and the remainder, 7,698,201 lbs., was smuggled into England, and that between 4,000,000 and 5,000,000 pounds of tea was annually manufactured in England. If the whole of the China tea annually consumed in England could be brought into the Company's hands, thirty-eight large ships per year would be employed instead of only eighteen. In order to bring this about and to eliminate smuggling, he proposed to take the duties off tea and replace them by a window tax.[11]

Richardson presented this plan to various members of the Government and of Parliament, who in general approved of it.[12] By this time the Government, faced with dire financial necessity, had taken fright at the progress of smuggling, which encouraged lawlessness and defrauded the revenue of immense sums, estimated at £2,000,000 per year.[13] The King's message on November 11, 1783, called attention to the frauds upon the revenue caused by smuggling and requested Parliament to provide remedies. On the 21st, Parliament passed a resolution providing for the appointment of a committee of fifteen to investigate the problem of smuggling. It was elected with William Eden as chairman and on the 27th it held its first meeting.[14] In the meantime the Court of Directors had been considering Richardson's plan, and on December 17 the Court ordered that the Chairman and the Deputy Chairman should wait upon the First Lord of the Treasury and the Chancellor of the Exchequer and request their good offices in carrying it out.[15]

At this junction the North-Fox Ministry, the successor to the Shelburne Ministry, was replaced by the King's nominee, William Pitt. This Ministry was too weak to carry successful legislation through until

---

[11] IO, *Home Miscellaneous*, LXI, 103-104, 138-42; G. L. Staunton, *Embassy from the King of Great Britain to the Emperor of China* (London, 1797), II, 617-23.

[12] IO, *Home Miscellaneous*, LXI, 117-19, 152.

[13] *Commons Journal, 1783*, XXXIX, 853.

[14] *Ibid.*, pp. 709, 738, 740, 741.

[15] IO, *Home Miscellaneous*, LXI, 113, 149-50.

after the general election in May, 1784, which returned it to power with a working majority.[16] In the meantime the Committee on Smuggling had been hard at work. On December 24, 1783, it presented its first report dealing with England. The report gave a detailed account of how smuggling was carried on and the extent to which it was practised in England. The Committee proposed a resolution, deploring the alarming growth of smuggling and calling upon the House to give the matter its earliest attention; this was passed on February 11, 1784.[17] The second report, which related to Scotland and confirmed the first, was presented on March 1, 1784.[18] The third report, which proposed changes in the existing laws to prevent smuggling, the reduction of duties on tea, and the substitution of a tax on windows, was presented on March 23.[19]

The Pitt Ministry was too much occupied with its Government of India Bill to give immediate attention to the problem of smuggling, and not until June 2, 1784, were the three reports from the Committee on Smuggling taken up. On June 21 Pitt introduced several resolutions relative to the tea duties. The resolutions, as originally introduced and passed by the House on June 22, provided that existing duties on tea were to be replaced by a window tax and by duties ranging from 12½ per cent on bohea tea to 40 per cent on congo.[20]

As finally passed, the bill provided for a uniform duty of 12½ per cent on the sales value of all tea sold at the Company's sales, and a window tax. In return for this boon, and in order that the public might be safeguarded, the Company was required to make four sales each year and to put up at least 5,000,000 lbs. at the first sale, 2,500,000 at the second, and thereafter such quantities as were judged sufficient for the demand. At the first four sales bohea was to be put up for sale at 1/7 per lb., congo at 2/5, souchong and singlo at 3/3, and hyson at 4/11, and the tea was to be sold if one penny per pound was bid on the upset price. After that the Company was to offer its teas at a price

[16] *Commons Journal*, XL, 1-3; *Parliamentary History*, XII, 450-51, and XIII, 307, and XIV, 1-4.

[17] *Commons Journal*, XXXIX, 853, 911; PP, *Sessional Reports, 1783-84*, VI, No. 58.

[18] *Commons Journal*, XXXIX, 964; PP, *Sessional Reports, 1783-84*, VI, No. 59.

[19] *Commons Journal*, XXXIX, 1048; PP, *Sessional Reports, 1783-84*, VI, No. 60.

[20] *Commons Journal*, XL, 67-68, 240-47; *Parliamentary History*, XV, 230-40.

not exceeding the prime cost and charges and was always to keep on hand a stock equal to at least one year's consumption.[21]

This measure was far-reaching. The quantity of tea sold at the Company's sales increased from 5,857,882 lbs. in 1783 to 10,148,257 lbs. in 1784 and to 15,081,737 lbs. in 1785. The sales amount then went slowly up until it reached 20,750,994 lbs. in 1796. The sales value of the Company's exports from China (despite the decrease in the price of tea) more than doubled in five years,[22] and because the quantity of British goods which the Chinese would buy was directly dependent upon the quantity of Chinese goods purchased by the British, the sales value of goods imported into China by the Company doubled in five years and nearly quadrupled in ten years. Similarly, the exports from India to China doubled in a single season and increased by seven times in three seasons.[23]

As the British trade flourished, that of its foreign rivals decreased. The quantity of tea exported from Canton by foreign European Companies, which was 19,072,300 lbs. in 1783-84, decreased to 10,165,160 in 1786-87, and to 2,291,560 in 1790-91.[24] The price of bohea tea at the Company's sales decreased from 2/10 per lb. in 1783 to 1/6 per lb. in 1787; hyson decreased from 7/8 per lb. in 1783 to 5/9 in 1787, and the average price of all teas decreased from 3/10 per lb. in 1783 to 2/10 per lb. in 1787.[25] This decrease in wholesale cost of tea naturally led to a considerable extension of its consumption. It also should be noted that these commercial results had a direct bearing (as will be noted later) upon the sending of the first British embassy to China.[26]

Finally, it is worth pointing out that the main benefits of this act did not accrue to the Company alone. Its average yearly net profits upon the China trade for the five years preceding the Commutation Act were £239,289; for the five years following the Act they were £558,413 per year.[27] The chief benefit accrued to the Country traders through the expansion of the cotton trade and to the nation in the reduction of tea prices, the increased sale of its woollens and metals

---

[21] 24 Geo. III, cap. 38.

[22] Appendices V and VII.

[23] Appendices IV and XII.

[24] CMC, X, Nos. 401, 402, 433; Milburn, *op. cit.,* II, 486; David Macpherson, *Annals of Commerce* (London, 1805), IV, 337.

[25] Wissett, *Compendium,* II, section on tea.

[26] Chap. V, Section 2.

[27] Appendix VIII.

in China, and the increased number of seamen and workers which the expanded trade employed. There is no better example in history for illustrating the beneficial results of a wise commercial policy.

3. The Company's Trade: A General View (1760-1800).

Figure 2 gives a very graphic view of the Company's trade with China. In 1760-61 the total value of its merchandise trade at Canton (imports and exports) was T. 901,371. It rose gradually until it reached the total of T. 3,036,671 in 1771-72 and then fell off to T. 866,016 in 1774-75. It then rose gradually to T. 2,505,221 in 1780-81, but in 1782-83 it dropped to T. 1,044,796, largely because several of the ships destined for Canton were detained in Indian ports. The arrival of the cargoes of these ships account for the high figure of T. 2,866,316 in 1783-84, but in 1784-85 it settled back to T. 2,519,434. The average for the first ten years was T. 1,675,943 and for the next fifteen years T. 2,059,757. The average for the whole twenty-five-year period prior to 1785 was T. 1,906,231.[28] It is worthy of notice that in 1779-80 and 1781-83, years when the Company's average fell low, the Country trade was also at a low ebb—a fact which shows to a marked degree the interdependence of the two.

Under the influence of the Commutation Act the Company's trade shot skyward, reaching the enormous figure of T. 6,095,825 in 1787-88. It then declined to T. 5,292,234 in 1791-92. This decline was caused partly by troubled conditions in Europe and by the overstocked condition of the tea market, partly because some of the ships sent to Canton did not arrive, and partly because the Country trade for the season was more than halved—the resources available to the Company at Canton thus being decreased. It should be noted that the value of imports did not decline during this season, but actually increased. The entire decline was in exports. The value of trade rose rapidly again, however, reaching a peak of T. 8,349,289 in 1796-97. The average for the fifteen-year period from 1785 to 1800 was T. 5,978,650, or 190 per cent greater than for the fifteen years prior to 1785.

It is of special importance that the value of exports for the five years 1791-92 through 1795-96 declined, and that the actual increase in the value of the total trade for these years was caused by an increase in imports. During the ten years from 1790 to 1800, imports in goods

---

[28] Appendices IV, VI.

equalled half of the exports, a thing never before known in the trade between Europe and China. Throughout the first half of the eighteenth century, roughly 90 per cent of the Company's imports were bullion, and only 10 per cent were goods. During the twenty years from 1775 to 1795, goods composed about 65 per cent and bullion 35 per cent of the Company's imports. This remarkable change was caused partly by the American and European war, which during the early part of the period closed the market for Spanish dollars, partly by the enormous increase in the market for British woollens after 1790, but mainly by the fact that the Company found means, which will be discussed later,[29] for drawing the residue of the Country trade into its treasury to be used in financing its exports. Between 1760 and 1775 the Company imported bullion to the value of T. 9,780,937 and goods to the value of T. 7,516,587. During the next ten years, when war was going on, it imported bullion to the amount of T. 723,776, most of which was from India, and goods to the value of T. 4,583,308. During the ten years from 1785 to 1795, when large sums were needed to finance the expanded tea trade, it imported bullion to the amount of T. 10,862,218, and goods to the value of T. 15,428,542.[30]

From 1764 until 1785 exports from Canton showed no material increase, but after that period they increased rapidly, reaching a peak of T. 6,248,940 in 1796-97. Imports, on the other hand, increased steadily until 1771-72, after which they declined until 1783-84. From this date they rose steadily, reaching their highest figure of T. 2,546,225 in 1799-1800. In 1760-61 the ratio of exports to imports was 3.9 to 1, in 1775-76, 2.56 to 1, in 1785-86, 4.28 to 1, in 1794-95, 2.12 to 1, and in 1799-1800, 1.57 to 1. This shows fairly well the tendency during the period. Exports reacted much more quickly to the Commutation Act, but merchandise imports gradually responded until, by the end of the period, they had made the gap between themselves and exports less than it had been in the history of the trade.[31]

The Company's imports sold at a steady loss after 1775. During a few years they sold at a profit, but for the twenty-year period from 1775 to 1795 the average annual loss was T. 24,039 or 2.3 per cent per annum upon the total cost. Imports actually sold at a profit upon the prime cost, but after handling charges, interest, insurance, and the

---

[29] Chap. IV, Section 3.
[30] Appendices IV, IX.
[31] Appendices IV, VI.

supercargoes' commission were figured in they showed the above loss.[32] Charges for freight were not figured against imports but were charged against exports. This loss on imports was of no great consequence to the Company. Its great profit was made on its exports, and imports were used only as a means of financing exports and meeting the demands at home that it export British manufactures. An increase in quantity' of goods exported to China, not profit upon them, was the policy of the Company; and well might it have such a policy, considering the profit it made upon its exports, and the fact that it lost even more upon bullion and bills—the only other means it had for financing the trade. The bullion which it imported between 1775 and 1795 realized an average yearly loss of T. 55,511, or 5.27 per cent; on an average it lost 8.33 per cent on the bills which it issued.[33]

When we turn to the Company's export trade, a different story appears. After all charges—interest, insurance, freight outwards and homewards, and the supercaroges' commission—are included, its exports from China sold at an average yearly profit of £333,316 or 29 per cent upon the total cost for the ten years from 1775 to 1785, and for £488,802 or 21 per cent for the ten years from 1785 to 1795. The average yearly profit for the whole period was T. 1,233,177, or 24.5 per cent.[34] Upon its total trade with China (imports and exports—bullion included), its average annual profit for the twenty-year period was £204,479 or T. 613,437. This amounted to an annual profit of 28 per cent upon the actual money invested in the trade.[35]

In summary, one can say that the total value of the Company's merchandise trade with China increased by 593 per cent between 1760 and 1800. Imports into China increased by 1200 per cent and exports from China by 470 per cent. The major part of this increase came after 1784-85. Over the twenty-year period from 1775 to 1795 imports in goods provided 35 per cent of the money invested in exports, and bullion equalled 20 per cent, a total of 55 per cent. Of the remaining 45 per cent, about 36 per cent came from the Country trade through bills of exchange, 5⅓ per cent from engagements with the Indian Presidencies, 3 per cent from the Private trade in the form of certificates, slightly over ⅓ per cent from freight, and slightly less than ⅓

---

[32] Appendix IV.
[33] For bullion, see Appendix IX, and for bills, consider the value of each dollar at 5/- and the average exchange rate at which they were issued 5/5.
[34] Appendix VII.
[35] Appendix VIII.

per cent from bonds.[36] The relatively greater increase of the merchandise import over the export showed that the Company's policy of dumping English goods into the Chinese market at less than cost was bringing results, and that a real demand for British woollens was gradually developing.

4. *The Company's Import Trade in Goods (1775-1795).*

From England the Company imported woollens, lead, tin, and a small amount of copper. From Bombay it brought raw cotton, from Madras and Bombay sandalwood and small quantities of redwood, from Benkulen pepper, and on one occasion it brought opium from Bengal. The total value of goods imported during the twenty years from 1775 to 1795 was T. 20,011,850, of which 90 per cent came from England and 10 per cent came from India and Benkulen. English woollens composed 75.8 per cent of the above total, British metals 14 per cent, and miscellaneous produce from England 0.2 per cent. Of the 10 per cent which came from the East, pepper provided 4.7 per cent, cotton 3.5 per cent, opium 1.2 per cent and sandalwood and redwood 0.6 per cent.[37] It should be noted that prior to 1783 Indian produce played a much more important part in the trade than after that date. Figure 3 will show more clearly than words the progress and relative importance of the Company's imports in woollens, metals, and Indian produce.

Woollens were by far the most important article of merchandise imported by the Company. Over the twenty years from 1775 to 1795 woollens to the value of T. 15,224,639 were imported. They constituted nearly 84½ per cent of the total merchandise imported from England, and metals constituted only 15½ per cent, divided as follows: tin 7.1 per cent, lead 7 per cent, and copper 1.4 per cent.[38] The woollens were of three sorts: long ells, broadcloth, and camlet; at various times the Company attempted to introduce other varieties, but without success.

From the point of view of both quantity and total value, long ells were the most important of the woollens imported. The value of long ells imported during the twenty-year period was T. 9,897,584 or 65 per cent of the total woolens imported. According to the price at which

[36] Appendices IV, VI, IX, X.
[37] Appendices I, II, III, IV.
[38] Appendices I, II.

they sold (T. 7 per piece from 1776 to 1783 and from then onwards, T. 7.5 per piece) long ells must have been an inferior type of woollen cloth. Judging from the name, they were an ell (48 inches) in width, and they were probably 24 yards long, for in 1792 each cloth contained

Figure 3.

East India Company's Imports into Canton (1760-1800)*.

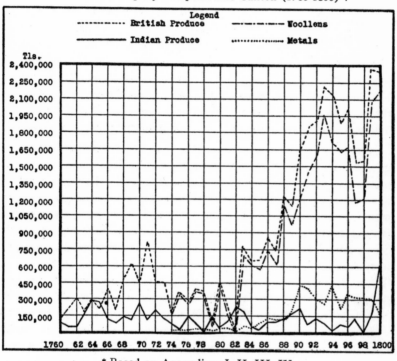

* Based on Appendices I, II, III, IV.

24 yards. They were shipped to China in bales containing 20 pieces. Their importation remained fairly low, averaging about 30,000 pieces per season, until after 1785, when they began a steady rise, reaching 177,155 pieces in 1793-94. They sold at a loss of 3.2 per cent upon the total cost throughout the period excepting the season 1794-95, when the overstocked market caused the Chinese to reduce the price to T. 6.7 per piece. Prior to 1788-89 the Company imported only one variety of long ells, but in that year it introduced a superior variety, which

was regularly imported in small quantities after 1790 and sold for T. 9 per piece.[39]

The fine, smooth, densely woven broadcloth was the second most important of the woollens imported by the Company. Over the twenty-year period the value of broadcloth imported was T. 4,558,321 or 30 per cent of the total woollens imported. It was of three varieties: worsters, which sold at T. 1 per yard; supers, which sold at an average of T. 1.45 per yard; and superfines, which sold at an average of T. 2.50 per yard. Each cloth contained about 35 yards, or 90 covids, and three cloths were packed in a bale. Prior to 1783 the importation averaged about 2,000 cloths per year; it rose to about 4,000 per year between 1783 and 1790, and then increased rapidly to 7,151 cloths in 1793-94. Broadcloth also sold at a steady loss throughout the period, the total loss being T. 465,013, or an average of 9⅓ per cent upon the total cost. It actually sold at a slight profit upon prime cost.[40]

Camlet cloth constituted a poor third in the triumvirate of woollens imported by the Company. It provided nearly 5 per cent of the woollens imported by the Company, and miscellaneous varieties provided one tenth of one per cent. Judging from the price (T. 36 per piece) at which the ordinary worsted camlet sold throughout the greater part of the period, it was in quality somewhere between the long ell and the broadcloth. The inferior quality camlet imported by the Company had to compete with the superior brand brought by the Dutch, but, nevertheless, it was the only woollen cloth which sold at a profit throughout the period. The total profit realized upon it was T. 165,424, or 29 per cent. During most of the period the Company imported only the worsted camlet, but in 1788-89 it introduced an imitation Dutch camlet, which was imported in small quantities for several years, and sold at prices between T. 40 and T. 44 per piece. In 1794-95 this was replaced by a mohair camlet, which sold for T. 33 per piece. Each piece contained 55 yards, and 20 pieces were packed in each bale. Prior to 1783 the average importation was about 300 pieces per year; it then rose to 1,250 per year for three seasons, and by 1794-95 reached 5,020 pieces.[41]

---

[39] Appendix I and the *Canton Diaries* as indicated in the notes to Appendix I; CMC, V, No. 225.

[40] Appendix I and the *Canton Diaries,* as indicated in the notes to Appendix I.

[41] Appendix I and *Canton Diaries,* as indicated in the notes to Appendix I.

Over the whole of the twenty-year period, the Company lost T. 903,088 (5.6 per cent) upon its woollens. This, however, was part of a settled policy of dumping them into the market in order to provide funds for the homeward investments, and in order to drive out Dutch and other European competition. The market was constantly overstocked after 1788, when the rapid increase in the woollen trade began. The Court of Directors insisted that barter transactions should not be made, and so the supercargoes sold the woollens at a stipulated price and kept a distinct account of their sales; but in reality the price which the Chinese merchants would give for woollens depended upon the price they received for their teas. If the supercargoes tried to raise the price of woollens, the merchants advanced the price of tea. The only method by which the supercargoes could force the sale of woollens was to make the quantity of tea which they bought from a given merchant dependent upon the quantity of woollens which he took. Contracts for tea were regularly made in this manner.[42]

The Company carefully supervised the preparation of its woollens for the Chinese market and was especially careful to maintain the quality and specifications so that there would be no complaint. This policy was worthwhile, for in time the Company's mark became the mark of quality, and it was said that its woollens were sent to the northward without ever having been opened, the merchants having the utmost confidence that the number of pieces and quality were exactly as stamped upon the bale. There was no real market for woollens at Canton because of the warm climate, and they had to be sent to the north where the cold climate made them desirable. In the course of time the Company's policy bore fruit; arteries of trade to the north were opened, and a genuine demand for British woollens developed.

Although metals constituted only 15½ per cent of the Company's imports from England, they were an important branch of the trade. The Company did not attempt to force the sale of metals, and they consequently sold at a slight profit above all costs. Some seasons they showed a loss, but for the twenty-year period they registered a net gain of T. 154,230 or slightly over 6 per cent. Lead, which had long been a staple article of export to China from Europe, was imported in ever-increasing quantities throughout the period. Its lowest year was

[42] Morse, *Chronicle*, II, 20, 28, 40, 96-97, 127, 174, 198, 210, and Morse, "The Provision of Funds for the East India Company's Trade at Canton during the Eighteenth Century," *Journal of the Royal Asiatic Society*, April, 1922, pp. 238-39.

1779-80, when only 1,667 piculs were imported, and its best year was 1786-87, when 35,640 piculs were imported. Its sales price ranged between 4 and 6 taels per picul, the average being less than 5. Lead constituted slightly over 46 per cent of the metals imported by the Company during the period, and it sold at an average profit of 8 per cent." A considerable percentage of the lead imported was used for lining camphor boxes and tea cannisters.

Tin, although not imported until the season 1789-90, quickly became the most important of the metals. During the six remaining seasons of the period, tin to the value of T. 1,280,106 or 47 per cent of the total metals was imported. The profit realized upon it was T. 57,468 or 4¾ per cent above all costs. Tin from the island of Banka was always in demand at Canton and had long been brought by the Country traders and by the Dutch. The first British tin from the mines in Cornwall was introduced by the Company in 1789-90, when 925 piculs were sold at the market price of T. 15.5 per picul. According to Meares, George Unwin of the Royal Navy was responsible for the introduction of English tin into China. It is quite certain, however, that in 1789 the Company entered into an agreement with the Cornwall tin producers, who were facing ruin because of the declining demand for Cornish tin upon the Continent, to export 800 tons of tin annually at £75 per ton, provided a sale could be found for it in India and China. British tin was considered less malleable than Banka tin, which was preferred, but a comparison of the market price and the price which the Company received for its tin reveals no particular differences, the price of each ranging between 14 and 16 taels per picul."

As an article of importation, English copper was of slight importance. Considerable copper was imported from Japan in the junk trade and was preferred to European copper. The first English copper was brought in Private trade in 1786-87, when 24 piculs were imported. In the same year the Company entered into an agreement with copper producers in England, that when prices fell below a certain level in England the Company would export what the producers could supply. Under this agreement considerable quantities were imported into China between 1787-88 and 1791-92. The first consignment (21 tons) sold for T. 7,217, a profit of T. 701. During the five seasons that it was im-

---

" Appendix II.
" Appendix II; John Meares, *Voyage . . . from China to the North West Coast of America* (London, 1790), pp. xc-xcv; PP, *Accounts and Papers, 1792-93*, No. 774b, p. 6; Wissett, *Compendium*, II, 4.

ported, a total of 9,952 piculs were brought, and, selling at T. 18 per picul, realized T. 181,117, a net profit of T. 3,859, or 2.2 per cent. Copper constituted 7 per cent of the metals imported during the period.[45] It should be borne in mind that the main expansion in the metal trade came after 1789, when the Company began the importation of tin and copper in considerable quantities, and that it began the importation of these metals at a time when it was straining every resource to finance the phenomenal expansion of the tea trade.

Indian produce, which had been of considerable importance in the Company's trade prior to 1775, constituted but 10 per cent of its imports between 1775 and 1795. Every season except two saw some Indian produce brought on the Company's account, but throughout the period its importation showed no increase. In 1760-61 the sales value of Indian produce was T. 71,371. Its highest mark was reached in 1782-83, when a cargo of opium realized T. 237,082, a loss of 18.7 per cent. The trade then dropped to T. 19,219 in 1794-95 but rose to T. 162,817 in 1799-1800. During the period from 1775 to 1795 the total sales value of Indian produce was T. 2,024,666, a yearly average of T. 101,233. It is hard to see why the Company did not encourage this trade, especially as it realized a net profit of T. 311,906, or 18 per cent over the twenty-year period. It is certain that the Company could have introduced much greater quantities of raw cotton from Bombay at considerable profit. However, the Indian Presidencies either did not wish to be troubled with the provision of large shipments or could not finance them, and so preferred to encourage the Country traders, by which means the proceeds ultimately reached the Company's treasury at Canton (but at a loss instead of a profit).[46]

In point of value pepper occupied first place among the Indian imports, constituting 46.8 per cent of the total between 1775 and 1795. With the exception of the season 1776-77, when it came from Bombay and Madras, all the pepper came from Benkulen (Fort Marlborough). The average cost of the pepper was 6d. per lb., and it sold in Canton at prices ranging from T. 10 to T. 16 per picul. If it sold for T. 12 per picul or above, it realized a profit, and during only four out of the thirteen seasons that it was imported did it sell below T. 12. It had to compete with pepper brought by the Dutch and in the Country and

---

[45] Appendix II; Morse, *Chronicle*, II, 136-37; IOCCD, LXXXV (1786-87), table of imports in Company's ships.

[46] Appendix III.

Private trades, but over the whole period its sales value amounted to
T. 948,309, recording a net profit of T. 107,493 or 12.7 per cent.[47]

Raw cotton from Bombay was the second most important Indian
import, and the only one which showed a tendency to expand. Its
sales value for the period was T. 707,980, amounting to 35 per cent of
the total Indian produce. It was imported during fourteen of the
twenty seasons, and sold for a loss but once. It sold at prices ranging
between 9 and 15 taels per picul, and realized a total profit of
T. 226,496 or 47 per cent.[48] Redwood was imported twice from Madras
and once from Bombay. It sold at a profit of 100 per cent the first
time, at a slight loss when imported from Bombay, and again at 100
per cent profit upon its last importation. Sandalwood was imported
during six seasons from Bombay and sold at a profit during four of the
seasons, when the price was above T. 20 per picul. Taken together,
sandalwood and redwood equalled 6¼ per cent of the total Indian
import and sold for a net profit of T. 24,948 or 24.7 per cent. The
remaining 12 per cent of the Indian produce imported was made up
by the one shipment of opium, and by a pearl which sold for T. 5,400,
a profit of T. 64.[49]

5. *Attempts to Introduce New Articles into China.*

On the whole, the East India Company was rather lax about attempting to introduce new articles into the Chinese market. It preferred to deal only in articles which found an extensive sale, and left
minor produce and the experimentation in new products to the Private
traders. The attitude of the supercargoes toward experimentation in
new articles was well shown by the Secret and Superintending Committee on February 3, 1794, which stated that it considered the list of
articles of trade recommended by Lord Macartney as better suited to
the speculation of individual traders than adapted to the extensive
scale of the Company. To this Lord Macartney quite properly replied
that, as the China trade was very largely a closed monopoly, he considered it incumbent upon the Company to undertake the introduction
of new products.[50] That the Court of Directors in general followed the
policy suggested by the supercargoes can be judged from the few at-

---

[47] Appendix III.
[48] Appendix III.
[49] Appendix III.
[50] CMC, VII, No. 322; IOCM, XCII, 529-32.

tempts made by the Company, except with respect to different varieties of woollens, to introduce new articles into China.

It has been noted already that the first British copper was introduced in Private trade. The same was true of cottons and steel. Thirteen piculs of cotton yarn were first brought in the Country trade in 1777-78; sixteen were brought the next year, and in 1780-81, 191 piculs were introduced (presumably from India) in Private trade. In 1781-82, 200 pieces of muslin were brought in the Country trade and 48 pieces in Private trade. These were probably from India, but in 1783-84, 327 pieces of muslin and 223 pieces of gingham, both of Manchester manufacture, were brought in Private trade. They apparently did not sell at a satisfactory profit, for no more were brought until 1792-93, when 330 pieces of muslin were imported.[51]

In the meantime the Company had shown signs of initiative. In 1886-87 some patterns of "Norwich, Manchester and Halifax Stuffs" arrived. They were shown to the merchants, who considered them too expensive and not as well suited to the Chinese market as the less elegant Chinese manufacture. In 1788-89 more samples of "Norwich, Halifax, and Manchester Goods" arrived. Shy Kinqua said that the velvets and velverets were useless, but indicated that he would not object to a small trial indent of denims and royal ribs, two cotton cloths of Manchester manufacture. In consequence of this, 50 pieces of denims invoiced at £317 (prime cost £289), and 50 pieces of royal ribs invoiced at £295 (prime cost £268) arrived in 1790-91. They were disposed of at T. 1000 for each variety, a net profit of T. 164 upon the invoice cost and T. 110 or 5.8 per cent upon the total cost. Because they were "not approved of" by the Chinese merchants, however, the Company refrained from sending any more.[52]

No attempts were made by the Company to introduce iron or steel during the period. In 1786-87, 641 piculs of iron were brought in the Country trade, and in 1792-93, 35 piculs of steel were brought in Private trade. In 1778-79 the Company brought 8 pieces of gold and silver tissue invoiced at £440 (total cost T. 1,398), which sold at a loss of T. 71 and in 1794-95 they brought 172 pieces of Irish linens which realized a loss of T. 72 upon the total cost of T. 2,619. Their only other adventures into the field of the unknown were three shipments of furs. The first, in 1777-78, was damaged on the way out and sold

[51] IOCCD, tables of trade in Vols. 62, 64, 71, 74, 78, 104.
[52] IOCCD, XCV, 118 and XCIX, 5; Morse, *Chronicle*, II, 120, 152, 179-80; PP, *Accounts and Papers, 1792-93*, No. 774.

at a net loss of T. 6,756 upon the total cost of T. 11,076. The next year a second consignment arrived from London, invoiced at £3,586, and it sold at a loss of nearly 49 per cent. Discouraged by this, the Company did not attempt this trade again until 1793-94, when a consignment, invoiced at £12,075, sold for T. 16,057, a loss of 56 per cent upon the total cost. It is hard to account for this last failure of the Company to sell its furs at a profit, unless it be attributed to lack of initiative on the part of the supercargoes in discovering good buyers, for the Private traders were bringing large shipments of furs from London at this time with apparent success.[53]

The Company made several unsuccessful experiments at introducing new types of woollens. In 1777-78, four pieces of felts sold for T. 295, and the next season fourteen pieces of duroys sold at a profit of nearly 53 per cent. These beginnings were not followed up. Flannels and drabs introduced in 1784-85 sold at a loss, as did forty pieces of camaroons introduced in 1787-88. In 1786, fourteen pieces of tabinets sold at a slight profit. But three years later 140 pieces sold at a loss. In 1793-94, two bales of embossed cloths sold at a profit, and as a consequence they were imported in small quantities for several seasons. During the period miscellaneous woollens to the value of T. 14,030 were imported and realized a net loss of T. 777 or 5.3 per cent.[54]

6. *The Company's Export Trade (1760-1800).*

As the Company exported only five articles from Canton (tea, raw silk, chinaware, nankeens, and sago), an analysis of its export trade is much simpler than of its import trade. As has already been noted, the value of exports made a phenomenal rise after the passage of the Commutation Act. This fact can be seen most clearly in Figure 4, which shows the progress of the Company's trade in each one of its staple exports from 1760 to 1800. This figure, together with Appendices V and VI, shows emphatically to what extent tea dominated the Company's export trade. Raw silk, the exportation of which was prohibited during the early years of the period, increased to T. 673,400 in 1767-68 and then declined to T. 169,077 in 1785-86. It jumped to T. 849,914 the following year, after which it steadily declined. China-

---

[53] IOCCD, tables of trade in Vols. 62, 64, 67, 78, 85, 91, 104, 107, 109, 115; Morse, *Chronicle*, II, 28, 30, 205, 256.

[54] IOCCD, invoices of ships and tables of trade in Vols. 62, 64, 80, 85, 87, 97.

ware and sago showed a slight tendency to increase until their exportation was stopped in 1791; and nankeens, which at no time amounted to more than an infinitesimal part of the total exports, showed a steady increase.

Figure 4.

East India Company's Exports from Canton (1760-1800)*.

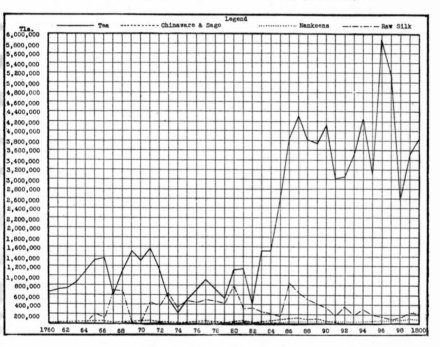

* Based on Appendices V, VI.

Tea was, in fact, the god to which everything else was sacrificed. Tea alone was an object of almost universal domestic consumption in England which did not compete with home manufacture, and from it the Company drew over 90 per cent of its commercial profits. Every precaution was taken to preserve it as a strict monopoly; every effort was made to expand it at the expense of foreign competitors, and every available resource was tapped in order to provide funds to finance its rapid expansion. During the fifteen years from 1760 to 1775 the total value of tea exported from Canton was T. 14,746,909, or 76 per cent of the Company's total exports. During the next ten years the value of tea was T. 8,774,060, or 66 per cent of the total exports. During the ten years 1785 to 1795 the total value of tea was T. 36,173,374, or 88.3 per cent of the total exports. During the whole thirty-five-year period nearly 60 million taels' worth of tea was exported, which amounted to 81 per cent of the Company's exports.[55] There were two main varieties of tea: black and green. Generally speaking, the black teas were inferior to and cheaper than green teas, and throughout the period about 70 per cent of the teas exported by the Company were black. There were four major varieties of black tea: bohea, congo, souchong, and pekoe, all of which came in the main from the Bohea Mountains in Fukien province. All teas, whether green or black, were the leaves of the same plant or shrub, the difference being due to the time of picking and the manner of preparation.[56]

Prior to 1785, bohea was by far the most important of the black teas exported. Between 1775 and 1785, it constituted about 77 per cent of the black teas and 53 per cent of all teas exported. After 1785, because of the decrease in the price of teas in England, it declined in importance and was replaced by congo, a somewhat superior and more expensive black tea. Between 1785 and 1795 bohea constituted but 31 per cent of the black teas and 21 per cent of the total teas exported. It was the cheapest of the black teas and sold in Canton throughout the period at prices varying between 12 and 14 taels per picul. Prior to the Commutation Act, its price at the Company's sales was from 2/5 to 2/10 per lb., but after this Act its average price was about 1/7 per lb. It was probably made from the second, third and fourth gatherings of tea and was consumed by the poorer classes in both England and China.[57]

Congo was the second variety of black tea. It was more carefully prepared, of a larger leaf, and less dusty than bohea. It became very popular in England after the Commutation Act had reduced its sales price from an average of about 4/10 per lb. to about 3/2. Between 1785 and 1795, it constituted roughly 60 per cent of the black teas and 40 per cent of the total teas exported from Canton by the Company.

---

[55] Appendix V.

[56] *Chinese Repository*, VIII, 132-64; Davis, *The Chinese* (1836), II, 336-37; Milburn, *op. cit.*, II, 521-27.

[57] IOCCD, tables of trade and prices throughout the volumes from 1775 to 1800; Wissett, *Compendium*, II, section on tea.

Its sales price at Canton averaged T. 21 per picul prior to 1785 and T. 25 per picul after 1785. Congo-campoi was a superior variety of congo which sold on the average for about T. 31 per picul. Souchong was a superior black tea carefully prepared from the first and youngest leaves picked. Its sales price at Canton varied between 30 and 50 taels per picul, and prior to the Commutation Act it sold at about 6/- per lb. at the Company's sales but afterwards at about 4/2. Pekoe, the most excellent of all black teas, did not constitute over 1 per cent of the black teas exported and sold at prices ranging from 45 to 60 taels per picul at Canton.[58]

Green teas constituted about 30 per cent of the teas exported from Canton by the Company. Of the green teas, singlo constituted about 40 per cent, twankay 25 per cent, hyson skin 10 per cent, and hyson 25 per cent. Most of the green teas came from a hilly region dividing the provinces of Chekiang and Anhwei. Singlo was the most inferior of the green teas, and its consumption expanded considerably after the Commutation Act reduced its average price at the Company's sales from 4/9 to 2/10. The increased demand caused its quality to deteriorate, which ultimately (after 1790) led to a rapid decline in its popularity. Its average cost price, both before and after 1785, was T. 21 per picul. Twankay was a superior variety of singlo which increased in popularity as singlo declined. Its sales price in England was about the same as singlo, but in China its average cost price prior to 1785 was T. 23 per picul, and after that date T. 26 per picul. Hyson skin consisted of the rejected leaves of hyson tea and sold in Canton at an average price of T. 26 per picul. Hyson was the most excellent of all teas exported from Canton. It was made from the first gathering of tea, and was of a small, close twisted, bluish green leaf. Its cost price varied between 45 and 60 taels per picul, and after the Commutation Act it sold at the Company's sales for prices varying from 5 to 6 shillings per lb.[59]

In view of the often reiterated contention of the Company that the re-establishment of the Co-hong in 1780 led to a great rise in tea prices, it is worthwhile to consider the matter upon the basis of the prices preserved in the Company's own records. Averaging the prices for four periods, we obtain the following results:[60]

---

[58] See note 57.

[59] For a discussion of teas see CMC, IX, No. 364.

[60] IOCCD, tables of prices in the volumes from 1775 to 1795. The Co-hong was abolished in 1771 but re-established in 1780; see Chap. V, Sect. 1.

Variety of Tea		Average 1775-80	Average 1780-85	Average 1785-90	Average 1790-95
Bohea	Tls. per picul	13.2	13.4	13.4	12
Black teas	Tls. per picul	23	23	28	26.4
Hyson	Tls. per picul	52.8	50	52.2	56
Green teas	Tls. per picul	29	31.4	32	32.8
All teas	Tls. per picul	26	27.4	30	30

From this it appears that there was no appreciable change between 1780 and 1785 in bohea, black teas, or hyson. The other varieties of green tea showed a slight increase, as did the average for all tea. Between 1785 and 1790, however, a considerable increase is to be noted in all teas except bohea, the one variety in which the Company's purchases showed a relative decline. One therefore concludes that, although the creation of the Co-hong did cause a slight increase in prices, the major rise did not come until five years later and was the result of the Commutation Act and the increased demands of the Company for tea. By 1790 a new level had been struck, so that between 1790 and 1795 the average for all teas remained the same as for the previous period, with black teas declining a little and green teas increasing a little.

The profits realized by the Company from its tea trade were great. Over the ten years from 1775 to 1785, the total value of tea sold was £11,809,112, the net profit being £2,792,910, or 31 per cent. Over the next ten years the total value of tea sold was £24,412,793, the profit being £5,865,923, or 31.6 per cent. The average yearly profit for the twenty years was £432,942, or 31.4 per cent above all costs.[61] In view of the importance of the tea trade, the Court of Directors in 1790 sent out a tea expert, Charles Arthur, to assist in the examination and appreciation of teas.[62]

Figure 4 and Appendix VI show that raw silk was the second most important article exported from Canton by the Company. Chinese silk rather than tea had been the article which originally attracted British ships to China, and during the early part of the eighteenth century it was of much greater importance than tea. As the demand for tea in England increased, however, the relative importance of silk declined.

[61] Appendix V.
[62] Morse, *Chronicle*, II, 181.

During the seasons 1760 to 1763 none was exported, because of an Imperial prohibition and the limited funds of the supercargoes; but in 1764 the reduction of the duty on raw silk imported into England to 1/3 per lb. of 24 ounces encouraged the Company to resume its exportation.[63] Between 1771 and 1774 the average yearly exportation was 1,600 piculs; for the next five years the average exportation was 1,733 piculs; between 1780 and 1785, it declined to 1,385 piculs per year; it then rose to 1,840 piculs per year between 1785 and 1790; and finally it dropped to an average of 1,101 piculs for the next five years.[64]

Between 1775 and 1785 the average yearly value of silk exported was T. 416,170, or 31.2 per cent of the total yearly value of the Company's exports. During the next ten years the average value of the exportation dropped to T. 397,024, or only 9.7 per cent of the exports. During the whole twenty-year period raw silk composed 14.9 per cent of the Company's exports.[65] Raw silk thus showed not only a relative but an actual decline in quantity after 1790. From Appendix VI it appears that this decline began after the peak season of 1786, in which 2,841 piculs were exported. The absolute decline in the silk trade was caused by an increase of the duties in England to 3/- per lb. in 1787, and by its replacement in the British markets by Italian and Turkish thrown silk.[66] The silk exported by the Company was the superior variety manufactured near Nanking. Its average cost price steadily increased until it reached a peak of T. 327 per picul in 1785, after which it steadily declined.[67]

From the point of view of cost and sales value, but not from the standpoint of profit, chinaware and sago occupied third place among the Company's exports from Canton. Chinaware, which was exported as flooring for tea, was packed in sago to prevent breakage. For the ten-year period, 1775 to 1785, the average annual value of chinaware and sago exported was T. 31,273, and, as the exportation of teas increased, chinaware showed a temporary increase, the average for the ten years from 1785 to 1795 being T. 54,395. Chinaware, however, was very bulky and in proportion to value exceedingly expensive to carry. Furthermore, the demand for Oriental porcelain was on the decline, be-

---

[63] *Shih Liao Hsün K'an,* Ch. 18, memorial dated Ch'ien Lung 24-6-25; Milburn, *op. cit.,* II, 251.

[64] Morse, *Chronicle,* V, 150, 156, 165, 176, 186; IOCCD, tables of the Company's trade in the annual volumes indicated in Appendix I.

[65] Appendix VI.

[66] Milburn, *op. cit.,* II, 251, 254-56.

[67] IOCCD, LXXXI, tables of prices.

cause it was imitated by European and English manufactures and the British government loaded it with ever-increasing duties, amounting to 47½ per cent in 1787 and to 109⅓ per cent after 1799. As a consequence of these factors, it sold at an ever-increasing loss.[68] In view of this, the Court of Directors sent out orders to decrease the quantity of chinaware purchased, and on August 4, 1791, sent out positive orders that after that season no more was to be sent on the Company's account.[69] The last sago was exported in 1785-86, and the last shipment of chinaware went home in the spring of 1792. Because of the decreased demand, the Company then had stocks on hand which were not entirely sold out until 1798.

Although nankeens, a brownish-yellow cotton cloth, manufactured near Nanking, constituted less than 1 per cent of the Company's exports, the trade showed a steady increase after 1775. From this date until 1786 the ordinary exportation was 20,000 pieces per year, but in that year it was doubled. In 1792 it was increased to 60,000 pieces, in 1796 to 119,000 pieces, and in 1799 to 200,000 pieces. This increased exportation was caused in part by the tariff policy of the British government. Prior to 1787, the duty amounted to nearly 50 per cent, but after that date it amounted to only 18 per cent, with a 10 per cent drawback upon re-exportation.[70] Roughly one third of the nankeens imported into England were re-exported.[71] Before 1789, the nankeens exported by the Company were 14 covids (5½ yds.) long by 1 covid (14.1 inches) wide. They were packed in bales of 100 pieces which averaged about a picul in weight, and by 1786 the price per bale had risen from T. 38 in 1775 to T. 48. In 1789 the Company began the exportation of nankeens 18 covids (7 yds.) long by 1 covid wide, which cost T. 62 per bale of 100 pieces, and in 1790 it added a new variety, 12 covids (4⅔ yds.) by 1 covid, which cost T. 40 per bale.[72]

Before attention is turned to the Private, Country, and Foreign trade, a final summary of the Company's export trade will be desirable. The average annual prime cost value from 1775 to 1785 was T. 1,332,426, and the average profit was £333,316, or 29 per cent per annum. During the next ten years the average prime cost value was

[68] Wissett, *Compendium*, II, section on duties.
[69] CMD, XII, Court to Select Committee, Aug. 4, 1791.
[70] IOCCD, Company's contracts for nankeens scattered throughout the volumes from 1775-1795; Wissett, *Compendium*, II, section on duties.
[71] PP, *Sessional Reports, Papers, etc., 1812-13*, VIII, No. 191, p. 479; Macgregor *Commercial Statistics*, IV, 420, and V, 33.
[72] IOCCD, XCV, XCVII, XCVIX, contracts for nankeens.

T. 4,095,813, an increase of 207 per cent over the previous ten years. Average annual profits amounted to £488,802, or 21 per cent."[73] This shows clearly that the increase in the China trade, although leading to a greater gross profit, was attained only at a decrease in the rate of profit. This fact is accounted for by the rise in prices at Canton resulting from increased demand and by close government regulation at home, which kept the sales price down.

---

[73] Appendices VI, VII.

CHAPTER IV

PRIVATE, COUNTRY, AND FOREIGN TRADE AND THE
STRUGGLE FOR CONTROL OF THE CHINA TRADE
(1764-1800)

1. *Private Trade at Canton (1764-1800).*

Although Private trade constituted only about 15 per cent of the total British trade at Canton during the period, it was of considerable importance for several reasons. First of all, the Private traders dealt in all manner of minor articles for which there was a definite demand at Canton and with which the Company did not wish to be concerned. In the second place, through the Private trade the Company found a cheap although sometimes troublesome way of reimbursing and encouraging the commanders and officers of its ships. In the third place, the Private trade, through its surplus of imports over exports, helped to finance the Company's trade. Finally, it was the only means by which the average British citizen, without shares in the Company's stock, could participate in the China trade.

Although the Private trade showed a considerable increase during the period, as can be seen from Figure 5, it tended to fluctuate a great deal and showed an actual as well as a relative decline between 1772 and 1783. The average annual value of the trade (imports and exports) for the six years 1764-1770 was T. 748,277; for the fifteeen years 1770-1785, it declined to T. 570,920 and then rose to an average of T. 1,127,810 for the last fifteen years of the period. If the average for the years 1764 to 1767 and 1796 to 1799 be taken as bases of comparison, the total trade showed an increase of 71 per cent. Imports showed an increase of 99 per cent for the same years and exports an increase of only 47 per cent. The most striking thing about the Private trade, however, was its relative decline when compared with the Company and Country trade. It constituted 26 per cent of the total British trade in 1764-65 but dropped to 7 per cent in 1774-75, rose to 14 per cent in 1780-81, and then fell off to 8 per cent in 1795-96.[1]

The decline during the middle part of the period corresponds to the years in which the Company's trade was in an unhealthy condition, and the number of ships sent by the Company, which really determined the size of the Private trade, was small. The relative decline over the

---

[1] Appendix XI.

whole period, although due in part to a decline in the demand in England for articles carried in the Private trade and to the exceptional growth of the Country trade in raw cotton and opium, must be attributed fundamentally to the increase in the size of ships used by the Company. In 1764 the Company loaded fourteen ships of an average size of 499 tons, and in 1799 it loaded fifteen ships of an average size of 1200 tons.[2] The increase in the tonnage capacity of the Company's ships decreased the number necessary to carry its ever-increasing trade and so automatically decreased the relative importance of the Private trade. The greater increase in Private trade imports than in exports during the period is largely accounted for by the growth of the ginseng and fur trade after 1785.

The variety of articles imported in Private trade was almost unlimited. Many of them never found their way into the Chinese customs house books, and so no record of them is preserved. In 1811 we have a list of fifty-six articles exported from England to China in Private trade. Of these, forty-five articles valued at £42,387 were British produce, and eleven articles valued at £17,851 were European and American produce. Raw cotton, furs, ginseng, dyes (blue and cochineal), metals, woods, cloth cuttings, and pepper were the most important articles imported during the period under discussion.[3] Articles imported in Private trade came from England, North America, and Asia. In 1785-86 the value and the distribution were as follows: British produce T. 86,564 (Prussian blue T. 24,000, lead T. 16,328, cloth cuttings T. 18,538, window glass T. 23,840, flints T. 4,000), North American produce T. 144,556 (ginseng T. 92,620, fine fur T. 1,400, rabbit skins T. 37,936, cochineal T. 12,600), and Asiatic produce T. 195,623 (cotton T. 74,012, tin T. 32,976, woods T. 55,250, pepper T. 4,210, sharks' fins T. 6,800, putchuck T. 4,131, elephants' teeth T. 2,967, miscellaneous T. 15,277), making a total of T. 426,725.[4]

The average of the figures for the seasons 1775-76, 1785-86, and 1795-96 shows that roughly 26 per cent of the goods imported came from England, 31 per cent from North America, and 43 per cent from

---

[2] Morse, *Chronicle,* V, and II, tables of shipping in the back.

[3] Macgregor, *op. cit.,* V, 35-38; IOCCD, LXXXVII, tables of trade, for the articles imported in a typical year.

[4] Appendix XI and IOCCD, LXXXIII, tables of trade. Only the quantities of articles imported in the Company's ships in Private trade are given in the *Canton Diaries.* The value is obtained by multiplying the quantity of each article by the Canton current price which is given in the same volume. All values for the Private and Country trade have been obtained by this method.

Asia. Over the whole period, Private import trade showed an increase of 99 per cent, but this increase was not distributed equally among the three sources of produce. In 1775-76 the percentages were as follows: English 36, North American 23, Asiatic 41. From this it appears that the importation of English produce suffered relatively, the proportion of Asiatic produce increased slightly, and North American produce increased a great deal.

The relatively greater expansion of the trade in North American produce was caused by the introduction of much greater quantities of ginseng and by the development of an extensive trade in fine furs after 1785. Rabbit skins had been a staple article of Private trade from the beginning, and in 1785 a beginning was made in the fine fur trade with 350 beaver skins. This trade grew rapidly and consisted mainly of beaver, fox, and otter skins brought from Canada to England and then shipped to China. From 1792 onward seal skins were also brought, and occasionally marten and sea-otter skins were imported. The peak year was reached in 1793-94, when 108,471 fine furs were imported and 311,100 rabbit skins. Cochineal was a West Indian insect from which was made a dye used in the preparation of silk goods.[5]

Besides the articles already mentioned as coming from England, bees'-wax, watches, clocks, knives, cutlery of various sorts, and glass-ware such as looking glasses, plate glass, and wine glasses, were brought. Prussian blue was a blue dye, and smaltz was an oxide of cobalt melted with silex and potash and was used for painting on por-celain. It is certain that camlets were smuggled in Private trade, but no satisfactory figures on the subject are obtainable. It also seems certain that small quantities of silver were regularly brought from England; and numerous miscellaneous articles—such as copper, cotton cloth, and iron and steel—were tried from time to time.[6]

Cotton from Bombay, tin from Banka, and woods from Bombay and Madras (sandalwood, redwood, and blackwood or ebony) were the most important articles of import from Asia, cotton easily being the most important article brought in Private trade. A description of articles imported from Asia may be found in Milburn's *Oriental Commerce* (II, 216, 497-545). Besides those already mentioned, rattans, betel-nut, olibanum and other gums, stick-lac, sago, *bêche de mer*, cutch, fish maws, snuff, spices, rose maloes, cornelians or agates, and various

---

[5] IOCCD, LVIII, LXXXIII, CIV, CVII, tables of imports in the Company's ships; Morse, *Chronicle*, V, 155, and II, 185, 193, 256.

[6] Milburn, *Oriental Commerce*, II, 479.

types of Indian cotton piece-goods, such as Madras long cloths and handkerchiefs, and Bengal palampores and handkerchiefs, were imported at various times in Private trade.

The value of exports in Private trade never equalled the value of merchandise imported. The main features and general character of the export trade may be judged from the figures for the season 1785-1786. During this season the total value of exports was T. 315,510, divided as follows: tea T. 96,000, nankeens T. 30,750, woven silks T. 29,800, chinaware T. 27,340, rhubarb T. 20,130, cassia and buds T. 76,288, sugar and candy T. 9,352, sago T. 1,040, and miscellaneous T. 24,810.[7] There are figures from the season 1793-94 onwards for the value of Private trade goods sold at the Company's sales in London. During this season the value of Private trade was £258,981, in 1794-95 £209,715, in 1797-98 £319,236, and in 1800-01 £268,701. During the season 1795-96, 1,344,794 lbs. of tea were sold for £314,139, the value of nankeens sold was £16,281, chinaware £11,024, and miscellaneous items £9,663—making a total of £351,107.[8]

As in the Company's trade, tea was the most important article exported, though its relative importance steadily increased throughout the period. Only the more expensive teas, souchong (black) and hyson (green), were exported in Private trade. At the beginning of the period chinaware was as important as tea, if not more so, but its exportation gradually declined for reasons already given in the discussion of the Company's trade. The export of silk piece-goods showed a tendency to decline throughout the period, whereas the export of nankeens steadily increased until 1790, after which it underwent a temporary eclipse. The exportation of rhubarb increased, and the trade in sugar and sugar candy, most of which went to India, was a steadily expanding one. The export of cassia and cassia buds increased steadily until 1786-87 and then underwent a sudden decline. Besides the above-mentioned articles, the following were exported in varying quantities during the period: turmeric, gamboge, galangal, rattans, mother-of-pearl ware, lacquered ware, quicksilver, fans, whanghees, soy, mats, borax, and silk thread.[9]

---

[7] Appendix XI, and IOCCD, LXXXIII, as in note 4 of this chapter.

[8] PP, *Sessional Reports, Papers, etc., 1812*, VI, No. 148, pp. 80-81, 102; Milburn, *Oriental Commerce*, II, 480; Macgregor, *Commercial Statistics*, IV, 412-13, and V, 33-34, 79-81; Wissett, *Compendium*, II, section on tea.

[9] IOCCD, tables of exports in the Company's ships, scattered throughout the volumes from 1775 to 1790.

Figure 5.
Private and Country Trade at Canton (1770-1800)*.

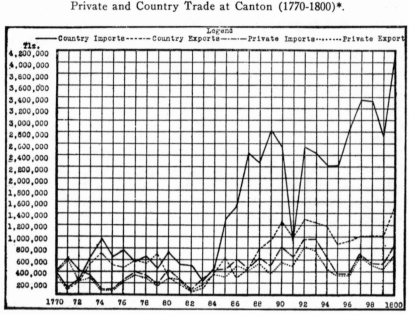

* Based on Appendices XI, XII.

2. *Country Trade at Canton (1764-1800).*

In 1764-65 the Country trade contributed 12 per cent of the total British trade at Canton; in 1775-76 it amounted to 40 per cent; in 1785-86 it receded to 30 per cent; and in 1795-96 its proportion was 33 per cent. Throughout the period it contributed about 30 per cent of the total British trade. It was primarily an import trade in contrast to the Company's, which was primarily an export trade. In 1764-65 imports in the Country trade exceeded exports by 16 per cent, and this disparity continued to grow throughout the period, amounting in 1775-76 to 18 per cent, in 1785-86 to 104 per cent, and in 1795-96 to 148 per cent. In 1775-76 the Country trade contributed nearly 50 per cent of all British imports and but 30 per cent of the exports; in 1795-96 it provided 48 per cent of the imports and 18 per cent of the exports.[10]

As can be seen from Figure 5, the Country import trade remained around T. 250,000 until 1773-74, when it rose to T. 632,000. This new

---

[10] Appendix XII.

high level was generally maintained until 1782-83, when for three years the average fell below T. 400,000. It jumped to T. 1,284,873 in 1785-86 and continued to rise until it reached T. 3,372,207 in 1797-98, the high-water mark for the period. Its general character may be judged from the average value of articles imported during the three seasons 1775-76, 1785-86, and 1795-96. The average annual value of the trade for these three seasons was T. 1,384,653, divided as follows: cotton T. 708,038, opium T. 213,398, tin T. 95,939, pepper T. 60,574, camphor T. 50,666, sharks' fins T. 31,655, woods T. 29,299, putchuck T. 26,490, elephants' teeth T. 12,486, birds' nests T. 5,266, olibanum T. 4,339, fish maws T. 2,677, rattans T. 1,584, and miscellaneous T. 149,909.[11]

As can be seen from Appendix XII, raw cotton (from Bombay) was by far the most important article imported in the Country trade. During the period from 1775 to 1800 it constituted at least one-half of the total merchandise imported in the Country trade, although in 1775-76 it was exceeded in importance by tin from the island of Banka. Throughout the period from 1775 to 1800 tin actually occupied third place among the Country imports. Figures for opium are practically unobtainable, but the best estimates indicate that it occupied second place among the imports and contributed perhaps 15 per cent of the total for the period. Pepper occupied fourth place among the imports, followed in order by camphor from Sumatra and Borneo, woods (mainly sandalwood, with small quantities of blackwood, redwood, and sapan wood) from Bombay and Madras, and sharks' fins and putchuck from Bombay. The cotton trade was a rapidly expanding one, and the trade in opium, woods, sharks' fins, olibanum, rattans, and elephants' teeth showed a steady growth. Tin, pepper, putchuck, fish maws, and camphor showed no marked increase.[12]

During this period the greater percentage of the Country trade was between Bombay and Canton. Generally speaking, six out of every ten Country ships were from Bombay, whereas only two came from Madras and two from Bengal. The produce which was brought in Country trade came from five general regions. Arabia and the Persian Gulf contributed cornelians (agates), cow bezoar, cutch, olibanum, myrrh,

---

[11] IOCCD, LVIII, LXXXIII, CXV, tables of Country trade and tables of the current price at Canton. The values are obtained by multiplying the quantity imported by the current price.

[12] Appendix XII and IOCCD, tables of Country trade for the seasons from 1775 to 1800.

putchuck, rose maloes, and sharks' fins. Most of these articles were brought to China by the Parsee merchants from Bombay, and to a lesser extent they came via Madras. Bombay, Surat, and the Malabar coast contributed cotton, cotton piece-goods, sandalwood, false amber, cow bezoar, elephants' teeth (ivory), gogul, olibanum, pearls, and sharks' fins. From Madras and the Coromandel coast came sandalwood, redwood, blackwood (Ceylon), cotton piece-goods, elephants' teeth, pearls, sharks' fins, pepper, mace, and false amber.

Cotton piece-goods, opium, rice, elephants' teeth, and stick lac came from Bengal; and a great assortment of articles were brought from the East Indian Islands and the Malay Archipelago by ships from Bengal, Madras, and Bombay. Birds' nests, camphor, dragons' blood, bengamin, rattans, sago, betel-nut, and pepper came from Java, Sumatra, and Borneo. Spices came from the Moluccas and Banda Islands, and amber, bees'-wax, *bêche de mer,* coral, fish maws, mother-of-pearl, and tortoise shell were brought from the various islands and the Archipelago. Tin came from the Island of Banka and elephants' teeth from Borneo and Siam. Practically all the cotton came from Bombay or Surat, but small quantities came from Madras after being transshipped. None came from Bengal at this time. Opium was brought from Bengal, Goa, and Daman by the Portuguese and from Bengal by Country traders, and small quantities may have been smuggled from the Malabar coast by the Parsee.[13]

In return for these articles the Canton market offered a great variety of things which the Indian Presidencies wanted, but never in sufficient quantities to make the trade balance. The difference would have been made up in bullion had not the Company needed the favorable Indian balance to finance its tea trade. The tea appetite of the English for many years saved China from the consequences of this balance of trade in favor of India. In fact, this insatiable desire for tea really created the favorable Indian balance, for it is doubtful that the trade in raw cotton, which actually caused the scales to swing in favor of India, would ever have expanded to such proportions had the Company not needed the residue which it left at Canton.

The curve of the export trade roughly followed that of the import trade, although its rate of increase was much slower. The relative value of the various articles sent by China to India may be shown by averag-

---

[13] Milburn, *op. cit.*, II, 497-545; Morrison's *Commercial Guide* (1844), pp. 131-44 gives a description of the articles mentioned above.

ing the trade for the three seasons 1775-76, 1785-86, and 1795-96. The average annual value of the export trade during these years was T. 673,158, divided as follows: raw silk T. 133,247, tutenague T. 100,729, sugar T. 90,401, sugar candy T. 87,352, tea T. 77,025, woven silks T. 63,943, chinaware T. 29,317, camphor T. 26,217, quicksilver T. 15,127, nankeens T. 14,293, alum T. 6,945, cassia and buds T. 6,220, China root T. 870, and miscellaneous T. 21,495.[14] Sugar and sugar candy together were the most important exports, constituting roughly 26 per cent of the total. Next in succession followed raw silk and tutenague, which throughout the period contributed roughly 20 per cent each. Tea made a poor fourth with 12 per cent, and woven silks amounted to about 10 per cent. Camphor and chinaware each contributed about 4 per cent, and quicksilver, nankeens, alum, and cassia lagged behind with 1 to 2 per cent each.

Besides the articles mentioned above, small quantities of dammar, turmeric, beads, gamboge, galangal, rhubarb, mother-of-pearl ware, lacquered ware, cochineal, hams, writing paper, mats, woods, spices, umbrellas, fireworks, glue, silk stockings, drugs and sweetmeats were from time to time exported. The annually exported quantity of each of the articles mentioned above tended to fluctuate a good deal, but over the period all of them, with the exceptions of tea and raw silk, showed a slow but steady increase. Tea and raw silk remained about the same throughout the period.[15] Such articles as tea, chinaware, and lacquered ware were exported primarily for the use of Europeans in India, but it seems probable that some proportion of the raw silk, nankeens, cassia, and drugs exported ultimately went to England via India. Tutenague, sugar, sugar candy, alum, Chinese camphor, quicksilver, and China root were apparently exported primarily for Indian consumption. What proportions of these exports went to the various Indian Presidencies is impossible to say, for many of the ships from Bombay and Madras returned via Bengal and Madras.

The number of London and Indian firms and individuals engaged in the Country trade at this time was large. From the lists of bills issued by the supercargoes and preserved in the *Canton Diaries,* it is possible to pick out and trace the evolution of some of the leading firms. Two early firms of importance were those of *Crichton and Smith* and *Hutton and Gordon,* both of whom began business in the late 1760's. Both

---

[14] IOCCD, as in note 11 of this chapter.
[15] *Ibid.,* tables of the Country trade in the volumes from 1775 to 1800; Milburn, *op. cit.,* II, 45, 147, 482, 497-545.

firms loaned money extensively to Chinese merchants, lost heavily as a result of the Hongist's bankruptcies of 1779, and shortly afterwards ceased to do business in China. Another early firm was *Messrs. Rumbold, Charlton and Raikes,* which appeared in 1775. By 1787 we find it under the name of William and Thomas Raikes and Salomons, and during 1791 and 1792, the last years in which it appeared, the name was William and Thomas Raikes and Samuel Ibbetson. Another prominent firm began in 1778 as John Hunter, Thomas Parry and James King and in 1784 included Hunter, Larkins, Vansittart, and Law. By 1787 Larkins had dropped out, but the firm of *Hunter, Vansittart and Law* (all of London) continued until 1791. Hunter's name was also linked with William Hornby's in 1787 and 1788, but in 1796 he was a member of Hunter and Tasker. His name also appeared alone in 1781, 1789, 1790, 1791, 1793, 1794, and 1795.

The firm of *Samuel Smith and Sons* appeared in 1778 and continued for several years, but in 1791, 1792, and 1793 it became Smith and Atkinson and then returned to the original name. The firm of *Lambert and Ross* first appeared in 1778 under the name of Ross, Mill and Ross. In 1788 the name of Anthony Lambert appeared, and thenceforward the firm of Lambert and Ross appeared regularly until after 1796. In 1778 also appeared *Messrs. Hoares and Co.* under Bland, Barnet, Hoares and Co. By 1781 Bland and Barnet had dropped out, but the firm continued to do business until 1797. The name of John Forbes appeared in 1781 alone and in conjunction with Libbald, Lockyer and Forbes. Forbes continued to trade alone until 1795, when the firm of *Forbes, Smith (James) and Co.* of Bombay was formed. It was replaced in 1804 by Forbes and Co.

The names of William Fairlie and John Fergusson appeared individually between 1781 and 1790, but in 1788 and 1790 the firm of *Fairlie, Fergusson and Co.* of Calcutta, did business at Canton. Between 1784 and 1788 the firm of *Gildart and Reid* (John Reid, Imperial Consul) did business at Canton. In 1789 and 1790 the names of Andrew and John Reid appeared and in 1793 the name of David Reid (as Danish Consul). Between 1792 and 1795 Reid and Fairlie united to form *Fairlie, Reid and Co.,* which was replaced from 1796 onward by *Fairlie, Gilmore and Co.* Reid later united with Beale to form Beale and Reid.

The year 1787 saw the beginning of several firms. Daniel Beale, an unlicensed Country trader and former purser on one of the Company's ships, arrived at Canton as Prussian Consul and continued to reside there for some years. During 1787, 1788, and 1789 he and John Henry Cox, also an unlicensed trader resident at Macao, did business separately, but in 1790 and 1791 they united in the firm of *Cox and Beale.*[16] After that, Beale did business alone and with his brother Thomas until after the formation of *Reid and Beale* of Calcutta in 1801. In 1804 this gave place to *Beale and Magnac,* which continued for some years.

Colvin, Bazett and Co. began in 1787 as Bayne and Colvin. Bazett was added in 1789, whereas Bayne dropped out, leaving Colvin and Bazett of Calcutta to do a regular business thereafter. Horsley and Palmer appeared in 1788, became Hall and Palmer the next year, and operated as William Palmer in 1790 and 1791. In 1802 it became *Palmer and Co.* of Calcutta. In 1793 Alexander Bruce, a former supercargo, began doing business at Canton, and from 1796 onward *Bruce, Fawcett and Co.* of Bombay and London did regular business at Canton. Ewan Law of London did business with various firms after 1784, but in 1798 the firm of *Law, Bruce and Co.* of Token House Yard, London, was formed.

The following is a list of other important firms which did business at Canton, together with the dates between which they carried on their most extensive trading, as shown in the list of bills.

1. William and Thomas Lushington (1775-1806).
2. Messrs. Drummond and Co. (1778-94).
3. Capt. James Farquaharson (1778-1804).
4. Capt. Joseph Cotton (1778-94), sometimes Tatnell & Cotton.
5. Alexander and John Duncan (1778-96), alone and with others.
6. Capt. William Mackintosh (1784-93).
7. William Paxton and Co. (1784-89).
8. Joseph Barretto and Co. (1787-----), Calcutta and Macao.

[16] John Reid, a Scotchman, was at Canton in 1783 and 1784 as Imperial Consul (Morse, *Chronicle,* II, 85; *Shaw's Journal,* p. 171), and from 1793 onward David Reid resided at Canton as Danish Consul (Morse, *Chronicle,* II, 206, 285, 311, 322). The Reids were probably brothers who had business connections in Bengal, and after 1792 they were represented in China by David, who worked in conjunction first with William Fairlie of Calcutta, and then with Thomas and Daniel Beale of Calcutta and Canton. For an account of the activities of Daniel Beale and John Henry Cox, see Morse, *Chronicle,* II, 85, 142, 150, 175, 187, 206, 285. In 1796 Thomas Beale, brother of Daniel, arrived at Canton as secretary to the Prussian Consul, and in 1798 he succeeded his brother as Prussian Consul. In 1802 Charles Magnac arrived as Prussian Vice-Consul, and soon the firm of Beale and Magnac was formed. It later became Magnac and Co. and finally evolved into Jardine, Matheson and Co., which is still in existence (Morse *Chronicle,* II, 285, 311, 390).

9. Edmund Boehm and Co. (1787-93).
10. John Call (M.P.) (1787-94), New Bond St., London.
11. Cockerell and Trail (1787-1804).
12. Joseph Price and Co. (1787-90).
13. David Scott and Co. (1787-----), Calcutta.
14. Robert and William Dent (1787-96).
15. Messrs. Goslings, Bankers (1788-93), London.
16. Lance and Fitzhugh (1788-96), London. Former supercargoes.
17. William Marsden (1788-95).
18. John Duval and Sons (1789-1801).
19. Porcher and Redhead (1789-----).
20. Dady Nasserwanjee (1792-98), Bombay.
21. Alexander Adamson (1793-1805).

3. *How British Trade at Canton was Financed.*

As already noted, the Country and the Private trade were more than self-sufficient; that is, they imported goods to a greater value than they exported and so there was no problem of finding money to pay for their purchases. With the Company's trade the situation was entirely different. During the twenty years between 1775 and 1795 the total sales value of goods and bullion imported into China by the Company was T. 31,597,844. During the same period the total invoice value of goods and stores exported was T. 56,516,560. The question at once arises as to where the supercargoes obtained the difference, T. 24,918,716, between the value of imports and exports. A glance at the balance in favor of the Country and Private trade will reveal the answer. Over the same period the Country trade showed a favorable balance of T. 13,644,563 and the Private trade a favorable balance of T. 1,762,730, a total of T. 15,407,293. In addition, the Country trade is known to have imported $1,718,920 in silver and the Private trade $466,196, and considerable unrecorded amounts were almost certainly sent.[17]

From this it is obvious that the residue of the Country and Private trade was used by the Company to finance its trade. The only question remaining to be answered is: How did the Company make this residue available for its use? The methods employed have already been indicated to a certain extent, and Doctor H. B. Morse has so thoroughly explained them in an article in *The Journal of the Royal Asiatic*

---

[17] Appendices IV, VI, IX, XI, XII.

Society[18] that a detailed discussion upon the subject would be idle. Only a brief statement of the methods will therefore be given, together with an indication of the relative importance and success of each.

Of the total funds needed to finance the Company's export trade and to pay running expenses at Canton for the years from 1775 to 1795, *goods* imported provided T. 20,011,850, over 34 per cent, and *bullion* provided T. 11,585,994, or nearly 20 per cent. All the bullion imported from England came in the form of Spanish dollars, and their availability in London depended upon the continuation of peace in Europe. Consequently, between 1775 and 1783, when England was at war, little silver was imported, and practically all that was brought to Canton on the Company's account came from India in the form of Spanish dollars, gold mohurs, pagodas, other Indian coins, and gold dust. India and Benkulen sent T. 588,108, or slightly over 5 per cent of the total bullion imported. Between 1786-87 and 1792-93, when peace prevailed in Europe, large quantities of Spanish dollars came from England. They were invoiced at from 5/1½ per ounce to 5/2½ per ounce. Altogether T. 10,997,886, or 95 per cent of the total bullion, came from England.[19]

Bills of Exchange on the Court of Directors in London were the most important source from which funds were secured. The Company obtained T. 22,627,742, or nearly 36 per cent of its funds from this source. For the most part the bills were issued in favor of Indian and London merchants in return for cash paid into the Company's treasury at Canton. Most of them were payable at 365 days sight, and issued at an exchange ranging between 5/- and 5/6 per Spanish dollar. Some were issued at 730 days sight at exchanges ranging between 5/3 and 5/7. Bills issued in favor of London firms went directly to London to be redeemed, but those in favor of Indian merchants went to India, where they were sold to persons wishing to transfer money to England and so were eventually presented in London for payment.[20]

Most of the cash paid into the Company's treasury in return for these bills came from the sale of goods brought in the Country trade. However, in times of emergency, especially during the early years of the period, this was insufficient, and the Indian Presidencies adopted other means of sending cash to Canton. For example, in 1776 the

---

[18] "The Provision of Funds for the East India Company's Trade at Canton during the Eighteenth Century," April, 1922, pp. 227-35.
[19] Appendix IX.
[20] Appendix X and the lists of bills given in the *Canton Diaries* from 1775 to 1800.

Governor-General's Council at Fort William invited *subscriptions* to a fund, the subscribers to be paid by bills on London. Through this method 966,666⅔ arcot rupees (420,520 dollars) were received at Calcutta and sent to Canton in a King's frigate.[21] In 1779 the Councils of Bombay and Fort St. George (Madras) adopted a modified form of this subscription plan and invited private merchants to send silver to Canton freight-free and at the Company's risk to be paid into the Canton treasury in return for bills on London.[22]

The *freight-free privilege* was another means employed to get money into the Company's treasury. By this method the Indian Presidencies allowed Country merchants to send goods to Canton upon the Company's ships freight-free, and, in return for this favor, they were to pay the proceeds into the Company's treasury and receive bills on London.[23]

Another means by which bills were made to realize purchasing value at Canton without the actual transfer of money was *transfers in the treasury*. This method was a modified form of barter and arose

at a time when the want of Specie rendered it an object of reciprocal convenience to the Company, the Merchant, & the Remitter, & was an order from the [Chinese] Merchant to whom the Company was indebted to pay the amount of the Balance owing or any part thereof to an Individual who [had] at the same time a demand on the Merchant, which payment it [was] always understood [was] to be made by a Bill of Exchange on the Hon'ble Court of Directors.[24]

The issue of tranfers in the treasury developed extensively after 1786 in consequence of the prohibition upon the issue of bills on Bengal by the Governor-General.

Although *bills on the Indian Presidencies* had been used prior to 1775, the year 1786 saw the only issue during the period under consideration (1775-1795), when bills amounting to nearly 7 lacs of rupees, T. 244,995, were issued at an exchange of $39 = 100 current rupees. Lord Cornwallis reprimanded the supercargoes for this and prohibited further issue in the future.[25] This one issue amounted to nearly 1 per cent of the total funds received during the period.

Engagements of the Indian Presidencies was the next most important source of funds, realizing during the period T. 3,011,323, or 5⅓

---

[21] Morse, *Chronicle*, II, 7.
[22] *Ibid.*, II, 36-37, 40-42.
[23] *Ibid.*, II, 9.
[24] *Ibid.*, II, 143-44.
[25] *Ibid.*, II, 121, 142; Appendix X.

per cent of the total. These engagements assumed various forms, but in general they consisted of advances of money from the Indian governments to Country merchants, who bought goods with them. The goods were shipped to Canton, and the proceeds, to the amount originally advanced, were paid into the Canton treasury. In Calcutta the government often delivered opium to Country merchants to be sent to China, the proceeds from which, to the value of the goods originally delivered, were to be paid into the Company's treasury at Canton.[26]

Certificates, which really amounted to bills upon the Court of Directors, issued to commanders and officers in return for cash paid into the Company's treasury were another important source of funds. During the period a total of T. 1,658,803, or 3 per cent of the total receipts, was obtained through this medium. The certificates were made payable half at 90 days' and half at 365 days' sight, and were issued at the exchange of the season. The use of other sources of remittance to England by Private traders was virtually forbidden, and by this means the Company obtained practically all of the residue of the Private trade.[27]

Freight paid by Country traders for goods shipped from India to China on the Company's ships provided T. 221,956, or about ⅓ per cent of the funds.

Bonds realized T. 170,926, or slightly less than ⅓ per cent. The bonds were issued at various times to Portuguese, Spanish, and Country traders at Canton and to the supercargoes. The rates of interest were generally very high, amounting in 1795 to 10 per cent.[28]

It is also of interest to know by whom the money received in exchange for bills was paid into the Company's treasury. Since the Company forbade the residence of "private English" at Canton, the Country trade had to be transacted through supercargoes sent with the ships or by agents in Canton. Private English residents at Canton under cover of a foreign commission and Portuguese at Macao sometimes acted as agents, but most of this business was done by the junior supercargoes of the Company. The money received in return for bills was thus paid in by the Company's supercargoes, by commanders of Company ships under special license, by supercargoes and captains of Country ships, by Portuguese and other foreign mechants, and by "private English."

[26] Appendix X; Morse, *Chronicle*, II, 31, 121.
[27] Appendix X.
[28] Appendix X; Morse, *Chronicle*, II, 32, 266.

From the list of bills issued it is possible to obtain the names of the persons who paid in the money.

During the whole period the Company's supercargoes probably paid in a greater percentage of the money than did any other group. In 1775 they paid.in T. 107,515, commanders of ships T. 8,637, and Country traders T. 322,528. In 1781-82 the supercargoes paid in but $331,366 out of a total of $1,432,472, but as the period advanced they paid in greater percentages.[29] From 1775 to 1783 W. H. Pigou was the most important of the supercargoes, and in 1784 and 1789 Lance and Fitzhugh were most important. Between 1787 and 1792 the agencies of Hall and Peach and of Parkin and Smith did practically all the business for the supercargoes. In 1791 the Court sent out orders that a House of Trade, to consist of two or three junior supercargoes, was to be formed to conduct the commission business, the profits to be divided among the supercargoes. This agency was formed in 1792 as Drummond and Sparkes and continued to do all the business for the supercargoes until 1796.[30]

Among the most important of the commanders who paid in money were Capt. Walter Watson (1778-84), Capt. William Mackintosh (1784-93), Capt. John William Wood (1787-91), and Capt. Lestock Wilson (1793-96). Several prominent "private English" who resided at Canton and Macao in defiance of the Court's orders paid money into the Company's treasury. George Smith, of Guildford, Surrey, and Madras, resided in China continuously from 1772 until the spring of 1782. He was finally forced to return to England in 1782, and in 1787 we find him in England requesting Colonel Cathcart to collect the debts which certain Chinese merchants owed him. Another George Smith, of Kingston, Surrey, and Bombay and Calcutta, first appeared in China during the year 1759. He remained there more or less continuously until 1765,when he returned to England. He did not go back to China for nineteen years, when he appeared again as supercargo of the *Lady Hughes* in the seasons 1784-85 and 1786-87. This latter George Smith was in Calcutta on September 10, 1787, when his namesake was in England.[31]

[29] Morse, *Chronicle*, II, 5, 26; IOCCD, LXXIV, 58-70.
[30] Morse, *Chronicle*, II, 196-97, 206, 285.
[31] For Geo. Smith of Guildford, Surrey, *ibid.*, V, 148, 162, 166, 172, 179, 191 and II, 4, 11, 33, 46, 54, 66-67. For Geo. Smith of Kingston, Surrey, Morse, *Chronicle*, V, 72, 102, 108. 115 and II, 99-100; IO, *Home Miscellaneous,* CCCCXXXIV, 11-12 and IOC, XIX, Geo. Smith to Dundas, Canton, Nov. 26 and Dec. 12, 1786, and Calcutta, Sept. 10, 1787.

John Henry Cox, of Bengal, who arrived at Macao in 1781, continued to reside in China until the spring of 1788, when he was forced to leave. Between 1778 and 1787 he paid in considerable sums, and in 1784 he was in partnership with Hugh Parkin, a supercargo. In 1787 Daniel Beale, a former purser on one of the Company's ships, arrived and took up his residence under cover of a commission as Prussian Consul. He resided at Canton until 1797 and regularly paid in large sums. Between 1789 and 1792 the firm of Cox and Beale carried on business at Canton, Cox presumably coming from India each season as a Country trader.[32]

From 1792 onwards, Manoel de Souza, a Portuguese resident at Macao, paid in considerable sums, and two Parsee named Edeljee Bomanjee (1787-98) and Dady Nasserwanjee (1788-94) appeared prominently. The names of numerous Country traders appeared, and the following is a list of the most prominent together with the dates between which they paid in money: Thomas Dickinson (1778-93), John Reid (1781-92), John Smith (1787-93), Duncan, Parker and Smith (1788-95), Bruce, Simpson and Watson (1789-95), Thomas Bruce (1792-95), John Elmore (1791-92), and Robert Hamilton (1792-97).

From the data at hand it is possible to draw up a balance sheet of the Company's transactions at Canton during the twenty years from 1775 to 1795:[33]

Receipts	Tls.	Payments	Tls.
Carry over 1775	340,395	Goods	54,282,381
Goods—English	17,987,184	Charges	2,110,424
Indian	2,024,666	Stores	123,755
Bullion—England	10,997,886	Bonds and Bills	500,537
India	588,108	Advances to Ships	820,800
Bills—London	22,627,742	Msc. Expense	514,212
Bengal	244,995		
Indian Engagements	3,011,323	Total	58,352,109
Certificates	1,658,803		
Freight	221,956	Balance Remaining	
Bonds	170,926	1795	1,521,875
	59,873,984		59,873,984

[32] Morse, *Chronicle*, V, 85, 142, 150, 175, 187, 206, 285.
[33] Advances to ships while at Canton are estimated at the charter-party rate of £200 per month. 304 ships were at Canton during the period, and their average stay was about 18 weeks per ship. Miscellaneous expense has been added to bring about the balance. Under it would come expenses attending the Macartney Embassy, various unrecorded bills paid and stores sent to India, expenses attending certain ships sent to India, advances to the supercargoes on their commissions, and minor unrecorded charges.

4. *Continental European and American Trade at Canton and the Struggle for Control of the China Trade (1764-1800).*

The British were not without strong competition in the China trade. The French established a successful factory at Canton in 1698, one year before the English, and the Dutch had indirect connections with Canton through Batavia from early in the seventeenth century. Their first direct ship from Holland to Canton arrived in 1729. Two years later, in 1731, the first Danish ships came, and in the following year the first Swedish ships arrived.[34] These five nations—England, France, Holland, Denmark, and Sweden—competed for the mastery of the China trade throughout the eighteenth century, and it was not until the very end of the period that the British emerged victorious. Between 1779 and 1795 new rivals appeared in the Imperialists, the Prussians, the Italians, the Americans, and the Spanish. Because of the importance of this foreign competition in influencing the Company's and the British government's policies toward China and the China trade, it seems advisable to devote some space to an analysis of the trade of these various countries. Figures 6 and 7 give a general view of foreign European and American trade from 1764 to 1800 and will serve as a starting point for this analysis.

The first important thing to notice is the steady growth of the total Continental trade in merchandise from 1772 until 1783 (with the exception of the war years, 1780 to 1783) and then its steady decline to a record low level in 1795. Starting with a value of T. 2,640,150 in 1764-65, it remained at about this level until 1772-73, when it rose to T. 3,006,310. It then increased steadily, except for the season 1775-76, until T. 3,656,340 was reached in 1779. It then decreased to T. 1,831,630 in 1781-82, because the European war interrupted the French and the Dutch trade. The Danes and the Swedes profited by this interruption, and persons sailing under Imperial, Tuscan, and Prussian flags seized this opportunity of sending ships to China. In consequence, a peak season of T. 5,454,744 was reached in 1783-84, when the cessation of hostilities enabled eight French ships—as well as two Prussian, five Imperial, three Swedish, and three Danish ships—to arrive. The arrival of four Dutch and four Portuguese ships the next season caused the average to remain high at T. 4,140,020. The season of 1785-86 was also an exceptionally good one, there being thirteen Continental European ships at Canton carrying a total trade of T. 4,294,450, but the following

---

[34] Morse, *Chronicle,* I, 91-92, 193, 203, 212.

season saw a decline, which continued steadily until the all-time low mark T. 693,150 was reached in 1795-96. Despite the war years, when French and Dutch ships were not at Canton, Continental European trade between 1775 and 1785 averaged about T. 3,530,000 per year. Between 1785 and 1795 it averaged about T. 2,560,000 per year.[35]

The second important thing to notice is the development of Spanish trade (between Manila and Canton) and American trade after 1784. One Spanish ship arrived in 1783 and four arrived in 1785, after which ships came regularly, averaging two per year for the last ten years of the period. The first American ship arrived in 1784, five came in 1786, and after that they came in increasing numbers. The development of the Spanish and American trade just about offset the decline of the Continental trade, their combined yearly average from 1784 until 1795 being about one million taels.[36] Spanish trade, however, did not compete to any extent with the British, and the American trade offered only indirect competition through its replacement of British teas in North America and the West Indies and to a very limited extent at this time upon the Continent.

A third important thing to consider was the influence which European wars had upon the Continental trade. Between 1779 and 1783 there were no French ships at Canton, because France had come to the support of the Americans in their war for independence. For the same reason there were no Dutch ships at Canton between 1781 and 1784. French and Dutch misfortune reacted favorably on the Danish and Swedish trade without being of any real benefit to the British, and it is certain that the revival of a Prussian trade and, to a considerable extent, the beginning of Italian trade were but attempts of the Dutch and the French to carry on a contraband trade.[37] The beginning of the Wars of the French Revolution ended the reviving French trade after 1792, while the last Dutch and Italian ships sailed from Canton in the spring of 1795. This war also gave the Americans an opportunity to carry on an extensive contraband trade between China and Europe.

As can be judged from Figure 6, the life-blood of Continental trade was tea. Over 80 per cent of the Continental exports were tea;

---

[35] E. H. Pritchard, "The Struggle for Control of the China Trade during the Eighteenth Century," *Pacific Historical Review*, III (Sept., 1934), tables, pp. 292-94; Morse, *Chronicle*, II, 40, 50, 84, 95, 111.

[36] Pritchard, *loc. cit.*; IOCCD, Vols. 78, 83, 85, 95, 99, 102, 104, 109, 115, tables of trade, for the Spanish trade; Morse, as cited in note 37.

[37] Morse, *Chronicle*, II, 40, 50, 61, 74, 84, 95, 111, 136, 184, 187, 193, 201, 205.

Figure 6.
Tea Exported from Canton (1768-1796)*.

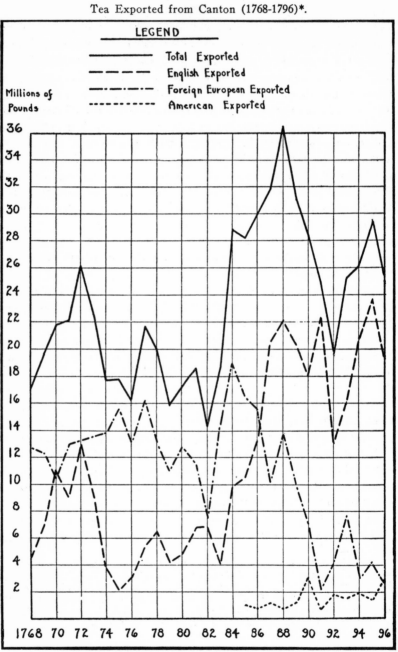

* Milburn, *Oriental Commerce*, II, 486.

after the Commutation Act struck so successfully at the smuggling of tea into England, the life-blood was removed from the French, Danish, and Swedish trades, and they declined. With the exception of the Dutch, who imported about twice as much merchandise as they did bullion, all Continental countries were very largely dependent upon bullion to finance their exports. Nearly 80 per cent of the French, Swedish, and Danish imports was bullion, but slightly less than 60 per cent of the total imports by Continental countries was bullion.[38] The Dutch occupied a favorable position because of their East India possessions, which enabled them to send large quantities of tin, pepper, sandalwood, and spices to Canton.

As intimated in the last paragraph, the Dutch were the strongest competitors of the British in the China trade because their trade was in every way legitimate and organically sound. They had an old and well-organized trade with the Far East, an extensive home and Continental market for their teas and China goods, and well-organized commercial centers in the East Indies which provided them with goods for the Canton market. Dutch exports, which were about T. 863,280 (imports T. 551,940) in 1764-65, remained at about the same level until 1776-77, when they rose to T. 1,012,490 (imports T. 356,680) ; they reached their highest level of T. 1,420,130 (imports T. 470,990) in 1786-87. The Commutation Act hurt but did not ruin Dutch trade. Its downfall was accomplished by the Wars of the French Revolution, and no more Dutch ships reached Canton after the season of 1794-95. The principal imports were tin, pepper, cloves, sandalwood, woollens, and silver. Tea, raw silk, woven silks, nankeens, and chinaware were the chief exports as in the British trade.[39]

The French trade, like the Dutch, was a legitimate one, for France offered a good market for Chinese goods despite the fact that the tea habit had not taken deep root in France. French trade, however, was handicapped by a lack of East India possessions from which to draw articles for the Canton market and by financial weaknesses and vacillating commercial policies at home. The numerous wars with England also hurt French trade. Starting with an export trade of T. 349,350

---

[38] Pritchard, *loc. cit.* As will be noted from the tables referred to, Continental exports, except the Dutch, were many times larger than imports. This difference had to be made up in the main by the importation of silver. For silver imported, see Morse, *Chronicle*, II, 12, 29, 35, 40, 50, 61, 74, 84.

[39] Pritchard, *loc. cit.*; IOCCD, LXXXIII, tables of foreign European trade for a typical year.

(imports T. 97,680) in 1764-65, French trade rose to T. 1,251,110 (imports T. 120,000) in 1776-77. It ceased entirely from 1779 to 1783, then rose to T. 1,044,690 (imports T. 98,000) in 1784-85, and then declined steadily until the renewal of war with England ended it after the season 1792-93. Silver, woollens, lead, Prussian blue, and blackwood (from Mauritius) were staple imports, and to the Dutch exports should be added tutenague.[40]

The Swedish and the Danish trade had no organic basis. The home market for Chinese goods was small, and neither had valuable possessions in the East from which to draw products for the Canton market. The life of the trade of these two countries depended to a large extent upon the finding of an illegal market for teas in England and upon the Continent; accordingly, after the Commutation Act their trade declined and was on the point of dying when the Wars of the French Revolution gave it new life. Danish exports rose from T. 473,840 (imports T. 37,530) in 1764-65 to T. 1,125,000 (imports T. 374,620) in 1782-83, after which they declined steadily. Swedish exports rose from T. 252,760 (imports T. 13,770) in 1764-65 to T. 1,200,540 (imports T. 142,800) in 1785-86, after which they declined rapidly. Besides silver, the only staple Swedish and Danish imports were lead and other metals, amber, and Prussian blue. Tea was the main article exported, and to the Dutch list should be added rhubarb and tutenague.[41]

The Imperial, the Prussian, the Genoese, and the Tuscan trade was entirely transitory. Expeditions were generally fitted out under these foreign flags by disgruntled English or French who hoped to profit by war-time conditions or by the smuggling trade into England. The ships under Genoese, Tuscan, and Prussian colors between 1787 and 1794 belonged without exception to Country traders who were attempting to avoid the regulations of the British Company. From 1779 to 1783 there were seven Imperial ships at Canton importing goods to the value of T. 582,823 (bullion T. 729,000) and exporting goods to the value of T. 980,429. Three ships under the Tuscan flag were at Canton, one in 1782, one in 1787, and one in 1792. They imported goods amounting to T. 194,912 and exported goods valued at about T. 351,129. The five Genoese ships at Canton between 1792 and 1794 seem to have been engaged in the Northwest fur trade and imported goods valued at T. 876,460 and exported goods to the value of T. 326,386. The six

---

[40] Pritchard, *op. cit.,* pp. 285, 292-94; IOCCD, LXIV, tables of European trade for a typical year.

[41] Pritchard, *loc. cit.*; IOCCD, as in note 39.

ships under the Prussian flag at Canton from 1783 to 1791, two of which were certainly on Dutch account, imported goods to the value of T. 488,739 (bullion T. 210,000) and exported T. 809,869 worth of merchandise.[42]

The Spanish trade which began in 1783 was non-competitive with the English, as it aimed to procure articles for export across the Pacific to Spanish America. It imported little save bullion and tropical woods, and its exports were almost entirely confined to fabrics such as woven silks, nankeens, Canton cloths, and grass cloth. In 1785 it imported bullion amounting to T. 415,000 and goods equal to about T. 92,970 and exported goods to the value of about T. 462,555. In 1795-96 the bullion and the goods imported equalled T. 300,000 and T. 8,576, respectively, and exports amounted to about T. 287,076.[43]

Since the story of the beginning of American trade has been told so well by Doctor Latourette[44] and others, it seems useless to discuss it here. The *Canton Diaries* do provide figures from which a rough estimate of its value may be obtained, but, as the author has already given these figures elsewhere, they need not be repeated in detail here. American exports rose from T. 79,320 in 1784-85 to T. 1,720,000 in 1799-1800, and the value of merchandise imports rose from T. 136,450 to T. 757,750 during the same period. The difference had to be made up by the importation of bullion.[45]

The struggle between England and her Continental rivals for control of the China trade during the eighteenth century has been dealt with indirectly at several points already, and as the author has discussed the matter more in detail elsewhere,[46] it is necessary only to summarize the final decisive years here. The struggle centered about the control of the tea trade, and, because Great Britain consumed the largest percentage of tea imported into Europe, the British government held the deciding ace in the form of the duties on tea. To reduce the duties charged on tea imported into England would kill the smuggling trade and hence

---

[42] IOCCD, Vols. 67, 71, 75, 78, 83, 87, 102, 104, 107, 109, tables of Continental trade and the Canton current price list; Pritchard, *loc. cit.*
[43] IOCCD, Vols. 78, 83, 85, 95, 99, 102, 104, 107, 109, 115, tables of Continental trade and price list.
[44] Kenneth Scott Latourette, *History of Early Relations between the United States and China* (*Transactions of the Connecticut Academy of Arts and Sciences,* XXII) (New Haven, 1917) and *Voyages of American Ships to China, 1784-1844* (New Haven, 1927); F. R. Dulles, *The Old China Trade* (Boston, 1930).
[45] Pritchard, *op. cit.*, pp. 292-94.
[46] *Ibid.*, pp. 280-95.

cause the Continental competition to die. To leave the duties at a high level would make the Continental trade flourish.

Figure 7.
Foreign Exports from Canton (1764-1806)*.

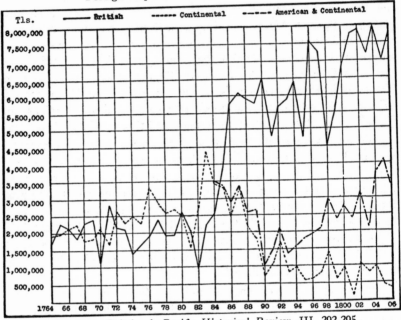

* Based on Pritchard, *Pacific Historical Review*, III, 292-295.

A glance at Figure 6 will show exactly what happened in the tea trade between 1767 and 1796, and Figure 7 will illustrate what happened to the commerce of the nations concerned. Despite the handicap imposed upon the Company's rivals by the Seven Years War, the annual quantity of tea sold at the Company's sales between 1760 and 1767 was only 4,333,267 lbs.; the duties on it amounted to 90 per cent. At the end of the period the Company had over 15,000,000 pounds of tea on hand and was faced with financial ruin. In order to relieve it the government passed the Idemnity Act, whereby for five years the excise duty of 1/- per pound was to be abolished on black and singlo teas and the whole customs duty of 23.93 per cent was to be drawn back on teas exported to Ireland and America. If the return from the duties fell below the average for the preceding five-year period, the Company was to make up the amount to the government. This amounted to a reduction of the duties to 64 per cent, and as a result the average annual sales for the next five years (1768-72) rose to 8,075,794 lbs. During the corresponding period the Company exported annually from China 9,088,109 lbs. of tea, and its Continental rivals 11,565,468 lbs; in other words, despite the reduced duties, the price of tea in England was still so high as to make smuggling profitable.[47]

In spite of the revival of the Company's trade, the Idemnity Act had not worked satisfactorily and the Company was forced to idemnify the government and buyers £686,399. In consequence, the old duties were restored in 1773, and the outbreak of the American Revolution caused the government to load new duties on tea. The average duty between 1773 and 1777 was 106 per cent. The Company's trade went into a rapid decline, and that of its rivals flourished as smuggling increased. The fortunes of the Company touched bottom during the years 1776, 1777, and 1778, when the yearly average of tea sold at its sales was but 4,977,068 lbs., whereas the yearly average of tea exported from Canton by its rivals was 14,085,400 lbs. A decrease in the duties in 1779 and 1780 helped the Company, but, as the government was in need of money, the duties were increased in 1781 and 1782. Consequently, the years 1781, 1782, and 1783 saw the Company's trade decline, and its financial affairs were brought to the verge of bankruptcy in 1783. The annual sales during these three years amounted to 5,721,655 lbs., whereas the return of France and Holland to the Canton market enabled its rivals to export 14,719,015 lbs. per year for the five years between 1780 and 1784.[48]

The peak of the Continental trade was reached in the season of 1783-84, when 19,072,300 lbs. of tea were exported from Canton. During the thirteen years before 1785 the average annual value of British exports from Canton had been T. 1,974,954 and that of their rivals T. 2,749,620.[49] The Company and the government after the return of peace were thus faced squarely with the problem: either the duties on tea had to be lowered or British trade with China would be ruined, and the government's tea revenue would be much decreased and its authority set at naught by the smugglers. The Fox-North coalition

---

[47] Milburn, *Oriental Commerce,* II, 538-39; Wissett, *Compendium,* II, section on tea.

[48] Milburn, *op. cit.,* II, 534; Wissett, *Compendium,* II, section on tea; *Parliamentary History, 1782-3,* XXIII, 572-82, 646-47, 795-801.

[49] Pritchard, *op. cit.,* pp. 292-95.

had in contemplation measures for the reduction of duties on tea when they were replaced by the Pitt Ministry. Pitt himself lent a willing ear to the proposals of the industrial and commercial interests of the country, and Henry Dundas, chief member of the newly created Board of Control, was especially interested in expanding British trade in the East.

Consequently, the government and the Company formulated a policy, perhaps unconsciously at first, but later on very consciously, which aimed at the ruin of England's rivals in the India and China trade, and at making London the European distributing center for all Asiatic products. The first step in this direction was the Commutation Act; the second, the forcing of greater quantities of English goods into the Chinese market in return for larger contracts for tea; the third, the Eden Treaty with France in 1786 (which had as its primary purpose the opening of France to British manufactures) ; and the fourth, an Embassy to China, which aimed at the opening of the northern ports of that country to trade for the benefit of the Company and in the hope that British manufactured articles would find an extended sale there.

The success of the Commutation Act is clearly shown in Figures 6 and 7. The lowered duties ruined the smugglers, on whom Danish, Swedish, Imperial, and to a certain extent, French trade lived, and ensured the British market to the Company; in fact, the lowered prices enabled teas imported by the Company to be exported to the Continent. For a few years the foreign companies tried to keep up the competition, but they were soon forced to capitulate, and their trade, with the exception of that of the Dutch, declined rapidly. Between 1785 and 1790 the annual amount of tea exported by the Company from Canton increased to 18,864,218 lbs., whereas that of its rivals decreased to 10,979,950 lbs. During the next five years the Company's annual exportation increased to over 19½ million pounds, whereas that of its Continental rivals decreased to 4½ million pounds.[60]

The ruin which the Commutation Act began was completed by the Revolutionary Wars, which eliminated France in 1792 and Holland in 1794. Swedish and Danish trade were for a time revived by the Wars, but they never again offered successful competition to the English. The newly developed Spanish trade at Canton did not compete with the British, and the American trade, although it was growing rapidly

---

[60] *Ibid.*; Milburn, *op. cit.*, II, 486; Appendix V.

and had largely displaced the English in the American market, was not yet more than a cloud upon the horizon. In 1795, England, with her control of the seas, stood triumphant in the century-long conflict for mastery of the China trade.

5. Commercial and Industrial Expansion of England during the Eighteenth Century.

Before the semi-political events at Canton leading directly to the sending of the first British embassy to China are discussed, it is necessary to consider certain economic developments in England—the beginning of the Industrial Revolution in north England—which in a general way influenced the sending of the first embassy. At the beginning of the eighteenth century England had to share with Holland, France, and the Scandinavian countries commercial and industrial supremacy. By the end of the century she was undisputed mistress in both of these fields. At the opening of the eighteenth century the most important industries in England were the manufacture of woollen and leather goods, followed by the production of silk, linen, tin, lead, and iron articles. At the close of the century the leather, tin and linen industries were on the decline, and the slowly growing woollen and silk industries were being eclipsed by the rapidly expanding cotton and iron and steel industries. The manufacture of porcelain and glass had also risen to respectable heights, but the lead industry was stationary.

These changes had been brought about by a multiplicity of forces, but suffice it to say here that the establishment of a sound financial structure in the Bank of England, the beneficial effects of the Navigation Acts, the commercial power of the East India Company, England's extensive Colonial Empire, and her control of the seas, had all contributed to the growth of her commercial supremacy. This latter created a surplus capital necessary to industrial growth, and the increase in population (from $5\frac{1}{2}$ million in 1700 to $8\frac{3}{4}$ million in 1800)[51] provided a market for industrial production and a supply of ready labor.[52] The application of mechanical invention and the factory system to the cotton industry and of chemical invention and the factory system to

---

[51] W. Cunningham, *Growth of English Commerce and Industry* (London, 1892), Pt. 2, p. 935.

[52] *Ibid.*, Pt. 1; P. Mantoux, *The Industrial Revolution* (New York, n.d.), pp. 47-140, 349-73; Frederick Dietz, *The Industrial Revolution* (New York, 1927), pp. 1-40.

iron and steel production enabled these industries to take the lead.[53]

The character of this industrial and commercial change can be judged from a few figures. The value of British imports and exports increased during the century from £6,010,000 in 1697 to £62,690,000 in 1800,[54] over ten times; and the tonnage clearing out of English ports increased from 245,000 tons to 2,130,000 tons during the same period.[55] The value of exported woollens increased from £2,933,292 in 1699 to £6,487,000 in 1802, only 2¼ times.[56] In 1699 woollens composed 43 per cent of the total exports; in 1802 they composed but 17 per cent, and 1/6 of all woollens exported went to China.

The exportation of cotton goods, which amounted to but £5,915 in 1697, remained low during the greater part of the century, rose to £355,060 in 1780, and then shot up to £7,624,505 (over a million pounds greater than woollens) in 1802. The value of cotton goods manufactured in England, which was considered as £960,000 before 1780, rose to £7,500,000 in the course of eight years.[57] The progress of pig iron production was equally rapid during the closing years of the century. Between 1720 and 1740 it remained stationary at about 17,000 tons per year, but with the coming of chemical improvements rose to 68,300 tons in 1788, to 125,079 tons in 1796, and to 258,206 tons in 1806.[58] It is also of importance to note that, though the Company exported a large percentage of the woollens produced to India and China, it did not, until after the close of the century, export cotton or iron goods, and then only in small quantities.[59]

The important thing about this industrial expansion was that most of it occurred after 1780 and that it was confined to the north and west of England—Manchester, Birmingham, Sheffield, and Leeds. The almost overnight rise of the cotton industry created a new crop of industrial barons who besieged Parliament and the government with

---

[53] Cunningham, *op. cit.*, Pt. 2; Mantoux, *op. cit.*, pp. 193-346; T. Ellison, *Cotton Trade of Great Britain* (London, 1886), p. 29.

[54] Anderson's *History of Commerce*, IV, 692-94; Leon Levi, *History of British Commerce* (London, 1872), pp. 491-93; Cunningham, *op. cit.*, pp. 694-96.

[55] George Chalmers, *Considerations on Commerce* . . . (London, 1811), Appendix 1; Levi, *op. cit.*, p. 500; Cunningham, *op. cit.*, pp. 696-97.

[56] Macpherson's *Annals of Commerce* (London, 1805), III, 602, and IV, 15, 489, 525; G. L. Craik, *History of British Commerce* (London, 1844), II, 47; Mantoux, *op. cit.*, p. 106.

[57] Macpherson's *Annals*, IV, 132; Ellison, *op. cit.*, p. 29; Cunningham, *op. cit.*, p. 639; Macgregor, *op. cit.*, IV, 753-54, 768.

[58] Mantoux, *op. cit.*, p. 278; H. Scrivenor, *Comprehensive History of the Iron Trade* (London, 1854), pp. 136, 256, 302.

[59] PP, *Sessional Reports, Papers, etc, 1812-13*, IX, No. 248, p. 463.

demands that it find markets for their swelling production. The commercial growth had been more evenly distributed over the century, but it too brought into prominence commercial cities in the north—Liverpool, Glasgow, and Hull. The net result of these changes was to transform England into a beehive of productive and expansive energy. New and powerful interests were created in the north which came to the government demanding protection, encouragement, and outlet for their productive energies—interests which looked with greedy eyes toward the East, from which the Company's monopoly excluded them. This spirit and pressure of the "cotton kings," both of which were reflected to a marked degree in the commercial policies of the Pitt administration,[60] helped to bring about the conditions that inspired the government to attempt to open all of China to British trade.

6. *Significance of these Commercial and Economic Developments.*

The enormous growth of British trade with China which took place between 1784 and 1795 was in the main the direct result of the lowering of the duties on tea. The exports of tea by the Company and the imports of raw cotton by the Country traders were the first to respond to the Commutation Act, but in the course of five or six years the Company's import trade at Canton also showed a marked advance, especially in woollens. An immediate effect of the expanding tea trade was the importation into China by the Company of large consignments of bullion, but, as the Country import trade grew and the Company's import trade in merchandise expanded, the importation of bullion decreased. After 1791 British trade was virtually self-sufficient (not dependent upon the importation of bullion), and the market for British metals and woollens, and Indian cotton and opium was expanding. During the period the Company's trade showed a steadily decreasing unfavorable balance, whereas the Country trade showed a steadily increasing favorable balance, the latter being the source from which the Company realized about 37 per cent of the funds necessary to finance its trade. By the end of the period the balance of British trade was on the point of turning against China for the first time in history.

The consequences of these commercial developments were far-reaching. As the Company's trade expanded and its profits grew, it became more desirous of maintaining and protecting the trade and of

---

[60] Mantoux, *op. cit.*, pp. 257-67; *The Commercial Policy of Pitt and Peel, 1785-1846* (London, 1847), pp. 5-6.

doing nothing which might endanger it. Conversely, as the China trade grew and the Company's profits expanded, the commercial and especially the rapidly developing cotton and metal industries in the north of England, which were excluded from participation in the China trade, became more jealous of the Company's monopoly and desired to participate in the trade. London and south England commercial and handicraft interests, which profited by the increased shipping of the Company and by its growing exportation of woollens, were more prone to support it. Furthermore, as the tea trade became more and more important to the nation and as the revenue realized from the total trade expanded, the government became more responsive to events in China which might endanger the trade, and, in accordance with its general policy of encouraging commercial and industrial expansion it interested itself in schemes for expanding the China trade. The expansion of trade seriously strained the system at Canton, and the confinement of trade to Canton placed a serious restraint upon its indefinite expansion—restraints which could be removed only by governmental action. Expansion of trade also increased the number of daily contacts at Canton between Englishmen and Chinese and multiplied the number of problems and conflicts which arose, thus making more evident the desirability of a treaty basis for the conduct of relations with China.

The growth of the Country trade also opened the eyes of Country traders to the restraints imposed by the Company and to the possibilities of a free trade to other parts of the Empire, and the Indian government found in the growing cotton and opium trade a valuable source of revenue. From the Chinese government's point of view the growing trade meant more revenue, more troublesome problems with the foreigner, and a greater danger of the influx of foreign ideas. To the Cantonese merchants it meant greater profits, but more danger of extortion from the officials, who saw in the increasing financial transactions a greater field for personal gain.

In England and in China, the conclusions drawn from the situation were diametrically opposite. The British government and Private traders wanted the trade expanded throughout the Empire, whereas the Chinese (Canton merchants, officials, and government) saw their best interests in keeping it strictly confined to Canton. The Company saw advantages in having it expanded to the north of China, but it was unwilling to undertake drastic measures which might endanger the trade or their monopoly. A final result, and one of more immediate influence upon the sending of the first British embassy to China, was the strain which the sudden expansion of the tea trade threw upon the Company's ability to finance the trade.

Chapter V

EVENTS LEADING TO THE FIRST BRITISH EMBASSY
TO CHINA (1760-1786)

1. *Financial Troubles with the Hong Merchants and the Proposal of an Embassy (1760-1782).*

In the three preceding chapters we have discussed three of the fundamental factors which led to the first British embassy to China. The dynamic force was the steady growth of the China trade and especially its rapid expansion after 1784, which carried with it immense advantages to the Company, to the Country and Private traders, to the marine and woollen interests of London and south England connected with the trade, to the government's revenue, and to the general public. The inactive factor, against which the commercial expansion continually knocked its head, was the restraining nature of the Chinese monopoly—the confinement of trade to the single port of Canton under troublesome and undefined restrictions, which at any moment might be so changed as to make the continuation of the trade impossible. Such restraints upon economic expansion did not suit the temper either of the government or of the commercial and industrial interests in late eighteenth century England. A third basic factor—although of less direct importance than the other two, but nevertheless of considerable importance in bringing about the state of mind which caused the government to send an embassy—was the commercial and industrial growth of England throughout the eighteenth century, culminating in the Industrial Revolution. These changes created in northern and western England marine and manufacturing interests which desired to participate in the India and China trade.[1]

The problem of this chapter is to trace the semi-political events at Canton which led directly to the sending of the first British embassy to China. The Co-hong of 1760 had been established in order to consolidate the power of the Hong merchants, to enable them to dictate terms to the foreign traders, to make them better able to meet the

---

[1] See Chap. VII, Sect. 5.

enormous responsibilities imposed upon them as securities for the foreigners and their ships, and to help them in meeting the financial demands of the mandarins and in providing presents for the officials and Imperial Court.[2] At about the same time the failure of a Chinese merchant to pay his debts led the foreigners to present a petition to the officials demanding redress. The Viceroy referred the matter to Peking, and in consequence one of the provisions of the Imperial Edict of 1760 forbade the borrowing of money from foreigners under pain of banishment to Ili and the confiscation of the property of the offender.[3]

Strengthened by the Co-hong, the Chinese merchants prospered for a number of years, and despite the Imperial prohibition borrowed large sums from Country traders in 1766-67. The rates of interest were exorbitant, ranging from 16 to 20 per cent and sometimes as high as 40 per cent per annum, but for a number of years the merchants met their obligations. The demands of the officials increased, however, and early in 1771 the supercargoes requested the Court of Directors to restrict the number of *sing-songs* brought in Private trade, which the mandarins forced the Hongists to purchase as presents, lest the merchants be ruined and the Company involved in their misfortune.[4]

Apparently without realizing it, the supercargoes had already taken the step which was to lead to disaster when they procured, after the payment of T. 100,000, the dissolution of the Co-hong on February 11, 1771. This dissolution broke the bargaining power of the Hongists; prices decreased, and the demands of the officials fell upon the merchants individually instead of collectively. Those who had borrowed and spent most extravagantly were unable to meet their obligations, and in consequence there was an influx of Country merchants who resided at Canton contrary to the Company's orders in an attempt to collect their debts.[5]

When the Co-hong was dissolved there appear to have been eleven Hong merchants organized into ten mercantile houses or Hongs— Puankhequa, Munqua, Shy Kinqua, Chowqua, Kewshaw, Yngshaw,

---

[2] This latter was said by the merchants in 1776 to amount to T. 500,000 (Morse, *Chronicle*, II, 16-17).

[3] CMC, II, No. 2; Morse, *Chronicle*, II, 54, 56, 57, and V, 94-96.

[4] CMC, II, No. 6; Morse, *Chronicle*, II, 44-46, and V, 154.

[5] CMC, II, No. 6; Morse, *Chronicle*, V, 153, for influx of Country merchants, pp. 162, 172, 180; Dalrymple, *Oriental Repertory*, II, 319.

Chetqua, Sy Anqua,[6] Coqua and Tinqua,[7] and Wayqua.[8] Chetqua, who was indebted to the Company in 1768, died in 1771, apparently leaving no unsettled debts. Wayqua, who was in debt to the Company when the Co-hong was dissolved, absconded in March, 1772, when the supercargoes petitioned the Viceroy in regard to his debt of T. 11,726. The affair was not settled until 1777, after a report had been sent to Peking by the Governor. Wayqua was ultimately found and imprisoned until the debt was paid, after which he was transported. T. 6,000 were paid by his brother and T. 5,216 were furnished by the officials.[9]

During 1773 and 1774, because of the financial difficulties of the Company in Europe, few bills were issued on London, and the Country traders, being unable to remit their money to England and being attracted by the extravagant offers of the floundering merchants, again lent extensive sums to the Chinese. In September, 1773, as Sy Anqua and Teowqua (Coqua) were unable to pay small sums which they had owed the Company since the preceding season, the supercargoes twice petitioned the Hoppo and Viceroy. By January 31, 1774, Teowqua (Coqua) had paid off his debt of T. 13,300, and Sy Anqua had reduced his from T. 17,025 to T. 7,251. Later in 1774 Puankhequa assumed Sy Anqua's debt to the Company and the affair was settled so far as the Company was concerned.[10] Late in 1774 Sy Anqua died in bankruptcy. The officials assessed his debts due to Country merchants at $222,000 (mainly to Hutton & Gordon), although his creditors claimed $300,000. His brother Seunqua was appointed to manage the business and assume the Hongist chop, and the debt without further interest was to be paid in ten annual instalments after Sy Anqua's son attained manhood. The creditors refused to accept the award.[11]

This placed all creditors in a fright, and, as their attempts to collect debts were unavailing, they refused to lend any more money. This

[6] Variously spelled—in 1768 Si Hunqua, in 1772-74 Sy Anqua; the firm consisted of two brothers Sy Anqua and Seunqua (Morse, *Chronicle*, V, 136-37, 159, 179-81, 186, 192, and II, 45, 55, 58).

[7] Coqua and Tinqua were sons of a retired Hong merchant, Suqua; both had Hongist chops, and with them were associated two other brothers, Tiqua and Chelqua (CMC, No. 6). It seems that prior to 1775 Coqua was spelled *Teowqua*, or if this is untrue, then there were twelve Hongists, of whom Teowqua was one (Morse, *Chronicle*, V, 159, 181, and II, 6, 25, 33-34, 45).

[8] Morse, *Chronicle*, V, 136-37, 141, 152, 159, 161, 168.

[9] CMD, XV, Nov. 18-20, 1777; Morse, *Chronicle*, V, 161, 172, 178, and II, 25.

[10] CMD, XV, Nov. 18-20, 1777, and VII, Dec. 17, 1777; Morse, *Chronicle*, V, 180-81, 186, 192.

[11] CMD, VII, Dec. 17, 1777; Morse, *Chronicle*, II, 45-46, 55-56.

created a situation reminiscent of that produced by the cessation of American loans to Germany after 1929. In both situations the continuation of payments was dependent upon the receipt of loans, and when these stopped, the Chinese merchants were unable to purchase goods and carry on business, to say nothing of paying old debts. To relieve themselves from this situation the merchants attempted in 1775 to restore the Co-hong and in 1776 to impose a tax of 10 per cent upon all exports and a similar tax upon pepper, lead, tin, putchuck, and cotton imported. On both occasions the supercargoes protested to the merchants and to the officials and were successful in preventing these proposed measures.[12]

Being unable to borrow money, prevented from forming a protective combination, and refused contracts because they could not pay their debts, a number of the merchants were left with nothing else to do but await the executioner. At the close of the season 1776-77 Coqua was indebted to Company merchants to the amount of several hundred thousand taels, and, because he was unable to discharge his obligations of T. 20,388 to the Company, it curtailed its business with him.

At the close of the season of 1777-78, Yngshaw was in difficulties and refused to renew his bonds to Country creditors. On February 3, 1778, he owed the Company T. 80,000 and Captain Parks of the Country ship *Favourite* T. 45,000. His business transactions had been curtailed because the Danish Company withheld $40,000 due to him for tea delivered, to offset his debt to private Danish merchants. In order to save him from bankruptcy, the Dutch Company advanced him T.30,000 and the English Company T. 42,000 on contracts for tea to be delivered in the fall, and Captain Parks was paid T. 25,000, the remaining T. 20,000 to be paid in goods the following season.[13]

The Company had ceased to do business with Coqua. By 1778 Tinqua and Chelqua, two other members of the firm, had absconded, and the active management of the business was in the hands of Tiqua (a poor business man) and Coqua, an idiot (according to Matthew Raper).[14] At the end of 1778 or early in 1779, the firm was declared bankrupt and all the property seized by the officials to pay the Emperor's duties and meet other obligations.

---

[12] Morse, *Chronicle*, II, 13-22; CMC, II, No. 6.
[13] Morse, *Chronicle*, II, 25-27, 30, 47.
[14] *Ibid.*, 33-34, 45; CMC, II, No. 6.

Thus at the close of the year 1777 the situation was becoming desperate. Of the eleven Hong merchants in 1771 Chetqua and Sy Anqua had died, the latter in bankruptcy, and although his business was conducted by Seunqua, the creditors would do no business with him. Wayqua had become bankrupt. Tinqua had absconded, and his firm, of which Coqua and Tiqua only remained, was soon to be declared bankrupt. Yngshaw was unable to pay his debts, and Kewshaw was also unable to pay his Country creditors, although he still made contracts with the Company. Only four merchants—Puankhequa, Chowqua, Munqua, and Shy Kinqua—were able to meet all of their obligations and conduct business in a dependable manner. Under these circumstances, four of the principal creditors—Charles Crommelin, Thomas Hutton, Charles Gordon, and George Smith—then resident at Canton, drew up, on December 17,1777, a representation and sent it to their agents and partners in London.[15]

After pointing out how the debts originated and indicating that both the Country trade and the loans which the Country traders had made to the Chinese were of immense advantage to the Company, the representation went on to say: that not only payment of bonds had been refused but their renewal except at reduced rates of interest had been refused; that the Hongists had fixed prices in a most unjust and arbitrary manner; that the merchants because of their lucrative trade were well able to meet their obligations; that every mode of legal redress had been denied and nothing but misrepresentation and deception had attended every complaint brought before a Chinese court; that every attempt to get redress by public action was attended by a declaration of bankruptcy, which resulted in the Chinese creditors being favored in preference to the foreign or in an unjust reduction of the amount due; and that representations sent to the officials through the merchants were either secreted or misrepresented. The representation continued that:

From all of which duly considered and maturely weighed, we are of positive opinion that no hopes of redress can be entertained from the Justice of the Chinese, unless our Complaints are properly made known to the Court of Peking and therefore that the only mode left us of obtaining the just and lawful property of the many British Subjects now under our management is by this plain and faithful representation of our case to the Court of Great Britain from which alone can be expected such a Power as shall make known and enforce these our

---

[15] CMC, II, No. 2; CMD, VII, Dec. 17, 1777.

lawful demands so unjustifiably kept back in a Country where an intercourse has been solicited, where justice is denied us, and where equity is not known.

Accompanying this representation was a paper showing the obligations due to Country merchants, amounting in all to about T. 3,000,000. These papers were carried to England by Charles Gordon, one of the principal creditors. He arrived in London some time during the summer of 1778, and a number of meetings of the creditors were held. A committee was deputed to inform the Ministry and request it to send an embassy to Peking. The Government apparently refused to take any action other than through the Company,[16] and in consequence the creditors—Mathew Purling, John Hunter, George Paterson, John Clements, and Thomas Raikes—presented a memorial to Sir George Wombwell, Chairman of the Court of Directors, requesting the Company's assistance in the collection of the debts. They stated that the debts represented accumulated fortunes in India which had been sent to China in order to be transferred home by means of bills, but as the Company's treasury was not always open they had been forced to lend their money to the Chinese; and that the money so employed was of great advantage to the Company, because it enabled the Chinese merchants to fulfill their obligations to the Company.[17]

Accompanying the memorial was a memorandum stating that from the supposed equitable maxims of the Chinese government, and especially from its recent edict settling the debts of Wayqua, it was thought that, if the distressed situation of the debtors were made known to the Court of Peking, redress would be certain. It then pointed out that, because of the corruption of the mandarins and merchants at Canton, it was impossible to send a representation through them, and proposed that a person with a commission from the English Crown should be sent in a King's Frigate from India to Tientsin and Peking to lay the matter before the Imperial Court. As a mode of liquidation, it proposed that debts remain at their present figure without any accumulation of interest, and that, as the profits of the Chinese merchants from the English trade amounted to over $700,000 annually, that sum should be paid into the Company's treasury each year on account of the creditors until the debts were liquidated, or, if the Chinese government wished

---

[16] CMD, IV, Council of Supercargoes to John Alexander Panton, October 7, 1779.

[17] CMD, VII, no paging and no date; Morse, *Chronicle*, II, 43.

to assume the obligations, it might remit the duties, which amounted to about $800,000 annually, until the debts were paid.[18]

The memorandum concluded by pointing out that there was danger of general bankruptcy among the Hong merchants, which would affect the Company as much as the Private merchants; that something should be done to improve the position of the Company's supercargoes, who were treated with disrespect; and that, as the French, who had recently established a Consulate at Canton and who were negotiating with the Portuguese for a cession of Macao, had sent a representative to Paris to solicit government aid in collecting debts, it was likely that an embassy would be sent which might gain privileges inimical to England. The Court of Directors apparently did not favor the proposal of an embassy, but on December 23, 1778, it sent instructions to the supercargoes to do all in their power, consistent with the interests of the Company, to assist the Private creditors since it considered the "Amount of the Money as a National Object." [19]

While these measures were in progress, the hotheads in India were taking the bit in their teeth. Two addresses were drawn up on July 8, 1779, soliciting the aid of Rear-Admiral Sir Edward Vernon in placing before the Hoppo and Viceroy a statement of the creditors' demands. One was from George Smith, George Monbray, Alexander Cuthbert, Andrew Ross, Alexander Jameson, Gilbert Pasley, and John Crichton; the other, from John Crichton alone. The latter contained a memorial to the Hoppo, which Crichton desired be delivered together with an address from the Admiral to the Hoppo. The memorial proposed that the existing bonds be renewed at a reduced interest of 12 per cent, and in return for this concession the debts were to be discharged in twelve annual instalments payable partly in goods and partly in money. The annual payment of interest was to be made compulsory, and the whole arrangement was to be enforced by the Chinese government.[20]

At the same time a letter was sent to the Governor (Sir Thomas Rumboldt) and Council of Fort St. George, requesting their assistance. The Governor and Council reprimanded the creditors for approaching the Admiral without first consulting them, and in reply to Admiral Vernon's letter of July 20, informing them that he intended sending an

---

[18] CMC, II, No. 2; CMD, VII, no page and no date.
[19] CMD, IV and VIII, Dec. 23, 1778, parags. 45-46; Morse, *Chronicle*, II, 43-44.
[20] CMD, IV, July 8, 1779.

address to the Viceroy of Canton by the Commander of H. M. *Sea Horse*, they suggested that the Commander should present the documents to the supercargoes and consult with them as how best to proceed.[21] Admiral Vernon, however, did not change his peremptory orders, and the *Sea Horse* sailed for China under command of Captain John Alexander Panton, where she arrived on September 23.

It is not known when the Court's letter of December 23, 1778, instructing the supercargoes to aid in settling the debts, reached China. The investigations, however, had already begun when the first regular ships of the season arrived on October 3, bringing two members of a newly appointed Select Committee (Thomas Fitzhugh and Thomas Bevan, the other member, Matthew Raper, already being in China) to manage the Company's affairs in China. The Committee found that debts, represented in bonds and accumulated interest for money lent and goods sold on credit, to the amount of $4,347,300 were claimed by Country traders and supercargoes representing Private merchants. Of this amount $539,224 was apparently owed to non-English in partnership with or represented by Englishmen, and $3,808,076 was owed to English, not more than $1,078,976 of which represented money and goods advanced. The difference represented accumulated interest compounded annually at 18 to 20 per cent. The debts were owing from one to eleven years, but most of them had been incurred within seven years.[22]

The claims on Coqua were $1,156,162, but, as the firm was already bankrupt and its property had been seized by the officials to meet various obligations, no counter claims were given. Seunqua was presented with claims to the amount of $648,359, mostly represented in the debts (and interest accumulated on them) of his brother, Sy Anqua. The mandarins in 1774 had assessed this debt at $222,000 and by this decision Seunqua was willing to abide. Yngshaw admitted that he had debts to the amount of $980,165 in 1777, after which he had refused to renew the bonds. The claims against him were $1,387,311. He offered to pay the principal in fifteen annual instalments, and interest amounting to $125,000 in six annual instalments after the end of the fifteen years. Kewshaw—who was kept solvent throughout the season

---

[21] CMD, IV, July 8, 20, 23, 28, 31, 1779.

[22] Morse, *Chronicle*, II, 44-46. The various creditors and their claims were as follows: Hutton and Gordon $1,776,638, Geo. Smith [and John Crichton] $789,379, James Frudd $304,545, A. Crommelin $73,818, Abm. Leslie $31,730, W. H. Pigou (supercargo, agent for others) $840,669, others $530,511.

only by a loan of T. 39,000 from the Company which was passed on to the accounts of Puankhequa, Munqua, Chowqua and Shy Kinqua—admitted debts of $321,110. The claims against him were $399,463, which he offered to discharge in ten annual instalments without further interest. The supercargoes advised the acceptance of these offers as the best available and in order to prevent the utter ruin of all the Canton merchants. Puankhequa and Munqua, who were solvent and whose credit was good, owed $244,710, which they were able to meet when it fell due. The remaining $511,295 was claimed from Chinese who were not Hongists.[23]

At this point constructive diplomatic efforts were set at naught by the interposition of the mailed fist. Captain Panton, despite the supercargoes' representation that his address to the mandarins would lead to the bankruptcy and banishment of several merchants, and to the establishment of an oppressive Co-hong, persisted in his orders. Consequently, on October 19, the supercargoes recorded a formal protest against Admiral Vernon and Captain Panton "for all losses of Goods, Monies, demorrage for detention of Ships, and every ill consequence that may (and we think will) attend the present premature representation to the Viceroy." [24]

On October 22, Captain Panton went into the City and was received by the Governor and Hoppo. He delivered the letter from Admiral Vernon, "demanding justice be done to His Majesty's oppressed Subjects in China, and two letters from Mr. Crichton humbly requesting justice in behalf of himself and others to whom the Chinese Merchants [were] indebted large sums of money," and himself asked "the Chinese Government in a respectful, friendly and firm manner, that His Majesty's Subjects [might] be justly paid the Debts owing to them." [25] The supercargoes of the other nations at the same time presented an address to the officials requesting that their business be not endangered by the action of Captain Panton. On November 6, the Captain received an answer that "Justice [would] be done agreeable to Imperial Laws," and on November 8 he sailed for Madras.[26]

---

[23] Morse, *Chronicle*, II, 45-47.
[24] CMD, IV, Oct. 6, 9, 19, 1779; Morse, *Chronicle*, II, 47-48.
[25] CMD, IV, Captain Panton's Memorial to the Viceroy.
[26] *Ibid.*, IV, Viceroy's Reply to Capt. Panton, Nov. 6, 1779; Morse, *Chronicle*, II, 48-49, 53.

On January 15, 1780, the Select Committee wrote to the Court of Directors explaining proceedings relative to the debts up to that point.[27] On the 17th Matthew Raper apparently addressed a private communication to someone at the India House (perhaps his uncle, John Raper), in which he enclosed a list of eighteen privileges "originally granted to the English" and annexed "a few remarks on the arbitrary deviation from them," and stated that it appeared to him that no redress would be attained "unless it be brought about by some extraordinary interposition"—an embassy, perhaps.[28] It also seems likely that two letters, one written prior to 1779, the other in 1779, to W. (a missionary at Macao) from a missionary at Peking (almost certainly Jean-Joseph de Grammont), were inclosed in Raper's letter.[29]

The first was in answer to some questions asking whether it would be possible to put the Europeans in China on a more equitable foundation. The missionary said that the only hope was for all the Europeans to unite in sending an embassy to Peking to request enlarged privileges and the right to maintain a diplomatic representative at Peking or Canton through whom their complaints might be made known. If this mode of redress was not favored, an agreement might be made with Portugal whereby all European trade could be removed to Macao and European laws enacted for its government. In the letter of 1779 the writer said that, if the Emperor were informed of the conditions of the Europeans, he would remedy the situation immediately; that, if he knew of the debts, he would secure their payment at once; that a private representation through one of the missionaries would be controverted by the mandarins and would only bring official wrath down upon all the missionaries; and that the only hope was for the Europeans to unite, a procedure that might accomplish something.

After Captain Panton's interruption, ordinary negotiations were resumed and a new statement of the indebtedness, uniformly calculated to the beginning of 1780, was handed in. This amounted to $4,400,222, of which Coqua owed $1,194,586, Yngshaw $1,383,976, Seunqua $634,784, Kewshaw $452,418, Munqua $158,451, Conqua (not a Hongist) $81,944, and other non-Hong merchants $494,063. On February

---

[27] CMD, VII, Canton general letter, Jan. 15, 1780.

[28] CMD, I, Jan. 17, 1780, near end of volume. Raper corresponded with Grammont, as is indicated in James Legge, *The Texts of Taoism* (Oxford, 1891), I, xiii.

[29] CMD, I, near end of volume, enclosed in a letter from Raper to the East India Company in Dec., 1791; IOCM, XCI, 29-31.

29 a joint communication was received from the Governor and Hoppo, which reminded the supercargoes of the decree of 1760 prohibiting the borrowing of money from foreigners (of which all the supercargoes and creditors claimed ignorance) and of the provision of Chinese law which said that accumulated interest should never be allowed to more than double the original principal. The supercargoes were asked to draw up a statement of the money lent, distinguishing between that lent before and after 1760. An interview was finally arranged and on March 22, 1780, Bevan, who spoke the mandarin language, and Raper were received by the Hoppo. He was surprised at the size of the accounts delivered by the supercargoes, which were much greater than the ones given to him by the merchants, but he indicated that he and the Governor were willing to secure payment of double the principal.[30]

As a result of this, and after negotiations between the creditors and debtors in April, Yngshaw offered to pay half the principal in yearly payments of $40,000 without further interest or security. Kewshaw proposed to pay his debt in ten annual payments without further interest or security. Seunqua resolved to abide by the decision of the mandarins in the year 1774. As Coqua's estate was already in the hands of the receiver, no proposals were made in regard to his debts. Munqua, whose firm was in sound condition, proposed to pay the whole of his debt in three yearly payments with interest at 5 per cent. The spirit of the creditors had been strengthened by the action of Captain Panton, and they refused to accept the proposals of Yngshaw and Kewshaw, but agreed to Munqua's proposition. Considering the precarious situation of Yngshaw and Kewshaw and the fact that the officials undertook to insure these payments, the proposals were remarkably generous.[31]

After this breakdown of negotiations, affairs at Canton awaited the decision of Peking upon Admiral Vernon's letter, which had been forwarded to the Capital together with a memorial from the Governor (acting Viceroy) reporting the affair as it appeared to him. Several of the creditors, being much encouraged by the effects of Admiral Vernon's letter, wrote to India in November and December, 1779, suggesting that a second representation should be sent by the naval authorities the following season.[32] In consequence, the creditors at Madras obtained the support of Admiral Sir Edward Hughes, who despite the

---

[30] Morse, *Chronicle*, II, 53-55.
[31] Morse, *Chronicle*, II, 55-56.
[32] CMD, IV, Nov. 8 and Dec. 4, 1779; Morse, *Chronicle*, II, 57.

opposition of the Governor and Council of Fort St. George, directed Captain Panton to deliver a second representation to the Viceroy and demand a statement of his intentions regarding the debts.[33] The *Sea Horse* sailed for China as convoy for merchant ships on June 19,1780, and reached Canton some two months later. Captain Panton had an audience with the Viceroy and delivered the letter from Admiral Hughes, but he received no explicit assurances.[34]

The second letter from India was useless, because the wheels of Chinese justice had moved. The representations sent to Peking had been referred to the joint investigation of the *Li Pu* (Civil Office) and *Hing Pu* (Justice). Upon their recommendations an Imperial edict was issued on July 7, 1780, in consequence of which Yngshaw and Kewshaw were thrown into prison, their property was confiscated to pay arrears of the Imperial duties said to amount to T. 150,000, and the remainder was to be used in paying their mercantile debts. All sums owing by them before 1760 were to be doubled and paid in ten annual instalments without further interest. It seems, however, that the debts were actually computed with interest until the end of 1779, and that half of the amount thus obtained was ordered to be paid in ten annual instalments.[35] In this way the amount was fixed at $817,738, of which the first payment was received on April 25, 1781. Seunqua's debt was to be settled according to the judgment of 1774 without further interest.

The Imperial edict also required that in future the Hong merchants should fix a uniform price and be under the supervision of a mandarin. In carrying this into execution, the merchants were required to meet at a certain place under the direction of a military mandarin in the Hoppo's office. In order to raise money to pay the debts and purchase presents for the mandarins, the merchants established a Consoo or Guild fund provided for by a voluntary levy upon themselves, which was shifted to foreign trade in the form of decreased prices for imports and increased charges for exports. The last step in the reestablishment of the Co-hong was taken in 1782, when the Hoppo forced the five newly created Hong merchants—Sinqua, Geowqua,

---

[33] CMD, IV, June 1, 9, 13, 16, 1780.

[34] *Ibid.*, IV, Letter from Canton, Oct. 29, 1780; Ft. St. George to Directors, Jan. 9, 1781; Morse, *Chronicle*, II, 56.

[35] CMD, VII, Vansittart and Law to Directors, Nov. 1, 1783; Morse, *Chronicle*, II, 57-59.

Pinqua, Seequa, and Lunshaw—to become jointly security for each other.[36]

As the Imperial decree did not provide for the settlement of Coqua's or non-Hong merchants' debts, a "Humble Petition" to the Emperor was drawn up by certain of the creditors late in 1781 or early in 1782 requesting that these debts be paid, and that the newly formed association of merchants should be abolished and the foreigners allowed to trade freely with all Canton merchants.[37] Whether or not this petition was ever sent to Peking is uncertain, but, because no settlement of these debts was obtained, George Vansittart and Ewan Law, acting as attorneys for the creditors, wrote to the Court of Directors on November 1, 1783, requesting the Company's assistance in obtaining a settlement of Coqua's debts. Inasmuch as the Court had been angered by the actions of the Country merchants in calling for Admiral Vernon's aid, the creditors were informed in 1785 that any further action in the matter would be detrimental to the Company's affairs.[38]

Thus ended a second drama which began with the dissolution of the Co-hong and the default of Wayqua in 1771, and did not end until six of the Hong merchants had been bankrupted, the wrath of Peking invoked, and the Co-hong re-established. Thanks to the Private creditors' usurious demands backed up by gun-boat diplomacy, of the $4,400,222 claimed by them not over $1,198,189, slightly more than the total principal, was ever required to be paid them. Had they not called in the aid of the Navy and had they accepted the supercargoes' advice in 1779, over twice this amount might have been realized, Yngshaw and Kewshaw saved from bankruptcy, and the establishment of the Co-hong and the Consoo fund prevented. The tragic demise of the Hongists was also caused "by their own vanity and extravagance," as the supercargoes said, and especially by the exactions of the mandarins. The Company must also bear a share of the blame because it was responsible for the abolition of the Co-hong and the introduction of the policy of appealing to the officials when the merchants could not meet their debts.

---

[36] Morse, *Chronicle,* II, 57-59, 69, 81, 82, 92.

[37] CMC, X, No. 430. Only an undated copy of this petition is preserved, but internal evidence shows that it followed shortly after the Imperial action on the other debts. It is initialed by A[braham] L[eslie], J[ohn] C[richton], T[homas] H[utton], C[harles] G[ordon], C[harles] C[rommelin], and G[eorge] S[mith], all of whom were in China at the time, and all of whom were creditors of Coqua (Morse, *Chronicle,* II, 51, 54, 66-67).

[38] CMD, VII, letters of Vansittart and Law, Nov. 1, 1783 and Feb. 8, 1785; IO, *Committee of Correspondence: Reports, 1785-88,* XV, 10.

From our present point of view, the whole affair was for several reasons of great importance. First of all, it led to several proposals that embassies be sent to China, at least one of which was made directly to the British government. Second, it led to the re-establishment of the Co-hong and the establishment of the Consoo fund in 1781, both of which, in the Company's opinion, were detrimental to their interest and raised prices. The Company was willing to take extensive measures to have them abolished. In the third place, it illustrated the unsatisfactory nature of the system by which trade was conducted and the inability of British subjects to obtain their own sort of justice in China. It suggested the advantages that might be gained from an official representative in China who had access to the Peking government and who had power to control the actions of British subjects in China. Finally, it created a considerable stir in India and in London and brought the British government into more direct contact with affairs at Canton.

2. *Financial Difficulties of the Company and Government: the Commutation Act and the Plan to Dominate the China Trade (1783-1786).*

At the close of the American War of Independence, both the British government and the East India Company were faced with bankruptcy. The war had cost England over £115,654,000, a considerable portion of which had been raised by the issue of bonds. As the disastrous war dragged on, confidence in the government's credit declined, and in January, 1783, its stocks had fallen to 56. The national debt in January, 1783, amounted to £215,717,709, whereas the annual income did not exceed £25,000,000, and each year saw a budget deficit and an increase in the debt. The value of England's foreign trade had fallen from £25,000,000 in 1775 to £18,500,000 in 1782.[39] The Mahratta War (1778-81) and financial mismanagement at home and in India had run the Company heavily into debt; and the European phase of the American War, growing foreign competition in the China trade, and excessive duties at home had caused the Company's commerce to decline from £4,514,075 in 1770 to £3,406,420 in 1783.[40] In 1783 its debts amounted to £10,343,692 (over three times its capital), and, because its income did not equal the current expenditure, it was

---

[39] J. Holland Rose, *William Pitt and the National Revival* (London, 1911), pp. 179-80; Levi, *op. cit.*, pp. 491-93.

[40] Macpherson, *India*, pp. 419-20.

forced on March 5, 1783, to petition Parliament for financial aid to the amount of £1,500,000.[41]

When William Pitt became Prime Minister in December, 1783, such were the conditions of the British government and the East India Company, whose fortunes were so closely interwoven that Burke earlier in March had said that to say the Company "was in a state of distress, was neither more nor less than saying the country was in a state of distress."[42] The honor of rescuing both from the dilemma must go to a great extent to Pitt and his colleagues. They did not originate all the constructive ideas, especially those relating to the Company, but they were wise enough to see where the difficulties lay and to adopt constructive proposals when they were brought forward. Pitt's policy was one of financial retrenchment and commercial and industrial expansion. In these two latter factors we have a basic force which caused the Pitt administration to favor a commercial embassy to China as part of a larger project of economic development.

One of his first moves in the re-habilitation of the government and the Company was the Commutation Act. Its immediate objects, according to Pitt, were to protect the government's revenue and promote the welfare of the Company by eliminating smuggling.[43] But, as smuggling was the source from which so many of the Continental countries drew the life-blood of their China trade, this statement meant nothing less than that England aimed to dominate the China trade. Pitt and the Company were well aware that, if the major portion of the lucrative China trade could be drawn into the Company's hands, many of its financial ills would be relieved, and the government's revenue in the end would also be benefited. Both government and Company, in a systematic way, set about achieving this end.

That England aimed to dominate the China trade is amply testified to in the documents relating to the Commutation Act, and in subsequent events. Richardson, in his original proposal of the Commutation Act, emphasized the fact that, if smuggling were eliminated, the Company would be able to carry three times as much tea as it then carried; that, as foreign trade declined, the Company would be assured of drawing the residue of the Country trade into its Canton treasury at lower exchanges, part of which residue was at present obtained by foreign

---

[41] *Parliamentary History*, 1782-83, XXIII, 572-82,1193, and XXIV, 165.
[42] *Ibid.*, XXIII, 646-47.
[43] *Parliamentary History, 1784*, XV, 230-33.

companies and used to the detriment of the English nation; and that the trade between India and China would be increased and the whole of it turned to the benefit of England.⁴⁴ The resolution introduced into the House of Commons on December 24, 1783, by Eden, Chairman of the Committee on Smuggling, emphasized the fact that smuggling threatened the destruction of the revenue and was highly injurious to regular commerce.⁴⁵

On February 11, 1784, Henry Beaufoy pointed out to the House that the Commutation Act involved considerations of highest importance to the manufacturing and commercial interests of the country, because at present many seamen and commercial elements of the country were working against it, instead of for it, and were exporting specie to Europe in return for French manufactures and products of the East Indies imported in foreign ships.⁴⁶ The third report of the Committee on Smuggling pointed out that a reduction of the tea duties would not only relieve the Company but would be a positive advantage to both the country and the Company by increasing navigation and stopping the great annual remittance then made to the Continent for tea.⁴⁷ On May 19 the King's message proposed "to frame such commercial regulations as may appear immediately necessary." ⁴⁸

Again on June 18, Eden pointed out that the clandestine trade was supporting foreign companies in their competition with the Company. On the 21st, Pitt insisted that the proposed Commutation Act would benefit the Company and nation by throwing the tea trade into their hands and by employing twenty more large ships and 2,000 more seamen, and that the revenue would be increased with an actual saving to the public.⁴⁹ Twenty days later, Alderman Watson of London frankly stated that the Act would strengthen the marine interests of the country and would enable the Company to defeat its foreign competitors, monopolize the tea trade, and even supplant the foreign companies in the Continental market.⁵⁰ Later in 1786 Pitt and Francis plainly said

---

⁴⁴ IO, *Home Miscellaneous*, LXI, 103-111, 140-48; G. L. Staunton, *Embassy*, II, 617-23.

⁴⁵ *Commons Journal, 1783*, XXXIX, 741.

⁴⁶ *Parliamentary History, 1784*, XIII, 104.

⁴⁷ PP, *Reports, 1783-84*, VI, No. 60, "Third Report of the Committee on Illicit Practices."

⁴⁸ *Parliamentary History, 1784*, XIV, 4.

⁴⁹ *Parliamentary History, 1784*, XV, 225, 230-33.

⁵⁰ *Ibid.*, XVI, 379.

that the object of the Act had been to secure the China tea trade for England.[51]

Whether the government had in mind a great expansion of the sale of British manufactures in China as a result of the Act, is not shown in the documents of 1784. On February 6, 1785, however, the super-cargoes, in commenting upon Richardson's plan, indicated that a con-siderable expansion of the woollen trade could now be contemplated "as the decrease of the foreign trade [would] naturally cause a decrease in the importation of foreign woollens." [52] How the British activity appeared to the foreigners is well summed up by Major Shaw on December 20, 1787:[53]

In the opinion of judicious observers, the English seem not only to be aiming at the monopoly of the tea trade to Europe, but to have in view the exclusive commerce of this division of the globe. The new plan of government for Bengal and its dependencies,- their late establishments, both to the eastward and westward,- the prohibition to their subjects in India against selling their ships to foreigners,- and, in short, their whole conduct, strongly favors the suspicion.

In carrying out this policy of monopolizing the China trade, and in order to help finance their increased purchases, the Company began to dump increased quantities of woollens into the Chinese market. The number of pieces exported from England to China rose from 28,417 in 1783 to 136,050 in 1790. The value of lead exported also rose from £4,579 in 1783 to £39,452 in 1788, and the exportation of copper was begun in 1786, and of tin in 1788.[54] Soon, however, several difficulties in the way of the complete success of the scheme made themselves evident. First of all, the government's revenue from the tea trade de-clined sharply after the Act. For the five years previous to the Com-mutation Act, the revenue received from tea had averaged £709,929 per annum. It fell to £324,738 in 1784-85 and to £285,460 in 1785-86 and rose only to £336,095 in 1786-87.[55] Although the government was protected from absolute loss by the window tax, it kept an anxious eye on the success of the policy.[56]

---

[51] *Parliamentary History, 1786-87*, XXVI, 159-60, 169.
[52] CMC, II, No. 8.
[53] *Shaw's Journal*, pp. 250-51.
[54] Appendices I, II; CMC, X, Nos. 398-99; PP, *Accounts and Papers, 1788*, XXI, No. 436.
[55] PP, *Accounts and Papers, 1788*, XXI, Nos. 483, 484.
[56] *Ibid.*, XXI, No. 469.

In the second place, the financial situation of the Company did not improve quickly. Revenues in India did not increase as expected, and expenditure remained high. Accordingly, the Court of Directors, in July, 1784, was forced to petition the government for relief from paying the £300,000 annuity required by the charter bill of 1781. This payment was also suspended in 1785 and 1786, and in the latter year the Company also requested permission to increase its capital stock by £800,000, making it £4,000,000. The expanding trade of the Company made necessary this increase in its capital. Before granting these relief measures, the government forced the Company to accept the limitation of its dividends to 8 per cent.[57] At the beginning of the year 1786, the Company's bonded debt in England was about £1,993,850 and its debts in India had been reduced only to £9,264,016, a total of £11,257,866.[58]

A third important problem arising out of the Commutation Act was that of finding means to finance the expanded trade. As we have seen, the Company sent more woollens and lead and began to send copper and tin, but these were entirely inadequate. The stress upon the financial machinery of Canton, although shown in most of the communications of the period, is even better illustrated in the financial status of the Canton treasury. At the beginning of the season 1784 the treasury had a credit balance of T. 214,121, at the beginning of the next season it had a debit balance of T. 222,766, in 1786 a debit balance of T. 864,307, and in 1787 a debit balance of T. 914,308.[59] As soon as the Commutation Act was passed, the Company wrote to India telling the Presidencies to give every aid in their power to the Canton factory, but Madras was helpless. The only help which Bombay could afford was through slightly increased shipments of cotton on the Company's account and the encouragement of larger private shipments in the hope that the proceeds would find their way into the Company's treasury. The situation in Bengal was little better. Bengal allowed bills to be drawn on itself in 1786, but Cornwallis stopped this at once, and the only successful help which it could afford was through the medium of the opium trade.[60]

At the end of the year 1784, the supercargoes, in a reply to a communication from the Governor General regarding means for helping

[57] *Parliamentary History, 1783-85,* XXIV, 1034-85, 1322-30, 1354; *ibid., 1786-88,* XXVI, 151-54.
[58] PP, *Accounts and Papers, 1787,* Nos. 405, 406.
[59] Morse, *Chronicle,* II, 94, 110, 118, 135.
[60] CMC, VIII, No. 8; PP, *Accounts and Papers, 1786,* X, No. 163.

Canton without embarrassing Bengal, made three suggestions: (1) that opium should be delivered to Country traders upon their giving bond that they would pay the produce into the Canton Treasury; (2) that, if the Bengal government's financial situation were such that it required the proceeds of the opium sale in its own treasury, then drawbacks should be given to those persons who would bind themselves to pay the proceeds into the Canton Treasury in return for bills on London; (3) that, if Bengal had more woollens on hand than were required, they should be sent to Canton.[61]

On April 29, 1785, the Governor General and Council wrote to the Directors that they had advertised the sale of opium in November upon terms which would require the money received from it to be paid into the Canton Treasury, and suggested three methods whereby the opium trade could be made to supply Canton. They first proposed the creation of an Opium Corporation to control production and exportation. It should establish a distributing center in the East and be required to pay at least $800,000 per year into the Canton Treasury in return for bills on London. The second proposal was to maintain a monopoly of the trade as at present but for the Company to establish distributing bases at Batavia, Rhio, and possibly Macao, whose agents would pay the proceeds into the Canton Treasury. The third proposal was to sell opium only to persons who would give security for paying the proceeds from its sale into the Canton Treasury. This latter proposal, which the Court and Board of Control ultimately approved, was adopted as a working basis until instructions were received from London.[62]

Increased supplies of pepper were also sent from Benkulen to China, and bonds were issued at Canton. The supercargoes were able to get increased sums from the Country trade and to draw remittances out of the hands of foreign companies by offering bills on London at 5/6 per dollar. The total sums received at Canton in the form of bills, certificates, and bonds rose from T. 576,393 in 1784 to T. 2,889,452 in 1787. In spite of all these efforts the Company was forced to export enormous sums in bullion from England—£704,254 in 1785, £694,962 in 1786, and £626,897 in 1787—and this large exportation aroused the opposition of certain members of Parliament in 1786.[63] But all efforts seemed to be insufficient. The debit balance steadily grew at Canton, and, if the Chinese merchants had not been willing to extend credit, the

[61] IOCCC, LXXIX, 115.
[62] PP, *Accounts and Papers, 1787,* No. 354.
[63] Appendices IX, X; *Parliamentary History, 1786-88,* XXXVI, 154-60.

increasing investments could never have been made. Thus at the beginning of the year 1787 in England it looked very much as if the attempt to monopolize the China trade was to be frustrated through inability to finance it.

A fourth disturbing element in 1787 was the continuation of foreign competition. In 1783-84 foreign competition had reached its zenith when twenty-one ships had exported 19,072,300 lbs. of tea, but in 1787 thirteen ships exported 13,578,000 lbs. of tea, and it was not until 1790 that the exportation of tea by Continental countries fell below the three million pound mark.[64] Nor were the reports sent home by the supercargoes encouraging. Thus in 1786 the supercargoes wrote: "The competition of Foreigners is not yet diminished, notwithstanding the alterations which have taken place in the Duties on Tea." The letters also complained of high prices because of the foreign competition and the high prices demanded by the inland tea merchants.[65] The creation in 1785 of a new *Compagnie des Indes* also indicated that France at least was preparing to keep up the competition; and on February 16, 1787, the supercargoes wrote home telling of the arrival of the French mission from Pondicherry under D'Entrecasteaux with the object of improving French trade with China and, as they thought, the establishment of a commercial base in Cochin China.[66]

The government and Parliament were keeping an eye on the China trade, as can be judged from the numerous papers submitted to Parliament relating to China. These papers showed the continuation of foreign competition, the difficulties in obtaining good teas at low prices, the quantities of tea imported, sold, and the duties realized, and the great difficulties which the supercargoes and the Indian Presidencies were having in providing Canton with cash.[67] Altogether the reports from China suggested to the government the advisability of taking measures which would aid the Company in supplying funds and still further handicap the Continental companies in their competition.

Other disturbing news was received from Canton which showed the general unsatisfactory nature of the system and of trade. Activities of the Co-hong in lowering prices on imports and raising prices on exports were reported; difficulties were encountered in finding a ready

---

[64] Milburn, *Oriental Commerce*, II, 486.
[65] PP, *Accounts and Papers, 1788,* XXI, No. 465.
[66] *Ibid.*; Morse, *Chronicle,* II, 134.
[67] PP, *Accounts and Papers, 1785,* No. 72; *ibid., 1786,* X, Nos. 154, 158-63; *ibid., 1787,* XVII, Nos. 334, 354, 372, 403, 406.

market for the increased quantities of woollens and lead; the officials tried to force the supercargoes to do business with Eequa, a merchant whom they could not depend on, and the supercargoes were especially annoyed by the limitation of the shipment of silk to 100 piculs per ship and by the stopping of trade several times during 1785 and 1786.[68]

At the same moment that these discouraging and alarming reports were arriving from China, the rapidly expanding cotton industry was beginning to bring pressure to bear on the government to afford it more protection and encouragement. The cotton manufacturers objected to the importation of Indian and Chinese cotton materials, and they wanted new markets. Already in 1787 the first signs of the cotton trade crisis of 1788 were beginning to show themselves and made the manufacturers more solicitous of advantage than ever.[69] They received their first great boon in the Eden free trade treaty with France, signed on September 26, 1786. The treaty also was a step in the government's general policy of industrial and commercial expansion and a part of the scheme for monopolizing the China trade as it made for freer entry into France of East India products (calicoes and silks excluded) brought by the Company to England and re-exported.[70]

Altogether the situation in regard to the China trade, as it appeared to observers in England at the beginning of the year 1787, was not especially encouraging. The government's revenue from the trade was not increasing as anticipated; the Company's finances were still in an unsatisfactory condition; foreign competition was still strong, and rumors of French designs were current; the Company was having difficulties in raising money to finance the trade, and the exportation of bullion was arousing criticism; British goods were not selling well in China, and teas and silks of good quality were hard to get at reasonable prices; the China trade, always dependent upon the caprice of the officials, was now also dependent upon the confidence of the merchants who were extending credit to the Company; at home, industrial interests were attacking the Company and demanding a market for goods which could not be sold at Canton.

Under such circumstances, it is not surprising that both the Company and the government should turn their thoughts to an embassy, which, by direct appeal to Peking, might put the China trade on a treaty

[68] Morse, *Chronicle*, II, Chaps. 39-41, especially pp. 96-98, 110-11, 120, 126-31.
[69] *Commons Journal, 1780-82*, XXXVIII, 893; Mantoux, *op. cit.*, pp. 262-63; Ellison, *op. cit.*, pp. 50ff.
[70] *Parliamentary History, 1786-88*, XXVI, 233-54, 267-72.

basis and open new ports to trade where the Company could get a ready supply of tea and silk at lower prices and where English produce might find a more ready outlet. Thus the pressure at home would be relieved, and the Company's financial problems in China would be solved. Such a treaty would give the English an advantage in the China trade and insure the defeat of their rivals. Finally, an expanded trade would also benefit the government's revenue.

3. *Treatment of H. M. Ships and the Activity of Country Ships in China (1765-1785).*

In Chapter II the generally unsatisfactory nature of the Canton system was pointed out, and in the previous sections of this chapter various events in the commercial sphere, which aroused concern in England and tended to encourage the sending of a British mission to China, have been discussed. In this and the following sections, attention is called to a number of semi-diplomatic events, culminating in the *Lady Hughes* affair, which illustrated the uneasy footing on which English relations with China rested, and which directly indicated the advisability of an attempt to put Anglo-Chinese relations upon a treaty basis.

The first of these events group themselves about the treatment of H.M. ships. As noted earlier, the Chinese forbade foreign ships of war to enter the Bogue. Warships were forced to anchor alongside Lintin Island or in Chuenpi anchorage, where the situation for re-fitting, careening, and provisioning was unsatisfactory. If H. M. ships were permitted to proceed to Whampoa, the Chinese insisted on treating them as merchant ships and measuring them, a procedure which was, according to European opinion, disrespectful to men-of-war and which was invariably opposed by their commanders, often to the detriment of trade.

In March, 1765, H.M.S. *Argo* arrived at Whampoa from Calcutta with ten lakhs of rupees on board. She was allowed to remain quietly at Whampoa, until after the first tea contracts were made late in April. The Hoppo then informed the supercargoes that he intended to measure the ship. To this Captain Affleck denied his consent, but the Hoppo refused to dispense with the measuring. In consequence, trade was stopped, and on June 27 Captain Affleck sent a protest to the Viceroy giving reasons for his refusal, and claiming the same privileges as those granted the H.M.S. *Centurion* in 1741-42.[11] In reply the officials pointed out that the former ship had "put into Port through stress of weather," whereas the *Argo* "brought money on a mercantile account," in which latter case there was no justification for dispensing with the measuring.[12]

On July 12 the supercargoes wrote to Captain Affleck indicating that their trade was being seriously injured by his refusal to allow the ship to be measured, and that the officials threatened to report the matter to Peking, an action that might lead to the ruin of a number of Hong merchants or the permanent cessation of trade. They requested him to allow the ship to be measured. Since the existence of the trade was endangered, Captain Affleck gave up the point, and the ship was measured.[13]

On September 16, 1776, H.M.S. *Sea Horse* arrived at Macao from Madras with nine lakhs of rupees. Captain Farmer demanded the status of a King's ship and offered to allow the Chinese to examine the vessel, but refused to allow her to be measured. On the 21st she passed the Bogue to avoid the danger of typhoons. The Chinese officials assumed an "attitude of passive resistance and covert hostility," and refused to give her a pilot, to supply her with fresh provisions and water, or to grant a chop for the unloading of the treasure. She remained at the second bar until October 17, when, at the measuring of the *Norfolk*, the supercargoes apologized to the Hoppo about some other difficulties. This put him in such a good humor that he told them he would not "demand a Dollar for the measurage and usual Presents for the Man-of-War," and on the 25th a chop for unloading the treasure was issued. By keeping the ship at the second bar, the captain had avoided the problem of measuring, but the favorable settlement of the whole affair depended upon the whim of the Hoppo.[14]

The outbreak of war between France and England in 1778 brought a number of King's ships into Chinese waters to act as convoys to the Indiamen. The *Sea Horse* was at Canton again in September, 1778, with treasure from Madras, but she apparently remained outside Whampoa and difficulties were avoided. In December, 1779, H.M.S. *Resolution* and *Discovery* arrived in a disabled condition from the

---

[11] The *Centurion*, after a great deal of difficulty, was allowed to proceed to Whampoa to be re-fitted without being measured, *supra*, p. 116.
[12] Morse, *Chronicle*, V, 127-30; Auber, *op. cit.*, p. 176; Eames, *op. cit.*, pp. 90-91; Martin, *China*, II, 15; Morse, *International Relations*, I, 97.
[13] Morse, *Chronicle*, V, 128-29.
[14] Morse, *Chronicle*, II, 19-22.

Cape of Good Hope. They remained outside of Whampoa and were granted facilities for careening, re-fitting, and provisioning. The *Sea Horse* was this year again at Canton, bearing the memorial which Captain Panton delivered to the Viceroy. She appears to have remained outside the second bar, as she did also in 1780.[75]

Although no difficulties were created by these latter H.M. ships, the circumstance of their being forced to remain outside Whampoa was most unsatisfactory so far as the English were concerned. If necessity required that King's ships proceed to Whampoa, there was always the certainty that the Chinese would demand to measure them, and the refusal of this demand would lead to a temporary embarrassment of trade and perhaps to its total annihilation. Such circumstances were not pleasing to the world's greatest sea power.

The war also led to other events which demonstrated the unsatisfactory nature of the British situation in China, and brought out clearly the difficulties arising through the absence of an official representative in China with power to command all British subjects. For several years prior to 1781 Country ships had come laden with goods, paid their receipts into the Company's treasury, and departed without cargoes. This was in violation of Chinese law, which required ships to carry away cargoes paying duties equal in amount to the duties on their imported cargoes. In 1781 a number of Country ships were employed by the Portuguese to carry Dutch goods from Macao to Batavia. The Chinese protested against their leaving Whampoa without cargoes, and the Hoppo directed a very abusive communication to the Company's supercargoes ordering them to put a stop to the practice or be held responsible for the duties on such ships and not to receive further money from Country traders.[76]

This demand was especially dangerous because the supercargoes had no means of forcing the Country ships to do their bidding, and further, because the success of their own trade depended upon the receipt of money from the Country trade. They wrote to the Court of Directors complaining of their inability to control the Country ships. The situation was further complicated by the piratical activities of Captain John McClary, commanding the Country ship *Dadoloy* of Bengal. On May 20, 1781, Captain McClary seized a sloop near Macao which he suspected of being Spanish property, but upon going to Macao he

---

[75] *Ibid.*, II, 36, 43, 47, 49, 51, 56.
[76] Morse, *Chronicle*, II, 62-63.

was seized, thrown into prison, and forced to pay $70,000 by the Portuguese officials before he was released. Angered by this, he proceeded to Whampoa, where, on August 17, he seized the Dutch Country ship *Felix*. McClary made preparations to take the prize from Whampoa by force, but the Chinese assembled troops to resist such action. It was finally arranged that the prize crew should abandon the ship, and the "Chinese gallantly invaded the prize, which was thus rescued from the pirate's hands." [77] In reward for his condescension Captain McClary was allowed to keep a chest of pearls and gold valued at 89,128 rupees.

During the course of the episode the Governor demanded that the supercargoes compel McClary to make restitution, to give compensation, and to keep the peace in the future. Upon being informed that they had no power to control Country ships or private merchants, the Governor called the English "a lying and troublesome People," blamed the supercargoes for McClary's activities, and announced that they would be held responsible in the future for the misdeeds of all English. Vexed by their situation, the supercargoes wrote to the Court:

We have many times seen the whole Trade of the Company under an Embargo on the most trifling pretence; and we think it may hereafter suffer the most material detriment; from the Wickedness or Folly of Country Commanders . . . These [the mandarins] sometimes permit to pass unnoticed; & sometimes make it a pretence for oppressing the Hong Merchants: but when it becomes a matter of too great magnitude to be passed over, the Company are [*sic*] held responsible. [78]

The next year, 1782, Captain McClary, in company with the *Death and Glory* privateer, seized two ships from Macao, and also plundered a Chinese junk near Banka belonging to Chowqua, one of the principal Hong merchants. McClary did not come to Canton, but the officials, fearing that he might come, instructed the supercargoes to keep McClary's ship away and to keep their own warships from coming to Whampoa, upon pain of being severely punished. The Portuguese, Dutch, and Hong merchants put in claims against McClary, which the supercargoes referred to the Governor-General, who in 1783 had McClary arrested. But he was released, as there were "no valid grounds for a criminal indictment," although the Governor-General promised to afford every assistance to the aggrieved parties if they wished to carry on civil suit against McClary. [79]

---

[77] Morse, *Chronicle*, II, 63-64.
[78] *Ibid.*, II, 65.
[79] Morse, *Chronicle*, II, 79-80, 86-87.

In view of these circumstances the Chinese became very cautious about allowing any ships without cargoes to proceed to Whampoa. The Company's gun-brig *Rodney* and dispatch vessel *Fox,* which were convoying the ships, were forced to remain at Macao in 1781. In 1783 the supercargoes had great difficulty in obtaining permission for the Company's packet *Antelope,* which arrived in a damaged condition, to receive provisions and supplies even outside the Bogue and at Macao.[80] The whole situation was fraught with danger both to the Company's trade and to the Country trade, and the Court of Directors took steps to increase the powers of the supercargoes over Country and Private traders.

On December 11, 1781, a general commission was sent out empowering the supercargoes to seize persons residing in China contrary to the Company's wishes and in violation of their covenants with the Company.[81] On December 24, 1782, the Company's Counsel delivered an opinion relative to the McClary case, stating that the Company's servants would have been justified in using force to aid the Chinese magistrates in seizing McClary. In consequence, orders were sent out in 1783, 1784 and 1785 directing the supercargoes to exercise a strict control over Country traders and to proceed against persons residing in China contrary to the Company's charter.[82] In view of these orders, the supercargoes, in 1785, detained Captain Richardson of the Country ship *Bellona* until he paid the port duties.

In 1786 the Company was able to get a statute passed by Parliament vesting in the supercargoes all powers relative to the control over "private English" which were possessed by the Court of Directors.[83] The whole matter of jurisdiction over "private English" and especially the McClary case came under a careful review by the Board of Control late in 1785,[84] which leads one to believe that the difficulties created by the lack of competent official jurisdiction over British subjects in China were important considerations in the minds of governmental officials when the decision was taken to send an embassy to China. Support is lent to this belief by a sentence in Colonel Cathcart's instructions, which

[80] *Ibid.,* pp. 81, 87.
[81] CMD, IX, Jan. 3-11, 1780 and VII, May 12, 1780.
[82] CMD, IX, Jan. 25, 1782, parags. 54-57; Dec. 24, 1782, Counsel's opinion on McClary case; Jan. 15, 1783, parag. 41; Dec. 9, 1784, parag. 34; Jan. 25, 1785, parag. 5; Dec. 30, 1785, parags. 18, 33, 39.
[83] 26 Geo. III, cap. 57, sec. 35.
[84] IOC, XX, Solicitor's report to the Board of Control on the Powers of the Company's Supercargoes over Country Ships, first part of the volume.

stated that if a cession of territory were obtained from China "competent Powers would of course be given from our own Legislature, so as
effectually to prevent or punish the Disorders of Our People, which
the Company's supra cargoes in their limited Sphere of Action must
see committed with impunity." [85]

4. *The Question of Criminal Jurisdiction: the Lady Hughes Affair (1772-1785)*.

The events which most impressed upon the Company and government the desirability of putting their relations with China on a treaty
basis were connected with the problem of criminal jurisdiction. The
question of submitting foreigners to Chinese law had been a moot point
throughout the eighteenth century, but the whole question was brought
to a head by the execution of Europeans in 1773, 1780, 1783, and 1785.
On December 17, 1772, a Chinese was wounded in an affray between
the sailors of the *Lord Camden* and some natives. The pilot's chop
for the ship was held up for nineteen days, but the recovery of the
injured person prevented serious trouble. [86]

Late in the same year a Chinese was killed at Macao; an Englishman, Francis Scott, was charged with the murder. The Portuguese
trial completely exculpated him, but the Chinese threatened dire venge-
ance upon Macao if he were not given up. Early in 1773 he was surrendered to the Chinese, by whom he was tried, convicted, and executed, although there was not the slightest evidence of his guilt. This
was the first execution of an Englishman by the Chinese, and it was
considered a bad precedent. [87]

In 1780 there were several affrays between sailors of different
nationalities at Canton, and in one a French seasan killed a Portuguese
sailor belonging to the *Stormont*. The murderer took refuge in the
French Consulate, where he remained for many days, but after some
negotiation and serious threats by the Chinese he was surrendered. On
the morning of December 14, 1780, he was publicly strangled, and the
Select Committee commented upon the execution in the following
manner:

---

[85] Morse, *Chronicle*, II, 165.

[86] Morse, *Chronicle*, V, 173-75; Davis, *Chinese* (1836), I, 60; Auber, *op. cit.*,
p. 178; Eames, *op. cit.*, p. 94.

[87] Morse, *Chronicle*, V, 182-85 and *International Relations*, I, 101-102; Davis,
Chinese (1836), I, 61; Eames, *op. cit.*, p. 94.

This is the first instance of one European being executed for the murder of another, in this Country, and appears to be a very dangerous Precedent; as it may involve Europeans in inextricable difficulties; if even by accident one man should kill another. The man executed today could have had no trial of common justice.[88]

On February 23, 1782, a twelve-year-old boy accidentally shot a Chinese with a gun which he had secured to frighten a man who was throwing crackers at him. Because of being under the age of responsibility, the boy was freed. A year later a Portuguese at Macao stabbed a Chinese, and after much controversy he was publicly shot by the Portuguese under the supervision of Chinese officials.[89] These cases served to show the determination of the mandarins to apply Chinese law to foreigners and to put the European community in a state of chronic fear. The crisis which had been brewing in the events of the past fifteen years came to a head in the *Lady Hughes* affair of 1784-85.

The *Lady Hughes* was a Country ship from Bombay commanded by Captain W. Williams; her supercargo was George Smith. On November 24, 1784, when she fired a salute, three minor mandarins in a chop boat alongside were so severely injured that one died on the following day, and a second died shortly. On November 25, W. H. Pigou, the British chief, was informed by minor officials that the gunner should be sent to Canton to be examined. The Chinese implied that it was not a capital offense and that the person would be released after a public examination. The supercargoes, however—remembering the fate of the Frenchman in 1780, having been told that the gunner had absconded, and thinking that someone else would have to take his place—proposed that the examination be held in the factories.[90]

On November 26 the mandarins called again to urge the surrender of the man. Puankhequa, talking for them, said that no official competent to try the case would come to the factories, that the man must appear before the Governor's tribunal, and that if the man were brought to the factories the officials would come with men and seize him. The supercargoes replied that they would not allow armed men to enter the factories, and the merchants and officials retired after requesting

---

[88] CMC, II, No. 2; Morse, *Chronicle,* II, 59-60; Martin, *op. cit.,* II, 15-16; Auber, *op cit.,* p. 181; Eames, *op. cit.,* pp. 95-96.

[89] Morse, *Chronicle,* II, 72-73, 86.

[90] IOCCC, LXXIX (1784), 118-37; Auber, *op. cit.,* pp. 183-87; Martin, *op. cit.,* II, 16-17; Eames, *op. cit.,* pp. 96-97; Davis, *The Chinese* (1836), I, 66-67; Morse, *Chronicle,* II, 99-107; Keeton, *op. cit.,* I, 40-42; *Shaw's Journal,* pp. 186-95; Henri Cordier, *Histoire des relations de la Chine avec les puissances occidentales* (Paris, 1901), I, 13.

that Smith should not leave the factories for several days. At eleven o'clock in the evening they returned to say that the mandarins had agreed that the examination should be held in the factories under the direction of the *Namhoi Hien* without military escort.

The next day the supercargoes were alarmed to hear that Smith had been lured from the factory, seized, and carried into the city under a guard of soldiers. Furthermore, trade was stopped, the linguists and merchants were nowhere to be found, and all avenues leading to the quay were barricaded and filled with soldiers. It was obvious that the Chinese were planning to apply pressure to bring about compliance with their demands. The British, supported by the French, Dutch, Danes, and Americans, determined to resist such pressure and to prevent such a dangerous precedent being established by its success. Despite a messenger from the Governor saying that he merely wished to question Smith and that he would be released in a short time, the supercargoes of all nations ordered their ships' pinnaces manned, armed, and sent up to the factories.

Later in the evening a minor mandarin came with a mandate from the Governor saying that the guilty person must appear before him for examination, that the foreigners should not resist Chinese law, that Smith had promised to write to Whampoa to demand the gunner, that Smith would be released as soon as the gunner arrived, and that if they resisted he would surround them with troops and cut off their retreat. On November 28 all the nations united in sending a letter to the Governor by the Hong merchants, requesting the release of Smith. In reply the Governor requested a conference with the nations other than the English who had signed the letter. He expressed surprise at their joining the English and tried to get them to abandon the English. They refused to do this, because they felt that the cause of the English was their cause in such affairs. The Governor said that he did not wish to punish all the foreigners and told them if a man were surrendered the whole affair would be ended. In the meantime the factories had been surrounded by troops and armed boats and all routes of escape blocked.

The Governor was so much upset by the united opposition of the foreigners that he would gladly have settled the matter, but he had gone so far that he now could not withdraw and save his face. At ten o'clock in the evening a linguist arrived with a letter from Smith to Captain Williams, directing that the gunner or someone else be sent to the factory to be examined, and that the ship should under no circumstances leave the port until the affair was settled. Captain Mackintosh was sent with the linguist to see that the message was delivered to the Captain of the *Lady Hughes*. He departed with orders to demand of Captain Williams the surrender of the man, and if the *Lady Hughes* should attempt to sail, to prevent it by such methods as he deemed proper.

On November 30 a conference was held with the mandarins during which Galbert, a Frenchman, acted as interpreter. The supercargoes indicated their fears that the gunner had escaped on *Le Necker*, which had sailed the day after Smith was seized. After abusing them for deception, the mandarins said that if the man were not delivered supplies would be stopped, trade suspended, and the ships not permitted to return to England. The supercargoes offered to send down several boats with men to search all the ships for the gunner. The mandarins were pleased by this and desired that five boats be sent, but that Pigou remain at the factory. The mandarins also said that the affair must be settled in two days or Smith would be held. The supercargoes seized this opportunity of freeing themselves of further responsibilty by recommending him to the benevolence of the Chinese. Captain Stephen Williams was sent to bring back the unfortunate gunner if he could be found and the commander of the ship prevailed upon to give him up. The supercargoes also seized this occasion to send back most of the armed guard.

Hardly had Captain Williams departed when Captain Mackintosh arrived with the gunner, who had remained on the *Lady Hughes* during the entire affair. The supercargoes of all nations sent a request to the Governor that the gunner be treated with clemency as the whole affair was an accident. The mandarins told them that there was no cause for worry about his fate, and that nothing would be done until the Emperor's decision was received. Smith, who returned in about an hour after the man was surrendered, reported that he had been well treated. In their account of the affair in a letter of December 9, the supercargoes stated that it was obvious that the Chinese had intended to seize the British chief had Smith's detention proved ineffective. They also requested that their powers over the officers of Country ships and Country traders be more clearly defined.

Trade was re-opened on December 6, and the *Lady Hughes* sailed the next day. No more was heard of the matter until January 8, 1785, when the supercargoes were summoned before the Provincial Judge.

He gave them a lecture on the graciousness of the Emperor, who, he said, was much displeased by their actions; and he further told them that they must submit to the Imperial decision, which was especially moderate in demanding but one life for two. Shortly afterwards they learned that the man had been strangled at about the same time they were receiving this harangue.

This termination of the affair threw the foreign community into a fit of terror, and the supercargoes wrote very gloomy letters to the Court relative to the future of the trade and to the disagreeable situation of foreigners in China. On February 5, 1785, they commented in detail upon the injustice of the affair and the ill which it forebode. They pointed out that a similar incident might place them in a state of personal danger from which "we shall not be able to extricate ourselves . . . without doing that, which must for ever disgrace us, or abandoning this important commerce." They continued with an account of the execution of the Frenchman in 1780 and other illustrations from Chinese judicial methods which showed that in "case of death a man must be given up . . . or if he be refused the Supra Cargo of the Ship, or Chief of the Nation must answer for his crime. . . . This appears so reasonable to the Chinese that we believe no Magistrate can ever recede from it." They further suggested that if similar incidents occurred in the future, their only recourse would be to retire to their ships and quit the port, which might lead the Chinese to prohibit trade.[91]

The indignities we personally suffer :- the vexations and impediments in our business; we have been taught by gradual encroachment to bear :- but if the Trade be once lost; and the necessities of England oblige her to regain it; we apprehend it can be done only by a submission, that must be disgraceful; or by the use of force, which however successful, must be productive of very serious calamities.- We think that no application to the Chinese Government for any, the most reasonable privilege would be successful unless made in a manner that would awe them: The Privilege with respect to their administration of justice should be, we think, that in case of Murder, the perpetrator should be tried by us, in the presence of a Chinese Magistrate: that if he be found guilty, he should be delivered up; but if innocent that we should be allowed to protect him — Should the act prove to be only Manslaughter that they agree to some adequate punishment, such as imprisonment for a year, or whatever else may be previously regulated between us :- that in case the delinquents have really escaped, no substitute shall be demanded; but that they will trust us in making the most diligent search for him; or assisting them to do it; . . .

<hr>

[91] IOCCC, LXXIX, 169-74 and for other comments on the affair 102-05, 108, 153-57; Morse, *Chronicle*, II, 105-07.

The Foreign Nations we understand, have made similar representations to their superiors — they have considered this from the beginning a common cause — and feel with us how exposed the situation of all Europeans is at this Port.

Not being content with these recommendations, the supercargoes, in a letter to William Richardson on February 6, after commenting upon the possibilities of the proposed Commutation Act and the financial difficulties in the way of its success, continued, "Among other Considerations respecting this trade it is much to be lamented that it is not, independent of mere Commercial reasons, on more secure & permanent footing" as the *Lady Hughes* affair clearly indicated.[92] Should

the Honble. Court determine in consequence to take some measures for our Security & protection it must be considered as a first principle that no Person sent in the name of the Company *only* will be of sufficient weight to effect the Purpose; they must procure a respectable person to be sent in ye King's name who should have force sufficient to secure himself from insult & after stopping at Macao to communicate with the Council, should proceed directly to the nearest Port to Pekin where only he can attract the notice of the Court & be secure from the misrepresentations of provincial Mandarins; . . . Whether anything will be done or not, we think the Council cannot in justice be censured for Communicating their apprehensions of danger which self interestedness might have concealed till some unfortunate accident should make it apparent & the consequences irremediable: let us hope too that it shall not be called an unnecessary alarm proceeding from premature & groundless fear, which is in reality the effect of the most certain conviction & assurances but too well founded.

In its reply of February 24, 1786, the Court censured the supercargoes for their conduct in the affair and told them that resistance to the Chinese government was useless, that they had absolute power to seize Private traders and jurisdiction over Country ships, that in cases of accidental death they were to apply to the Hong merchants to settle the affair by financial means, and that in the cases of murder they were to aid the Chinese officials in apprehending the criminal.[93] Measures were, nevertheless, set on foot in England to carry out the recommendations of the supercargoes.

---

[92] CMC, VIII, No. 2.
[93] CMD, III, Court to supercargoes, Feb. 24, 1786; Auber, *op. cit.,* pp. 188-91; Eames, *op. cit.,* p. 97.

5. *Growing Connections between India and China: the Smith-Dundas Correspondence (1774-1786).*

Besides the events already mentioned, the growing political and commercial connections between India and China were additional considerations, causing the government to decide to send an embassy to Peking. The expansion of British power in India brought them into contact with Nepal and Tibet. Nepal, which was ruled by a Goorkha tribe allied with Tibet, was in a constant internal turmoil which endangered good relations with India, and the Governor-General of India was interested in opening commercial relations with Tibet. In 1772 a Goorkha tribe invaded Behar, and in response to an appeal from the Rajah, Warren Hastings sent into the country a force which repelled the invaders. The Dalai Lama, religious ruler of Tibet, thereupon wrote a letter to Warren Hastings interceding in behalf of the Goorkhas. Hastings seized the opportunity to send a mission to Lhasa with the object of opening commercial relations. The mission set out in 1774 and returned in 1775 without having accomplished anything definite.[94]

The Dalai Lama, however, was very friendly, and when he went to Peking in 1779, he called the Emperor's attention to his friend, Warren Hastings, whom he wished the Emperor to know and be friendly with. The Emperor promised to write a letter to Hastings in such a vein as the Lama might suggest. The Lama, however, died of smallpox in 1780 at Peking and so this attempt of Hastings to open a commercial connection with China through Tibet and Nepal failed. In 1782 Hastings dispatched Captain Turner to see the new Lama, and to attempt the opening of intercourse. He was well received, and remained for about a year at Lhasa, but satisfactory relations were not established. Thus the situation remained when Hastings' governorship ended in 1785.[95]

The commercial connections between India and Canton were also assuming such proportions that they could not lightly be jeopardized. The expansion of this trade in merchandise from T. 352,500 in 1764 to T. 1,912,940 in 1785 has already been noted. At the same time the opium trade was growing steadily and was becoming one of the Bengal government's most valuable sources of revenue. The net revenue derived from the opium monopoly, amounting to 125,453 current rupees

---

[94] R. S. Gundry, *China and Her Neighbors* (London, 1893), pp. 324-30.
[95] *Ibid.*, pp. 329-30; CMC, II, Nos. 5, 7.

in 1774-75, rose to 1,172,326 current rupees in 1786-87.[96] The opium trade, however, had to be carried on by smuggling, and the Indian government would have favored any change in the nature of British commercial connections with China which would have made the trade easier to conduct. The importance of Indian considerations in bringing about the embassy is testified to by a sentence in Colonel Cathcart's instructions, which says that the prosperity of India "would be promoted by procuring a secure vent for [its] Products and Manufactures in the extensive Empire of China, at the same time that the Produce of such Sales would furnish Resources for the Investment to Europe." [97]

The creation of the Board of Control in 1784 was a further link in establishing closer connections between affairs in India and China. The Board was a definite organ of government to deal with the affairs of the Company and with British affairs in the East. Henry Dundas, its most active member and admittedly the authority upon Eastern affairs in the Pitt Government, was well acquainted with commercial and political matters affecting the Company's affairs in India and China. He understood the commercial connections between the Country trade and the financing of the Company's trade; he aimed to use the China trade as a means of remitting home both the excess territorial revenue of India and the accumulated private fortunes in India, and above all he wanted to promote the progress of British commerce in India and China.[98]

Not content with the information which he could demand from the Company, Dundas had private agents in India and China to collect information for him, among whom was the Country trader George Smith of Kingston, Surrey. On February 16, 1783, Smith wrote to Dundas outlining a plan "for the better vegetation of the Company's trade with China" and of the Country trade. He pointed out the precarious situation of the Company's trade with China, which was dependent upon the sufferance of the mandarins, and the great injury which had recently been done to Country merchants through the unjust debt settlement. He considered this a matter of national concern, believed that if Peking were accurately informed of the state of affairs justice would be done,

---

[96] PP, *Sessional Reports, Papers, etc., 1810,* V, No. 363, pp. 80-81.

[97] Morse, *Chronicle,* II, 160.

[98] *Papers Respecting the Negotiation for the Renewal of the Company's Charter, 1793,* April 23, 1793, Section XXIII, Dundas' proposals.

and proposed that a British embassy be sent to Peking at the expense of the Company. Its objects should be:[99]

(1) A treaty of friendship and commerce, and permission to trade at Amoy and Ningpo;

(2) The extension of the sale of British manufactures, woollens, and firearms in China;

(3) The abolition of the 1950 taels *cumshaw*, and a clear statement of the Imperial duties;

(4) The establishment of standard prices for imports and exports on the basis of averages of the previous ten years, seasonal variations thus being eliminated.

(5) The recognition and enforcement by the Chinese government of contracts legally entered into by the Chinese merchants;

(6) A secret offensive and defensive alliance against France and Russia.

Once such a treaty were concluded, the supercargoes should be instructed to enter into contracts with the Chinese merchants for all the tea to be exported from China. Such a procedure would insure to the Company a complete monopoly of the China trade and compel other European countries to purchase their teas and China goods from London; it would forestall the attempts of America to trade with China, and it would open the Chinese market for British goods, especially woollens and firearms, where an indefinite expansion might be expected.

Leaving the proposal to the consideration of Dundas, Smith sailed for India and China. On November 26, 1786, at Canton, he wrote to Dundas dwelling upon the possibilities of expanding British trade (especially in woollens) with China; the advantages to India of an increased trade; measures to be pursued to supply the Canton treasury with cash (he suggested bills on Bengal) and to draw the trade away from foreign countries. He discussed at great length the restraints on trade, the growing impositions of the mandarins upon the Chinese merchants and foreigners, the steady increase of prices, and the general insecurity of the trade. He concluded: "and should these grievances be continued the Trade of this Country so very beneficial to us, must be greatly clogged, for which reason it appears to me Sir, that nothing less than an Embassy can remove the Evils now so justly complained of." [100] In a letter of December 12, 1786, he proposed that the Company's chief supercargo should be commissioned H.M. Consul, with full power to

---

[99] IO, *Home Miscellaneous*, CCCCXXXIV, 15ff.
[100] IOC, XIX, Smith to Dundas, Nov. 26, 1786.

control British subjects.[101] It is not impossible that these last two letters reached Dundas before actual steps had been taken to send the Cathcart Embassy, and if so they doubtless served as the final deciding factor in causing the government to send an embassy to China.

6. *Conclusion and Summary.*

The events in China between the years 1757 and 1761 confined foreign trade to the single port of Canton under very odious and re-straining conditions, sanctioned and legalized by Imperial decree. The restrictions made impossible a satisfactory expansion of trade, the Imperial decree made change impossible except by appeal to Peking, and the Skottowe mission from the Court of Directors in 1761 showed the impossibility of change through the agency of a commercial mission sent by the Company. For a time the English were content to let mat-ters stand as they were, attempting as best they might to resist the activities of the Co-hong and the impositions of the mandarins.

The abolition of the Co-hong in 1771 was hailed as a great achieve-ment, but in reality it made certain the bankruptcy of a number of the Hong merchants, a situation that led to the crisis of 1779 and 1780. The final result of this crisis was the serious injury of the trade by the reduction of the number of merchants, the annoyance of the mandarins at Canton and Peking, the clear demonstration of the futility of and damage done by the interference of naval officers, the arousing of the Country merchants who demanded redress and an embassy to China, the establishment of the Consoo levy on trade, and the re-establishment of the Co-hong under official control with power to 'fix prices at will.

With the passage of the Commutation Act of 1784 to relieve the Company and government of financial distress, they embarked upon an active policy of monopolizing the China trade and making London the emporium for Asiatic trade. The success of this policy was endangered by the restraints and restrictions at Canton which at times threatened the very existence of the trade, by the apparent determination of for-eign nations,to take measures to counteract the British move, by the increase of prices at Canton and the difficulties of getting satisfactory goods, by the unrestrained activities of Country merchants, and by the great difficulty which the Company encountered in getting cash to finance the trade.

---

[101] *Ibid.*, XIX, Smith to Dundas, Dec. 12, 1786.

The government's attention had been called to Chinese affairs not only by the Commutation Act, the debts controversy, and the proposals of an embassy by the creditors, but by the various incidents relating to the treatment of H.M. ships, by the difficulties and dangers created at Canton through the irresponsible acts of Country traders, by the several executions of foreigners under conditions which violated European ideas of justice, and by the growing connections between India and China. Furthermore, the chief member of the Board of Control, who was especially ambitious to do something startling in Eastern affairs, had received private information as to how the China trade could be improved through the sending of an embassy. This long train of events and the extensive list of objections to the system at Canton were brought to a focus by the *Lady Hughes* affair, which filled the supercargoes with fear and dismay and seemed to threaten the very existence of the trade which the English were trying to monopolize.

In their letters to Richardson and the Court of Directors in February, 1785, the supercargoes linked the continuance of the trade and the success of the Commutation Act with an embassy which should procure enlarged commercial privileges, the rights of extraterritorial jurisdiction, the abolition of existing abuses, and security for the future. At the same time interests at home demanded expanded markets, and the government needed more revenue. Reports from China relating to the seasons of 1785-86 and 1786-87 were not encouraging from a commercial point of view, and many minor difficulties with the merchants and officials did not relieve the fear for the security of the foreign community and for the trade, a fear that had been created by the *Lady Hughes* affair. The outlook for the future of the China trade and the success of the Commutation Act appeared so black in England during the winter of 1786-87 that, considering the fact that informed persons believed the Emperor would remedy the situation if he knew the real state of affairs, it is little wonder that both Company and government turned their attentions to an embassy, as the only means of securing the success of these plans and of putting their relations with China on a firm and more honorable foundation.

CHAPTER VI

THE CATHCART EMBASSY AND EVENTS FOLLOWING IT
(1787-1791).

1. *Preliminary Negotiation Relative to the Cathcart Mission (Spring to July 31, 1787).*

Saxe Bannister asserts that the Cathcart Embassy originated in an invitation addressed by the Chinese Court to the agents of the Company at Canton.[1] The invitation of the Chinese, which did not come from the Court of Peking, but was only a proposal from the Viceroy and Hoppo that a deputation should be sent from the European community to congratulate the Emperor upon his eightieth birthday, was not delivered until October, 1789.[2] One true statement made by Bannister is that the idea of sending an embassy was "warmly" supported by Pitt and Dundas.

There are no extant records to show who actually took the first step in bringing about the Cathcart Embassy, but one is led to believe by the prominent part which Dundas and Pitt took in the early arrangements that the proposal was first made by Dundas, who obtained the support of Pitt, and that the idea was "warmly" seconded by the Court of Directors, who felt that something had to be done to improve the Company's situation in China. This idea is supported by a number of facts: the interest which Dundas took in Chinese affairs; his receipt of information about China and a proposal of an embassy from George Smith; his access to the Company's papers, among which were the supercargoes' proposals of an embassy, as well as the solicitors' report in the autumn of 1785 or 1786 to the Board of Control on the jurisdiction of the Company's supercargoes over Country ships, which contained full references to and extracts from the supercargoes' recommendations in consequence of the *Lady Hughes* affair;[3] and a sentence in one of Cathcart's letters to Dundas, which referred to the Embassy as "Your Public Measure."[4] It is not improbable, however, that indirect feelers had been sent out by the Court of Directors, but there are no records

---

[1] Saxe Bannister, *A Journal of the First French Embassy to China, 1698-1700* (London, 1859), xliv-lvi.
[2] Morse, *Chronicle*, II, 177.
[3] IOC, XX, solicitors' report near beginning of the volume.
[4] IOC, XC, Cathcart to Dundas, Nov. 1, 1787.

to show that it ever approached the government with an official request that an embassy be sent.

Lt. Colonel Charles Cathcart, M.P., a distinguished officer and quartermaster-general to the Bengal Army, who had but recently returned to Europe after negotiating a convention with the Governor of Mauritius,[5] was approached by the government sometime during the spring of 1787 relative to his willingness to serve as Ambassador.[6] Sir George Leonard Staunton, who had been Secretary to Lord Macartney while the latter was Governor of Madras (1780-85) and who had negotiated the treaty of peace with the Tippoo Sultan in 1784, applied to Dundas for the appointment as ambassador to China "but Colonel Cathcart [a Scotchman and protégé of Dundas] had the preference."[7] Cathcart, who evidently responded favorably to the proposal, busied himself with a preliminary study of the problem. He discussed with supercargoes then in England the procedure to be followed and studied the Company's China records. On June 20, 1787, he addressed his preliminary proposals to Henry Dundas.[8]

His principal objects of inquiry were, "As to the Mode in which the Mission should be appointed—and the Place which would best suit the Commerce of Great Britain as a Depot in China." As to the first, he concluded "that the only Chance of success in negotiating with the Court of Peking [would] arise from the Mission being in the Name of the King, and that any attempt thro' the Servants of the Company only, would be ineffectual." He expressed the utmost sympathy with the attitude of the supercargoes in China and with their fear that the trade might be lost, felt sure that the government could rely on their cooperation, and believed a large frigate to be the "only proper Conveyance to mark and distinguish a Mission from the King. The Measure

---

[5] BM, *Additional Manuscripts* (*Auckland Papers*, LVII), No. 344,468, pp. 353-61.

[6] IO, *China: Cathcart Embassy*, XC, Greville to Court of Directors, Jan., 1789. Practically all the documents relating to the Cathcart Embassy are contained in this volume. Hereafter it will be referred to as IOCCE. Additional information is contained in a paper to be found in Volume XX under date of April 18, 1815, entitled "Memorandum of Contents of a Fools-Cap Book bound in Velum lettered at the back in MS. 'Cathcart's Embassy.'" It is merely the table of contents of a volume extant in 1815. Many of the documents mentioned in it have since been destroyed, but valuable information can be obtained even from this list of papers. It will be referred to as IOC, XX, "Memorandum" in notes to follow.

[7] G. T. Staunton, *Memoir . . . of the late Sir George Leonard Staunton* (London, 1823), p. 315.

[8] IOCCE, XC, Cathcart to Dundas, June 20, 1787. This letter is printed in Morse, *Chronicle*, II, 157-59, under the date August 18, which must be a misprint.

being adopted, very little Preparation appear[ed] necessary further than the Selection of Officers, and a well considered Letter, accompanied by a Present."

The Object of the Mission being to extend our Commerce, under the Protection of the Chinese Government; it appears of the greatest Consequence to avoid, or at least not to press, Requests exciting Jealousy. On this Principle, it would perhaps be the best Policy to leave the Selection of the Place of Depot to the Chinese, — only stating to them that we require a healthy Situation accessible and safe for Shipping, convenient for the Dispersion of our Manufactures and for the Collection of Tea's, Chinaware and other Returns the Produce of the Eastern Provinces; and if they will not grant a convenient privileged Depot, we must remedy as many of the Defects of our present Situation as possible.

In Cathcart's opinion, Macao might be ceded by the Portuguese and the Hong merchants induced to go there, but it was remote from the tea and raw-silk-producing areas, and, as it was not completely free from the jurisdiction of the Chinese, they might refuse to confirm the English in the Portuguese privileges. Amoy was favorably situated so far as the sale and purchase of goods were concerned, but as it was desirable to have a place where the English could exercise jurisdiction, it seemed advisable to obtain an island outside the Empire, yet accessible to the junk trade. Such an establishment could not be expected "unless the Assurance of better Control over our own People is promised on this occasion, by His Majesty, and confirmed by the Legislature," for at present the Chinese could not confide in a nation whose sailors were "subject to no Law or authorized Coercion and Subordination."

Once the general outlines of the mission were adopted, the settlement of the ceremonial and presents would be an easy matter, he thought. Although he disliked "idle Parade," he was convinced that the success of the mission would depend on the "decorum" with which it was conducted. Its "Formation and Establishment" ought to be such as to give no reason to the Chinese to feel that they had been "slighted or insulted." He would prefer to ascertain beforehand the full expense of the Embassy and so to transact it without making use of the "Powers respecting a Contingent Bill," apparently confided to him by the Directors, who it seems had already agreed to bear the expense of the mission. After the Embassy had reached Canton and the necessary information was obtained, he favored proceeding to Tientsin by sea, where the Embassy could disembark.

Colonel Cathcart concluded his remarks by indicating his wishes regarding the personnel of the Embassy. As Captain of H.M. Ship he proposed Captain Erasmus Gower, a distinguished officer, who had been twice around the world, who had served with distinction in the Indian fleet from 1781 to 1784, and who was then stationed at New-foundland.[9] The second in command should be Lieutenant Rutherford, a friend of Captain Gower. He wished to have Lieutenant Young, who had accompanied him to Mauritius and who was at the time in India, as Secretary to the Embassy, and Captain Patrick Alexander Agnew, who was then in the Company's service and was to return to India, as his private secretary. He was a confidential friend whom Cathcart could dispatch from Peking to Canton if necessary, but if the reception should be especially favorable, he could return to India by way of Tibet with propositions relative to the opening of commercial relations between that country and Bengal. As naturalist and scientist he wished a German professor of Economy, Herr Fabricius, who could study Chinese industrial and agricultural arts for the benefit of England. Finally, for interpreter he proposed a Frenchman, M. Galbert, who had been educated and lived many years at Peking.

From this date until July 19 there are no further records relative to proceedings, but from a letter of this date and from subsequent letters,[10] it is apparent that Cathcart had conferences with the Directors relative to the resignation of his appointment as quartermaster-general to the Bengal army, and with Pitt relative to possible times for the sailing of the Embassy and about the inclusion in his instructions of references to the debts owed by the Chinese to private individuals. He also sought information from former supercargoes relative to the presents to be sent to the Emperor, and on the above-mentioned date he suggested that a letter in which the name of the Emperor had been left blank should be taken along to be filled in with the name of the new Emperor should Ch'ien Lung die before the Embassy arrived.

On Sunday, July 25, after morning service, Cathcart discussed with Pitt the possibility of having the mission sail by the middle of October and proceed by Cape Horn in order to reach Macao in April. He sug-gested the appointment of Captain Truebridge in place of Gower, who could not return in time, and asked Pitt to request Earl Howe to have the frigate properly equipped and ready for sea at Plymouth or Fal-

---

[9] *Biographical Memoir of Sir Erasmus Gower* (London, 1800-10), pp. 1-25.
[10] IOCCE, XC, Cathcart to Dundas, July 19, 25, 1787.

mouth by late September.[11] The preliminary outlines of the Embassy had been completed by the end of July, and on the 30th Dundas wrote to the Chairman and Deputy outlining the plans. In consequence, on the 31st, the Court of Directors empowered the Chairs to expend £20,000 for the objects of the mission.[12]

2. *The Debts of Chinese Merchants and the Drafting of the Instructions to the Ambassador (May to August 31, 1787).*

The private creditors of the Chinese merchants had been much displeased by the Imperial award in 1780, and as already noted, approached the Court of Directors for help in 1783 without success.[13] On December 13, 1786, Captain Richard Parks, a captain of one of the Company's ships, requested the Court's aid in the collection of a purely commercial debt for goods delivered on bond to Yngshaw in 1779, amounting to T. 5,080. On January 2, 1787, the Company declined to help him for fear of injury to its commerce.[14] In May, 1787, George Vansittart and Ewan Law, assignees of George Smith, requested the Company's assistance in collecting the whole of the debts due to George Smith, and especially the debt of Coqua, none of which had been paid. Accompanying this request was a "Narrative of Proceedings for recovery of debts owing by Chinese Merchants to British Subjects," drawn up by George Smith.[15] As the Court had already resolutely determined not to help the private creditors, whose unrestrained actions in China had given them so much trouble, it delayed answering this request for some time.

The creditors, because the Company showed no intention of helping them, approached Pitt and Dundas with a request that Smith be allowed to accompany the Embassy. In his letter of July 19 to Dundas, Cathcart referred to the advisability of including in his instructions some paragraphs relative to the debts, but on August 3, 1787, Dundas addressed a letter to George Smith stating:[16]

---

[11] IOCCE, XC, Cathcart to Dundas, July 25, 1787.

[12] IOC, XX, "Memorandum," July 30 and 31, 1787.

[13] *Supra,* Chap. V, Sec. 1.

[14] CMD, VII, Parks to Directors, Dec. 13, 1786; IO, *Committee of Correspondence: Reports,* XV, 199.

[15] CMD, VII, Vansittart and Law to Directors, May, 1787, and Smith's "Narrative," pp. 145-223.

[16] IOCCE, XC, Cathcart to Dundas, Aug. 18, 1787, and Smith to Cathcart, Nov. 20, 1787.

that after full consideration of the subject, it is thought improper to load the intended Mission with any Official Instructions relative to the Debts . . ., far less to take any of you as Coadjustors in the Mission, but if any of you will at any time wait upon Colonel Cathcart, he will, with my approbation, be glad to receive every information from you, and to be of any service to you that lays in his Power, not inconsistent with the important object of his Mission.

In consequence of this letter Cathcart had a conference with some of the creditors on August 15, in which he indicated his inability to help them unless he were given the bonds together with full freedom to act as he considered most advisable. Smith indicated that, if the government would consider Vansittart, Law, Hunter, and himself as proper agents to represent the creditors, he was of the opinion that he could by individual applications get the necessary consent from most of the creditors and have the above-listed men named as a committee to transact the business with the government. To this Cathcart agreed, subject to the consent of government, but told them that, if the creditors would not repose responsibility in the proposed committee and refused to give up their bonds to the Ambassador, it would be impossible for him to enter into negotiations with the Chinese government relative to the debts."

Cathcart wrote to Dundas on August 18, recommending that the above-mentioned proposal be accepted. On the 26th Dundas approved the creditor's plan and Cathcart's recommendations to them. This letter was received by the Colonel on August 31, and with Pitt's consent he wrote on the same day to Smith stating that the government had no objection to the proposed committee requesting the creditors to delegate to it full powers to treat with the government and to send secret instructions to their agents in China relative to a plan for the recovery of the debts."

Three days before, on August 28, the Committee of Correspondence of the East India Company acted upon Vansittart and Law's request of May. The Committee stated that the creditors in question had lent money to the Chinese contrary to law at exorbitant rates of interest, which, piling up, came to compose the greater part of the debt; that Smith and many others of the creditors had resided in China contrary to the Company's charter and in defiance of the Company's orders;

---

[17] IOCCE, XC, Cathcart to Dundas, Aug. 18, 1787.

[18] *Ibid.*, XC, Dundas to Cathcart, Aug. 26, 1787, and Cathcart to Dundas, Aug. 31, 1787.

that some of them had offended against the Chinese government in a most grievous way; that, contrary to the Company's wishes, they had procured the intervention of Captain Panton, which had reacted unfavorably upon the Company's affairs through the creation of the Consoo levy on trade; that by these actions they had forfeited all rights to complaint or help; and that any attempt to help them would only bring adversity upon the Company's affairs. In view of these facts, they recommended that the request for assistance be refused by the Directors.[19]

The drafting of the original instructions to the Ambassador, which was done by Henry Dundas, was in progress as early as July 19, because on this day Cathcart referred to debts and the policy to be pursued in case of the death of the Emperor as subjects which should be dealt with in the instructions. The Company prevented the inclusion in Cathcart's instructions of any specific commands regarding the private debts which would force him to bring the matter to the attention of the Chinese government.[20] The preliminary instructions were completed and in the hands of the Company and the Ambassador before August 16, the day on which the Chairman and the Deputy Chairman (John Matteux and Nathaniel Smith), assisted by the Company's solicitor, held a conference with Cathcart.

The Chairs especially objected to a paragraph in the instructions which directed the Ambassador, "should a new Establishment be conceded, [to] endeavor to obtain free Permission of Ingress and Regress for Ships of all Nations, upon paying certain settled Duties, if so required by the Chinese Government." Cathcart replied that, as he remembered his conversations with Dundas, the Ambassador was "to take Possession in the Name of the King of Great Britain, and for the use of the East India Company during the Currency of their Charter." He assured them that he believed the above-mentioned provision was not aimed to and would not interfere with their exclusive privileges nor keep them from controlling the number of Private ships licensed to go to China, and that the aim of the Embassy was to benefit the Company and the country. Not content with these assurances the Chairs wrote to Pitt on August 23 expressing their doubts about the instructions and requesting that foreign ships be excluded from the

---

[19] IO, *Committee of Correspondence: Reports*, XV, 275-79.
[20] IOCCE, XC, Cathcart to Dundas, July 19, 1787 and note 16 above.

acquired area unless licensed by the Company as should ships of Private English.[21]

On August 18 Cathcart wrote to Dundas regarding the Chairs' objections. In replying, on the 26th, Dundas stated that the Company should be assured by the government that the exclusive benefits of the grant would go to them so long as their present charter lasted; that when the charter was renewed the future status of the settlement would be a matter to be settled between the Company and the government, and that the Company could be assured of the right to use such an establishment so long as it continued to be interested in trading. But he went on to say:[22]

It would, in my apprehension, be absurd if we can obtain a Settlement from the Emperor of China, to take the grant of it on any more limited terms than he is willing to give. Our obtaining the Grant without any restrictions, does not lay us under any obligations to communicate the benefits either to other Nations, or even to British Subjects, other than the East India Company; but surely the Chairman and Deputy Chairman cannot seriously mean that in negotiating with the Emperor of China the King of Great Britain is to accept a Settlement with such restrictions in it, as of necessity obliges him to carry on the trade of China by an exclusive Company. It may or may not be expedient to do so, but sure I am, the Government of China have no right to be made Parties in that Question of Commercial Policy . . .

On August 31 Cathcart communicated this letter to Pitt, who had already used similar arguments and given similar assurances to placate the Company. He agreed to a slightly changed wording which preserved to the English freedom either to admit or to exclude the ships of foreign nations. As finally accepted with the hearty approval of the Chairs the sentence read, "Should a new Establishment be conceded, you will take it in the name of the King of Great Britain." [23]

The King's letter to the Emperor was also in preliminary draft before the end of August. The original intention had been to present with it certain personal gifts to the Emperor, but after consultation with the supercargoes, it was concluded that no gift which could be offered to the Emperor would be accepted. It was decided, therefore, to enclose the King's letter in a handsome ornamented gold box (which cost £885) provided by the Directors, "more as a mark of attention than in

[21] IOCCE, XC, Cathcart to Dundas, Aug. 18 and 31, 1787; IOC, XX, "Memorandum," Aug. 16, 21, 23, 1787.
[22] IOCCE, XC, Dundas to Cathcart, Aug. 26, 1787.
[23] *Ibid.*, XC, Cathcart to Dundas, Aug. 31, 1787; final instructions are in Morse, *Chronicle*, II, 165.

the Light of a Present." [24] This necessitated the elimination of the final paragraph of the King's letter, which originally read, "I have sent a few presents from this Country, not as being worthy of Your Majesty's Notice, but as marks of my regard and friendly disposition to Your Imperial Majesty." The change was made in the hand of Henry Dundas, and the last paragraph of the final letter read, "We have instructed Our Ambassador to take every Method in his power to mark Our regard and friendly disposition to Your Majesty, and it will give Us the utmost Satisfaction to learn that our wishes in that respect have been amply complied with." [25]

3. *The Ambassador's Salary and Internal Arrangements of the Embassy (August 7 to October, 1787).*

As Cathcart had early in the negotiations expressed his desire that the full expenses of the Embassy should be ascertained beforehand so that he would not have to depend upon contingent allowances, the Court requested him to draw up an estimate of the expenditure. In a letter of August 7 he outlined his ideas on the subject. [26] As a first principle in securing the success of the Embassy he believed that it should be distinguished from all previous missions of its kind. It should aim to impress upon the minds of the Chinese that British subjects were controlled by British laws, that all mariners were not a rabble, and that the mission was to inspire confidence and not to procure redress and concession by the promotion of awe and dread.

To achieve these ends it was necessary to be especially careful in choosing the personnel of the Embassy, so that their actions and discipline would contrast with that of the trading ships which the Chinese have heretofore had contact with. As Private trade would not be allowed, the members of his suite should be paid respectable salaries, and the usual allowances granted by the Company to the officers of H.M. Ships should not be encroached on. It would be necessary to take out valuable presents, among which should be specimens of British manufactures. He was not yet well enough informed on this subject

---

[24] IOCCE, XC, Cathcart to Chairs, Aug. 24, 1787, and Cathcart to Dundas, Aug. 31, 1787.

[25] For first draft with Dundas' changes, IOC, XX, no paging; for the final draft IOCCE, XC, under date of Nov. 30, 1787; Morse, *Chronicle*, II, 167-69; a published copy of the first draft appears in Bannister, *op. cit.*, pp. 227-29.

[26] IOCCE, XC, Cathcart to Chairman (John Matteux), Aug. 7, 1787.

to make an accurate estimate of the cost, but he believed it would amount to six or eight thousand pounds.

As to the method of paying the expenses of the Embassy, he recommended two alternatives: (1) that the Company assign certain fixed salaries to the persons attending the mission and send along a comptroller of the extra expense, or (2) that the Company grant to him a sum out of which he should pay the salaries of the establishment and provide for the table and contingent expenses while they were on shipboard. This would amount to not less than £7,500 to £8,000 per annum. The expenses of the Embassy while it was in China should be paid by the Company's supercargoes. In either alternative, he requested to have credit upon the Company in London for the amount of the specified salaries or for the sum granted to him, one quarter to be paid in advance and the remainder to be paid on sight when due.

These proposals and matters relating to the presents were discussed at several conferences with the Chairs,[27] and on August 23 they strongly pressed Cathcart to reduce the proposed annual expense to £6,000. On the following day he agreed to reduce his demand to £6,000, provided the Company would idemnify him on his return if this amount proved insufficient. He promised to be careful of expenses, but felt certain that they must not be stingy if the Embassy was to succeed. He was glad to find that the Court agreed with him as to the presents, and was of the impression that the first audience, in order to prevent the appearance of a tribute mission, should be confined to the delivery of the King's letter. Presents to the value of £4,000 or £5,000 should be kept in reserve to give to the various officers of state.[28]

On August 28 the Chairs stated that in order to put the Embassy upon the respectable footing which the importance of the negotiations required, they would pay £6,000 a year for the duration of the Embassy for the "Salaries and Maintenance" of the Ambassador and his suite exclusive of table and travelling expenses while it would be in China. The salaries were to begin upon embarkation and cease upon the return of the Embassy to England. They hoped that this sum would be adequate, but if "it shall hereafter be made apparent to the Court of Directors that it was not so, we doubt not (altho' we cannot engage) that the Court of Directors will grant such indemnification as shall be

---

[27] IOCCE, XC, Cathcart to Chairs, Aug. 7, 1787, and Cathcart to Dundas, Aug. 18, 1787.
[28] IOCCE, XC, Minutes of a Conference between Cathcart and Chairs, Aug. 23, 1787, and Cathcart to Chairman, Aug. 24, 1787.

proper." [29] In a letter of August 31 to Dundas, Cathcart expressed his satisfaction at this arrangement.

During the whole course of proceedings, the Chairs and Cathcart drew heavily upon the suggestions and recommendations of the various China supercargoes who were in England. Conferences were held with several of them, including Thomas Fitzhugh, James Flint and Matthew Raper. On August 29 Fitzhugh addressed a letter to the Deputy Chairman suggesting that the Embassy should land at Canton, because all other embassies except the Russian had done so and because Chinese custom demanded it. Tientsin was more conveniently located, but because of the Flint expedition to that place he believed the Chinese would be very much prejudiced against another English ship proceeding there. He felt that the Embassy would be well received in so far as the "pride and singular forms of the Chinese allowed," but that the Chinese prostrations would be insisted on, as proved by experience of other embassies. While at Peking the Ambassador would be closely guarded and no one allowed to see him except by permission, and his complaints would be disregarded and no additional trade privileges would be granted. [30]

The Chinese Government is proud and insolent. It looks with contempt on all foreign nations. Its ignorance of their force give it confidence in its own strength, which by experience it knows to be superior to the boardering Hordes of Tartars with whom it is commonly engaged in War; nor do I think it looks on Embassies in any other light than acknowledgments of inferiority.

Fitzhugh concluded his remarks with a few hints to the effect that presents should be given to the Viceroy and the high officials at Canton in order to win their goodwill; that presents should be given to the missionaries who would translate the King's letter, which should be in Latin and English; that an interpreter (Galbert) should be taken along, as the Chinese linguists were poor; that the expense of the Embassy while it was in China would be paid by the Emperor, and that he believed the best time to send an embassy would be upon the accession of a new Emperor. Subsequent events prove only how true were most of Fitzhugh's observations and prognostications.

James Flint took an active part in the selection of the presents, and on October 12 he called the attention of the Chairs to a rumored French

[29] IOCCE, XC, Chairs to Cathcart, Aug. 28, 1787, and Cathcart to Dundas, Aug. 31, 1787.
[30] IOCCE, XC, Thomas Fitzhugh to Nath. Smith, Aug. 29, 1787.

settlement in Cochin China inimical to the British. On the 22nd of the same month he pointed out the jealousies of the Chinese and the precautions to be taken to obviate them. For his services he was allowed £25 by the court.[31] Since Flint's exclusion from China made him ineligible to act as interpreter and, because Bevan was unable to go, the services of M. Galbert were sought. He was ultimately located at Avignon, and it would appear that Captain Agnew was sent to engage him.[32] On the 30th of August, Cathcart was able to inform the Chairs that M. Galbert had been engaged. He arrived in England and was presented to the Chairman on September 7. His suggestions were sought on a number of matters, especially as to the titles to be used in addressing the Emperor.[33]

The discussions over the presents to be sent were spread over several months. It was finally decided, because of the supercargoes' recommendations, that a present should not be given to the Emperor, but it was generally agreed that presents should be taken along to distribute among the officials. It was considered advisable to take along samples of British manufacture in order to stimulate a sale for them in China and to impress the Chinese with the advanced state of British industry. Various scientific, mathematical, and philosophical instruments and some prints were to be taken along to impress the Chinese with British progress in the arts and sciences. The amount to be spent on presents was fixed at £4,000 by the end of August.[34] The list of presents as finally delivered to Cathcart together with their value was as follows:[35]

Eight bales of superfine broadcloth	£610	Mathematical and philosophical instruments	£488
Guns	469	Glass lustres	676
Cutlery	51	Gold box	885
Wedgewood pottery	33	Watches	374
Prints (Boydell's)	32	Chronometers	175
Pocket books	51	Theodolites	76
Perfumery	28	Antiques	46
Rappee snuff	17	Charges	16
Pencils	11		
Flag staff	7	Total	£4,045

[31] IOC, XX, "Memorandum," Aug. 31, Sept. 6, Oct. 12, 22, Dec. 10 and late in Dec., 1787.

[32] IOCCE, XC, Agnew to Dundas, Kirkdale, France, Sept. 4, 1787.

[33] IOC, XX, "Memorandum," Aug. 30 and Sept. 7, 1787; IOCCE, XC, Cathcart to Chairs, Nov. 1, 1787, Chairman to Cathcart, Nov. 8, 1787, and Cathcart to Dundas, Nov. 22, 1787.

[34] IOCCE, XC, Cathcart to Chairs, Aug. 7, 1787, and Cathcart to Dundas, Aug. 31, 1787.

[35] CMC, VIII, No. 343.

Among the original members of the personnel of the Embassy proposed by Cathcart, it was apparently impossible to obtain the services of the German professor, Fabricius, and in his place was substituted Dr. John Ewart as physician and scientist. Lieutenant Young, who was then in India, received the appointment as Secretary of the Embassy and was to join it off Macao. Captain Agnew became Cathcart's secretary, but retained his commission in the Indian army with full pay "as a Captain *on service* from the Date of his departure [embarkation] until his return to the Carnatic." The total annual salaries to be paid by Cathcart to the members of his suite amounted to £1,630.[36]

The choosing of the vessel and her commander caused considerable difficulty, as Captain Gower could not return from Newfoundland in time. Cathcart then suggested Captain Truebridge, and on August 7 he had a conference with Earl Howe, First Lord of the Admiralty, on the subject, but no extant records show when the final decision was made. The matter was probably settled before the end of September; H.M.S. *Vestal*, frigate with twenty-eight guns, was chosen to carry the Ambassador to China, and she was to be commanded by Captain Sir Richard Strachan, Bart. The second in command was to be Lieutenant Rutherford. The salaries of the captain and officers of the frigate were to be paid by the Admiralty until the ship sighted Java Head on the way out, after which until Java Head were passed on the return voyage they were to be paid by the Company.[37] A military guard did not attend the Ambassador.

4. *Final Discussions with the Private Creditors (September 12, 1787 to February 23, 1788).*

In view of Colonel Cathcart's offer to do what he could toward the collection of the debts due to the private English if the creditors would appoint a committee to represent them and deliver to him the original bonds, Smith, Vansittart, and Law set about the task of getting the creditors to accept the proposal. George Smith had apparently been declared bankrupt sometime prior to May, 1787, and Vansittart, Law, and Hunter had been appointed as assignees to his estate.[38] The

[36] IOCCE, XC, Cathcart to Chairs, Aug. 7 and Nov. 1, 1787, Cathcart to Dundas, July 25 and Nov. 1, 1787, Agnew to Dundas, Sept. 4, 1787, Greville to Chairman, Oct. 12, 1788, and Jan. 1789; IOC, XX, "Memorandum," Sept. 12, 1787; CMC, III, No. 59; Morse, *Chronicle*, II, 155, 166, 169.
[37] IOCCE, XC, Cathcart to Chairs, Nov. 1, 1787; CMC, V, No. 192, and references as in note 36.
[38] CMD, VII, Vansittart and Law to Directors, May, 1787.

first difficulty was encountered in getting the consent of Hunter, who, as a Director of the East India Company, refused the "Aid proferred by the Government." Nevertheless, a circular letter was drawn up to be sent to the various creditors requesting them to agree to the appointment of Smith, Vansittart, and Law as a committee with full power to make arrangements with the government, and a "Covenant and Agreement" was drawn up vesting the necessary powers in the proposed committee.[39]

Hunter remained obdurate until Law and Vansittart interviewed him on October 24 and threatened to protest against him. He then requested a copy of the proposed "Covenant and Agreement" and a week to consider it. On the same day it appears that Smith met some of the creditors, with the result that on November 13 a covenant was drawn up and agreed to by certain of the creditors.[40] On November 1, Hunter had written to the Chairs "demurring as an Assignee to the Estate of Mr. G. Smith against entrusting any person to receive the large amount due to Mr. Smith's Estate, from Chinese Merchants, unless with approbation of the Company."[41] In reply the Chairs referred him to the various resolutions of the Directors upon the subject.

Confronted with the fact that he alone was holding up the proceedings, Hunter, on November 15, agreed to the compounding of Smith's debt, but objected to the inclusion of Smith as one of the proposed committee. Vansittart transmitted this information to Smith and suggested that the circular letter should be sent at once, and that the deeds relative to the compounding of his debts could be drawn up later. Since Hunter's demands required that Smith's name be struck out of the letters and the "Covenant and Agreement," the latter wrote to Cathcart on November 19 requesting his permission for the proposed changes, and stating that in view of the delay it would be impossible to deliver the necessary papers to the Ambassador before the middle or end of December. Cathcart indicated that the proposed changes were immaterial to him, but that, as he expected to sail towards the end of November, it seemed impossible for the creditors to transmit the proper materials and documents to him.[42]

---

[39] IOCCE, XC, Smith to Cathcart, Nov. 19 and 20, 1787.

[40] *Ibid.*, XC, Smith to Cathcart, Nov. 20, 1787, and covenant between the British creditors, Feb. 19, 1788.

[41] IOC, XX, "Memorandum," Nov. 1 and 3, 1787.

[42] IOCCE, XC, Smith to Cathcart, 19, 1787, and Cathcart to Smith, Nov. 19, 1787.

In a final appeal to the Ambassador, Smith threw the blame for delay on Hunter and requested permission to transmit the necessary powers to Cathcart by one of the Company's ships later in the season.[43] In replying on November 21, Cathcart said that he had transmitted Smith's letters to Dundas; that, until the committee had been appointed by the creditors, nothing could be done; that, once it was appointed and had been granted the necessary powers, it should approach the government about the transmission of the papers to him, and that, if the government saw fit to have them sent, he would be glad to act according to the line of action already outlined.[44]

With these assurances, Smith, Vansittart, and Law sent out the circular letter and proceeded with the business, but it was not until February 19, 1788, that they were able to execute the Covenant with the creditors. The Covenant appointed Vansittart and Law a committee to transact business relative to the Chinese debts with the British government, and delegated to them full power to liquidate the whole amount of the debts or to compound them upon the most advantageous terms—powers which they could delegate to anyone they chose.[45] On the same day Vansittart and Law transmitted to Cathcart a copy of the Covenant and delegated to him full power to adjust the debts with the Chinese government as appeared to him most advantageous to the creditors. They called his attention to the statement of the debts as they stood in 1779, and requested that if possible he would collect interest on the debts between that date and 1788. On February 23, Wil-

---

[43] *Ibid.*, XC, Smith to Cathcart, Nov. 20, 1787.

[44] IOCCE, XC, Cathcart to Smith, Nov. 21, 1787.

[45] *Ibid.*, XC, "Covenant and Agreement Twixt the British Creditors of the Chinese Merchants at Canton and George Vansittart and Ewan Law," Feb. 19, 1788. It was signed by the following creditors or by attorney for them: M. Purling, Bazett, John Clements, R. Parks, Robert Barclay, Thos. Seward, C. E. Pigou, W. H. Pigou, Francis Wood, G. Stratton, Andrew Reid, John Griffith, Capt. Pat. Maitland, W. Holland, John and Edw. Holland, Rev. John Thomas, Daniel Corneille, Capt. Peter Pigou (deceased), Hon. William Elphinston, Capt. James Dundas, Charles Smith (deceased), Stephen Briggs, Gov. Roddarn, Hon. Edw. Monckton, George Smith (of Madras), Alexander Tod, Gilbert Pasley (deceased), John Burges, William Larkins, Charles Desvoeux, Robert Stewart, H. Bazett, John Brasier, George Peterson, G. Stainforth, John Roger, William Fraser, Geo. Dawson, John Blake, Frances Mantresor, John Sulivan, Henry Brooke, and William Brown, Thomas Thomas, William Money, James Farquharson, trustees of estate of Hutton and Gordon of Canton; George Vansittart, Ewan Law, for themselves and, with John Hunter, assignees of the estate of George Smith, late of Canton; George Smith and David Scott, executors to Mrs. Mary Church, executrix to Richard Church of Bombay. The George Smith of Madras, Canton, and Guildford, Surrey, is the one referred to wherever the name appears.

liam Cabell, Secretary to the Board of Control, forwarded these documents to Colonel Cathcart by order of Dundas.[46]

5. *Final Preparations for the Embassy (October to December 21, 1787).*

The original plan was that the Embassy should sail during the early part of October or at least by the middle of that month. No advanced intelligence of its coming was to be sent out. It was to proceed to Macao or Canton, and, after conference with the supercargoes, to announce its arrival to the Chinese government, and then to proceed to the northward "as circumstances should determine." What route it intended to take is not certain, the only route mentioned being that by Cape Horn. On October 3 one learns that the sailing had been postponed until November 20, and Cathcart actually did not leave London until December 2.[47]

Why the sailing was delayed is uncertain. The instructions and the internal arrangements of the Embassy were practically completed by the end of August, and the interpreter had arrived and most of the presents were in hand by the middle of September. It is possible but unlikely that a satisfactory frigate could not be ready by early October, and it is very unlikely that the delay was occasioned by a desire to allow the private creditors to compose their differences. Nor does a complete explanation occur in Cathcart's letter of November 1, in which he indicated that because they had obtained the services of M. Galbert it would be unnecessary to proceed to Canton as formerly planned, but that they could now proceed directly to a northern port if he so desired.[48] The most plausible explanation is that the route by Cape Horn was abandoned in favor of that by the Cape of Good Hope. By this route no advantage would be gained by sailing before late November or early December.

Cathcart appears to have been officially appointed as Ambassador during October, and early in November an order was sent to the Admiralty from the State Department requiring that a frigate of twenty-eight guns be prepared for distant service, her commander to be instructed to obey such orders as he should receive from the State De-

---

[46] IOCCE, XC, Vansittart and Law to Cathcart, Feb. 19, 1788, and Cabell to Cathcart, Feb. 23, 1788.

[47] IOCCE, XC, Cathcart to Dundas, July 25, 1787, Cathcart to Chairs, Nov. 1, 1787, Cathcart to Smith, Nov. 19, 1787, and Cathcart to Lord Sydney, Dec. 2, 1787.

[48] IOCCE, XC, Cathcart to Chairs, Nov. 1, 1787.

partment.[49] On November 1 the Ambassador wrote to the Chairs requesting that £5,000 be put upon the *Vestal* to be used by him while in China, should he decide to proceed directly to the northward without touching Canton. He requested permission to draw upon this sum for any extraordinary emergency which might arise during the voyage, and wished to use at least £600 of it to purchase salted provisions, wine, stores, surgical instruments, and medicine, which would be needed if he should proceed directly to the northward. He also requested an advance of £2,000 out of his salary, because it was necessary for him to make certain advances to men in his suite and to purchase certain articles for his personal outfit. He further requested that M. Galbert's travelling expenses from Avignon to London and his living expenses during his stay in London be paid, and he hoped the Chairs would authorize him to assure Galbert of reward at the end of the Embassy if his services had been satisfactory.[50]

On the same day the Ambassador explained to Dundas that, as the whole expenses of the suite were to fall upon him, it had been necessary for him to make his arrangements on the assumption that he and his executors should be paid his salary until the Embassy had returned to England. It had been necessary for him to make such engagements with the gentlemen of his suite that should he die on the way their salaries should continue until they had it in their power to return to their regiments in India or to England. Such being the situation, he requested power to appoint Lieutenant Young *"Chargé des Affaires"* in the event of his death, with full powers to continue the mission, and should his death occur before Lieutenant Young joined the Embassy, he wished power to appoint Captain Agnew to that position until the Lieutenant arrived. He also recommended Galbert to a pension or pecuniary reward if his services proved satisfactory.[51] These requests were in general agreed to, although it was provided that should the Ambassador die before he reached China and had actually proceeded to the execution of his mission the Embassy should return directly to England.[52]

---

[49] *Ibid.,* XC, Cathcart to Dundas, Nov. 1, 1787, and order to the Admiralty, Nov., 1787.

[50] *Ibid.,* XC, Cathcart to Chairs, Nov. 1, 1787.

[51] *Ibid.,* XC, Cathcart to Dundas, Nov. 1, 1787.

[52] *Ibid.,* XC, Supplementary Instructions to Capt. Strachan, Nov. 30, 1787; Morse, *Chronicle,* II, 170.

The Chairs finally agreed to put the £5,000 requested by Cathcart on the *Vestal*. They also agreed that he might use part of the money to repair the frigate in case of emergency, and they allowed him to use £600 in the purchase of supplies. M. Galbert's expenses were to be paid, but they would not undertake to assure him of a reward, and they would advance Cathcart but one-fourth of his salary, £1,500. He was requested to keep a strict account of all expenditure, to keep a diary and journal to be delivered to them on his return, to transmit information to them under cover of Thomas Morton whenever possible, and to keep a strict account of all presents delivered.[53]

Cathcart was in general satisfied with these arrangements, but objected to serving both *"God and Mammon,"* as he regarded the Chairs' request that he transmit to them a diary in addition to the official one which he must keep for the government. In replying to the Chairs on November 12, he stated that, if the sum of £600 was used in the purchase of supplies before sailing, but £4,400 need be put on the ship. He indicated that he had vested full power of attorney in Messrs. Drummond, who were to receive his salary and meet his engagements until the return of the Embassy. Cathcart also received a verbal promise that his salary would be continued in all events until the return of the Embassy.[54]

In view of the Chairs' refusal to advance him more than £1,500, he was forced to borrow £800 from Messrs. Drummond upon his and Lord Cathcart's bond to meet incidental expenses before sailing, and in order to take £500 in cash with him for personal expenses. Before leaving, he purchased, with cash and credit, supplies relating to the Embassy which together with the above-mentioned bond amounted to £3,200. Of this latter sum £600 represented cash purchases, and £2,600 was left in the form of bills falling due in six, nine, and twelve months, which were to be paid out of his salary. On November 27 Cathcart transmitted to the Chairs a bill amounting to £539 for supplies purchased, of which the Chairs evidently paid but £500, in lieu of which sum they embarked on the *Vestal* but $17,600 (less than £4,500).[55]

[53] IOCCE, XC, Chairman to Cathcart, Nov. 8, 1787; IOC, XX, "Memorandum," Nov. 3, 1787.

[54] IOCCE, XC, Cathcart to Dundas, Nov. 9, 1787, and Cathcart to Chairs, Nov. 12, 1787.

[55] *Ibid.*, Greville to Chairs, Oct. 12, 1788, Greville to Nat. Smith, Jan. 1789, Cathcart to Chairs, Nov. 27, 1787.

On November 22, Cathcart discussed with Galbert the appropriate titles to be applied to the Emperor in the King's letter. M. Galbert stated that Son of Heaven and Ten Thousand Years, the latter meaning Eternal, were often used, but he recommended that "Kien Long, Emperor of China, etc. etc. etc.," be used, and that it be left to the translators to put in the appropriate titles. This advice was followed. On the day following, the Chairs sent a "Secret and Confidential" letter to Henry Browne, chief of the Council at Canton, "communicating particulars respecting Col. C[athcart]'s Mission." [56]

All arrangements for the Embassy being completed, the instructions to the Ambassador, his credentials in Latin, the King's letter to the Emperor, and Sir Richard Strachan's instructions were signed on November 30 and were transmitted to Cathcart. Orders were also sent to the Admiralty, commanding them to direct the Commander of the *Vestal* to receive on board the Ambassador and his suite. On the 2nd of December Cathcart started for Portsmouth, where he arrived and embarked on the 4th. On the 7th he informed the Chairs that he was embarked and ready to sail; from this date his salary began. In acknowledging the receipt of his instructions from Lord Sydney, Cathcart transmitted copies of his final correspondence with Smith and requested to be informed if Parliament took steps to provide the powers relative to the control over British subjects in China which he was instructed to tell the Chinese government would be given. [57]

On December 21 the *Vestal*, with an eight months' supply of stores on board, sailed from Spithead bound for some point off Macao, where she would pick up Lieutenant Young and receive advices from Canton. She then aimed to proceed to a northern port, whence she would announce her arrival to the Emperor. The *Vestal* was to be employed in surveying the coast and islands off the northern part of China while the Ambassador was at Peking. [58]

---

[56] *Ibid.*, Cathcart to Dundas, Nov. 22, 1787; IOC, XX, "Memorandum," Nov. 23 and about Dec. 10, 1787.

[57] IOCCE, XC, Order to Lords of Admiralty, Nov. 30, 1787, Evan Nepean (under Secretary of State) to Cathcart, Dec. 1, 1787, Cathcart to Nepean, Dec. 1, 2, 4, 1787, Cathcart to Lord Sydney, Dec. 2, 1787; IOC, XX, "Memorandum," Dec. 7, 1787.

[58] IOCCE, XC, Strachan to Sydney, Dec. 4, 9, 21, 1787, Cathcart to Nepean, Dec. 10, 21, 1787; IOC, XX, "Memorandum," Nov. 30 to Dec. 21, 1787; Morse, *Chronicle*, II, 162.

6. *The Instructions to the Ambassador and Sir Richard Strachan and the King's Letter (November 30, 1787).*

The Cathcart Embassy, the first ever sent from the British Crown to a Far Eastern Potentate, was primarily a commercial mission. Its aim was distinctly national, and although the concessions which it hoped to receive were to be assured to the East India Company for the duration of its charter, its purpose was not merely the assistance of the Company. Its great object was to put Anglo-Chinese relations upon a treaty basis, and thereby to eliminate the disturbances and uncertainties of the existing system. If possible, northern Chinese ports were to be opened to British trade under prescribed conditions, and a convenient depot was to be obtained where British jurisdiction could be exercised. If these points could not be obtained, the reform of the existing system, embodied in a written agreement with the Chinese government, was to be attempted.

The instructions first called the Ambassador's attention to "those Objects" which had conspired to enhance the importance of the Embassy :[59]

First; The Measures lately taken by Government for drawing the Tea Trade out of the hands of the Other European Nations . . .; and Secondly an attention to the Prosperity of Our Territorial Possessions in India, which would be promoted by procuring a secure vent for their Products and Manufactures in the extensive Empire of China.

Next the "discouraging" circumstances under which trade was conducted, "hazardous to . . . Agents employed in conducting it, and precarious to the various Interests involved in it," were alluded to.

At Canton . . . the fair competition of the Market is destroyed by associations of the Chinese, Our Supercargoes are denied open access to the Tribunals of the Country and the fair Execution of its Laws, and are kept altogether in a most arbitrary and cruel state of depression.

The more general objects of the mission were next pointed out. The Ambassador was to endeavor to ascertain whether these evils had "arisen from any settled Policy of the Imperial Government, or from an ill founded Jealousy of Our National Influence, or whether they are created merely by the Corruption and Abuses of a distant Provincial

---

[59] Although the instructions to Cathcart were written by Dundas, they were signed by Lord Sydney, Secretary of State, because Dundas at that time did not have Ministerial rank. The original instructions signed by Dundas are in Bannister, *op. cit.*, pp. 209-26, and the final instructions signed by Sydney without change are in IOCCE, XC, Nov. 30, 1787; Morse, *Chronicle*, II, 160-67.

Administration." Whatever the causes of the abuses might be, the Ambassador was to endeavor to obtain a remedy for them. He was also to discover whether a "studious [desire] to avoid any intimate connection or Intercourse with Europeans . . . operates upon the Imperial Government of Peking." A common prejudice prevailed to this effect, but the writings of various travellers among the Chinese, the "reputed wisdom of the Chinese Administration," and the experience of the Russians with China, led one to believe that the idea was caused by "Commercial Jealousy, aided by the Tyranny and corruption of distant Delegates, under a despotic Sovereign and the general depravity of the Inhabitants" at Canton.

But if, contrary to these suppositions and inferences, such Jealousy should really exist, as it can proceed only from fear, and a sense of their own internal weakness, natural to a vicious People and a despotic Power, it will depend upon your management to obviate it by Declarations the most free and unqualified, that in seeking a connection with China, We have no view but commerce, to be protected by the Chinese Government, subject to its Laws and Regulations, and formed upon a permanent Principle mutually beneficial.

The Ambassador was to endeavor to ascertain the practicability of increasing British exports to China, either by the increase of present assortments or by the introduction of new products of British manufacture. He was to acquire all information possible without exciting jealousy as to the "present Strength, Policy and Government of the Empire . . . , and what intercourse has taken place of late Years, between the Emperor of China and any other European state."

The specific objects of his mission were next described. He was advised not to attempt "to gain upon the Chinese Administration by Artifice or Deception, or by Representations found upon the intricacies of either European or Indian Politicks" but to give assurances of England's friendly and pacific inclinations and rely upon an "honest" and faithful statement of facts to produce the desired effects upon the Emperor. First, he was to emphasize the mutual benefits to be gained from an extended commerce between the two nations.

Second, he was to request the cession "of a small tract of Ground, or detached Island in some more convenient situation than Canton" to serve as a depot for British commerce, where they would be "able to restrain the irregularities which are occasionally committed by the seamen of the Company's Ships and those of Private Traders." Should the establishment be ceded it was to be taken in the name of the King, and the Ambassador was to

endeavor to obtain it in the most beneficial terms, with power of regulating the Police, and exercising Jurisdiction over Our own Dependents, for which competent Powers would of course be given from Our own Legislature . . . . Should it be required that no native Chinese be subject to be punished by Our Jurisdiction, or should any particular modification of this Power be exacted, it is not material to insist upon it, provided British Subjects can be exempted from the Chinese Jurisdiction for Crimes they may commit and that the British Chief be not held responsible if any culprit should escape the pursuit of Justice, and after search has been made by British and Chinese Officers acting in conjunction.

Great care was to be taken to fix the settlement at a place that was convenient and safe for shipping, and that would facilitate the vend of British products and the purchase of teas. As to the exact location of such an establishment, however, the Ambassador was to use his discretion as circumstances and later advices might require.

Third, the Ambassador was to represent the purely commercial views of the English; they did not wish territory, fortifications, or defenses, but merely desired the protection of their merchants and trade. He was to "obviate any Prejudice which may accrue, from the Argument of Our Present Dominion in India" (especially as it was the great object of other European nations to inspire the Emperor and ministers of China with a fear of England because of her expansion in India), by stating that it had arisen almost without their seeking through the necessity of defending themselves against the oppressions of revolted Nabobs, who formed cabals with other European nations and who disregarded privileges granted to the English by various Indian Emperors. He was to handle the question of the opium trade with "great circumspection" but was to agree to its prohibition if necessary, leaving the Bengal opium "to take its chances in an open market, or to find a consumption in the dispersed and circuitous traffic of the Eastern Seas."

[In the fourth place,] the difficulties and vexations under which Our trade has long labored at Canton, must be forcibly represented as proceeding from the malversations of the Viceroy and Merchants and ministers of Justice, in contravention of the Orders and Intentions of The Imperial Court, all which His Britannic Majesty chose rather to lay before The Emperor Himself, in full confidence of Redress, from His Wisdom and Justice, than suffer his Subjects to take any measures for redressing themselves . . .

[Fifth,] If . . . all your attempts to obtain a new Establishment should be decidedly ineffectual; You must turn your whole Attention to the relief of Our present Embarassments at Canton, by an Extension of our Privileges, and a Revision of the Unjust Proceedings which have taken place there to Our prejudice and discredit. . . .

[Sixth,] In case the Embassy should have an amical and prosperous termination it may be proposed to His Imperial Majesty to receive an occasional or perpetual minister from The King of Great Britain and to send one on his own part, to the Court of London, in the assurance that all proper Honors will be paid to any person who may be deputed in that sacred character. . . .

[Finally,] Whatever may be the decision of the Imperial Government, unless, indeed it should be a rejection of all our requests, it will be desirable to obtain it in writing, under such formalities as may enable Us to carry it with some Eclat to the Province where the illtreatment of our Subjects has originated.

The Ambassador was to use his discretion as to which route to pursue in proceeding to Peking, but as the route by Canton would enable the merchants and mandarins to embarrass the Embassy, he was advised to proceed by sea directly to an eastern or northeastern port, and from there to announce his arrival and request a safe conduct to Peking. If he chose he could dispatch one of the lieutenants of the frigate with the messenger who announced at Peking the Ambassador's arrival. If it seemed expedient, the Embassy might touch at Macao or Canton to collect information and procure advices from the supercargoes or private individuals and then proceed to the northward, and if it was necessary it could disembark at Canton and proceed to Peking by land.

Should the Ambassador be allowed to go to Peking he was to proceed with as much ceremony as possible. He was to procure an audience with the Emperor as soon as possible, "Conforming to all Ceremonials of the Court, which may not commit the Honor of Your Sovereign, or lessen your own Dignity, so as to endanger the Success of Your negotiation" and being prudent and considerate not to allow "trifling Punctilio" to stand in the way of important benefits. If personal curiosity caused the Emperor to converse with him on the "manners or Circumstances of Europe or Other Countries" he was to "turn such a Contingency to proper Advantage." Should the Ambassador meet any intelligent Portuguese, Spanish, or Italian missionary, free from national attachment or personal prejudice, he was if possible to be attached to the service.

The presents which he took with him were to be delivered with discretion, and should necessity require more he should provide them by drafts on the Company or its treasury at Canton. He was to take every opportunity of communicating with Lord Cornwallis, Governor-General of India, and be guided by instructions from him. A diary was to be kept from the time of his arrival in China, in which were to be recorded all circumstances or occurrences upon "Political and Commercial, and even Nautical Subjects." He was to have free access to and permission to take copies of the Company's correspondence with its supercargoes in China.

A copy of Cathcart's instructions from the Court of Directors is nowhere extant, but they were presumably given him at the same time as his other instructions. Judging from those given to Lord Macartney in 1792, they emphasized his function as a commercial agent for the Company, requested him to gather information relative to the promotion of trade, and recommended the reform of abuses, but cautioned him to do nothing which might endanger the trade or cause an increase in the difficulties.[60]

The King's letter to the Emperor was addressed to "Kien Long, the Most August Sovereign etc. etc. etc. Emperor of China." It referred to the beneficial effects of a well-regulated trade and believed that the Emperor was convinced of the advisability of encouraging the exchange of commodities upon "fair and equitable principles, consistent with the honor and safety of both Sovereigns." It regretted that there never had been an intercourse between the two sovereigns in order to "ratify and invigorate" their friendship, and so to encourage the speedy remedy of "inconveniences and misunderstandings" which arose between their subjects. Because of this the King was sending "Charles Cathcart Esqr. a Gentleman of Noble Birth, etc. etc. etc.," as Ambassador to the Emperor's "Sublime Court," with instructions to indicate the King's friendly disposition toward the Emperor. It entreated the Emperor to give the Ambassador a "gracious reception and a favourable ear to his representations."[61]

We rely on Your Majesty's wisdom and justice, that you will afford Our Subjects, as long as They conduct themselves with propriety, a secure Residence within your Dominions, and a fair access to Your Markets, under

[60] IOC, XX, "Memorandum," "Proposed Instructions to Col. Cathcart from the Court," pp. 106-125. For Macartney's instructions, see WSCPMD, No. 1.
[61] IOCCE, XC, King's letter of Nov. 30, 1787; Morse, *Chronicle*, II, 167-68; Bannister, *op. cit.*, pp. 227-29.

such Laws and Regulations as Your Majesty shall think right, that their Lives and Properties shall be safe under your Imperial Protection: that one man shall not suffer for another's Crime, but that every necessary Measure shall be taken on the part of Your Majesty's Government, as it certainly shall on Ours, to bring to condign punishment, all Persons who may transgress the Law, and any way disturb the Peace and Friendship subsisting between Us. . . . May the Almighty have you in His Holy Protection.

Sir Richard Strachan's instructions were dated at Whitehall, November 30, 1787, and signed by Lord Sydney.[62] He was commanded to put to sea as soon as possible after Colonel Cathcart should have embarked upon the *Vestal,* and to proceed in her with as much expedition as possible to such port on the Chinese coast as the Ambassador might direct. He was to consider himself attached to this particular service until the Ambassador had finished the business of the Embassy, was to allow the ship to be employed in any service which the Ambassador required, and in general was to conform to the wishes and directions of the Ambassador. He was cautioned to be especially careful to keep his men under control, to conform to the port regulations of the Chinese, and in every way to avoid giving offense which might endanger the Embassy.

In a supplementary instruction of the same date, attention was called to the indisposition of the Ambassador, and he was instructed "that in case of the Lieut. Colonel's demise previous to your arrival in China, you are the instant it may happen to make the best of your way back to the first Port you can reach in England, and to transmit information thereof to me." [63] If the Ambassador reached his place of destination before his possible demise, the conclusion of the mission would fall under the management of the Secretary of the Embassy, and Sir Richard was to comply with his directions until the mission was finished.

7. *The Demise of the Ambassador and the Embassy (1787-88).*

According to letters received from Cathcart, the *Vestal* sailed from Spithead on Sunday, December 21, 1787. Her "Journal" begins the next day, and on the 23rd she encountered a heavy storm in which she suffered considerable damage, and some of the water and beef casks and all of the hay bags had to be thrown overboard. She sighted Maderia on January 2, 1788, and the following day anchored in

---

[62] IOCCE, XC, Nov. 30, 1787; Morse, *Chronicle,* II, 169-70.
[63] Morse, *Chronicle,* II, 170.

Funchal Road in order to make repairs. How much the damage done during the storm cost Cathcart is uncertain, but it amounted to several hundred pounds. Cathcart was dying of consumption when he left England, and tired out by the long journey to Portsmouth, he took to bed as soon as he had embarked. In writing from Maderia, he said that the voyage had been "considerable exercise" for an invalid, but that he believed himself to be better than when he left England. The *Vestal* sailed from Funchal Road on January 6.[64]

On January 14 the Cape Verde Islands were sighted. After crossing the equator, the ship met unfavorable winds, and the Embassy was becalmed for two weeks; on February 4 dysentery began to break out among the sailors. By March 7 "the Flux," as they called it, was raging, and forty-six of the ship's company were ill. In view of these circumstances, as well as to make permanent repairs on the ship, she put into Cape Town on March 11, where she received a good welcome from the Dutch governor, Van de Graaft. The sick were disembarked and the repair of the vessel was undertaken.[65]

In writing to Nepean on March 15, Cathcart reported that the ravages of dysentery had been stopped by the landing, but said, "I cannot inform you of any great Progress in my Recovery. My Cough turns out to be nervious [sic], and I cannot shake it off. However I hold out, and think myself likely to do so; and nothing can give me a better chance of Recovery than constant Change of air at sea." [66] In a private letter to John Lewis on March 28, Strachan wrote: [67]

Colonel Cathcart is unwell, and though we are ready to proceed on our voyage, I shall stay ten days longer to let our people gain strength and to accommodate the Colonel who thinks he is better since he arrived here. I fear he can't live, he is very much reduced and to all appearance in the last stage of a Consumption. I shall be extremely sorry if any accident happen to him on account of the service we are going upon, and from the great regard and respect I have for him.

The *Vestal* sailed on April 8, most of her crew having recovered, although five who were too unwell to move had to be left at the Cape. On May 27 the Straits of Sunda were reached, and the day following the ship dropped a single anchor in Angier Road, where she lay putting

---

[64] IOCCE, XC, "Journal of the *Vestal*," Dec. 22, 1787 to Jan. 2, 1788, Cathcart to Nepean, Jan. 5, 1788, Strachan to Sydney, Jan. 6, 1788, Greville to Chairs, Oct. 12, 1788.
[65] IOCCE, XC, "Journal of the *Vestal*," Jan. 6 to March 12, 1788.
[66] *Ibid.*, XC, Cathcart to [Nepean], March 15, 1788.
[67] *Ibid.*, XC, Strachan to John Lewis, March 28, 1788.

in wood, water, and food.[68] On the same day Cathcart wrote to Strachan requesting him to direct his course to Macao, as in the

Opinion of my Physician, the debilitated state of my Health, renders it impossible for me to proceed to the North East Coast of China without recruiting my Health on Shore. . . . I must also request that you will remain a few days at this place, as Doctor Ewart wishes me to try what effect the Air of the Shore may have on my disorder.[69]

The *Vestal* remained at anchor until June 6, when she sailed into the Straits of Banka and dropped anchor on the 9th, and on the 10th, "at ½ past 8 departed this Life, The Honble-Lieutenant Colonel Cathcart." The ship returned to Angier Road, and on the 16th his remains were deposited under the Dutch flag. The body was "sent on shore to be interned at 10 A.M. while minute guns were fired from the time the corpse left the ship until it was interned and fired [*sic*] 3 vollies of small arms, the ceremony lasted an hour."[70] As Sir Richard's instructions required his immediate return to England, Captain Agnew, who assumed control of Cathcart's public papers, wrote to the supercargoes at Canton and to Lord Cornwallis giving an account of the gloomy event. The *Vestal* sailed for England on June 18, but, as a distemper broke out among the men, she was forced to put into Cape Town on July 28, after having lost six men. By August 16 she was ready to sail, but Lieutenant Rutherford was too ill to go and had to be left behind.[71]

The *Vestal* reached the Channel on October 7, but the weather took a last parting blow at the unfortunate mission and forced the *Vestal* to put into Plymouth on October 8, 1788. At some time during the return voyage M. Galbert also died; thus one of the few persons in Europe capable of acting as interpreters was eliminated. Lord Sydney was informed of Cathcart's death and the return of the Embassy by Sir Richard and Captain Agnew on the same day, and Captain Agnew also informed Dundas and the Court of Directors. Strachan also fell ill after his return, but had to stand the routine court martial which examined into his conduct during the voyage.[72]

---

[68] IOCCE, XC, "Journal of *Vestal*," April 8 to May 28, 1788.
[69] *Ibid.*, XC, Cathcart to Strachan, May 28, 1788.
[70] *Ibid.*, "Journal of *Vestal*," June 6 to June 16, 1788.
[71] *Ibid.*, June 17 to August 17, 1788, Strachan to Sydney, Oct. 8, 1788, Agnew to Dundas, Oct. 8, 1788.
[72] IOCCE, XC, Strachan to Sydney, Oct. 8, 1788, Agnew to Sydney and Dundas, Oct. 8, 1788, Agnew to Sydney, Nov. 11, 1788, Sydney to Agnew, Nov. 12, 1788, Strachan to Nepean, Dec. 14, 1788, Smith to Nepean, Feb. 9, 1789, Morton to Nepean, Feb. 23, and 25, 1789; IOC, XX, "Memorandum," Oct. 15, and Nov. 8, 1788.

Cathcart's last days were clouded by financial worries. He had made his plans with the idea that the Embassy would last three years, and in consequence had incurred considerable debts which were to be paid out of his salary as it fell due. Knowing the state of his health, he had asked the government to make adequate provisions for the continuation of the Embassy in case of his death, which they failed to do. By the time of his death the payments on his salary were insufficient to meet the creditors. The payment due to Cathcart on March 7, 1788, was withheld by the Company in lieu of the £1,500 advanced him in November, 1787. The salary installments falling due on June 7 and September 7, 1788, were paid, but the Embassy returned before his December allowance was paid.

Including the £500 paid for supplies in November, 1787, and £230 taken by Cathcart for personal use from the silver on board the *Vestal*, he received from the Company £5,230. The expenses which he personally incurred in connection with the Embassy were known to amount to £5,833 plus an indefinite amount expended in cash by him before sailing and sums paid by his brother to M. Galbert's executors as reimbursement for his travelling expenses from Avignon and living expenses in London, which the Company had agreed to pay but apparently never did. The total personal expenses incurred by Cathcart thus amounted to not less than £7,000, and his receipts from the Company to but £5,230.[73]

The matter was first brought to the attention of the Chairman, Nathaniel Smith, on October 12, 1788, by C. F. Greville, a close friend of Cathcart and one of his executors. Lord Cathcart, the Colonel's brother, also wrote to Dundas about it on October 17, as did the Duke of Athole on October 22. The Court, however, disturbed by the failure of the Embassy and the large sums already expended, took no notice of it, and a detailed and reasoned statement from Greville in January, 1789, was also disregarded. On September 16, 1789, the facts in the case were laid before the India Board. As nothing was done, Lord Cathcart drew up a statement of his brother's claims against the Company on March 12, 1793, which appears to have been for the use of the government, but so far as records show no money was ever paid to his estate either by the Company or by the government.

---

[73] IOCCE, XC, Greville to Chairs, Oct. 12, 1788 and Jan. 1789, and Lord Cathcart's Memorandum, March 12, 1793; IOC, XX, "Memorandum," April 12, June 3, Sept. 25, 1788.

The direct violation of a written agreement to pay Galbert's expenses and to recompense Cathcart if his salary proved insufficient, and the violation of a verbal agreement to pay Cathcart's salary under all circumstances until the Embassy returned to England (he was not paid anything for the two months from September 6 to October 8) should be an everlasting shame on the name of the East India Company. To be sure, the Embassy cost it £9,046 (including the presents, of which £3,306 was again used at the time of the Macartney Embassy)[74] from which it received nothing, but this was in part caused by the unstatesmanlike procedure of sending out a dying man without taking adequate means to insure under all circumstances the continuation of the Embassy. For this mistake the government must bear the chief responsibility. Had Cathcart lived until Lieutenant Young joined the Embassy at Canton, the commission would probably have been executed, and Cathcart would not have died in financial disgrace.

8. *The Abandonment and the Revival of the Idea of Sending an Embassy to China (1788-91).*

No sooner had the news of the death of Cathcart reached England than a movement for sending another mission was set on foot. So far as the government was concerned, most of the reasons which had brought about the sending of the Cathcart Mission still existed. Furthermore, the *Vestal* was still in port prepared for the service, the necessary presents were already in hand, the necessary plans, instructions, and documents prepared, and most of the necessary personnel for the mission were ready for service. From the government's point of view the only thing necessary was the choosing of a new ambassador. In addition, other events had transpired since the departure of the Cathcart Embassy which made the government still more eager to open a more extensive trade with China.

First of all, the government and Parliament had carried on a thorough examination of the China trade and the working of the Commutation Act in May, 1788. A large amount of documentary and statistical material relative to China had been demanded of the Company, and no less than twenty-three "Accounts and Papers" were sub-

---

[74] IOCCE, XC, Lord Cathcart to Dundas, Oct. 17, 1788, Duke of Athole to Dundas, Oct. 22, 1788, Greville to William Cabell (Secretary of the Board of Control), Sept. 16, 1789; CMC, VIII, No. 343; note 73.

mitted to Parliament relative to the China trade.[75] These papers went into every detail of the trade and showed that the government's revenue from tea had been just about halved by the Commutation Act; that, although the Company's trade had been greatly increased, it was having great difficulties in raising money and had to export large quantities of bullion from England; and that foreign competition was still continuing at Canton. The extracts from the supercargoes' letters presented to Parliament spoke in discouraging terms of the foreign competition, the high prices, and the difficulty of getting satisfactory teas.

At the same time a crisis caused by overproduction occurred in the cotton industry. The throwing open of Arkwright's patent in 1785 had led to feverish expansion in the industry, with the result that the market became glutted in 1788, prices fell, and the cotton-goods producers were faced with ruin. Descending upon the government like a pack of hungry wolves, they demanded protection and the discovery of new markets. They drew up a petition attacking the Company and demanding a prohibition upon the importation of Indian and Chinese manufactured goods. A conference was arranged between delegates of the cotton manufacturers and the Court of Directors in which the former requested that the Company cease the importation of cottons manufactured in India and China and that it undertake to import raw cotton from India for the use of the manufacturers.[76]

The Company refused to comply with their demands regarding the importation of manufactured cotton goods, because (1) the competition of Eastern cottons actually was not the cause of their present difficulties, which were due to overproduction; (2) seventeen-twentieths of the calicoes and three-fifths of the muslins imported by the Company were re-exported anyhow; (3) if the Company gave up the trade it would fall into the hands of foreign competitors to the detriment of British shipping; (4) a cessation of the Indian piece-goods trade would ruin the Indian producers and endanger the Company's revenue in India; (5) and a decrease in the Company's imports would mean a decrease in its exports and so would injure other British industries which depended upon it. As to the demand that Indian raw cotton be imported, it promised to make the experiment, but held out no hope

---

[75] PP, *Accounts and Papers, 1788,* XXI, submitted to Parliament on May 22 and 23, Nos. 462-84.

[76] Mantoux, *op. cit.,* pp. 260-63; PP, *Accounts and Papers, 1792-93,* No. 774, "Reports of the Select Committee of the Directors on the Cotton Trade," and "Court's Memorial on Cotton Manufacture in 1788."

that it could do this profitably or that this material would be satisfactory for use in British manufacture.

As a consequence of these factors, the government was more eager than ever to send out an embassy in the hope of increasing the trade with China, improving the government's revenue, finding new markets for the outlet of British manufactures, and so silencing the hubbub at home and stopping the attack upon the Company, whose interests were so closely identified with those of the government. The Company, however, was not so favorable. It did not wish to spend more money on an already costly undertaking, the advantages of which it was beginning to doubt. Furthermore, in view of the attack upon it, it was afraid that advantages gained from China might be turned to its disadvantage, and it could already see that the battle for the control of the China trade was won and that further intervention was unnecessary.

The first proposal of a new embassy was made by C. F. Greville, with the knowledge and approbation of Pitt, to the Chairman of the Company (Nathaniel Smith) on October 12, 1788, in connection with his proposal for the settlement of Cathcart's debts. He suggested that Lieutenant Young and Captain Agnew should be appointed jointly and severally envoys to the Emperor, and that they should proceed to execute Cathcart's mission using the equipment and presents which he had taken. In view of Galbert's death, the embassy would have to go by way of Canton to procure an interpreter. If this procedure was adopted, the money on the *Vestal* would not be needed and could be given to Cathcart's estate—part as the last installment of his salary and part as equipage money.[77]

On October 15 Dundas, in a letter to Nepean, said that he hoped the death of Cathcart would not prove fatal to the mission, which he considered a very important one.[78] Conferences were certainly held between Pitt, Sydney, and the Chairs, but evidently the last-mentioned were not especially cordial to the idea of a new embassy, and the government did not approve of Young or Agnew as ambassadors.[79] On October 22 Lord Macartney wrote to Pitt recommending Sir George Leonard Staunton as a possible successor to Cathcart.[80] There are no more

[77] IOCCE, XC, Greville to Chairman, Oct. 12, 1788; IOC, XX, for the same and an additional letter to Smith showing that Pitt had seen the documents and was going to discuss the matter with the Chairs.
[78] IOCCE, XC, Dundas to Nepean, Oct. 15, 1788.
[79] IOCCE, XC, Smith to [Nepean], Oct. 10, 1788, arranging for meetings with Pitt and Sydney.
[80] G. T. Staunton, *Memoir of G. L. Staunton*, pp. 320-21.

records relating to the proposed embassy until February 8, 1789, when the Board of Control was informed that another mission was to be sent.[81] Records are not available to show what happened during the next five months, but various discussions were held, and arrangements were made for sending another mission.

On July 2 a letter from the Committee of Secrecy to the secretary of the Company directed him to "examine the several Packages received from the *Vestal*" and to "replace or repair such as might be spoiled or damaged."[82] Six days later a secret letter was sent from William Wyndham Grenville, who had succeeded Lord Sydney as Secretary of State, to the Board of Control saying, that his Majesty's Ministers had thought it expedient to attempt another embassy. With this in view, the *Vestal* had been ordered to be equipped to convey a deputation to China, but the diffiiculty of finding a person in England to go out as head of the deputation had induced the Ministers to intrust the nomination of the ambassador to Lord Cornwallis. The communication inclosed a draft letter to Lord Cornwallis to be sent out upon the *Vestal*, which would be ready to sail in ten days. The board was directed to take necessary measures to put this proposal into effect.[83]

The proposed letter to the Governor-General ordered him to appoint a person to continue the deputation to China, and to give to that person such instructions in addition to those given to Cathcart as his local knowledge should cause him to think necessary. A thing to be especially impressed upon the mind of the person chosen was the necessity of extending the sale of British manufactures. The Company found difficulty in selling its goods at Canton, but the northern part of China was being furnished with British products (North American furs, woollens, glass, hardware) through Russia. Every endeavor should be made to turn this traffic into channels more favorable to British subjects. Cathcart had been instructed to agree if necessary to a prohibition of the importation of opium by British subjects into China, but such a prohibition was not to apply to native inhabitants of that part of India belonging to England. Sir Richard Strachan, by whom he would receive this letter, was to place himself under orders of the Governor-General for the prosecution of the mission.[84]

---

[81] Bannister, *op. cit.*, "Introduction." He refers to Vol. 193 of the records of the *Board of Control*, which is no longer extant.

[82] IOC, XX, "Memorandum," July 2, 1789.

[83] IOCCE, XC, Grenville to Board of Control, July 8, 1789; see also the same letter signed by Grenville in IOC, XX.

[84] IOCCE, XC, draft letter to Lord Cornwallis, July 8, 1789.

A copy of this last letter is to be found in the China records in the India Office, signed by Henry Dundas and marked "not sent." The only other communication upon the subject is a secret letter from Nepean to William Devaynes (Chairman of the Directors), dated August 10, 1789, informing him that the execution of the plan of sending an embassy to China was for the present suspended.[85] The *Vestal*, nevertheless, sailed to India with dispatches but without the presents. She must have carried less mandatory orders to Cornwallis, because on April 12, 1790, he wrote home stating that, as he had no reason to expect any material advantage from deputing any person to China, he had not employed the *Vestal* on that service.[86]

The question arises as to why the proposed embassy was suspended, and why, if discretionary orders were sent to Cornwallis, he did not act upon them. The decision to abandon the embassy was taken between July 8 and August 10, 1789. A consideration of contemporary events in France leads one to believe that the sudden revolutionary activity in that country so clouded the European horizon that it was considered inadvisable to dispatch the mission. So far as one can see, there are no other reasons for the abandonment of the plan. Cornwallis, being in closer contact with Canton, probably had a genuine feeling that no good would come from an embassy. Furthermore, a war had broken out in India late in 1789 with the Tippoo Sultan,[87] which was occupying the energies of the Governor-General, and, in view of the troubled situation in Europe, he probably deemed it advisable to keep the *Vestal* close at hand for service in the Indian fleet.

Events moved on in China and England. In October, 1789, the Hoppo proposed to the President of the Select Committee that "two Persons of each Nation be deputed to go to Pekin, to join in" congratulating the Emperor upon the attainment of his eightieth birthday. The Select Committee expressed fear that they might be detained at Peking and that they would be forced to perform the *kotow*. They were reassured on the first point but their fears on the second were confirmed. Bruce ultimately made a tender of his services, but, as the proposal had not come from Peking and was only an idea of the Viceroy, it was ultimately abandoned.[88] News of this reached England by May,

---

[85] IOC, XX, Dundas to Lord Cornwallis, marked "not sent"; IOCCE, XC, Nepean to Devaynes.

[86] MSS. Public Record Office, *Colonial Office: East Indies, 1788-92,* 77/26, April 12, 1790, received in England Sept. 8, 1790 (précis only).

[87] *Commons Journal,* XLVI, 256.

[88] Morse, *Chronicle,* II, 177-78.

1790, and the Directors wrote to the Select Committee reprimanding them for hesitating in taking advantage of the proposal, telling them that they should conform to the ceremonials of the Court, and closed by saying, "[we] shall expect to hear of the Departure of a proper Delegation to Peking." [89]

In the opinion of the government the proposal discussed above was an indication that Peking would welcome an embassy from England, and other considerations impressed upon their minds the advisability of a mission which might obtain an extended market for British manufactures. As has been already noted, the cotton and iron industries were experiencing mushroom growth at this time, and often at the expense of other old-established industries. As a consequence, representatives of all interests were calling upon the government for aid and protection. [90] In view of the need of new markets, the Lords of Trade began early in the summer of 1791 a thorough investigation into the possibilities of expanding British trade. They held a conference with the Court of Directors and requested information on the exportation of British manufactures to India, China, Japan, and Persia, especially in regard to the possibilities of increasing exportation to these countries. A Select Committee was appointed by the Directors to investigate these matters. Reports on India and China were submitted in September, 1791, and on Japan and Persia in January, 1792. [91]

After going into a detailed analysis of the China trade, the reports concluded that the exportation of woollens, metals, or other articles could not be increased except by the negotiation of favorable treaties. They maintained that there was no hope of trade to Japan or Persia, and that cotton manufactures were not in demand in India or China, because these countries produced cotton goods more cheaply than England. They did not express a definite opinion as to the advisability of sending a mission to China, but they objected strenuously to any change in the existing system either by allowing private individuals to send out goods from England or by trying to gain new advantages which might endanger their present satisfactory situation. They said that the Company was doing all that was possible toward the expansion of British manufactures in the East. From these facts it was evident that

---

[89] CMD, II, Court to Select Committee, May 10, 1790; Morse, *Chronicle,* II, 181-82.

[90] Mantoux, *op. cit.,* pp. 258-63.

[91] PP, *Accounts and Papers, 1792-93,* XXXVIII, No. 774 (bl-3), Reports on India, China, Japan and Persia.

the government could expect no substantial help from the Company in extending the sale of British goods, and that the idea of sending out a commercial mission to China was part of a general scheme for promoting the sale of British manufactures.

In June, 1791, Henry Dundas was promoted to the position of Home Secretary, but retained his position in the Board of Control as well. Armed with the powers of a Secretary of State, Dundas once again set about the realization of his favorite scheme of an embassy to China. He was encouraged by the publication of a book by a Country trader,[92] which spoke in glowing terms of the possibilities of expanding British trade, especially in woollens and tin, to the north of China, Japan, and Korea, and of developing the fur trade between the Northwest Coast and China, if only an embassy were dispatched to negotiate the necessary treaties. His ideas were supported by various private reports received from China, which tended to show that the supercargoes were slothful and inattentive to business, and that if proper energy were exercised an increased trade could be developed.[93]

In his and the government's mind practically all the reasons which had led to the Cathcart Embassy still existed.[94] In addition, there was now the belief that such an embassy would be well received; there was an unsatisfactory flow of silver from England to China;[95] there was available an experienced diplomat, nobleman, and friend of Henry Dundas, Lord Macartney, who had been without employment since 1786; there were intellectual advantages which might be gained from a friendly intercourse with China; there was the possibility that "success might prove highly advantageous to the Board of Control [i.e. Henry Dundas],"[96] and above all else there was the imperative necessity of finding new markets to quiet the demands of the industrialists and encourage English industry and commerce.

It was true that the political situation in Europe was very unsettled, but it had been so for several years. Furthermore, it was true that European competition had been greatly reduced at Canton and that the

---

[92] John Meares, *Voyages made in the Years 1788 and 1789, from China to the North West Coast of America* (London, 1790), pp. lxviii-lxxxvi.

[93] CMC, II, No. 16; BM, *Additional Manuscripts* (*Liverpool Papers,* CLXIII), No. 38,352, pp. 391-92.

[94] For a general review of the reasons for the Macartney Embassy see G. L. Staunton, *Embassy* (1797), I, 13-27; Eames, *op. cit.,* pp. 117-18.

[95] John Barrow, *Some Account of the Public Life . . . of the Earl of Macartney* (London, 1807), I, 339-41; Meares, *op. cit.,* pp. xciv-vi.

[96] W. Winterbotham, *An Historical . . . View of the Empire of China* (London, 1795), pp. 1-2.

Company's China trade and its Canton treasury were now in a prosperous condition.[97] Still there was the prospect of American competition. Nor did the Company look with favor upon the proposal of an embassy, because it might endanger the advantages they had already gained, and they saw no reason for expending money which might "shake" if not "annihilate" a "fabric which is the Wonder of the Present, as it must be of every future Age . . . in case Projects suggested by Adventurers shall be adopted upon the dangerous Principle of Experiment."[98]

These latter objections were minor ones compared with the possibilities of the realization of Dundas' great ambition, and so they were swept aside. The government (especially Dundas and Pitt) decided to send to the East the greatest commercial embassy that England had ever sent. The Ambassador was to be armed with powers not only to negotiate with the Emperor of China but with the rulers of Japan, Indo-China, and all the islands of the East Indies. Lord Macartney was approached at least as early as October, 1791, and preliminary discussions were in full swing by the end of November.[99]

---

[97] At the beginning of the season 1791 the Company's treasury had a credit balance of T. 1,460,718 and at the beginning of the next season a credit balance of T. 2,063,818. Morse, *Chronicle,* II, 184, 192.

[98] PP, *Accounts and Papers, 1792-93,* XXXVII, No. 774 (b2), "Second Report of the Select Committee of the Court of Directors on the Trade to the East Indies (China and Japan), Dec. 29, 1791," end of report.

[99] G. T. Staunton, *Memoir of G. L. Staunton,* pp. 332-37.

CHAPTER VII

PREPARATIONS FOR THE MACARTNEY EMBASSY
(1791-1792)

1. *Preliminary Discussions and Proposals (October, 1791 - January 19, 1792).*

The idea of attempting another Embassy to China had been definitely formulated by the early part of October, 1791, as it appears that Lord Macartney was approached about this time by the government on the subject of his willingness to serve as Ambassador. George Lord Macartney was a distinguished diplomat and colonial administrator. He was born near Belfast on May 14, 1737, and was trained for the diplomatic service by two years of travel and study on the Continent. He had served as Ambassador to Russia, as a member of the Irish and British Parliaments, as Chief Secretary for Ireland, and as Governor of the West Indian Island of Grenada, where he established a life-long friendship with George Leonard Staunton. In December, 1780, he accepted the post of Governor of Madras, with Staunton as his Chief Secretary. After five years, he returned to England and was offered the Governor-Generalship of Bengal. He was uninterested in the appointment unless given very extensive powers, and, as he was opposed by Hasting's supporters, the appointment ultimately was given to Lord Cornwallis. The East India Company voted him a life annuity of £1,500, and until his selection as Ambassador to China he held no more public positions.[1] In 1791 he was undoubtedly the most eligible man in England to serve as an Ambassador to China.

As soon as Macartney was approached about the Embassy he appears to have written to Sir George Leonard Staunton, then at Edinburgh, requesting his return to London, for Staunton hurriedly left his family on the 19th or 20th of October and returned to the south.[2] It also appears that the subject had been broached to the East India Company, because on October 13, Thomas Morton, Secretary at the India House, sent out a list of nineteen queries to former supercargoes,

---

[1] John Barrow, *Account of the Public Life . . . of the Earl of Macartney* (London, 1807) ; Helen M. Robbins, *Our First Ambassador to China* (London, 1908) ; *Dictionary of National Biography.*
[2] G. T. Staunton, *Memoir of G. L. Staunton*, pp. 332-37.

then resident in England, relative to affairs in China. The queries were of a general nature and designed to obtain information which the Court could use for any purpose it desired, such as the preparation of the reports for the Lords of Trade or the preparation of an Embassy.[*]

In general, the answers to the queries tended to show the unsatisfactory nature of the Canton system and the dangers to which both the supercargoes and the trade were subjected. They also indicated that no extensive immediate expansion of British trade to China could be expected under the existing system, and that there was no likelihood of new products being successfully introduced into the Chinese market. They confirmed the advantages which the Company was said to have over its foreign rivals, and generally added support to the Company's contention that no beneficial expansion of the trade might be expected outside its monopoly. In sending in his reply on November 21, William Fitzhugh, in a private letter to Thomas Morton, called particular attention to the restraints and impositions, especially the charge on the migration from Canton to Macao, which had risen from $1,700 in 1774 to $12,000 in 1790. He said that these impositions had originated with the minor mandarins at Canton and that they could be removed and the trade protected only by the establishment of a respectable intercourse with Peking.

It appears that Lord Macartney did not wish to undertake the mission unless there was a fair chance of success. Both he and the government were of the opinion that the Company's affairs in China were improperly managed and that their management must be reformed as a first step in securing the success of the mission. Their view was supported by William Richardson, Secretary at the India House. The Chairs, however, did not wish to take drastic measures without careful consideration, and proceedings dragged.[⁴] Preliminary negotiations continued throughout November and by early December the government seems to have decided that a Select Committee should be sent to Canton to take over the management of the Company's affairs. On December 14 Richardson wrote to Macartney expressing his satisfaction at the plan adopted by the government. He recommended that the Select Committee at Canton consist of three men with ample power and that Staunton be president. He further suggested that Captain Mackintosh, Commander of one of the Company's East Indiamen, and Charles

---

[*] CMD, I. The queries and answers occupy the whole volume.
[⁴] See notes 5 and 6.

Arthur, the tea inspector at Canton, be the other two members of the committee. He was sure that, if matters were properly managed, British exports to China could be greatly increased, and the costs of exports from China could be decreased and the trade soon be made to balance. He enclosed an extract of a letter from James Drummond, a writer at Canton, which showed how inefficiently the Company's affairs were run.[5]

Four days later Macartney wrote the following interesting lines to Staunton:

The other matter [the Embassy] . . . seems to wear a more favorable appearance; but till I have seen Mr. Dundas, and the business be more opened and explained it is not easy, even on this point, to form a proper judgment. Our friend Richardson is eager, sanguine, and active, and from his superior intelligence of these affairs, ought certainly to have great weight: but is he likely to have as much weight as he ought to have? And will there not be fifty knaves and blockheads, who on the first hint of what is in agitation, will, by means of connection and other circumstances, intrude themselves into the business, destroy all the credit that able and honest men might acquire in it, and defeat all the benefits intended to the public. You, who are on the spot, can judge of all this, better than I can at a distance; but certainly neither I, nor any wise man, would wish to embark in the vessel, unless there was a fair prospect of making an honorable and prosperous voyage. I am myself pleased with the idea, and should therefore be sorry to find myself disappointed.[6]

On December 20 Matthew Raper transmitted to Richardson a copy of a letter in Italian which he had recently received from a missionary at Peking, dated November 12, 1790. It was ultimately sent to Dundas and Macartney, accompanied by Père Grammont's letters of 1779 suggesting an embassy to China.[7] The letter was unsigned, but may have been written by Grammont or by Louis Poirot, a French missionary well acquainted with Italian and then living at Peking. It stated that the present was not the proper time for an embassy. The celebration of the Emperor's eightieth birthday (1790) would have been an opportune time, but, that being past, it would be advisable to wait until the accession of a new Emperor. The most proper procedure would be to

---

[5] CMC, Nos. 20, 21, 16.
[6] G. T. Staunton, *Memoir of G. L. Staunton*, pp. 337-38. To be found on pages 603-619 of Volume 93 of the India Office collection on China is a "List of Papers contained in two vols. obtained from the India House on the subject of Lord Macartney's Embassy to China." As some of the papers referred to in this list are no longer extant, reference will sometimes be made to it as IOCM, XCIII, "List of Papers."
[7] *Supra*, p. 208.

make an arrangement with Portugal, whereby the Senate of Macao should propose to the Viceroy the sending of an embassy. By this method the intrigues of the merchants at Canton and of the nationally prejudiced missionaries at Peking might be avoided. The ambassador should be a man of capacity, accompanied by an able interpreter and a handsome retinue; and rare and curious presents, such as new mechanical inventions, paintings, and fine yellow cloth, should be brought.[8]

On the same day Richardson wrote to Macartney stating that he was

clearly of opinion that whether the Directors appoint *proper* Supracargoes or not, the King should have a resident Consul at Canton a man of good sense & firmness, he would keep the Supracargoes, Captains etc. in some order. Sir G[eorge] S[taunton] might be Consul & President of the Council.[9]

On December 22 Dundas and Macartney had a conference at the Secretary of State's office, and apparently the final decision was taken upon sending the Embassy to China. In consequence, Dundas asked Macartney to give his sentiments on the best way of making the Embassy a success.[10] Macartney immediately busied himself with collecting information on which to base his ideas. He was supplied with extensive materials from the India House and from the office of the Board of Control. Among the latter papers was a letter from Samuel Garbett (a Birmingham metal manufacturer and associate of Mathew Boulton)[11] to Dundas, dated October 31, 1791, with six enclosures.[12] Neither the letter nor the enclosures are extant, but they are of interest in showing the early connections between the northern industrialists and the Embassy.

On January 4, 1792,[13] Macartney set forth his ideas about the Embassy. It should be announced in such a way as not to be unpalatable to the Chinese, and therefore its obstensible object should not be to obtain redress of grievances. Its object could be announced as a visit to the most Civilized, as well as most Ancient and Populous Nation on the Globe, in order to observe its celebrated institutions, and to communicate and receive the benefits, which must result from an unrestrained and friendly intercourse between that country and [England].

[8] E. H. Pritchard, "Letters from Missionaries at Peking Relating to the Macartney Embassy," *T'oung Pao*, XXXI (1934), 4-6; CMC, Nos. 6, 14; IOCM, XCI, 25-31.
[9] CMC, No. 21.
[10] *Ibid.*, Nos. 22, 23.
[11] Mantoux, *op. cit.*, pp. 309, 381.
[12] CMC, No. 24.
[13] IOCM, XCI, 37-52.

Such a statement would allay fear, provide the proper flattery, and give the desirable philosophical background. The Chinese should be impressed with the wisdom and justice of the English King, and with British power and resources, which might lead to the negotiation of a treaty of friendship and alliance. To preserve the treaty and prevent misunderstandings, resident ministers at Peking and London should be arranged for if possible.

The commercial objectives should include:

(1) The abolition of restraints and extortions laid upon trade at Canton;

(2) The opening of new ports for trade near the primary commodity-producing areas;

(3) The abolition of import and export duties or at least their reduction to the rate at which they were when trade began;

(4) The granting of a convenient trade depot where the traders might remain from season to season;

(5) The obtaining of an edict stipulating that the Company's agents were not to be held responsible for the misconduct of individuals, and that innocent persons should not in the future be made to suffer for the deeds of criminals who might have escaped; the Company's agents undertaking not to assist in such escape, but on the contrary to afford every assistance towards the recovery of the guilty person;

(6) The encouragement of the introduction of British manufactures into China not only by opening new ports, but by procuring the repeal of regulations which tended to discourage their introduction, and also by inducing a taste at Peking for articles of British workmanship hitherto unknown there.

Lord Macartney next turned to the make-up of the Embassy. It should be conducted with much pomp and éclat, although dignity and decorum should be maintained. It should be carried out by a King's ship and if possible be accompanied from Malacca by part of the Indian Fleet. The retinue should consist of men to aid in the negotiations, and men of the arts and sciences provided with instruments and machines to make experiments and demonstrations that had not been seen before in Peking. These men could gather information and study Chinese methods of manufacture and production. It would also be advisable to have a military guard and a few light field pieces to impress the Emperor with both the pomp and the power of the English, for his recognition of the latter might facilitate the negotiations.

It would be necessary to take along the customary presents for the Emperor and chief mandarins. A "discreet and seasonable generosity" might have to be exercised toward minor officials, and it would "be useful to conciliate the good will of the Missionaries at Peking, by some trifling supplies of European articles." It would be advisable to take an interpreter with the Embassy, and it seemed likely that a confidential agent sent to the Continent as a private traveler might find a satisfactory person.

He felt that it would be desirable to have a British Consul at Canton to announce the Embassy, and that it would be wise to have new men sent to Canton as head of the Company's establishment to reform abuses and cooperate with the Consul. In order to secure cooperation, the Ambassador should be given power to control the factory. A letter to the Emperor of Japan should be sent and intercourse with that country might be attempted; the threat of such intercourse might produce beneficial results in the negotiations with the Emperor of China. Finally, because many unforeseen events might occur, the Ambassador should be given a good deal of discretionary power, guarding always the interests of the King and not hazarding advantages already obtained.

A conference was held between Macartney and Dundas on January 6, at which Dundas expressed his general approval of the plan, asked the Ambassador to draw up a tableau of the Embassy, and desired that preparations be hurried in order that it might sail about April 1. Macartney replied on the 7th, stating that he thought it advisable to take three artificers with knowledge of "metallurgy," weaving, and pottery who could study with advantage to England the progress of these arts in China, and be of especial help to the Birmingham, Manchester, and Staffordshire manufacturers. He also requested that he be left entirely to himself in the choosing of the personnel of the Embassy, in order to ensure harmony and strict devotion to the Ambassador.[14] The tableau included the following persons:[15]

1 Ambassador	3 Artificers (metallurgy, weaving, pottery)
1 Secretary	
2 Under-secretaries	10 Servants
2 Interpreters	6 Musicians
1 Comptroller	
1 Surgeon	30 Total civil suite
1 Scientist	35 Light infantry
1 Mechanic	15 Artillerymen
1 Painter and draughtsman	3 Commissioned officers
	83 Total Embassy

[14] IOCM, XCI, 57-59, 101.
[15] *Ibid.*, pp. 61-62.

On January 8 Dundas authorized Macartney to proceed at once to get an interpreter.[16] Staunton was immediately dispatched to Paris to search for one, and by the 11th he was already at Calais.[17] At a meeting on the 10th Macartney and Dundas discussed the plans for the Embassy in detail. Later in the same day Macartney requested that a ship of fifty guns be commissioned for the service, and that Sir Erasmus Gower be appointed to command her.[18] It is worthwhile noting that Macartney resisted a request of Richardson that his son-in-law be given an appointment on the ship which was to carry the Embassy.[19]

On January 12 the Chairman and the Deputy Chairman (John Smith Burges and Francis Baring) waited upon Pitt and Dundas, and were officially told of the Embassy and requested to finance it. They "expressed grave doubts as to the probability of a substantial and permanent advantage being derived by the Company or the Country at large from the measure," but, as the ministers were determined and they considered Macartney especially competent, they agreed to consider the measure further.[20] On the 16th they had another conference with Dundas, at which they apparently lent their support to the proposal, but stated that they would have to obtain the approval of the Court of Directors.[21] The ministers, however, wanted to keep the affair a secret, and objected to the publicity which a discussion of the matter in the Court of Directors would create. Consequently, Dundas requested the Chairs to explain to the Directors that a measure was in "contemplation considered to be of much importance to this Country in its commerce with China," and to request of the Court authorization "to take such steps in concurrence with His Majesty's ministers as may appear expedient for promoting the object in view."[22] On the 19th the Chairs met the Directors and explained in confidence that a mission to China was in contemplation, requested that they be appointed a secret committee to negotiate with the government, and that £20,000 be voted to be applied at their discretion in promoting the mission. The name of the Ambassador was not mentioned. The proposal was unanimously adopted, and, with full financial and discretion-

---

[16] CMC, No. 30.
[17] G. T. Staunton, *Memoir of G. L. Staunton*, p. 338.
[18] CMC, No. 33.
[19] *Ibid.*, No. 32.
[20] IOCM, XCIII, "List of Papers," Jan. 12, 1792; Auber, *op. cit.*, p. 193.
[21] CMC, No. 35; IOCM, XCIII, "List of Papers," Jan. 16, 1792.
[22] IOC, XX, Dundas to Chairman, Jan. 17, 1792.

ary powers in the hands of the Chairs, the way was open to proceed with the plan."

2. The Controversy between Macartney and the Chairs over the Arrangements for the Embassy (January 20-February 14, 1792).

On January 20 the Chairs wrote to Dundas giving their opinions upon Macartney's proposals. They agreed with him as to the manner in which the Embassy should be announced and as to his plan for the extension of arts, sciences, and useful knowledge. In general, they agreed with his statement of abuses and objectives to be attained, but requested that conversations be held with the Company's supercargoes before the final decision was taken on these matters. They offered no definite opinion upon the size of the establishment until after the matter of salaries had been considered. They were very doubtful as to the advisability of the military guard, especially as the presence of artillery might arouse the suspicion and distrust of the Chinese. They definitely opposed the idea of sending out a British Consul, and refused to give Macartney control over their Canton establishment. They promised to secure cooperation between the Ambassador and their supercargoes by sending out most positive orders to that effect and by adopting other proposals which seemed advisable. They wanted assurance that the measure would not affect their present rights and privileges. They also asked to be released from the payment of the expenses of the ship-of-war."

On the same day Baring and Macartney met to discuss the salaries to be allowed members of the Embassy. Baring also expressed the Chairs' objection to the sending out of a British Consul and urged that Sir George Staunton be sent out as head of the Company's Select Committee at Canton. Macartney intimated that he believed Staunton was already determined to accompany the Embassy," but on the following day he wrote to Staunton transmitting the proposal. He said that he did not wish to stand in the way of Staunton's advancement, but felt sure that they would achieve the greatest success by remaining together in the undertaking. He also hoped that Staunton would be successful in finding an interpreter in Naples, as there were no fit persons in Göttenburg, Copenhagen, or Lisbon. Staunton ultimately

²³ CMC, Nos. 39, 41; IOCM, XCIII, "List of Papers," Jan. 19, 1792.
²⁴ IOCM, XCI, 63-70.
²⁵ CMC, Nos. 40, 41, 42.

wrote declining Baring's offer, much to Macartney's personal satisfaction.[26]

On January 23 Macartney gave his opinion of the Chairs' letter in a private communication to Dundas. He said that he would welcome information from the supercargoes, but doubted that one could learn much about China from them. Since the Company's supercargoes were on good terms with the Canton magistrates, and as the Company seemed to rely on them very much, he trusted their cooperation could be assured without extending his complete control over them. He was quite sure that the guard would not arouse distrust, especially as the field pieces were to be left as a gift to the Emperor. The Company must be the judge of the commercial advantages to be obtained, but the government should judge to what extent the wishes of the Company were to be subservient to political considerations. He felt that as this was the first British Embassy to China a good appearance must be made and that the Company should share the major expense, but that in order to maintain proper dignity the government should provide a few things, such as the King's picture, the canopy, and the plate.[27]

Throughout these early proceedings Macartney relied heavily upon the opinions and information supplied him by Richardson, Mackintosh, and George Rose (of the Treasury), and the presence of the latter and of Pitt in the discussions suggests the close connections between the Embassy and the revenue needs of the government. Macartney had grave doubts about the capacities of the Company's supercargoes, and as to the likelihood of their thorough cooperation with him. In consequence he intrigued with Mackintosh to obtain from the India House information which would either verify his view or dispel his doubts. Obviously with Macartney's knowledge, Mackintosh transmitted to Rose on January 24 a list of papers, "which would serve to answer the Chairman's letter." He requested that, in order to prevent the possibility of the detection of the source, Rose should have the list copied before sending it on to the Board of Control, which would demand the papers from the India House.[28]

---

[26] G. T. Staunton, *Memoir of G. L. Staunton,* pp. 48-50, 338-40; CMC, No. 72.

[27] CMC, No. 44; IOCM, XCI, 75-78.

[28] IOCM, XCI, 79-83. Among the papers demanded were the following: (1) "Copies of all paragraphs in Complaint contained in the Directors Letters to their Supercargoes for 10 or 12 years back" (already transmitted to Macartney through Richardson and Cobb). (2) "The examination of any supercargoes at the India House by Court or Committees relative to China."

On the same day Richardson, in transmitting various bits of information to Macartney, pointed out than Chinchew, a port to the north which had a good harbor, had once been open to trade.[29] On January 25 Macartney wrote to Baring commenting upon the presents selected for the Cathcart Embassy. Certain of the mathematical and mechanical articles would be suitable if repaired so as to appear quite new. The guns, pistols, pocket books, and opera glasses would be more suitable if mounted and ornamented with silver. All clocks should be new and undamaged, and the amount of yellow articles should be increased.[30]

On January 26 Richardson directed a very interesting letter to Rose. He was of the decided opinion that Macartney should be given control over the Company's servants in China and over any new factories which might be opened in Japan. He proposed that Macartney, with a respectable council, should be made superintendent and director of all British affairs in Asia. Under such able direction the trade of Great Britain and the Company with Asia could be greatly extended, especially if the Company would abolish the practice of "hereditary bottoms," which made its shipping very expensive and inefficient. He believed that Macartney should have a salary equal to that of the Governor-General of Bengal (£25,000) in order to ensure his prestige.[31]

On January 27 Macartney and Baring discussed the questions of presents and salaries. The Ambassador was given permission to proceed with the preparation of the presents, but no agreement was reached on salaries. Macartney believed that his salary should be £16,000 a year, the amount which he had received as Governor of Madras. His original idea also provided that the Secretary should receive £4,000, other attendants, musicians, and servants £3,500, and the guard £1,200; presents would cost £10,000, table expense £8,000, and contingents £300; hence the total cost for the first year would be £43,000. For the next two years, as no presents would be necessary, the expense of the establishment would be but £33,000 per annum. Baring considered this expense too great, especially the salary of the Ambassador, which would become a precedent for future missions. Macartney was especially sensitive upon the matter, feeling that his

[29] CMC, No. 49.
[30] CMC, Nos. 43, 44, 48, 53.
[31] CMC, No. 54.

personal prestige would suffer if he went beyond the Cape for less than he had once received.[32]

In a letter of January 28, Macartney dwelt upon the great advantages to the country and the Company which would probably flow from the Embassy, and hoped therefore that the Chairs would, upon a reconsideration of the tableau, see no reason for any material alterations. He also indicated his intention of taking along as presents some new and ingenious discoveries, such as a model steam engine, a spinning jenny, Smeeton's pullies, balloons, Bromah's patent locks, a rolling and printing press, and a set of globes. In commenting upon the Canton supercargoes, he said, "it is possible that more effectual measures may be contrived by the Court of Directors to ensure such co-operation or obedience as may be found necessary for their Servants in China, than any that I could presume to propose." [33] Biting sarcasm! Macartney was well informed on all subjects pertaining to the expedition and to the Company's affairs in China, and he knew it. He objected to interference in his plans, although always in a dignified way, and he generally obtained his desires.

Although Grenville, the Foreign Secretary, had refused to write a letter of introduction for Sir George Staunton to Sir William Hamilton, Ambassador at Naples, he had sent to Dundas a letter from Dr. Ewart (physician in the Cathcart Embassy), requesting appointment as Secretary to the Embassy. Dundas transmitted this to Macartney, remarking that "a Secretary in my opinion is no more a subject of recommendation than a Wife," but that Ewart might be of use in some other part of the arrangement.[34] Macartney's reply on January 31 was very pointed, and stated that with Dundas' knowledge he had appointed Staunton as Secretary of the Embassy; that many people had already applied for positions but that he had refused them, because there were many capable men who had been faithful to him, and to whom he was especially obligated because he had never had favor enough with the government to get even the smallest favor for any of them; that it had already been settled that he was to have complete freedom in choosing the personnel of the Embassy, but that if Dundas wished he would of course depart from this last principle.[35] After this Macartney was left entirely to himself in choosing the personnel of the mission.

---

[32] CMC, Nos. 50, 56, 61, 64, 437.
[33] IOCM, XCI, 87-92.
[34] CMC, Nos. 58, 59, 55, 56.
[35] IOCM, XCI, 93-96.

Proceedings were delayed by the opening of Parliament, but on February 7 Sir Erasmus Gower's appointment as commander of the man-of-war which was to carry the Embassy seems to have been arranged.[36] On the same day Baring conferred with Dundas about a proposal to appoint a new committee to reorganize the Company's affairs at Canton and to announce and cooperate with the Embassy. On the evening of the same day he called on Macartney and discussed at great length the question of the salary of the Ambassador and his Secretary.[37] On the day following, after a conference with the Chairman, Baring informed Macartney that the Chairs were under the necessity of setting a precedent in the matter of salaries to be paid Ambassadors. Under these circumstances it was necessary for him to "express a doubt whether the Sum of £10,000 per annum for yourself, and £2,000 to the Secretary, can be justified, if it shall be exceeded." [38]

On February 8 Dundas, Rose, and Macartney had a meeting, at which they were able to consider a proposal transmitted by Richardson to Macartney, for the appointment of a "Special Commission" at Canton. The proposal explained that complaints relative to the conduct of the Company's affairs in China had arisen which, although exaggerated, left no doubt as to the necessity of reform. A particular abuse was the practice of allowing supercargoes to act as commission agents for private individuals, because it caused them to neglect the Company's business and enabled them to amass large private fortunes and so to retire at the time when they were becoming most useful to the Company. In view of these facts it was proposed:[39]

(1) To abolish all private commissions under heavy penalty, and in their place to substitute a house of trade composed of two or three servants below the Council, who should do business for private individuals and charge a commission of 3 per cent on merchandise and 1 per cent on gold and silver to be divided among the supercargoes after a small amount had been deducted for themselves;

(2) To exercise every power vested in the Company to prevent private English from residing permanently at Canton;

(3) To reduce the size of the Select Committee at Canton from six to three persons;

---

[36] CMC, Nos. 65, 68, 71.
[37] CMC, No. 72.
[38] IOCM, XCI, 97-99.
[39] CMC, Nos. 76, 70, 73.

(4) To appoint a special commission of three to carry out this reorganization, to investigate generally the condition of trade and of the Company's servants, and to "promote other material considerations" [that is, the Embassy]; the head of this commission was also to be the new chairman of the Select Committee.

By this procedure the Chairs hoped to achieve an improvement in the management of their China affairs, satisfy Lord Macartney that the supercargoes would cooperate with the Embassy, and avoid the establishment of a British Consulate at Canton. On February 10 the Chairs officially informed Dundas of the proposal which was then before the Court. They denied a desire to enter into a controversy with Lord Macartney, inasmuch as they had confidence in his zeal, integrity, ability, and desire to make the Embassy a success, and although they agreed with him that their Canton administration needed to be reformed they did not favor the establishment of a Consulate at Canton. They left to the Ministers the decision as to how large the retinue should be and as to whether or not it would be advisable to take along the guard. They approved of the presents which Macartney had ordered.[40]

Among the various papers for February 9 there is a notation by E[rasmus] G[ower] which points out that because of the character of the monsoons in the China Seas there would be no advantage in sailing before July. Macartney and Dundas met on February 14, and presumably at this meeting the decision was taken to postpone the sailing of the Embassy until about August 1. The delay in procuring an interpreter and the advisability of having the proposed commissioners announce the Embassy and receive the Emperor's decision upon it before the Embassy reached China were additional reasons to those given by Gower for postponing its date of departure. By sailing on August 1, the Embassy would probably reach Pulo Condore, off the coast of Cochin China, by March 1, 1793, and there it could wait until the Emperor's permission to proceed to Peking had been received.[41]

3. *The Appointment of a Secret and Superintending Committee to Reform the Canton Establishment (February 14-May 5, 1792).*

With the exception of the question of the Ambassador's salary, the controversies between Macartney and the Chairs had now been settled. The latter had acquiesced in most points, but the matter of re-

---

[40] IOCM, XCI, 104-14; CMC, Nos. 78, 79, 81.
[41] CMC, Nos. 326-28, 387, 82; IOCM, XCI, 101.

form in and control over the Canton establishment had been compromised by the proposal to send out special commissioners. Macartney was at first cautious about accepting without reserve the proposal of the Chairs. On February 15 he wrote to Dundas asking that consideration of the proposal by the Court be postponed until Wednesday next (February 22) to give more time for examination.[42]

In the meantime, Dr. Ewart thrust himself into the picture again by proposing to Dundas on February 20 that he be sent to Canton to make arrangements for the arrival of the Embassy and by preparing, at Dundas' suggestion, a paper called "Facts and Considerations relative to the proposed Embassy to China." The paper, a copy of which was sent to Macartney, was a rather well-written piece of work which concluded from the experience of other missions that the Embassy could not go to Tientsin, but would have to disembark at Canton, and that it would be necessary to perform the *kotow*, which was really not a mark of submission.[43] In commenting on the paper, Macartney was very sarcastic, saying that there was nothing in it which could not be found in published books and which he had not already called to Dundas' attention, and that the man must think the Ambassador a novice who would find his ideas of some use. He then proceeded to comment on and criticize every paragraph of the paper and concluded by saying that the man whom the Court of Directors planned to send to Canton, because of his previous experience in China, would be far more competent than Ewart.[44]

The proposal to appoint special Commissioners was ultimately adopted by the Court of Directors, but not without opposition. Eight of the twenty-four directors handed in a written protest, which complained that the plan adopted was only a half measure. It objected to the establishment of a house of trade, to the appointment of a smaller Select Committee (under a man who had been implicated in former abuses) instead of a complete reorganization of the whole scheme, and to the appointment of a Superintending Committee, which instead of decreasing expenses only increased them.[45]

Macartney's doubts apparently vanished after consultation with Henry Browne, the man proposed as head both of the reduced Select Committee and of the Secret and Superintending Committee. The lat-

[42] IOCM, XCI, 121.
[43] *Ibid.*, XCI, 115-18, 133, 137-50, 151-54.
[44] *Ibid.*, XCI, 155-63.
[45] CMC, Nos. 99, 100.

ter, in its superintending capacity, was to carry out the reform and, in its secret capacity, was to make preparations for the Embassy. Browne had been President of the Select Committee at Canton from the spring of 1786 until January, 1789. Major Shaw described him as a very absent-minded but well-meaning man,[46] but Macartney seems to have been impressed by his appearance and assurances. Eyles Irwin and William Jackson (apparently from India) were the other two members of the Secret and Superintending Committee. They were each to receive a salary of £5,000 per year, and Browne was to receive £2,000 in cash plus ⅓ per cent commission on the Company's trade. Whether Dundas ever urged the name of Ewart as one of the Commissioners is not evident, but if so it is quite certain that both the Chairs and Macartney opposed it.[47]

The Chairs sent instructions to the Select Committee in China, dated March 15, 1792, informing them of the reduction in the size of the Committee, the appointment of the Secret and Superintending Committee, the abolition of private commissions, and the establishment of the house of trade. All the supercargoes were to be assembled once a fortnight to consider the proceedings of the Select Committee, and the supercargoes were ordered to cooperate in every way with the new Commissioners. The reduced Select Committee was to consist of Henry Browne, President, John Harrison, George Cuming, and Hugh Parkin; upon Browne's return home or possible death, Parkin was to become President.[48]

As might be expected, Macartney received a number of letters from various persons, including the Duke of Leeds and Mrs. Crewe, recommending either a brother-in-law, an unfortunate and misunderstood friend, or a capable and worthy individual, for appointment in the Embassy.[49] Incidentally, on March 7 he received an amusing unsigned request from a physician saying that:

A Gentleman in whom ardent curiosity has overpowered the strict Rules of Decorum and Propriety begs leave to offer his Service to Lord Macartney to attend him on his proposed Embassy to China . . . [But on March 14] Sudden and violent Indisposition has prevented his waiting on Lord Macartney to hear his pleasure. Reflection in a sick bed has helped to cool the excitement of a hot-headed young man, who fully perceives the impro-

---

[46] *Shaw's Journal*, pp. 244-45; Morse, *Chronicle*, II, 110, 151.
[47] CMD, XII, March 15, 1792; CMC, Nos. 91, 92.
[48] CMD, XII, March 15, 1792.
[49] CMC, Nos. 62, 75, 89.

priety of his conduct and . . . he humbly and respectfully asks pardon— Etranger Inconnu.[50]

By February 19 Captain Gower had selected the *Lion*, a frigate of sixty-four guns, to convey the Embassy, and on March 7 Dundas ordered her prepared for foreign service. Dundas and Macartney met on March 11 and discussed various matters relating to the new Commissioners. Dundas also approved Macartney's desire that the *Hindostan* (Captain William Mackintosh) should attend the Embassy to carry presents. Immediately after this conversation with Dundas, Macartney set about the preparation of a draft of the political instructions to the Commissioners. It was completed by March 17, the day on which it was mailed to Dundas together with a "Sketch of the Letter from the Directors to the Viceroy." [51]

The instructions to the Commissioners directed them to announce to the principal magistrates at Canton that the King of Great Britain, being very sorry that a deputation had not been sent to congratulate the Emperor upon his eightieth birthday,[52]

and being desirous of cultivating the friendship of the Emperor of China, and of improving the connexion, intercourse, and good correspondence between the Courts of London and Pekin, and of encreasing and extending the Commerce between their respective Subjects, had resolved to send his welbeloved Cousin and Counsellor the Right Honorable George Lord Macartney, Baron of Lissanoure, . . . as His Embassador extraordinary and plenipotentiary, to the Emperor of China, to represent his Person and to express in the strongest terms . . . his earnest wishes to promote the advantage and interest of the two Nations of Great Britain and China, and to establish a perpetual harmony and alliance between them.

The Commissioners were to add that the Ambassador was bringing many costly and delicate presents which might be injured by a long overland trip and that consequently he would proceed directly to Tientsin. The Canton officials were to be asked to report this information to Peking.

After this had been done, the Commissioners were to write an account of their reception by the Viceroy and of everything interesting to the Ambassador or to the Company's affairs, and dispatch the same to Macartney by every conveyance likely to meet him at Batavia, Angier Point, or elsewhere. The draft letter to the Viceroy, after

---

[50] CMC, Nos. 87, 90.
[51] IOCM, XCI, 129; CMC, Nos. 88, 91, 92, 94, 152.
[52] IOCM, XCI, 167-68.

offering greeting to him and giving in detail the titles of the King, continued in words identical with those used in the instructions to the Commissioners quoted above. It concluded with a request that the Viceroy transmit this information to the Emperor, trusting that he would issue orders for the proper reception of the Ambassador and ship when they arrived at Tientsin or on the neighbouring coast.[53]

Macartney and Baring met on the same day, March 17, and Baring was given a copy of the proposed letter and instructions. They also discussed the salaries to be allowed to certain of the retinue, and certain additional presents which were to be prepared. The Ambassador was requested to procure sundry presents and an estimate of the cost of three carriages which he wished to take along, two for the Emperor and one for himself. After this meeting further consideration of the tableau was discontinued until after the Commissioners sailed.[54]

The first draft of the Chairs' political instructions to the Commissioners was completed by the end of the first week in April and was transmitted to Dundas for his perusal. They incorporated Macartney's draft of instructions and added more information about the aims of the Embassy and about what the Commissioners were to do to help it. Dundas returned them, expressing a fear that they contained too much information.[55] On April 11 Baring sent a copy of the proposed draft to Macartney indicating Dundas' doubts. He also informed Macartney that the commercial instructions had been approved by Dundas and the Court. The following day Baring asked Dundas to consider how the political instructions should be altered.[56]

On April 13 Macartney returned the draft to Baring with a few "trifling alterations and additions." He saw no reason for not conveying Cathcart's instructions to the Commissioners, nor did he think there would be anything in his which the Commissioners might not know. He also thought it advisable that a cypher be given to the Commissioners and to the Ambassador to be used when necessary. On the 14th Macartney's remarks were sent to Dundas, and in the end Macartney and Baring had their way. Cathcart's instructions were given to the Commissioners, and the only alterations adopted were those suggested

---

[53] IOCM, XCI, 171-72.
[54] CMC, No. 92; IOCM, XCIII, "List of Papers," entries following Feb. 14, 1792.
[55] IOCM, XCI, 197-99; CMC, No. 106.
[56] CMC, No. 108; IOCM, XCI, 217-20.

by Macartney and a few circumlocutions in phraseology to satisfy Dundas.[57]

The final instructions to the Commissioners were approved by Dundas on April 24 and were dated and marked secret on the 25th. In addition to the instructions proposed by Macartney and already quoted, the Commissioners' attention was called to the accompanying letter from the Chairman to the Viceroy, which they could deliver or not as they deemed the more expedient. To avoid apprehension, they were to impress on the minds of the Chinese that the main object of the Embassy was to pay a compliment to the Emperor. The instructions then explained that its real objects were to obtain commercial privileges and remedy abuses. The Commissioners were told that remonstrances against trifling abuses might frustrate the endeavors of the Ambassador, that they were to be especially cautious in order not to offend the Chinese, and that it was especially important to secure a gracious reception for the Embassy.[58]

The instructions indicated that the mission hoped to obtain an establishment to the northward nearer to the tea-producing and woollens-consuming area, and that a competition between the two ports would lead to an abolition of the abuses at Canton and a breaking of the power of the Co-hong, and so make it unnecessary for the Ambassador to remonstrate directly against them. If the establishment was obtained, two old and experienced servants with some of the younger men were to be sent to manage it under such regulations as the Commissioners saw fit to establish. They were to cooperate in every way with the Ambassador, conform to his advice and requisitions, and transmit to him detailed information about the movements, cargoes, size, and so forth, of all ships at Canton, whether Chinese or foreign, and all other information about the trade between China and the outer world which they could obtain.

On Wednesday, April 11, at the meeting of the Court of Directors, Francis Baring was promoted to Chairman and John Smith Burges became Deputy Chairman. On the 19th Macartney met Baring for a little while and signified his wish that the Chairman's letter to the Viceroy be in Latin as well as in English.[59] The translation of the letter into Latin caused some delay, but it was completed on April 27. The letter

---

[57] IOCM, XCI, 201-16, 221-35.
[58] WSCPMD, No. 26; CMC, No. 117.
[59] IOCM, XCI, 197-99, 217-20, 233-35; CMC, Nos. 108, 109, 117.

was identical with Macartney's original draft described above.[60] On the 24th Macartney and the Chairs had final conferences with the Commissioners relative to their duties and functions, and on the 28th a large packet was delivered to Henry Browne. Besides many documents relating to the Embassy and to the Company's trade with China, it contained a special letter to Browne, Irwin, and Jackson in their capacity as Superintending Committee, dated April 11.[61]

It commanded them to inquire into the conduct of the Company's business and to instigate reforms directed toward economy and efficiency. They were to inquire into the advisability of having a large surplus of cash in the Company's treasury and the practice of issuing transfers in the treasury, and the desirability of decreasing remittances from India. They were to endeavor gradually to decrease the rate of exchange, and the abusive practice of private commission was to be abolished. They were to endeavor to increase the quality and decrease the price of articles purchased in China, and were to examine thoroughly the possibilities of increasing English exports to China. They were to reform the factory, reduce its expenses, and abolish as many minor abuses and charges as they could. They were to obtain as much information about the growth and production of tea, silk, and nankeens as possible, and in order that they might have ample power to carry out these duties, any two of the Committee were empowered to reprimand, suspend, or dismiss any servant below the Council. The *Thetis*, with the Commissioners on board, sailed on May 5, 1792.

4. *Detailed Preparations for the Embassy and the Promotion of Macartney to the Rank of Viscount (March 17-June 28, 1792).*

Once the Commissioners were on their way, it was possible to return to the interrupted preparations for the Embassy proper. Macartney's ideas as to whom he was to take with him on the Embassy had matured early. Every person was to be a capable, deserving, intelligent individual to whom Macartney was in some way indebted, and on whose complete cooperation and personal devotion the Ambassador could depend. It is practically certain that by March 17 the personnel of the Embassy was complete. Sir George Leonard Staunton, an old and trusted friend, was to be Secretary. Acheson Maxwell, who had

---

[60] IOCM, XCI, 333-36; CMC, No. 115.
[61] CMD, XII, April 11, 1792; IOCM, XCIII, "List of Papers," April 24-28, 1792; WSCPMD, No. 31.

been Macartney's private secretary in India, and Edward Winder, a distant relative of Macartney, were to be the two Under-secretaries, with salaries of £500 each. John Barrow, an ambitious jack-of-all-trades who considered himself something of a mathematician and scientist, and who owed his appointment to Staunton's patronage, was to be Comptroller, with a salary of £200.[62]

Dr. William Scott, a former naval surgeon, was to attend as surgeon and receive £200. Dr. Hugh Gillan, "a good scholar, a physician, [a chemist], and moreover, a Scotch Metaphysician," was to attend as physician and scientist. Dr. James Dinwiddi, "a Scotch Philosopher" and experimentalist in electricity and balloon flying, was to go along as "Machinist" with a salary of £200. Thomas Hickey was to attend as painter and William Alexander as draughtsman. The interpreters were to receive £150 each. Sir Erasmus Gower was to command the *Lion* and have freedom in choosing his under-officers, and Captain William Mackintosh was to command the Company's ship *Hindostan*. Major Benson, "a smart, correct, and active officer," was to attend as commander of the guard. Lieutenant Henry Parish was to command the artillery detachment. In the appointment of Lieutenant John Crewe, Macartney allowed sentimentality toward his favorite, Mrs. Crewe, "the celebrated wit and beauty of her day," to overcome his judgment. Her son was taken along after giving a solemn pledge that he would touch neither "cards or dice, or other instruments of gambling." It appears that he violated this pledge, spent his time in gambling, and left a debt of some thousands of pounds unpaid.[63]

Macartney had chosen Major Benson to command the guard and had promised him promotion to the rank of Lieutenant Colonel. The War Office, however, declined to advance him by brevet, nor would it advance him to a vacancy in violation of the time-honored practice of promotion by seniority, and other proposed expedients failed. After several unsuccessful talks with the War Office and because of a lack of energy in the matter on the part of Dundas, Macartney became very much annoyed.[64] Finally, on June 4 he wrote to Dundas telling him to mention to "The King" that in the original formation of the

[62] CMC, Nos. 92, 442, 437; IOCM, XCIII, "List of Papers," entries following Feb. 14, 1792; Helen M. Robbins, *Our First Ambassador to China* (London, 1908), pp. 184, 203; G. L. Staunton, *Embassy*, I, 32-38; *Auto-biographical Memoir of Sir John Barrow* (London, 1848).
[63] Robbins, *op. cit.*, pp. 178, 181, 184, 203; *Biographical Memoir of Sir Erasmus Gower* (London, 1800-10) ; and as in note 62.
[64] IOCM, XCI, 125, 173-90, 193-94; CMC, Nos. 114, 118.

Embassy it had been deemed necessary to have a guard commanded by Major Benson, who was to have the rank of Lieutenant Colonel to add dignity to the mission. "The point is for Mr. Dundas to obtain his Majesty's Consent to give Major Benson the Brevet rank of Lt. Colonel and to announce his Majesty's pleasure upon it to the Secretary of War as a *matter done."* [65] This produced results; Dundas came to life; "His Majesty" showed solicitude for the Embassy; the War Office overcame its scruples, and Major Benson became a Lieutenant Colonel.

On May 2 Macartney attended the Court of St. James in order that he might have the honor of being presented to kiss His Majesty's Hand, and on the 3rd he was officially appointed "Embassador Extraordinary and Plenipotentiary from the King of Great Britain to the Emperor of China." On the same day he was sworn a Privy Councillor in order to give him added prestige in the eyes of the Chinese, as well as to satisfy his own desires. Staunton was to be "Secretary to the Embassy and Minister Plenipotentiary in the absence of the Embassador," with the expressed power of carrying on the Embassy in case of the death or incapacity of the Ambassador. [66]

While all of the preparatory events had been taking place in London, Staunton was busily engaged upon the Continent in search of interpreters. His inquiries in Paris were fruitless, but he obtained information about the College for Chinese maintained at Naples by the society *De Propaganda Fide.* He crossed the Alps in the dead of winter and reached Rome, where he obtained from Cardinal Antonelli, of the *Propaganda,* letters of introduction to the Italian missionaries at Peking, as well as to the Curator of the Chinese College at Naples. In the meantime, Sir William Hamilton, Ambassador at Naples, had been informed, and it was settled before Staunton arrived that two young Chinese, Paolo Cho and Jacob Ly, who had completed their training for the priesthood, should go with Staunton to England. Hamilton wrote to Macartney on April 3 telling him of the arrangement. The men were, according to Staunton, "qualified to interpret between their own language and the Italian or Latin." Staunton was back in England with the interpreters before May 18. [67]

[65] IOCM, XCI, 253; CMC, Nos. 131, 132.
[66] CMC, No. 118; Robbins, *op. cit.,* pp. 178-79; Morse, *Chronicle,* II, 216; Barrow, *Macartney,* I, 347.
[67] CMC, Nos. 107, 442; IOCM, XCIII, "List of Papers," May 18, 1792; G. T. Staunton, *Memoir of G. L. Staunton,* pp. 48-50, 341-2; Barrow, *Macartney,* I, 345-46; Staunton, *Embassy,* I, 38-41; Robbins, *op. cit.,* pp. 175-76.

As early as March 11 Macartney obtained Dundas' approval of his plan to have the *Hindostan* accompany the Embassy. Toward the end of May he went to Portsmouth to inspect the *Lion,* which had been commissioned about May 1. After returning, he wrote to Dundas on the 29th, saying that the man-of-war was very satisfactory, but that it would be necessary to have one of the Company's largest ships to carry the presents and part of the suite. He recommended the *Hindostan,* commanded by Captain Mackintosh, because she was large and fast. He doubted not that the Court would cooperate if Dundas recommended the measure.[68] On June 10, at a conference between Dundas and Macartney, the former agreed that the *Hindostan* should attend the Embassy, and on the next day he wrote to Baring recommending the measure. The Court immediately prepared the ship for the desired service.[69]

Other preparations for the Embassy and the selection of the presents were being pushed along by Macartney, because he had to go to Ireland about the middle of June. After the arrival of the two Chinese, they were able to give helpful suggestions regarding the presents. Dr. Dinwiddi was employed from the first of May in preparing various of the mechanical devices and arranging for the electrical and scientific experiments which he meant to perform. On June 10 he requested Macartney to purchase an air pump, and mentioned other devices on which he was working, such as fireworks, a foundry, a planetarium, and curious watches. Among other curious and interesting things which the Ambassador intended to take along to amuse and impress the Chinese were celestial and terrestial globes, a fire engine, various works in steel, Irish globes, "optical deceptions," a telescope, a rolling chair, and a balloon.[70]

On June 11 Macartney informed Major Benson of the latter's promotion to Lieutenant Colonel by brevet. The guard was to consist of twenty light infantrymen, ten dismounted light dragoons, and twenty gunners from the Royal Artillery. As Macartney was to leave London soon, he wished Benson to complete the arrangements for the guard. On June 28 it was arranged that Benson should resign his position in the 60th regiment and attend the Embassy on Major's pay, his promotion to take place from the time of embarkation. On the same

---

[68] CMC, Nos. 88, 91, 92, 113, 118, 120.
[69] CMC, Nos. 131, 133; IOCM, XCI, 281-83 and XCIII, "List of Papers," June 13, 1792.
[70] CMC, Nos. 127, 128, 129, 136, 442.

day Macartney asked Dundas to request of the Board of Ordnance two light three-pounders, four one-pounders, and two howitzers for the use of the guard. These pieces were ultimately to be given to the Emperor as presents.[71]

Macartney determined to have two things in consequence of his undertaking the Embassy. First, he insisted upon a salary equal or nearly equal to his former stipend as Governor of Madras. Second, he demanded a promotion in rank both from personal desire and from a belief that added titles would give him prestige in the eyes of the Chinese. He was a Baron in the Irish nobility, and he wished to be given an Irish Earldom, although what he really wanted most was an English Peerage. Baring and Macartney thrashed out the problem of salary at various times. The Chairs recognized Macartney's claim to a good salary, but were determined not to set so expensive a precedent. Macartney insisted that he either receive £16,000 per annum or £12,000 as Ambassador and £10,000 as a gift in recognition of his services. He promised to abide by any decision which Dundas should make upon the subject. On May 30 the Chairs wrote to Dundas suggesting that Macartney might be satisfied with a salary of £10,000 and a present of £5,000.[72]

On June 4 Macartney wrote to Dundas about the Peerage and about his salary. He urged that the present mission demanded no less work or talents than were required of a Governor of Madras, and pointed out that even £16,000 did not represent the proportional difference between the pay received by the Company's supercargoes and the Ambassador which their rank indicated. He further urged that his wage need not set a precedent, because the first Embassy must naturally be the most expensive. In support of his claims to an Irish Earldom he urged his long and faithful service which had in no way been rewarded by increase in rank, and insisted that it would facilitate the work of the Embassy and that in the present case the Earldom would be more of an honor to His Majesty's first Ambassador to China than a grant to a private individual. Finally, he urged that as he had no children it would be only a temporary supercession to other claimants.[73]

On June 10 Macartney "waited upon Mr. Dundas at Somerset Place . . . and in his usual frank and Gentleman like manner he entered upon business immediately." Macartney was promised a salary of

[71] CMC, Nos. 132, 138, 145, 146.
[72] IOCM, XCI, 237-44.
[73] IOCM, XCI, 245-74.

£10,000 a year as Ambassador and an additional allowance of £5,000 per annum in recognition of his former services. He was also to receive plate, canopy, picture, and equipage from the Crown as did other Ambassadors. It was impossible in the first instance to make him an Earl, but he was to be at once made a Viscount and promoted to an Earldom as soon as one was made. The Chairs acquiesced in the decision about the salary and agreed that the allowance for the civil suite below the Ambassador and the Secretary should be £3,500. On June 28 Macartney became Viscount Macartney of Derrock, in the county of Antrim (Ireland).[74]

5. *The Northern Industrialists, the Private Creditors, and the Designs of Russia and Sweden (June 9-August 15, 1792).*

With these delicate matters settled, the preparations for the Embassy entered upon their final stage, and a new project was embarked upon which showed the close connection between the Embassy and the new industrial interests in the North. On June 23 Macartney wrote to Lord Hawkesbury, one of the Lords of Trade, stating that the Company wished to send out with the Embassy a small assortment of articles from the principal manufacturing cities of England, to be distributed among the chief merchants and persons at Peking, who might be likely to establish a taste for them. In replying on the 25th, Lord Hawkesbury gladly offered his services and requested that the Chairs and Lord Macartney meet him and persons of his staff to discuss the matter further.[75]

Several meetings were held, but it is evident that the Chairs did not agree with the Lords of Trade as to the extent and the type of articles to be sent out. It would appear that they did not favor collecting articles from the northern industrial districts. Finally, however, an agreement was reached and on July 19 a circular letter was sent to Mathew Boulton and Samuel Garbett of Birmingham and to individuals in other industrial towns. It requested them to make a collection of the principal specimens of the manufactures of Birmingham, Manchester, and surrounding towns, to be taken by the Ambassador with the aim of contributing to their sale in China. To each article was to

---

[74] CMC, Nos. 131, 144, 442; IOCM, XCI, 277-78, 281-83 and XCIII, "List of Papers," June 18, 1792; Robbins, *op. cit.,* p. 179; Barrow, *Macartney,* I, 347.
[75] CMC, Nos. 141-42.

be attached the price at which it could be sold in China, and the Company would pay the expenses of making the collection.[76]

These hustling industrialists immediately set to work to make an extensive collection. Garbett wrote on July 21 suggesting a large assortment of low-priced articles, and on the 25th Boulton indicated that a complete collection of Birmingham patterns would cost at least £1,000. Boulton, at Macartney's request, also tried to find a person qualified to manage the patterns to the best advantage in China. These ambitious schemes dismayed the Chairs, who at once sent back information that not over £150 was to be spent on the collection. Garbett was furious and insisted that unless specimens to the value of £3,000 were allowed he would not countenance the transaction. He did not wish the Company to pay a shilling, but merely requested permission for the manufacturers to send out the collection on their own account.[77]

Macartney finally persuaded the Chairs to increase the amount allowed to £400, but they refused to allow the manufacturers to send out goods on their own account. On July 30 he wrote to Boulton and Garbett stating that in addition to the £400 to be allowed, he had already procured some of Gill's sword blades and had ordered firearms from Birmingham. He also indicated that he had secured a satisfactory metallurgist. On June 26 the Mayor of Exeter had also written about supplying specimens, and early in August a Mr. Bristow wrote to Pitt requesting permission to send out some pattern boats made in the Chinese taste. Garbett, in several letters to Macartney, openly expressed his disgust at the Company's attitude.[78]

Boulton was more quiet about his disappointment and collected a small assortment of Birmingham hardware valued at £320, which he sent to the India House on August 1. On the 15th the correspondence was closed by a letter from Garbett wishing the Embassy success in order that it might lay the ground for a national extension of British manufactures to the East, which he believed could be done only by establishing depots free from the Company's control where all British traders might go. So ended the first attempt of the industrial cities of northern England to make an impression on the East. Hardware and sword blades to the value of £646 were sent from Birmingham, hardware valued at £125 was sent by Sheffield, and articles were also

---

[76] CMC, Nos. 151, 154; IOCM, XCIII, "List of Papers," June 19, 1792.
[77] CMC, Nos. 150, 154.
[78] CMC, Nos. 154, 159, 160, 162, 163, 164, 167, 168; IOCM, XCIII, "List of Papers," July 26, 1792.

sent from Leeds, Exeter, Norwich, Coventry, Gloucestershire (cloth), Wiltshire (cloth), Paisley, Manchester (cottons), and Trome.[79]

While this "strange interlude" with the northern industrialists was taking place, another set of interests, the creditors of Chinese merchants, were again making their voices heard in London. As early as May 28 Vansittart and Law had directed a long memorial to Pitt and Dundas requesting the government's aid in the collection of the debts. They called special attention to the debts of Coqua, who, it was reported, was now living in luxury. They ultimately had meetings with the Ministers and requested the Ambassador's assistance in obtaining redress. To the Company's objection that the debts had been contracted contrary to Chinese law, the creditors maintained that at the time they had not known this to be true, and that the Company also allowed opium to be sold in India to be imported into China contrary to Chinese law.[80]

Dundas laid the matter before the Chairs early in July, and, after some consideration, they returned a long account of all the proceedings relative to the debts and requested the Ministers to forbear mentioning the debts in their instructions to the Ambassador. This virtually ended the matter so far as the Ministers and the Ambassador were concerned. On August 2 George Smith suggested that the Ambassador might bring the matter before the Emperor after the other negotiations had been completed, and requested permission to accompany the Ambassador at his own expense. This request was refused, and a supplementary instruction to Macartney told him not to press for the debts, but to obtain all the information about them and the Emperor's attitude toward them which he could, and to determine how much interposition could be used for their recovery without injuring the Company.[81]

Early in April Macartney had learned of a Japanese who had been brought to Russia, and whom he hoped to get and take along as an interpreter. After some delay a special messenger was dispatched with a letter to Charles Whitworth, Ambassador to Russia, desiring him to obtain the Japanese if possible. Whitworth's reply, received in London on June 9, explained that he had already (in October, 1791) sent information about the Japanese which had apparently been intercepted. The person in question was master of a Japanese merchant vessel wrecked off the shores of Siberia. He had been brought to St. Peters-

[79] CMC, Nos. 168, 182, 184, 225; IOCM, XCI, 534-80.
[80] IOCM, XCI, 293-313, 315-16.
[81] IOCM, XCI, 319-22, 285; Morse, *Chronicle*, II, 243.

burg in May, 1791, by a Professor Lachsmann, who was director of mines in Siberia and who had been employed for several years by the government in reconnoitering the border of China, the Russian Island, and Kamchatka, and in drawing up memoirs and plans of operations. The Japanese had been guarded very closely, and after about five months had returned to Irkutsk with the professor.[82]

Through his secret agents, Whitworth had been able to collect a good deal of information about Russian plans in Siberia and eastern Asia. Professor Lachsmann's son had been commissioned *chargé d'affaires* to Japan, with instructions to return the Japanese to his native land and, if possible, to obtain permission to proceed to the Imperial Court. The Russian policy was to gather all possible intelligence, military and commercial, about China and Japan, because they must shortly seize the Amur region and perhaps Japan in order to supply their settlements in Kamchatka and encourage the fur trade. Arrangements had already been made with Spain to receive supplies from her settlements in Asia and America. At the time of Russia's recent dispute with China (1789-91), an army had actually been prepared to attack the Amur, but the plan had been given up for the present.[83]

Toward the end of July either the Swedish Ambassador or a secret service agent, having taken affright at the Embassy, sent home a long dispatch in regard to it. The dispatch, dated July 26, expressed the fear that the Embassy aimed at advantages which would entirely ruin Britain's rivals in the China trade. This being the situation, it suggested that an armed vessel be dispatched at once to Canton to inform the mandarins and merchants of the mission and to arouse their suspicion and jealousy in every way. The ulterior motives of the Embassy should be explained, and the mandarins told that it aimed to complain against them and their abuses. By such a procedure the official world would be aroused against the Embassy, its favorable reception interrupted, and its aims frustrated. Whether or not this dispatch reached Sweden is uncertain, but at any rate Sweden made no endeavors to embarrass the Embassy.[84]

During the latter part of July and early part of August several proposals from outside individuals as to how British trade might be expanded in the East were submitted to Macartney. The first of these

---

[82] CMC, Nos. 119, 359.
[83] CMC, Nos. 17, 119, 359.
[84] CMC, No. 235.

was submitted by W. Brereton on July 28. He was interested in promoting the infant colony of New South Wales and suggested that certain ships chartered for China should go first to New South Wales, load with timber, and then proceed to China, where they could be loaded with tea by the Company. The convicts at Port Jackson could be used for cutting down the trees and sawing them into planks. He also thought that a type of sea weed to be found in New Holland, valuable for its use in making ropes, might be introduced into China, and he wanted Macartney to arrange with the Emperor for the establishment of one or two Chinese colonies near Port Jackson.[85]

In replying to this proposal, Macartney pointed out that there was no demand for timber at Canton and that colonization schemes were impractical, because emigration from China was prohibited. Furthermore, he said, the ships which since the season of 1788-89 had followed the route suggested could carry timber if it was thought advisable. Sir Ralph Woodford also submitted a paper, which ultimately reached Macartney, suggesting the possibilities of trade between the Philippine Islands and the British Settlements in the East. Although Macartney pointed out that a free port at Manila would probably facilitate the introduction of British manufactures into Spanish America, the Company apparently did not favor the project.[86]

6. *Final Preparations for the Embassy and the Promise of Dutch Cooperation (July 29-September 26, 1792).*

Macartney wrote his own instructions with the aid of Sir George Staunton, as is shown by a letter to Dundas on July 29, 1792:

I have, as you were pleased to desire me, taken the liberty of putting upon paper the few ideas which have occurred to me in regard to the instructions, on which occasion I have had nothing to add to those you gave to the late Colonel Cathcart, except what the change in circumstances have rendered necessary.[87]

Macartney's draft incorporated the major portion of Cathcart's instructions, but was a much longer document and written in a more polished style. It added a number of introductory remarks about the value of British trade with China, for the sake of which, as well as for the commercial prosperity of the British nation, it was deemed advisable to

[85] CMC, No. 172.

[86] CMC, Nos. 171, 185, 218; IOCM, XCIII, "List of Papers," following date, Aug. 15, 1792; Morse, *Chronicle*, II, 151, 179, 256.

[87] CMC, Nos. 156, 157; G. T. Staunton, *Memoir of G. L. Staunton*, pp. 343-47.

send an Ambassador "to claim the Emperor of China's particular protection." It then called attention to the cultural advantages which
should be gained from a free communication with the oldest civilization in the world.[88]

The draft suggested that the Ambassador proceed directly to Tientsin unless otherwise advised by dispatches from the Commissioners
at Canton. Added emphasis was given to the necessity of endeavoring to
increase the exportation of British manufactures to China. A new paragraph pointed out the expediency of touching upon the coast of Japan
and the possibilities of trade, especially in sugar, with Cochin China.
Furthermore, the Ambassador might find it desirable to touch at various other islands and places in the East where a vend for British
manufactures might be found. Consequently, credentials to the rulers
of these various countries would be sent. Finally, a paragraph was
added indicating that Staunton was to have dormant credentials to be
used if the Ambassador should die or if it should be necessary to leave
someone at Peking or send some person in a public character to Japan,
Cochin China, or other places.

This draft was sent to Dundas for additions and corrections. Most
of his corrections, which were completed before August 22, were of
minor importance. He eliminated, for example, his own former remarks regarding measures for drawing the tea trade out of the hands
of other European nations. Instead of saying that the abuses at Canton should be forcefully represented, he said that they should be
represented if a favorable opportunity arose to present them without
criticizing the officials. He also inserted a line referring to the desirability of getting a second depot for trade, and he cut out a phrase which
Macartney had added referring to the use of opium as "pernicious."
As such, the final instructions stood without essential change from
those given to Cathcart, except for the emphasis given to the promotion
of British manufactures, the provision for visiting Japan, Cochin China,
and other places, the provision for succession in the event of the
Ambassador's death, and the provision for leaving Staunton as a resident minister if necessary.[89]

On July 31 Macartney sent to Dundas a draft of his credentials.
Cathcart's credentials had been used as a basis, but a great deal had

[88] CMC, Nos. 155, 158; IOCM, XCI, 341-74; Morse, *Chronicle*, II, 160-67.
[89] IOCM, XCI, 341-74; IOC, XX, Macartney's draft with Dundas' changes;
CMC, Nos. 155, 158, 194; Morse, *Chronicle*, II, 232-42.

been added and the whole letter was in much more flowery and complimentary language. Several paragraphs were added extolling the virtues
and achievements of the English King. The difficulties which arose between the subjects of the two countries at Canton, which could be
avoided if the English King had a properly authorized person in China
to control his subjects, were pointed out. It was also specifically indicated that the English hoped to maintain a permanent resident at
Peking, Staunton being accredited for this service. This draft was
adopted without change, and on August 18 Macartney sent to Dundas
a draft in Latin. He requested Dundas to make what changes he considered necessary and return it to him so that he could have it put into
Chinese by one of the interpreters. Dundas ultimately returned it
unchanged.[90]

On August 10 Baring sent to Macartney drafts of the covenants and
agreements to be entered into between the Company on the one hand
and Macartney and each member of his suite on the other. Macartney
found them "very proper" except for one or two omissions. After
being approved by Dundas, they were signed on August 29. The
Ambassador and each member of his suite signed separate covenants,
and bond was given for their fulfilment. The musicians and servants
did not enter into covenants, but bonds had to be signed for each of
them. By the covenants each member of the Embassy agreed to the
following provisions: not to carry on any private trade; not to borrow
money from the Chinese, not to lend money to them, nor to have any
commercial dealings with them except to procure food or necessities; to
behave in a civil manner toward natives and to recompense them for
any damages done; and not to take bribes or accept presents except
presents given in an official capacity. Violation of these covenants
gave the Company the right to recover damages in civil suits to
amounts specified in the covenants.[91]

On August 26 Macartney sent to Dundas drafts of his and
Staunton's credentials to the Emperor of Japan and to the King of
Cochin China, and general credentials to all the other Princes of the
East. Staunton's and Macartney's credentials to the Emperor of China
had been contained in the same document, but, because it was likely
that Staunton might be sent to these other places alone, it was deemed

---

[90] CMC, Nos. 161, 175, 176, 330; IOCM, XCI, 325-32; Morse, *Chronicle*, II,
244-47; Bannister, *op. cit.*, pp. 230-38.
[91] CMC, Nos. 177, 179, 190, 197; IOCM, XCIII, "List of Papers," following
date Aug. 15, 1792; WSCPMD, Nos. 9, 10, 11.

advisable to have them separate. They were approved by Dundas without material alteration and were then put into Latin as well as English.[92]

The draft of the Chairs' instructions to Macartney was finished by about August 20, but Macartney and Dundas found several points of objection. The Chairs wanted an understanding that, if a trading depot was ceded to the British, it would be turned over to them to administer, and they were also doubtful about the desirability of obtaining an establishment too near Peking. They had to give in on their first point, inasmuch as both Macartney and Dundas were determined that a government official should be sent out, if such an establishment were obtained, with sufficient power to control all British subjects. On the other point the Chairs had their way. A paragraph in their instructions to Macartney expressed a doubt as to the advisability of an establishment near Peking, since a disorder so near the capital might cause the whole trade to be prohibited.[93]

In order to avoid possible Dutch hostility to the Embassy, Lord Auckland, the Ambassador to Holland, was instructed to offer them assistance at Peking, and to request their assistance in obtaining relief from the grievances from which both Holland and England suffered. On July 3 Auckland wrote to Lord Grenville indicating that the "President and Advocate of the Committee for the China Trade of the Dutch East India Company" had expressed their appreciation of the offer and had promised to give orders to their factories to show Lord Macartney every attention. The Dutch Commissioners also drew up a memorial, which they delivered to Auckland on August 31, expressing at the same time their confidence that the aim of the Embassy was to promote the interests of other nations at Canton in so far as such a procedure was compatible with the interests of Great Britain.[94]

The memorial pointed out that the abuses under which the Dutch suffered were the same as those felt by the English, and requested the Ambassador to make a joint Dutch and English representation of their grievances to the Emperor. They specifically mentioned (1) the exactions and oppressions levied on trade and on the Chinese merchants by the mandarins, (2) the high charges on the passage from Canton to Macao, and (3) the prohibition upon year-round residence at Canton. They also stated that they would send orders to their agents

---

[92] CMC, Nos. 210, 329.
[93] CMC, Nos. 194, 199, 208, 218; IOCM, XCIII, "List of Papers," after date Aug. 15, 1792; WSCPMD, No. 1.
[94] CMC, Nos. 147, 148; BM, *Additional Manuscripts,* No. 34,444, p. 169.

in China and the East to supply Macartney with information and to cooperate with him in every way. The promise of Dutch cooperation suited the English, but the reference to specific grievances to be represented to the Emperor did not fall in line with the Company's or Macartney's views. Their aim was to obtain other more material concessions which would in time lead to the elimination of abuses at Canton, and they intended to use specific complaint only as a last recourse.[95]

Early in August Macartney informed Baring that Sir Erasmus Gower was desirous of securing a tender to accompany the *Lion*. He recommended the *Jackall*, which could be purchased for £1,500. On August 8 the Chairs gave their consent, since the *Jackall* was to be "officered, manned, and victualled" from the *Lion* and would therefore be no extra expense to the Company. The government was to pay the expenses of the *Lion* during the greater part of the voyage, although from the time she sighted Sumatra on the way outward until she lost sight of it on the return journey, the salaries of the officers and men were to be paid by the Company.[96]

The final arrangements for the guard caused considerable correspondence and delay. It would seem that this matter and the disagreement over the Chairs' instructions caused another delay in the sailing of the Embassy, which had once been provisionally set for the middle or the latter part of August. The War Office refused to allow the artillery detachment to move until the question of their pay and maintenance, which was to be provided by the Company, was settled. On August 25 Baring and Dundas indicated that the Company would pay to the guard the highest field allowances given to H.M. troops serving in India; that with regard to provisions they would be treated in the same manner as other troops going to India; that the pay to be allowed by the Company would begin when the ship sighted Sumatra on the outward voyage and end when it quitted Sumatra on the homeward voyage, and the troops would not be left in India unless they so desired. This settled the difficulty and the detachment, to consist of one sergeant, three corporals, one drummer, and fifteen gunners, was given permission to proceed to Portsmouth.[97]

---

[95] IOCM, XCI, 377-99; CMC, Nos. 230-31.
[96] CMC, Nos. 165, 170, 173, 175, 179, 190, 192; IOCM, XCIII, "List of Papers," following July 26, 1792.
[97] CMC, Nos. 152, 183, 186, 192, 195, 196, 200-06, 211.

Because the preparations for the Embassy were proving to be very expensive, the Directors on August 8 extended their note of credit to the Chairs to £30,000. A few days later $20,000 was put on the *Hindostan* for Macartney's use. A number of handsomely decorated firearms, valued at 740 guineas and including a pair of newly invented pistols which shot eight balls in succession, were added to the list of presents early in August. On the 29th Staunton was allowed £960 to cover the expenses of his trip to Italy, but the Chairs hoped to recover some of it from the missionaries at Peking, as expenses pertaining to the interpreters, who were to remain in China. Staunton's salary, because of the Chairs' objection to the £4,000 proposed, was not fixed until a few days before the Embassy sailed. Dundas finally fixed it at £3,000. All preparations being completed, Macartney, on September 4, settled his accounts with the Company, and the Embassy was ready to proceed.[98]

It therefore seems advisable to take a last glance at the tableau and presents. The original cost of the civil suite below the Ambassador and the Secretary suggested by Macartney and agreed to by the Chairs had been £3,500 per annum, which was later raised to £3,700. The total annual cost of the Embassy, less maintenance (which could not be accurately calculated) and the expense of the naval officers and men while they were in Far Eastern waters, was £23,410, as shown below— somewhat less than Macartney's original estimate. Others who attended the Embassy were: Francis Baring's son, John, young George Thomas Staunton, J. C. Hüttner, tutor to young Staunton, two Chinese missionaries, and six servants, making a total suite, exclusive of naval officers, of ninety-five persons.

The whole suite was paid by the Company, not by Macartney, although it would appear that he handled the financial arrangements of those below the Secretary. The Ambassador had absolute control over the suite with full powers to punish. For running expenses, Macartney had $20,000 in cash plus the power of issuing drafts upon the Court of Directors and upon the Select Committee at Canton, who were to place $50,000 at his disposal. The salaries of most of the civil suite began upon the date of embarkation, and the pay which the Company allowed the military and naval suite, as has been noted, began when Sumatra was sighted.[100]

[98] IOCM, XCIII, "List of Papers," Aug. 8, Sept. 4 and 5, 1792; CMC, Nos. 177, 179, 180, 185, 188, 219.
[100] WSCPMD, No. 1; IOCM, XCIII, "List of Papers," about Sept. 4, 1792.

TABLEAU OF THE EMBASSY [99]

Office	Person	Salary
Ambassador	Viscount Macartney	£15,000
Secretary	Sir George Staunton	3,000
Under-secretary	Acheson Maxwell	500
Under-secretary	Edward Winder	500
Interpreter	Paolo Cho	150
Interpreter	Jacob Ly	150
Comptroller	John Barrow	200
Physician	Dr. Hugh Gillan	400
Surgeon	Dr. William Scott	200
Machinist	Dr. James Dinwiddi	200
Painter	Thomas Hickey	200
Draughtsman	William Alexander	100
Artificer	Henry Eades	50
Musicians	Six	360
Servants	Ten	550
1st Courier	James Maclawrin	25
2nd Courier	Aneas Anderson	25
31	Total civil suite	**£21,610**
Lt. Colonel	George Benson	£685
Lieutenant	Henry Parish	182.10
Lieutenant	John Crewe	182.10
Dragoons	Ten	150
Artillery	Twenty	300
Infantry	Twenty	300
53	Total military suite	**£ 1,800. 0**
84	Total annual cost	**£23,410. 0***

*Exclusive of the naval officers, of whom Captain Gower received £500.

The original estimate for presents was £10,000, but this was considerably exceeded, as will be shown below. Great care had been taken in the selection of presents, in order duly to impress and gratify the Chinese. Recent inventions and curious devices of all descriptions were taken along, and a large assortment of British manufactures were taken for distribution at the capital in the hope of creating a demand for British goods. A compressed list of the presents appears in the table below.[101] The total cost of the Embassy to the Company before its departure was: presents £15,610, *Jackall* tender £1,450, dollars put on *Hindostan* £4,547, Staunton's expenses £960, presents to Viceroy of Canton

[99] CMC, Nos. 437, 442; WSCPMD, No. 1.
[101] IOCM, XCI, 543-90.

PRESENTS TAKEN BY THE MACARTNEY EMBASSY

Article	Value	Article	Value
Planetarium	£1,438	Carpets	£ 221
Globes	971	Mathematical instruments	124
Carriages	2,180	Printed satins	115
Lustres	949	Prints	256
Firearms	777	Wedgewood pottery	170
Curiosities	420	Chronometers	17
Samples of tea	16	Optical instruments	174
Broadcloth	1,026	Smeaton's pullies	45
Long ells	465	Merlin's chair	39
Camlets	145	Telescope	180
Silk cloths	229	Saddlery	259
Poplins and tabinets	164	Models of the sovereign	142
Birmingham goods	484	Measuring instruments	388
Swords	162	Chem. and electr. inst.	917
Sheffield goods	125	Stationery	210
Morocco skins	4		
Copperware	115		£13,124
Tinware	33	Cathcart's presents	£ 2,486
Window & plate glass	36		
			£15,610

£342, drafts drawn by Macartney at Portsmouth £800, advances on salaries (principally to Macartney), £8,162—a total of £31,871.[102]

Everything being thus complete and the Embassy ready to sail, the Ambassador's instructions were signed by Henry Dundas on September 8, and delivered to the Ambassador, along with his credentials to the various Far Eastern rulers, dated at St. James Palace on September 3. On the 8th or 10th a supplementary instruction was given by Dundas to Macartney, telling him not to press for a settlement of the debts. The Chairs' instructions to the Ambassador were signed by Francis Baring and John Smith Burges on September 8, and were delivered to him, together with thirty enclosures, on the 9th, and a large book-packet consisting of twenty volumes was sent to the *Lion* for him. The enclosures included Cathcart's instructions, letters to the supercargoes and to the Secret and Superintending Committee, a copy of the instructions to Captain Mackintosh, and copies of various charter-parties, deeds, covenants, and miscellaneous papers. The book-packet included extracts from the Company's records since the beginning of its China trade, copies of the nineteen queries put to supercargoes in October, 1791, and various other papers, all of which are at present in the Wason Collection on China at Cornell University.[103]

---

[102] WSCPMD, No. 1; CMC, No. 221; IOCM, XCII, 1-9.
[103] WSCPMD, Nos. 1, 6-11, 13-24, 26, 33; Morse, *Chronicle*, II, 232-47; CMC, No. 229.

Macartney set out for Portsmouth on September 11 and arrived there in eight hours. On the 13th he acknowledged the Chairs' instructions, promised to be careful not to lose any advantages which had already been gained, agreed to be very well advised before he obtained the abolition of the Co-hong, and thanked the Company for its courtesy and liberality. The Ambassador and his suite embarked on the 21st, and on September 26, having a fair wind, the whole squadron set sail.[104]

7. *Macartney and Gower's Instructions: Aims of the Embassy.*

The aims and objects of the mission are best set forth in the various instructions given to the Ambassador.[105] Since they so closely adhered to those given to Colonel Cathcart, which have already been outlined in detail, and since the few changes and additions made by Macartney have been noted, it will be sufficient to give a very brief statement of the aims of the Embassy as shown in the instructions. The Ambassador was to obtain all of the information—economic, political, military, intellectual, cultural, social, and philosophical—about China which he could. He was to endeavor to impress upon the Chinese the ability and reliability of the English in the hope of opening an extended intercourse, remedying abuses, and promoting commerce. He was to dispel all illusions about the territorial designs of the English, and he was to discover all that he could about the relations of China with other countries, especially those with Russia.

The special objects of the mission were:

(1) To obtain one or two cessions of territory near to the tea- and silk-producing and the woollen-consuming areas, where English traders might reside and where English jurisdiction might be exercised;

(2) To extend British trade and commerce throughout China if possible by negotiation of a commercial treaty and the opening of new ports under more favorable conditions than at Canton;

(3) To establish a resident Minister at Peking;

(4) To abolish existing abuses and to obtain assurances that they would not be revived;

(5) To create at Peking a stronger taste for known British products and a desire for hitherto unknown products;

(6) To open Japan, Cochin China, and the Eastern Islands to British trade by means of treaties.

---

[104] IOCM, XCII, 1-9; Robbins, *op. cit.*, p. 180.
[105] Morse, *Chronicle*, II, 232-43.

In other words, the aim of the mission was to open the whole East to British commerce and to put British relations with China on a treaty basis. The Ambassador was to cultivate the friendship of the Chinese and was to conform to all the ceremonials of the Chinese Court which did not commit the honor of his sovereign or lessen his own dignity. Discretion was left to him on this point and on the question of whether the Embassy should proceed straight to Tientsin or disembark at Canton. Provision was made for Staunton to become Ambassador if Macartney should die, be absent, or become incapacitated. No attempt was to be made to collect the private debts, but information was to be obtained about them which might lead to their future recovery.

When all of the verbiage is cut away from the King's letter, the following points stand out: that there were abuses in the trade which the King would like to have remedied; that he wished the lives of his citizens to be secure and desired that they should obtain justice; and that he would like to leave a resident Minister at Peking.[106]

The instructions to Gower, dated September 8, were almost identical with those given to Sir Richard Strachan. He was to take the Ambassador as near to Peking as possible, and if the Ambassador so desired, was to dispatch a Lieutenant with the messenger who announced the Embassy. If the Ambassador wished, he was to go to Canton, and he was to consider himself and his ship especially attached to the service of the Embassy and was to conform to the directions of the Ambassador. He was to take special care to avoid injuring the Chinese or giving offense to them in any way.[107]

The Chairs' instructions to Macartney[108] was a very long document, but the one refrain throughout was: be careful, don't be hasty, preserve the advantages we already have rather than risk them in the hopes of gaining greater plums. The Company was in a very advantageous position in China, and they knew it. In their mind the expedition held a double danger: it might cause the Chinese to suspend the trade entirely or, if it succeeded fully, it would cause private interest in England and India to raise such a commotion that the Company's commercial monopoly would be endangered. For these reasons they had not favored the mission, and when the government insisted, they naturally wished the Ambassador to tread cautiously. While he was away they

---

[106] *Ibid.*, pp. 244-47.
[107] IOCM, XCI, 401-06; CMC, V, Nos. 226, 227.
[108] WSCPMD, No. 1.

had to fight to maintain the Company's India trade monopoly, and had the whole East been opened, the growing pressure of the Country traders and of the new commercial and industrial interests in the north of England would have been too strong for the Company to resist.

They pointed out to Macartney that conditions had definitely improved in China since the Commutation Act and since the idea of an Embassy had first been proposed. The specific things which they wished him to aim at were:

(1) To be careful not to impair or injure their present position by complaining of abuses or denouncing individuals.

(2) To create a favorable impression of the British character, which would do more to benefit trade than commercial treaties.

(3) To obtain permission to trade at one or more ports north of Canton but not near Peking. The competition of such ports would automatically remedy the abuses at Canton.

(4) To be very thoroughly informed before he attempted to abolish the Co-hong. It no doubt increased prices and placed limitations upon the freedom of trade, but it had the advantages of affording security for debts and commercial bargains, and because of its power it was able to purchase and sell goods (woollens) which private Chinese merchants could not afford to handle. Before it was abolished the Ambassador should be sure that something substantial would take its place, that a specific statement of the Imperial duties would be given, and that foreigners would be protected from the exactions of the mandarins.

(5) To obtain all information possible about Chinese manufactures, products, and trade, with the object of using such knowledge to the advantage of the English at home and in India.

(6) To obtain if possible a "receptacle" at Canton where British sailors might reside, and where the Company would be able to control them and prevent brawls arising with the Chinese.

(7) To obtain information as to new articles which might be profitably exported from China to England. In opinion of the Chairs, the expansion of the sale of British woollens and Indian cotton would soon turn the balance of trade against China. This being the situation, it was necessary to discover new products to export from China.

(8) To attempt through the gaining of commercial concessions and the distribution of presents taken along to increase the demand for the assortments of British goods already sent out. The Chairs did not particularly favor the attempt to introduce new products into China.

(9) To find out about the exportation of Chinese piece-goods to Russia. In the Chairs' opinion Russia and central Europe were being supplied by this route to the detriment of the Company's piece-goods trade between India and London.

In concluding, the Chairs informed Macartney that the Commissioners at Canton had been instructed to keep $50,000 in readiness for his use. Some of it might have to be discreetly distributed to counteract fear and jealousy. In order to ensure his control over the personnel of the *Hindostan,* and so to prevent disorder detrimental to the Embassy, he was empowered to suspend or dismiss any officer of the ship who should be guilty of a breach of his covenants or of disobedience to the orders from the Secret Committee or from the Ambassador. They concluded:

> In the final letter we addressed to His Majesty's Ministers on the occasion of this Embassy we claimed on behalf of the Company a full and compleat reservation of their rights and privileges. The ability, integrity and zeal which your excellency has already manifested for the interest of the Company, induce us to rely that no measures will be taken which shall prejudice those rights and privileges.

The Company also gave the Ambassador memoranda dealing with the tea tree and with silk and nankeens. He was asked to collect information about the care of the silk worm, the culture of the mulberry tree, and Chinese methods of silk manufacture, with a view to their use in India. If possible he was to obtain some of the mulberry trees and a quantity of silk-moth eggs, to be sent to India and England with suitable directions for their cultivation and treatment. He should also procure drawings and models of the machines and implements used in silk manufacture. He was, if possible, to discover the method used in the dyeing and the manufacture of nankeens.[109]

With such instructions sailed the first British Ambassador ever to reach the capital of the Middle Kingdom. He had high hopes and great ambitions; he was thoroughly prepared for his task and he knew it, but both he and the Ministers were laboring under a false impression that the Peking administration was not really opposed to foreign intercourse. The Company's view, based on long experience, was more correct in these matters, but there was an essential conflict between the interests of the Company and those embodied in the Ambassador as a representative of the government. The government, feeling the pressure of growing commercial and industrial interests both in India and England, represented more the view of the age which was just beginning—an age of tremendous economic expansion. The Ambassador too, an intelligent and wide-awake man, saw the trends in England and

---

[109] CMC, No. 177; WSCPMD, No. 8.

was personally on the side of the expansionists. It was this view which led to the Embassy. The Company, on the other hand, was the product of another age. It was secure in the *status quo* and considered experiment dangerous; besides, it saw in the gaining of too many concessions its own doom. It represented the conservative vested interest, clinging to what it had. The Embassy, as visioned by the Ministers, with whom Macartney's sentiments agreed, represented the new spirit of the industrial age. As representative for these two conflicting views the Ambassador had a thorny path to tread—a task which became quite impossible when he reached the barrier of Chinese custom, tradition, and exclusiveness.

Chapter VIII

THE MACARTNEY EMBASSY IN CHINA (1792-93)

1. *Work of the Commissioners at Canton and the Chinese Attitude toward the Embassy (September 20, 1792—January 31, 1793).*

While the Embassy was pursuing its way toward China, the Secret and Superintending Committee was engaged in activties of interest at Canton. The Commissioners reached Canton on September 20, 1792, and on the 24th they requested Munqua and Puankhequa to attend them. The Commissioners explained that they had a very important letter to deliver to the Viceroy and requested the merchants to arrange an audience. The merchants expressed no surprise, as a rumor of the Embassy had already spread. The Commissioners were informed that the Viceroy (Fu K'ang-an) was absent putting down a revolt in Tibet, that the communication might be given to the Governor (Kuo Shih-hsün), and that the merchants must first inform the Hoppo (Sheng Chu). The Commissioners agreed to this and requested that they be allowed to sit during the audience with the Governor. The merchants expressed fears that the measure in contemplation might affect them or the trade adversely, but, upon being assured that it would be productive of good rather than of ill, they expressed satisfaction and went away to arrange the matter.[1]

An audience was arranged for October 10, and it was at first intimated that the Commissioners would be allowed to sit. But on the 9th the mandarins requested to know the rank of the person sending the letter, and, upon discovering that he was not a government official, they stated that the Commissioners could not be allowed to sit at the public audience, but that after it ended a private meeting with the Governor and the Hoppo to discuss the matter would be held, at which they would be allowed to sit. Whether the supercargoes were to remain standing or to be allowed to sit when received by the provincial officials was a question of long standing. On this occasion the Commissioners hoped to take advantage of the importance of the event to establish their contention, as well as not to compromise the dignity of the Embassy. They did, however, agree to this arrangement; but on

---

[1] IOCM, XCIII, 25-28; Yü K'un, *Yüeh Hai Kuan Chih* (about 1838). Ch. 7 deals with the mandarins.

the following morning they were informed that certain officials objected to the private sitting and so it could not be granted.[2]

Because it was now too late to make further objection without causing great delay, they set off to attend the Governor at his yamen. They were carried in sedan chairs and accompanied by Munqua and Puankhequa, who were to act as interpreters. They reached the Governor's establishment at about 10:30 A.M., and after an hour's wait were ushered into the mandarin's presence. The Governor and Hoppo sat facing the entrance—with the other Chinese officials upon the left (the side of honor). The Commissioners walked to within a few steps of the Governor, made a low bow, and took their places on the right. The two merchants dropped on one knee and bowed their heads to the ground. The letter was placed in the hands of the Governor by Browne. It was accepted in a very gracious manner; the Latin copy was given to a Chinese to translate, and the English copy was returned to the merchants to be translated with the help of the Commissioners, who were allowed to retire to a private apartment.[3]

They had difficulty in making the merchants understand the letter, but the Latin copy was apparently better translated, for about one o'clock the Commissioners were summoned to the audience hall, where the Governor, with great politeness and affability, questioned Browne. He wished to know the time of the departure of the Embassy from England and the probable time of its arrival, said that it was customary for embassies to come to Canton, requested the Commissioners to write to the Ambassador telling him to come to Canton, and asked for a list of the presents to be given to the Emperor. Browne replied that the Embassy had sailed about the middle of August, that it might reach Tientsin by the end of February, that, as the King had ordered the Embassy to go to Tientsin as a special mark of attention to the Emperor, the Commissioners could not tell the Ambassador to come to Canton, and that they knew nothing about the presents, which had not been prepared when they left.[4]

The Hoppo was especially displeased with this and insisted that the Embassy should come to Canton and that a list of presents must be given. The argument went on for about half an hour, when a discharge of cannon announcing the arrival of an Imperial edict relieved the situa-

[2] IOCM, XCIII, 28-35.
[3] *Ibid.*, pp. 35-39.
[4] *Ibid.*, pp. 39-43; Wang Chih-ch'un, *Kuo Ch'ao Jou Yüan Chi* (Canton, 1891), Ch. 6, p. 3.

tion. The Commissioners were requested to retire to avoid the *kotow* when the edict was received. At 2:30 they were called to take leave of the Governor, who informed them that the letter would be sent to the Emperor, and that they should hear further on the subject through the merchants. The next day, September 11, Munqua and Puankhequa attended, and proceeded to ask all manner of questions about the Embassy.

In the end a paper was drawn up stating that a very great mandarin, Lord Macartney, was being sent by the King as Ambassador; that the Commissioners had been told by Baring that the King regretted very much that no one had been sent to congratulate the Emperor on his eightieth birthday, and that therefore the Ambassador was now being sent to convey the King's regards and cement a friendship with the Emperor; that very considerable presents were being brought, but as to the details the Commissioners were uninformed, and that after the congratulations were given, the Commissioners understood, the King had instructed the Ambassador to discuss some matters of trade with the Emperor. The Commissioners also requested that the Ambassador might be given a proper reception and that pilots should be sent to conduct the King's ship to Tientsin.[5]

On September 14 the merchants and one of the Hoppo's secretaries came to ask the Commissioners where they thought the pilots should be stationed. The Commissioners suggested Chusan and Ninghai (near Weihaiwei in Shantung), and they thought the pilots should be stationed there about the first of February. The next evening the merchants came with a further message from the Governor asking for an account of the motives of the Embassy and the nature and value of the presents. The Commissioners indicated that they had already told all they knew about the aims of the Embassy, and that before their departure they had seen a planetarium and some carriages which were intended for the Emperor. This reply about the presents apparently satisfied the officials, but at noon on the 16th a deputation of minor mandarins came to find out about the aims of the Embassy. Every device was used to get information, and as a last resort the Commissioners were asked if they would be willing to go to Peking if the Emperor was not satisfied. Upon being given an affirmative answer, the deputation departed.[6]

---

[5] IOCM, XCIII, 43-49.
[6] *Ibid.*, pp. 49-54.

The merchants volunteered the information that the mandarins, particularly the Hoppo, were afraid the Embassy might draw trade to Ningpo and put them into ill repute at Peking, and that the deputation had been sent to confirm the merchants' report, which had displeased the Governor. It was decided that Irwin and Jackson should hold themselves in readiness to go to Peking.[7] The Governor was obviously much worried about sending to Peking a report about an Embassy which proposed to deviate from customary procedure on so many points. He finally sent a very humble memorial, together with Baring's letter, pointing out that he knew that embassies should come to Canton, but that the English now desired to go to Tientsin, nor had they, as was customary, given him a copy of the King's letter to the Emperor or a list of the presents. According to the Commissioners, the memorial was dispatched to Peking on October 20.[8]

On November 25 the Commissioners sent dispatches to the Chairs giving an account of proceedings to that date and telling of their work in beginning the reform of the factory. They indicated that since the delivery of the letter more attention had been paid to their representations, and that the Hoppo talked of reducing the exorbitant charges on the passage between Canton and Macao. From the merchants they had learned that the price of tea could be reduced by one or two taels per picul if an establishment were obtained at Chusan. They were setting aside T. 300,000 to be used if necessary in the service of the Embassy. They called attention to their need of an interpreter, which had been especially evident in the recent negotiations. They also discussed the disorderly behavior of the sailors and the duelling among the officers and recommended that the granting of leave to sailors should be discontinued.[9] On the same day they sent a short note to Lord Macartney, to be left at North Island in the Straits of Sunda, indicating that everything was "proceeding in a fair train."[10]

In the meantime, the Governor's memorial had found its way to Peking. It was referred to the Board of War, and on December 3, 1792, that board, in conformity with the Emperor's orders, issued an edict granting permission to the Embassy to proceed to Tientsin, ordering the officials to make preparations for its reception, and directing

---

[7] *Ibid.*, pp. 54-56.
[8] Yü, *op. cit.*, Ch. 23, pp. 3-4; IOCM, XCIII, 56; Wei Yuan, *Hai Kuo T'u Chih* (Introduction, 1852), Ch. 53, pp. 10-14.
[9] IOCM, XCIII, 5-22, especially 17-22; CMC, No. 319.
[10] IOCM, XCIII, 57-58.

that the Ambassador and his suite be conducted by a military mandarin to Peking.[11] According to Père Jean Joseph de Grammont, a French missionary at Peking, the Emperor expressed great satisfaction when the coming of the British Embassy was reported to him on December 3.[12]

The edict was slow in reaching Canton, but by December 14 a report had reached Canton that a mandarin of rank was on his way to that city with the Imperial edict. The Commissioners, therefore, determined to send by the *Sir Edward Hughes* a letter, partly in cypher, to be delivered to the Dutch Governor of Batavia for the Ambassador. The essential part of the letter, dated December 17, 1792, and written in cypher, was: "No answer yet from Peking to our application for pilots to be stationed at Cheusan & Ninghoy . . . a report is in the City of a great Mandarin coming to enquire further & the Tjontoc of Canton is thought to be the person, . . ."[13] On December 21 the edict reached Canton, and on the 25th the Commissioners were informed by "private but undoubted intelligence" that it had arrived and that its contents assured the favorable reception of the Embassy.[14]

The Commissioners obtained a transcript of the edict through the merchants before January 5, 1793, but, not being satisfied with this, they sent Munqua and Puankhequa to the Governor and Hoppo to request that it be communicated officially. Late in the afternoon of the 6th the merchants returned with a copy of the edict (in Chinese) in the form of an address from the *Namhoi Hien* to the merchants. On the same evening they despatched the *Earl of Wycombe* to Batavia with a letter to Macartney containing ten enclosures, one of which was the edict in Chinese. They directed the *Wycombe* to wait at Batavia until the 15th of February, when, if none of Macartney's squadron had reached that place, it was to leave the packet in the care of the Dutch Governor and proceed to England.[15]

The enclosures in the packet included copies of the Commissioners' proceedings both in their Secret and in their Superintending departments, an account of the Imperial duties, Co-hong charges and port charges, an estimate of their stock to March, 1794, and accounts of

[11] CMC, VIII, No. 335; IOCM, XCII, 19-22.
[12] CMC, No. 251; E. H. Pritchard, "Letters from Missionaries at Peking Relating to the Macartney Embassy," *T'oung Pao*, XXXI (1934), 8.
[13] CMC, No. 236; IOCM, XCIII, 77-82.
[14] IOCM, XCIII, 65-69, 84-86, 107.
[15] *Ibid.*, pp. 73-75, 105-18.

imports, sales, current prices, and foreign shipping at Canton in 1792. Their letter to the Ambassador indicated the impossibility of smuggling pilots to Batavia or of arranging to have them meet the Embassy at Macao; it called attention to the necessity for the Ambassador to arrange early with the Court at Peking for a free communication with the Commissioners, because otherwise the intrigues of the local officials would prevent it; and it specified that jealousy of the Embassy seemed to exist nowhere except at Canton. It also stated that, according to the merchants, the Emperor had ordered pilots to be sent to the principal ports to the north, and that he had sent a great mandarin to Tientsin to arrange for the Embassy's arrival.[16]

The letter further explained to what extent the Consoo levy or Co-hong tax increased the duties on trade, and that it was voluntarily levied by the merchants upon themselves to provide a fund from which to buy presents for the mandarins and the Emperor (an illegal use) and to pay the debts of bankrupt merchants, but said that the information was not of sufficient soundness to serve as a basis for a complaint to the Emperor. The letter also reported the decline of Continental commerce, complained of the recent competition of private English under the Genoese flag, said that the opening of a port to the northward would decrease the price of tea by the amount of the transit duties, and maintained that there was no hope of expanding British exports unless new ports were opened.

In addition, the letter informed the Ambassador of the establishment of the house of trade under Messrs. Drummond and Sparkes, and upheld the advisability of keeping a large supply of cash on hand, because it enabled them to make more favorable contracts. Finally, the Commissioners stated that they had been unable to obtain any information about silk culture or the manufacture of nankeens, except that it was impossible to produce the white Nanking silk at Canton. They requested Macartney to make enquiries upon the subject. On January 13 the edict was officially delivered by the *Namhoi Hien,* after which the Commissioners sent complimentary letters to all of the principal mandarins.[17]

---

[16] *Ibid.,* pp. 118-144.
[17] *Ibid.,* pp. 145-55.

2. *Voyage of the Embassy to Macao and Taku and Events in China (September 26, 1792—July 25, 1793).*

The squadron consisting of the *Lion,* man-of-war, the *Hindostan,* Indiaman, and the *Jackall,* brig, sailed from Spithead on September 26, 1792. The two large vessels lost sight of the *Jackall* the first evening out of Spithead, and saw no more of her until March 23, 1793, off the coast of Sumatra. The Embassy reached Madeira on the evening of October 10 and disembarked at Funchal Road, where it was royally entertained by the Governor. While there, Macartney drew drafts on the Company amounting to £959 for the purchase of wine. On the 18th the *Lion* and the *Hindostan* left Madeira and proceeded to Santa Cruz in the Island of Teneriffe and thence to Porto Praya in the Island of St. Jago (one of the Cape Verde Islands), where they were entertained by the Portuguese Governor. After five days, as the *Jackall* did not overtake them, they sailed for Rio de Janerio on November 7. They crossed the equator at noon on Sunday the 18th, and on December 1 the expedition dropped anchor in the harbor at Rio de Janerio.[18]

On November 22 Macartney had been "seized with a severe fit of the gout," from which he had not entirely recovered when the squadron sailed from Rio de Janerio on December 18. While at that port, the members of the Embassy were received by the Viceroy, and some of the gentlemen of the suite visited one of the convents, where they were "received with great ceremony and respect." On the 15th Macartney re-embarked, and on the 18th of December the squadron sailed.[19] On the 31st they passed the Island of Tristian d'Acunha, and on February 1, 1793, reached the Islands of Amsterdam and St. Paul. They stopped for a day at these Islands to allow the scientists to examine the volcanic formations, and on the Islands they found three Frenchmen and two Americans who were collecting seal-skins for the Canton market. On the 26th of February Java Head was sighted, and on March 1 the *Lion,* with her crew suffering from scurvy, anchored at North Island, where she found the *Hindostan,* from which she had become separated.[20]

---

[18] IOCM, XCII, 9-12; CMC, No. 327; Robbins, *op. cit.,* pp. 180-89.

[19] *Macartney's Journal* in Robbins, *op. cit.,* pp. 193-96. Hereafter reference will be made only to *Macartney's Journal,* the text given in Robbins being used. A slightly less accurate text is in Barrow's *Macartney,* Vol. I.

[20] Detailed accounts of the voyage are to be found in G. L. Staunton, *Embassy* (1797), I; *A Complete View of the Chinese Empire* (London, 1798); John Barrow, *A Voyage to Cochinchina, in the Years 1792 and 1793* (London, 1806); Samuel Holmes, *The Journal of . . . Lord Macartney's Embassy to China* (London, 1798); Aeneas Anderson, *A Narrative of the British Embassy to China* (London, 1795).

After taking on wood and water, the squadron proceeded to Batavia, where the *Lion* anchored on March 6. Titsingh and Wiegerman, two members of the Dutch Council, came on board with the dispatches for Macartney and compliments from Governor Van Aelting, and Wiegerman offered his house to Macartney while the latter would be at Batavia. The Ambassador was very much indisposed for several days and declined to come on shore. On the 8th he disembarked and attended the great festival given by the Governor in honor of the Prince of Orange's birthday. It consisted of gluttonous eating and drinking, and in the evening of an elaborate ball which went on until four in the morning, while "jolly dames took especial care that the strangers should be well pleased and well plied with wine, to which, at the same time, they were by no means backward in helping themselves." [21]

Such wining and dining did not agree with His Excellency, and on March 10 he returned to the *Lion* with a severe attack of the gout,[22] leaving his trusty Staunton to carry on business with the Dutch officials. On the 13th Staunton wrote to Macartney stating that the Governor wanted a copy of the Dutch memorial sent to London, because a transcript of it had not yet reached Batavia. According to the Governor Mr. Van Braham the Director of the Dutch Supercargoes at Macao is exceedingly alarmed about the Institution of your Mission, and is probably joined with other Europeans and Chinese at Canton in endeavoring to counteract its effects; that he had applied to the Gouvernment here to send a Counter Embassy etc.; that great pains are taking in China to excite the apprehension of the Chinese as to the secret views of the present Embassy; that the English Power in Hindostan is the subject of declamations against the progress of our ambition etc. etc.; that the General and Council will write to Mr. Van Braahm not only to disist from any intrigues against the Embassy, but to resist the Intrigues of others.[23]

Staunton indicated that the Governor would send the Dutch memorial on to Van Braam with orders to disclose it to no one, and that consent to this request would assure the Dutch of the good intentions of the English. The request appears to have been complied with, and on March 17 the Embassy sailed from Batavia much encouraged by the favorable reports of the Emperor's attitude received from Canton, and by a letter from the Dutch Governor, requiring Van Braam's

[21] *Macartney's Journal*, pp. 212-16; BM, *Additional Manuscripts (Journal of the Lion)*, No. 21,106, pp. 43 (79).
[22] Anderson, *op. cit.*, p. 35.
[23] CMC, No. 242.

cooperation. As they were leaving, the *Lion* struck a submerged rock, but without any damage. This event caused Macartney to purchase a new tender at the cost of $5,000, the *Nereide*, which was re-named the *Duke of Clarence*.[24]

After returning to North Island, the squadron was joined by the *Jackall* on March 23. On the 25th Macartney wrote to the Chairs informing them of events at Batavia, enclosing a Latin translation of the Emperor's edict, and stating that he would not touch at Canton, but would send one of the brigs in to get information. The ships cruised about the Straits until expected vessels arrived from Canton to carry the dispatches to England.[25] The squadron proceeded toward Cochin China on April 20, but, as the monsoon was unfavorable and the weather hot and rainy, the boats made slow progress. To make matters worse, fevers and dysentery broke out among the crew, so that on May 16 they came to anchor at Pulo Condore. As the anchorage was unsafe and the natives had taken to the hills upon their approach, the squadron sailed for Turon Bay, where it hoped to anchor and disembark the sick.[26]

On May 26 the vessels reached Turon Bay, where they found a Portuguese ship commanded by one Mansel Houme Cawalko (Duome in Barrow). The Cochin Chinese treated the English well, and presents were sent to the Ambassador from the Governor of the place and from the boy King, who lived inland. On June 4 Macartney went ashore to visit the Governor. Banqueting and the mutual exchange of compliments and presents followed. Macartney hoped to make a good impression to facilitate possible commerce, and to make easier the negotiations upon his intended return. On June 10 more presents and a letter were received from the King, to which Macartney replied on the 13th, promising to visit the King on his return homeward. Observations about the harbors and possibilities of trade were made during the stay. By June 15 most of the sick had recovered, and the Embassy set sail for Macao, where it arrived off the Grand Ladrone on June 20.[27]

[24] CMC, No. 248; Barrow, *Cochinchina*, pp. 160-207, especially 177; Staunton, *Embassy* (1797), I, 235-41; IOCM, XCII, 15-18; *Macartney's Journal*, p. 230.

[25] Anderson, *op. cit.*, pp. 45-47; *Macartney's Journal*, pp. 219-30; IOCM, XCII, 15-18.

[26] CMC, Nos. 340-41; Anderson, *op. cit.*, pp. 47-50; *Macartney's Journal*, pp. 231-34; Barrow, *Cochinchina*, p. 244.

[27] *Macartney's Journal*, pp. 234-44; Barrow, *Cochinchina*, pp. 247-79; Anderson, *op. cit.*, pp. 50-56; Staunton, *Historical Embassy* (1797), pp. 182-85.

Meanwhile events of interest had been transpiring at Canton. On March 15 Munqua came to the factory with a message to the effect that an edict had recently arrived from the Emperor intimating his pleasure at the coming of the Embassy, repeating his assurance that the Ambassador might go to any port in the Empire, and stating that he would be received by a guard to escort him to Peking.[28] On the 17th Munqua and Puankhequa waited on the Commissioners and requested in the name of the Governor to know when the Embassy had sailed and on what part of the coast it was likely to touch. In reply the Commissioners sent a letter explaining that it had probably sailed in August, and that, as the monsoons were unfavorable, the squadron had probably gone to the eastward of Formosa and would probably make the coast of Chekiang or might even then be at Tientsin. On the same day the Commissioners decided to retain the *Endeavour* (one of two surveying ships which had arrived in February) for the possible use of the Embassy.[29]

In the meantime an edict had been issued at Peking on March 24, stating that the English and Burmese tribute missions and the Mongolian Princes could be given a banquet together "in order to make manifest the munificence of the treatment of travelers from far places." On April 2 another edict was issued through the Council of State at Peking directing the Governors of Fukien, Chekiang, Kiangsu, and Shantung to have the garrisons of the coastal cities put into the best of conditions. Further, as there were no interpreters or Hong merchants in Fukien, Chekiang or Kiangsu, the Governor of Canton was ordered to prepare merchants and interpreters to be sent to these places if the ships brought trading goods. This was necessary in order to protect the English from being swindled by the natives. If the ships arrived in Shantung or Chihli this latter precaution would be unnecessary, since the English could come to the capital to trade and negotiate.[30]

When this news reached Canton early in May, it caused consternation among the merchants. On May 15 Munqua arrived at Macao, where the Commissioners then were, and explained that two Hong merchants and two interpreters had been ordered to hold themselves in readiness to go to any of the three aforementioned provinces should the Embassy arrive there. Many of the merchants, he reported, had bribed the Hoppo not to name them, but he, as head of the Co-hong,

[28] IOCM, XCII, 157-72.
[29] *Ibid.*, pp. 177-87.
[30] *Kao Tsung Shun Huang-ti Shêng Hsün,* Ch. 276, pp. 4-8.

had been positively commanded to go. He asked for a letter to Lord Macartney from the Commissioners and requested the Ambassador to be so kind as to intercede for his return to Canton without having to proceed to the capital. As the Commissioners knew that Macartney had interpreters and were convinced that trade would suffer by Munqua's extended absence, they wrote the desired letter. They also took other means to indicate to the officials that the Ambassador was provided with interpreters.[31]

On May 26 the Commissioners dispatched to the Chairs via the *Anna*, sailing to Bombay, a letter to be sent overland to London. It gave an account of the above-mentioned events at Canton, and indicated that the reports of the Embassy had had a very good effect on the officials and that in consequence the charge on going to Macao that spring had been reduced from $4,935 to $2,926.[32] On the 29th of May they received news by a Portuguese ship from Bengal that the Embassy had not sailed until late in September, 1792. On May 28, being convinced that the mission had already passed Macao, they determined to send the *Endeavour* to the northward with dispatches for the Ambassador. Captain Proctor was to proceed to Chusan, and, if the Embassy had passed there, he was to go to Tientsin and deliver the dispatches; but, if not, he was to cruise off the coast until June 30 in the hope of intercepting the squadron. If by that time he had not met them he was to go to Tientsin, and if they were not there he was to return to Macao at once.[33]

His sailing was delayed until June 1 because of the necessity of finding an interpreter. Finally the brother of a Chinese whom the Commissioners had recently obtained to teach the language to certain members of the factory agreed to go. He was disguised in European dress to avoid the danger of detection. Lieutenant Proctor carried with him a letter from the Commissioners to Lord Macartney dated June 1 with two enclosures: one a copy of their letter to Munqua, the other a copy of their last letter to the Chairs. They informed him of all that had happened since their last dispatch of January 6, and stated that he would be the best judge of whether Munqua would be the more valuable at Canton or at Peking. They also said that he could do what he thought best with the *Endeavour*, but indicated that it would be advisa-

[31] IOCM, XCIII, 188-93.
[32] IOCM, XCIII, 194-200; Morse, *Chronicle*, II, 208.
[33] IOCM, XCIII, 202-03, 211-12.

ble to have her sent back to Canton, so that she could carry more dispatches if necessary.[34]

On June 14 another edict was issued through the Council of State at Peking. It indicated that Cheng Jui, Imperial Salt Commissioner, had been stationed at Tientsin to receive the Ambassador and make all preparations for his trip to the capital. As yet no word of the Ambassador had been received by the trading ships from Chekiang or Kwangtung, but Cheng Jui was to go to Taku and make all arrangements for receiving the Ambassador and his tribute goods. Further, as the Emperor was to go to Jehol, the Ambassador was to be escorted there in great state by Cheng Jui and the local mandarins; there the Embassy would be entertained with the tribute bearers from Burma and the Mongolian Princes.[35]

On Thursday, June 20, the *Lion* came to anchor off the Grand Ladrone. The *Jackall* and *Clarence* were sent to Macao with Sir George Staunton, Maxwell, and Captain Mackintosh. Staunton carried a letter from Macartney to the Commissioners and the letter from the Governor of Batavia to Van Braam. Macartney's letter to the Commissioners, dated June 18, expressed satisfaction with their work and wished to know by what means he could draw on them for money in the future.[36]

The Commissioners met in conference with Staunton on the 21st. He was allowed to examine the record of their proceedings since their last dispatch to Batavia. He said that Padre Cho had become frightened, would not proceed to Peking, and had come ashore. In view of this, the Ambassador wished to obtain another Chinese, but the Commissioners recommended the person sent on the *Endeavour* as the only available man. They also offered to give Macartney $12,000 in cash, but Staunton declined it because the Embassy already had sufficient funds to reach Peking. They assured Staunton that Van Braam had done a good deal of talking, but were of the opinion that his activity had not been directed against the Embassy. They were of the decided opinion that all the other Europeans might be somewhat jealous, but were hoping to derive substantial benefits from the Embassy, as the Dutch had already escaped the extra charges between Canton and Macao.[37]

---

[34] IOCM, XCIII, 204-11.
[35] *Kao Tsung Shun Huang-ti Shêng Hsün*, Ch. 276, p. 16.
[36] IOCM, XCIII, 213-15; *Macartney's Journal*, p. 244; BM, *Additional Manuscripts (Journal of the Lion)*, No. 21,106, p. 67.
[37] IOCM, XCIII, 213-32.

From the Italian missionaries at Macao Staunton learned that the Portuguese were intriguing against the Embassy, because they feared that the English might get a separate establishment which would ruin Macao. From other sources the intrigues of the officials and the merchants, who were afraid that trade might be transferred from Canton to other ports, were confirmed. After receiving the Governor of Batavia's letter, Van Braam wished to see Macartney, but, upon being informed that this was impossible, he sent a letter instead. The Embassy had carried out, in addition to the two interpreters, two other Chinese Padres from Naples, Nyan and Vang, who were left at Macao. In order to continue the good will of the Italians, Macartney agreed to take to the north with him two other missionaries, a French Lazarist, Louis-François Lamiot and an Irish Lazarist, Robert Hanna, who had been waiting for some time to enter the Emperor's service. The Embassy was especially well looked upon by the Spanish, their chief, Señor Agoté, even sending Macartney a map of Macao.[38]

Staunton returned to the squadron on June 22, bearing this information and a letter from the supercargoes to Macartney. The letter indicated that there were no commercial houses in Peking in correspondence with those at Canton, and that, if Macartney's drafts on them were not accepted in Peking, they would have to send him cash by land conveyance. It also appears that Captain Mackintosh was able to arrange that two Chinese pilots, whom the squadron had brought back from the Straits of Sunda, should accompany the Embassy northward. Everything being thus auspiciously arranged, and supplies having been sent to the ships by the Commissioners, the whole squadron set sail for Chusan on June 23 with a favorable monsoon. Three days later a mandarin deputed by the Hoppo, who had heard of the arrival of the squadron, came to supply the Embassy with necessities at the Emperor's expense.[39]

On July 3 the squadron anchored in Chusan Road, and Staunton was sent on to the city to obtain pilots for Tientsin. This occasioned some delay because the Governor wished to give him pilots to carry the squadron only to the next province, but Staunton insisted on men to take them to Tientsin and threatened to interview the Viceroy at Ningpo if such pilots were not forthcoming. This produced results;

---

[38] IOCM, XCIII, 221-22 and XCII, 31-35; *Macartney's Journal*, p. 245; Staunton, *Embassy* (1797), I, 390-98.
[39] IOCM, XCIII, 220-35; *Macartney's Journal*, pp. 244-45; BM, *Additional Manuscripts*, No. 21,106, p. 68 (127).

two merchants were ultimately found who knew the whole route, and despite their pleas on bended knee to be exempt from the service they were forced to go. Staunton returned with them on July 7, and, upon being told the *Lion's* draft of water, they said that she could not proceed further than the Miaotao Islands near Tengchow, because the Gulf of Chihli was very shallow. While the ships were at anchor drawings of the harbor were taken.[40]

The squadron sailed on July 9, and on the 17th the *Hindostan* met the brig *Endeavour*, which was returning from Tientsin. On July 20 the Embassy reached Tengchow, after passing through numerous fogs and some rough weather. On this day Macartney caused to be read publicly to all the sailors of the several vessels, privately to the guard, and personally to other members of his suite, a "declaration and instruction to his train, and all others attending the Embassy." The declaration was aimed to secure good order and obedience in order to give the Chinese a favorable impression of British character. It required everyone to pay strict attention to orders, to conduct himself in a most orderly and discreet manner, and to offend the Chinese in no way, and gave to those in command complete power to inflict summary punishment. It concluded with a quotation of the unqualified power given by the Company to the Ambassador to carry these orders into effect. After being visited by the Governor of Tengchow, the squadron proceeded to Taku, where the *Lion* anchored on July 25.[41]

3. *From Taku to Tungchow and the Question of the Kotow (July 24—August 16, 1793).*

Before July 24 a memorial from Ch'ang Lin, Governor of Chekiang province, had reached Peking telling of the Embassy's departure from Chusan, for on this date an edict was issued indicating that the mission had left Chusan on August 7. It went on to say that:

in dealing with barbarian affairs, one must find a happy medium between extravagance and penury. The provinces generally either do too much or not enough. This time after the English tribute bearers arrive all entertainment decidedly should not be too lavish. But these tribute bearers have sailed far across the sea to come for the first time to see the brightness of our country; they cannot be compared with those who bring tribute regu-

---

[40] *Macartney's Journal*, pp. 245-48; IOCM, XCII, 35-40; Staunton, *Embassy* (1797), I, 403-37.
[41] *Macartney's Journal*, pp. 248-49; Anderson, *op. cit.*, pp. 234-42; IOCM, XCII, 40-47, 127-35; BM, *Additional Manuscripts*, No. 21,106, pp. 76-79.

larly every year from Burma, Annam and other places. Liang K'eng-t'ang [Viceroy of Chihli province] and Cheng Jui must take care of them suitably and not go so far in simplicity that the men from afar will be contemptuous . . . I command Cheng Jui to find out from the interpreters the number of chief and assistant envoys, and the number of men who will come with them to Jehol, and to make a list and quickly report, and let him also make a list of the officers and sailors who will be left to watch the main ship in the outer ocean, and report, so that presents can be prepared.[42]

The *Jackall*, with Hüttner (tutor to young Staunton), Lieutenant Campbell, and the interpreter Jacob Ly, who had been dressed in English clothes to disguise his race, had been sent on ahead on July 21 to make soundings at the mouth of the Peiho and to interview the mandarins. They reached the Peiho on the 23rd and the next day went ashore. They were met by Van (a military mandarin), Chou (a civil mandarin), and an elderly mandarin. Van (variously transliterated Fan or Wan) and Chou were two Imperial commissioners sent to receive the Embassy. After obtaining the names and ranks of the English deputation, the mandarins asked what kind of provisions the ships needed, how many people were on board, and whether there was any merchandise on board, which they said could be sold in Peking. The English were told to inform the Ambassador that everything was ready for his reception, and that as soon as the *Lion* approached, the two commissioners would come to greet him.[43]

After reporting this information, Hüttner and Lieutenant Proctor were sent back in the *Endeavour* with the Cantonese interpreter, Lorenzo, to make arrangements for boats to carry the baggage ashore. At an interview on July 28, Hüttner found that the presents would have to be taken from the *Lion* in junks and transported to a point beyond Taku, where they would be embarked on river barges for the rest of the journey. The mandarins agreed to furnish ten barges for the Ambassador and his suite and thirty for the presents. It was further arranged that twenty junks should be sent to the *Lion* for the presents and ten for the Ambassador and suite. Hüttner was also told to request of the Ambassador a copy of the King's letter to the Emperor and a

[42] *Kao Tsung Shun Huang-ti Shêng Hsün*, Ch. 276, pp. 17-18; *Chang Ku Ch'ung P'ien* (Peiping, 1930), II, pp. 8-9, gives Ch'ang Lin's memorial.

[43] CMC, No. 265; J. C. Hüttner, *Voyage à la Chine* (Paris, 1803), pp. 5-11; *Macartney's Journal*, pp. 249-50; Staunton, *Embassy* (1797), I, pp. 475-84. For information about Van and Chou, whose personal names are never given, see Liu Fu, *Ch'ien Lung Ying Shih Chin Chien Chi* (Shanghai, 1930), p. 13, and Hsiao (Siao) I-shan, *Ch'ing Tai T'ung Shih* (Shanghai, 1928), II, 752-60.

list of the presents. Upon expressing his doubt as to whether the Ambassador would grant this request, he was informed that it was the custom of the country, and that the Emperor would be angry if it was not complied with."

At noon on July 31 Van and Chou came on board the *Lion* to present their respects to the Ambassador, and brought with them a prodigious quantity of fresh meats, cereals, and green provisions. Arrangements for taking the baggage ashore were completed and Macartney agreed to give them a list of the presents.

These two mandarins seemed to be intelligent men, frank and easy in their dress, and communicative in their discourse.

They sat down to dinner with us, and though at first a little embarrassed by our knives and forks, soon got over the difficulty, and handled them with notable dexterity and execution upon some of the good things which they had brought us."

These two commissioners were upon this occasion inferior to the Tartar Legate, Chen Jui, who had been especially deputed to manage the affairs of the Embassy, and who, as they explained, would meet the Ambassador after he had disembarked. Van was a colonel and Chou was governor of the Tientsin district. They accompanied the Embassy throughout its stay in China and became very much attached to the Ambassador and suite."

The prevalence of sickness on the *Lion* (ninety-three men having been reported ill on the 27th) and the impossibility of finding a good anchorage in the Gulf of Chihli made a speedy departure to a suitable harbor necessary. It was arranged that Captain Mackintosh should accompany the Ambassador to Peking, where it was hoped he would be able to obtain permission to trade at Chusan, to which port the *Hindostan* was to go. Captain Gower was ordered to go to the Miaotao Islands and, if a satisfactory harbor could be found, to disembark his men until they recovered; if not, he was to proceed to Chusan for that purpose. As soon as his men had recovered he was to proceed to Yedo in Japan and deliver a letter which Macartney gave him. While there, he was to make nautical observations, discover harbors, learn to what extent the Japanese were averse to foreign

" CMC, No. 265; *Chang Ku Ch'ung P'ien*, III, 16-18. The Cantonese interpreter was called Antonio by Hüttner and Lorenzo by Captain Gower and Lord Macartney.

" *Macartney's Journal*, pp. 252-53.

" Hüttner, *op. cit.*, p. 10; Barrow, *Travels in China* (London, 1804), pp. 69-70; Staunton, *Embassy* (1797), I, pp. 485-92.

intercourse, and observe to what extent a market for British manufactures might be found in Japan and what products they had to give in return.[47]

From Japan he was to proceed to Manila and present a letter from Macartney to the Governor. He was to remain there until it was practicable to go farther south, collecting as much information about the state of the country and the disposition of the people as he could during his stay. From there he was to proceed to the Islands of Salutaya, Mindanao, Bunwoat, Gilolo, that part of the Celebes not under Dutch control, and Borneo. At all these places he was to make nautical observations, explore for harbors, cultivate the friendship of the natives, explain that Macartney intended to visit them later, and look out for the possibilities of trade. In this connection Macartney observed: "the great object of my mission is to spread the use of British manufactures throughout every part of Asia, from whence any valuable returns may be made to Europe." After this, Captain Gower was to return to Macao, where Macartney hoped to be by May, 1794.[48]

The letter to the Emperor of Japan, dated near Chusan on July 10, 1793, explained Macartney's appointment as Ambassador and said that he hoped to visit the Emperor the following year. The letter to the Governor of the Philippine Islands, dated August 1, asked him to give the *Lion* good treatment, assured him of the cordial relations between England and Spain, promised that the Ambassador would render service to Spanish subjects while he was in China, and hoped that he would be able to visit the Governor before he returned to Europe. Gower's reply to Macartney cheerfully agreed to carry out his orders and to take care that his men would not offend the natives, and requested that passes or letters of introduction might be obtained from the officials.[49]

On August 2 junks arrived and began to unload the presents, and Macartney gave the Chinese a list of the presents written in English, Latin, and Chinese, together with a description of the more important. The demand for a copy of the King's letter was resisted, but a paper containing the names and positions of members of the suite was given to the mandarins. On August 5 the Embassy disembarked and proceeded to the mouth of the Peiho, where it was received with much ceremony.[50]

[47] *Macartney's Journal,* p. 253; IOCM, XCII, 40-50, 137-47; Anderson, *op. cit.,* p. 58.
[48] IOCM, XCII, 137-47; CMC, Nos. 338, 339.
[49] IOCM, XCII, 151-53; CMC, Nos. 261, 267.
[50] IOCM, XCII, 155-70; CMC, No. 266; Staunton, *Embassy* (1797), I, 490-99; *Macartney's Journal,* pp. 254-55.

On August 6, the Viceroy of Chihli, Liang K'eng-t'ang, having arrived to visit the Ambassador, Macartney and Staunton went ashore and were conducted in great state by an escort of troops to the Viceroy. Mutual compliments were exchanged and then Macartney explained that he was quite willing to go to Jehol to pay his respects to the Emperor, but that as some of the presents might be damaged during so long a journey it would be advisable to leave the more delicate ones at Peking. He also requested a diploma from the Viceroy which would allow the *Lion* to go to Miaotao or Chusan and disembark the sick, and he emphasized the compliment intended by the English King in sending the Embassy and his personal desire to promote this sentiment. Macartney was particularly struck with the Viceroy's ease, politeness, dignity, and kindness, as well as with the "regularity, alertness, and dispatch" that accompanied the preparations for the trip up the river.[51]

On August 8 the necessary diplomas were received from the Viceroy and were dispatched to the *Lion*. Accordingly, on the 8th, the *Lion* and the *Hindostan*, accompanied by the *Clarence*, sailed for Miaotao. The harbor of this port was found so unsatisfactory that they proceeded to Chusan, where they arrived on August 27 and soon obtained permission to disembark. During August there were on the *Lion* 128 sick, of whom 78 recovered and 46 (*sic*) remained unfit. By the 9th, preparations for the journey up the river were completed. Macartney, therefore, dispatched the *Endeavour* (the *Jackall* apparently remaining, although it ultimately reached Chusan on September 17), and with it went Père Hanna and Père Lamiot. These two missionaries were not allowed to go to Peking except as members of the suite, and as such they would have had to leave with the Embassy.[52]

"At noon [on August 9] the gongs, or copper drums, began to beat . . . and . . . in less than an hour our whole fleet was under sail. . . . " On the 11th they reached Tientsin, where they were met by the Tartar Legate, Cheng Jui (called Chin-ta-gin by Macartney), who "discovered a perverse and unfriendly disposition" toward the concerns of the Embassy, and announced that it was to proceed to Tungchow by boat and afterwards by land with all of the presents to Jehol. Macartney agreed that the members of the suite would be will-

---

[51] *Macartney's Journal*, pp. 255-60; *Chang Ku Ch'ung P'ien*, III, pp. 18-20.
[52] *Macartney's Journal*, p. 260; Staunton, *Embassy* (1797), I, 513-18; BM, *Additional Manuscripts (Journal of the Lion)*, No. 21,106, pp. 80-88 (151-64); CMC, No. 268.

ing to go, but said that some of the presents would be damaged by such a journey. The Legate insisted, however, and it was not until the Viceroy had intervened that Cheng Jui would change his demand. It was finally decided to proceed to Peking, where the planetarium, globes, lenses, lustres, and clocks could be left, after which the Embassy, with the rest of the presents, would proceed to Jehol to be present at the Emperor's birthday on September 17.[53]

Toward evening the Embassy moved on. At this time the Ambassador received two letters from the French ex-Jesuit Grammont, one written on May 7 and one on August 6. They professed his sincere wish for the success of the Embassy, stated that he was doing all in his power to give the Chinese a favorable idea of the English, warned them against the intrigues of a Portuguese ex-Jesuit, Joseph-Bernard d'Almeida, a member of the Tribunal of Mathematics, who had been appointed interpreter to the Embassy, and suggested that the Ambassador request of the mandarins permission to select from among the missionaries a person to act as *factoton* to the Embassy. Macartney was rather suspicious of Grammont's offers, and, as the latter did not wish his name revealed, he sent no reply (Grammont's Chinese name was Leang Tong-ts'ai). Nevertheless, he seized the first opportunity of requesting that he might select a missionary to attend the Embassy. The mandarins promised to write the Court about it at once.[54]

The Embassy moved on up the Peiho with the banners of their barges carrying the conventional formula *"The Embassador bearing tribute from the Kingdom of England."* Macartney was aware of this fact; but, considering it not a matter of primary importance and fearing that a remonstrance would not be followed by redress, a circumstance which would have put a stop to his mission, he desisted from making a complaint. The Legate and Van and Chou visited the Ambassador almost every day, and on August 11, as the flotilla was nearing Tungchow, they came to inform him that the arrangements proposed by the Ambassador relative to the presents were agreeable to the Emperor; that two houses were being prepared for him, one in Peking and one near the Yüanmingyüan Palace (Summer Palace, six miles northwest of Peking), and that he could choose which he wished; that after the audience at Jehol the Embassy would return to Peking

---

[53] IOCM, XCII, 50-53; *Macartney's Journal*, pp. 260-63.
[54] CMC, Nos. 216, 251; Pritchard, *op. cit.*, pp. 6-13; *Macartney's Journal*, pp. 263-64.

and be followed shortly by the Emperor, and that, therefore, it would be unnecessary to take the howitzers and field pieces with them.[55]

After making these remarks, the conductors broached in a very adroit manner the subject of the ceremony to be performed before the Emperor. They discussed various modes of dress and remarked that the English should adopt the Chinese mode before appearing before the Court, inasmuch as the knee-buckles and garters would cause much inconvenience. Macartney observed that he supposed the Emperor would prefer the Ambassador to pay the same sort of obeisance to him that he would pay to his own King. The mandarins then supposed the ceremonies of the two Courts to be much alike, and went on to describe their own, which consisted of kneeling on both knees three times and at each kneeling making three prostrations (the *kotow*), a ceremony which "never had been, and never could be, dispensed with."

Macartney explained that the English custom was somewhat different, but that he had an earnest desire to be agreeable to the Emperor, although his first duty was to his King, and that, if they were really serious in their objection, he would give them a written answer after he had reached Peking. They went on to drop hints about the dangers of the long voyage, and to suppose that the King would be anxious to see him home again soon—on account of which the Emperor was returning earlier from Jehol than usual in order not to cause delay. Macartney replied that the King's letter would indicate what was expected of the Ambassador when he arrived home, and what time would be sufficient to transact the business he was charged with. He was asked if he had brought any personal presents for the Emperor, to which he replied that he had brought a coach, and that he would no doubt be able to find other presents to offer him at the New Year's Day, thus hinting that he aimed to remain for some time.[56]

As a result of this interview Cheng Jui memorialized the throne indicating that the English were ignorant of the proper obeisance to be performed before the Emperor, but that he was instructing them and having them practice the *kotow*. On August 18 an edict expressed confidence that the English would comply with the Court ceremonials and not "commit the blunder of being rude." Even before Cheng Jui had seen the English, he had evidently intimated that he intended to force them to practice the *kotow*, for on August 5 the Emperor indi-

---

[55] *Macartney's Journal*, pp. 264-66, 269; IOCM, XCII, 58-61; Staunton, *Embassy* (1797), II, 130.

[56] *Macartney's Journal*, pp. 266-67; Staunton, *Embassy* (1797), II, 135.

cated that he should not be too inconsiderate and exacting in dealing with the matter.[57]

On August 16 the Embassy reached Tungchow, where the land portage began, and on this day Grammont directed another letter to Macartney, reasserting his desire to help the Ambassador and requesting Macartney to obtain permission for him to attend the mission to Jehol.[58] At about this time Macartney learned through the friendly Chou and Van that it was believed the English had assisted the Goorkhas during recent fighting in Tibet, where the Emperor's troops had been employed to repel their invasion. Macartney at the time knew nothing of the particular circumstances, but assured them that the English would not have opposed a friendly nation like China, urged that Tibet was too far from Bengal for the English to send troops, and that most of the British troops had been busy fighting the Tippo Sultan in the south. From them he also learned that in the light of these events the chief ministers were inclined to suspect some sinister intention concealed beneath the proffers of gifts and friendship.[59]

4. *From Tungchow to Jehol and the Settlement of the Ceremonial (August 16—September 14, 1793).*

Some time was spent in transferring the baggage to land carriages at Tungchow, during which the Embassy was housed in a temple. On August 18 Van and Chou informed the Ambassador that the Emperor would permit him to select one of the missionaries to attend him, and that one of the Grand Secretaries (Colaos), together with a missionary, would meet the Embassy at Peking. On the following day Van and Chou returned to the question of the ceremony. They requested the Ambassador to practise it and gave a demonstration themselves. He declined, and they then asked the interpreter to do it, but he said that he could do only what the Ambassador directed. Cheng Jui continued to be distant and unfriendly despite Macartney's efforts to placate him. In the evening Henry Eades, the metallurgist, died of dysentery and was buried the next day.[60]

On August 21 the cavalcade set out for Peking, where some refreshments were taken, and then it proceeded through the city to the

---

[57] *Chang Ku Ch'ung P'ien,* V, pp. 25-31 and VII, p. 52.
[58] CMC, No. 217.
[59] IOCM, XCII, 53-56; *Macartney's Journal,* pp. 268-69; Staunton, *Historical Embassy* (1797), pp. 272-76.
[60] *Macartney's Journal,* pp. 269-75; Anderson, *op. cit.,* pp. 86-98.

Yüanmingyüan Palace, where it arrived about three o'clock in the afternoon, but no missionaries were sent to it. On the 22nd Cheng Jui announced that the Grand Secretary was on his way from Jehol and would soon arrive, and that the missionaries would be sent the next day. Observing that he was in good humor, the Ambassador indicated that the Embassy would probably find the surroundings in Peking more satisfactory and requested permission to be taken there. The Legate thought there would be no objection.

On the next day the Legate came with Joseph-Bernard d'Almeida, André Rodrigues (Portuguese ex-Jesuit), Louis de Poirot (French ex-Jesuit), Joseph Panzi (Italian ex-Jesuit), Peter Adeodato (Italian), Joseph Paris (French layman), and two or three other missionaries. D'Almeida, because of his influence with the chief minister, Ho Shen, whom he attended as a surgeon, had obtained the appointment as interpreter. As Macartney had been warned against him, and, as the man knew none of the modern European languages which Macartney did, his services were declined. This rejection threw d'Almeida into a rage, and he openly denounced the English to an Italian missionary, using Latin, which Macartney understood. The other missionaries were more friendly, and through one of them Macartney conveyed regrets to d'Almeida that his ignorance of Portuguese robbed him of so able an interpreter. Later d'Almeida came back and assured Macartney of his good will and favorable services.[61]

Shortly after this scene Van and Chou came to say that the Colao (variously called Chun and Keen [Kun?] San by Macartney—possibly Kung A), a cousin of the Emperor, had arrived, and that he and they were now to manage the affairs of the Embassy. In consequence, Van, the interpreter, and Maxwell went to Peking to view the palace intended for the Ambassador, while Chou took the Ambassador over the Yüanmingyüan Palace. Macartney seemed to have been much impressed by the palace and was interested to find a large clock there made by George Clarke, a watch-maker in Leadenhall Street. He was disquieted to find that Cheng Jui accompanied him almost continuously. In the evening Maxwell returned with a favorable report on the palace in Peking. The next day, August 24, it was arranged that Barrow and Dinwiddi should remain at the Summer Palace to put up the presents,

---

[61] *Macartney's Journal*, pp. 275-77; IOCM, XCII, 63-66; for details about the missionaries see CMC, Nos. 405, 426, 428 and Louis Pfister, *Notices . . . sur les Jesuites . . . de Chine* (Shanghai, 1932-34), II, 886-89, 965-74.

while the rest of the Embassy went to Jehol. Peter Adeodato came later to serve as interpreter to these men while the Embassy was away.[62]

A dispute arose during the same day because the English interfered with the rough handling of some of the delicate presents by the Chinese workmen. The Tartar Legate objected, saying that they were *cong-so (kung)*, tributes to the Emperor. The interpreter replied that they were not *cong-so* but *sung-lo*, presents. The Colao put an end to it by saying that *sung-lo* was proper enough. On the following day the Legate delivered to Macartney a letter from Captain Gower, sent from Tengchow. After Macartney had prepared an answer, which he requested the Legate to forward, the latter asked the contents of both. In order to placate him, Macartney had them both interpreted to him and observed "with great good-humor" that the English had no secrets. On August 26 the Embassy removed to Peking, where it found more spacious quarters, although the members were confined closely and not allowed to see anyone except in the presence of officials.[63]

On August 25 the Legate once again raised the question of the ceremony and desired Macartney to practise it before him, but the Ambassador put a stop to it by saying that he had a paper on the subject which he would deliver in a few days. He found difficulty in getting anyone to translate it because his own interpreter was unacquainted with the proper diplomatic form. After their return to Peking, however, Nicholas Joseph Raux, a French Lazarist, was sent on the 27th to wait upon and serve the Embassy. Macartney obtained considerable information from him, and through him was able to get a Chinese to translate his letter to Ho Shen upon the subject of the *kotow*. The Chinese, however, was fearful that the identity of the translator would be discovered from the writing, and so it was arranged that young George Staunton, who had made considerable progress in the writing and speaking of the language on the way out, should put it into Chinese characters.[64]

The note to Ho Shen, first minister, was dated August 28 and written in four languages: English, Latin, French, and Chinese. After expressing the esteem in which the English King held the Emperor and the Ambassador's desire to please the Emperor and fulfil the objects

---

[62] *Macartney's Journal*, pp. 278-80; Barrow, *China*, pp. 104-110.
[63] *Macartney's Journal*, pp. 280-82; IOCM, XCII, 64-66; Staunton, *Historical Embassy* (1797), pp. 312-22.
[64] *Macartney's Journal*, pp. 282-83; IOCM, XCII, 58-64; Staunton, *Embassy* (1797), II, 330-37.

of his mission, it indicated that the Ambassador would be punished by his King if his conduct could be construed as unbecoming to the rank of his master. To avoid this and yet conform to the ceremonies he agreed to perform "every exterior ceremony practised by His Imperial Majesty's Subjects" on condition that the Emperor order

that one of the Ministers of the Court, equal in station to the Embassador shall perform before His Britannic Majesty's Picture at large in his Royal Robes, and in the Embassadors possession now at Pekin, the same ceremonies, as shall be performed by the Embassador before the throne of His Imperial Majesty.[65]

On the same day an unsigned note was sent to Grammont indicating that his suggestions had been valuable, that they hoped he would continue to give them information, and that they had tried in vain several times to obtain his services for the trip to Jehol. On August 29 the paper relating to the ceremony was delivered to Cheng Jui to transmit to Ho Shen at Jehol. The Legate did not like the proposal, but Van and Chou favored it as an expedient. Later in the day Macartney received a kind note from the aged French ex-Jesuit Jean-Joseph-Marie Amiot, regretting that his infirmities prevented his seeing the Ambassador, giving good wishes, and promising all information and assistance in his power.[66]

Preparations were now being made for the journey to Jehol, and on August 30 Macartney purchased two especially handsome watches from Captain Mackintosh as presents for the Emperor. He also requested permission to be shown about the city, but was told to restrain his curiosity until his return from Peking. The same day he received a long letter from Grammont. It indicated that d'Almeida and Poirot had been sent to Jehol, and said that the best way to counteract the Portuguese's designs would be to leave the Chinese interpreter behind, so that d'Almeida could not divert him; Poirot would be able to convey their words directly to the Emperor. He also said that after returning from Jehol they would be expected to give presents to the four sons of the Emperor and to his eldest grandson, to A tchong tang (first minister), to Ho tchong tang (favorite minister), to Fou liou (another favorite minister), and to the President of the Board of Rites. He said that d'Almeida should have nothing to do with the distribution of their presents, and felt that Raux and Poirot had had too little experi-

---

[65] IOCM, XCII, 209-10.
[66] *Macartney's Journal*, pp. 283-84; CMC, Nos. 213, 405, 426, 428; Pfister's *Notices*, II, 837-60.

ence, but recommended himself, and asked Macartney to obtain from Ho Shen permission for Grammont to serve the Embassy on its return.[67]

From a conversation with Raux on the same day Macartney received confirmation of much of what Grammont had said and also of what he had received from Van and Chou about the management of government. A-kuei (called A-cou-i or A-chong-tong by Macartney) was the highest ranking minister but, being very old, took no part in affairs. Ho Shen (called Cho-chan-tong or Ho-chon-tong by Macartney and Staunton) was the Emperor's favorite minister, in whose hands practically all power rested. Fu Ch'ang-an (called Fou-li-ou by Macartney), brother to the Viceroy of Canton (Fu-K'ang-an, who had been fighting the rebels in Tibet and who had recently returned to Peking), was the minister second in favor. The three above-named men were Tartars, and the three other chief ministers, being Chinese, possessed little influence, although they were men of great ability.[68]

From one of the missionaries who accompanied Alesandro Govea, the Bishop of Peking, when he visited Macartney on August 30, the Ambassador learned that the Portuguese as a group were all violently opposed to the success of other nations. Grammont, who was allowed to see the Ambassador for a few minutes on August 31, stated that his inability to obtain free access to the English was due to Cheng Jui's jealousy and to the missionary's having talked so much in their favor. Macartney considered him a "clever fellow," but as he was said to be "of a restless, intriguing turn" was determined to be on guard against him. Sixty-nine persons accompanied the Ambassador to Jehol (twenty-one remained behind), forty of whom composed the guard. The two Secretaries, Dr. Gillan, Captain Mackintosh, William Alexander, Jacob Ly, Sir George Staunton and his son, and J. C. Hüttner went to Jehol; John Barrow, Dr. Dinwiddi, and some of the servants remained at the Yüanmingyüan Palace, and Dr. Scott, some members of the guard, and the sick remained in Peking.[69]

The cavalcade set out on Monday, September 2. On the 3rd, conversations with Van and Chou revealed that Macartney's letter to

[67] CMC, No. 214; Pritchard, *op. cit.*, pp. 17-22; *Macartney's Journal*, pp. 285-86.

[68] *Macartney's Journal*, pp. 286-87; Giles, *Chinese Biographical Dictionary*, Nos. 590, 657, 1583; G. T. Staunton, *Criminal Code*, pp. 498-502.

[69] *Macartney's Journal*, pp. 288-92, 296; IOCM, XCII, 67-70; CMC, Nos. 405, 426, 482.

Gower had not been forwarded, and later the Legate returned it, saying that he considered it to be of no importance. On September 5 the Embassy entered Jehol province by the Kupeikow pass. The English examined it with great interest, and Lieutenant Parish took its dimensions. Late in the day Chou told Macartney that he thought the proposal relative to the ceremony would be approved. On the 6th the members of the suite were entertained by some passages from one of the Tientsin gazettes, giving extravagant and unreal descriptions of the presents brought by the Ambassador. One present was described as "a singing bird as big as a hen, that [fed] upon charcoal, and [devoured] usually fifty pounds per day." On September 8 the Embassy entered Jehol in state, preceded by one hundred mandarins on horseback, and were housed in one of the Emperor's palaces.[70]

Soon after the Ambassador's arrival, Van and Chou came with Ho Shen's compliments and indicated that, as he had an injured knee, he would be pleased if Macartney would visit him. Macartney excused himself, saying that if necessary Sir George Staunton could go. The Legate also returned the paper relating to the ceremony, saying that it would be more effective if the Ambassador delivered it himself. Later in the day Staunton visited Ho Shen, who wished a copy of the King's letter to the Emperor, which was promised him. He then opened the subject of the ceremonial and revealed that Macartney's letter had been shown to him. He did not like the proposal, and he tried to contrive other means whereby Macartney could escape the censure of his King and yet conform to the Court ceremonials. During this discussion Staunton was allowed to sit, and the conference ended by Staunton's giving Macartney's letter on the subject to Ho Shen and desiring the Minister to give his written opinions upon the matter to the Ambassador for consideration.[71]

This interview revealed the Legate's duplicity; as a result and because of the fact that he had not visited the Ambassador on board the *Lion*, he appears to have been demoted three ranks. Whether or not Macartney's proposal was submitted to the Emperor is uncertain, but on September 9 a Court dispatch was issued indicating that the Emperor was "deeply displeased at heart" because the Ambassador was not conversant with the proper ceremonial. It directed the provincial of-

---

[70] *Macartney's Journal*, pp. 292-97; CMC, No. 358; Staunton, *Embassy* (1797), II, 150-208.
[71] *Macartney's Journal*, pp. 297-98; Staunton, *Embassy* (1797), II, 209-13; IOCM, XCII, 68-71.

ficials to treat the Embassy less ceremoniously on its return trip. On the same day the Legate and Van and Chou came to urge Macartney to perform the ceremony, but he insisted upon the propriety of "something to distinguish between the homage of tributary Princes and the ceremony used on the part of a great and independent Sovereign." He was later privately informed that the Emperor had not yet been told of his proposals, but that when he was informed he would probably adjust the matter as the Ambassador wished.[12]

On September 10 a still more drastic Court order was issued. It complained of procrastination, ignorance, and haughtiness on the part of the Ambassador, who feigned sickness and excused himself from practicing the ceremony. It specified that the Embassy was to be treated in a rather unfriendly fashion at Jehol, that the presents were not to be accepted, that after its return to Peking it was to be treated in a curt manner and dismissed, and that its provisions were to be cut down. In conformity with this, supplies were not delivered as usual to the Embassy, but a prompt complaint produced an immediate remedy.[13]

Later in the day the Legate, Van, and Chou resumed the discussion, and Macartney told them that it was not natural to expect him to show greater reverence for a foreign Prince than for his own Sovereign. They hinted that failure to comply with the ceremony might expose the Ambassador to personal danger, but when he informed them that he was willing to kneel on one knee and kiss the Emperor's hand as the obeisance which he would perform before his own sovereign, they seemed to think that would be satisfactory. Later in the day the Legate arrived and said that it was decided that the English ceremony should be performed, but he proposed that Macartney should kneel on both knees instead of one. Macartney replied that he would "kneel upon one knee only on those occasions when it was usual for the Chinese to prostrate themselves." The Legate assented to this, but said that the kissing of the Emperor's hand would have to be dispensed with, to which Macartney agreed.[14]

What machinations went on behind the scenes to produce this settlement is not evident from the available documents. The Emperor may have considered Macartney's final proposal as indicative of sufficient

[12] *Chang Ku Ch'ung P'ien*, VII, 52-53; *Macartney's Journal*, pp. 298-99.
[13] *Chang Ku Ch'ung P'ien*, VII, 53-55; Staunton, *Embassy* (1797), II, 213-20; Anderson, *op. cit.*, pp. 143-45.
[14] *Macartney's Journal*, pp. 299-300; IOCM, XCII, 68-71; Hüttner, *op. cit.*, pp. 70-79.

respect. At any rate on September 11 Macartney had a private meeting with Ho Shen, who was accompanied by Fu Ch'ang-an and other ministers. Ho Shen appeared very congenial, and after mutual compliments had been exchanged, he informed Macartney that because of the great distance which the Ambassador had traveled to pay his respects to the Emperor, he would be allowed to perform the English ceremony, that he would be permitted to deliver the King's letter into the Emperor's hands, and that the time for the first audience was set for Saturday, September 14. On the same day a Court dispatch was issued specifying that, as the English were now "Sincerely obedient and all follow[ed] the prescribed rules," they should be treated with consideration.[75]

During the course of the conversation with Ho Shen on September 11, Macartney emphasized the pacific intentions of England, attempted to allay Chinese fears about British aggression from India, dwelt upon the value of the commerce between the two nations, and discussed British relations with Russia. Ho Shen promised to discuss these matters further at a later date. On the same day the presents were unpacked and on September 12 they were delivered to the Imperial Palace. The presents delivered at this time included guns, swords, pistols, woollens, linen, cotton and silk cloth, carpets, pictures, and a telescope. Dr. Gillan was sent to install the telescope.[76]

5. *The Imperial Audiences at Jehol and Events at Canton (September 14—September 28, 1793).*

On the morning of September 14 the first audience with the Emperor was held. Besides the Ambassador, the other gentlemen of the Embassy were allowed to remain to witness the ceremony, but the servants and guards, after attending the Ambassador to the place of audience, were sent back to their quarters.[77] It will be of interest to let the Ambassador tell his own story of the reception in the words which he used in his official dispatch to Henry Dundas. On the morning of September 14

I went before daylight, as directed, to the Garden of the Palace of Geho, and after waiting a considerable time, which is a part of the etiquette, the Emperor appeared, about seven o'clock, seated in an open chair borne by

[75] *Chang Ku Ch'ung P'ien*, VII, 54-56; *Macartney's Journal*, pp. 300-302; Staunton, *Embassy* (1797), II, 220-39.
[76] IOCM, XCII, 70-74; CMC, No. 352; *Macartney's Journal*, pp. 302-303.
[77] Anderson, *op. cit.*, pp. 146-49; Holmes, *op. cit.*, pp. 143-45; Wang Chih-ch'un, *Kuo Ch'ao Jou Yüan Chih* (Canton, 1891), Ch. 6, pp. 3-4.

sixteen men, and preceded, accompanied and followed by Officers of his household, besides flag and high umbrella bearers, and music. He entered a large and magnificent tent intended for numerous assemblies, and supported by gilded and painted Pillars. He ascended the Throne by the front steps, consecrated to his use alone. The tent was filled by about eighty Tartars or other tributary Princes, besides many of his own family. I was conducted to the side of the Throne, holding his Majesty's letter in the gold box with both hands above my head, and mounting the side steps I delivered the box and letter into his Imperial Majesty's own hands and with one knee bent, as had been settled, I made the most reverential obeisance. The chief Persons close to his Person were the Colao [Ho Shen], the Vice-roy of Canton [Fu K'ang-an] who is his Son in law, and a brother of the Viceroy's [Fu Ch'ang-an] who all constantly spoke to him on their knees. He received me in a very gracious manner, and with the utmost appearance of satisfaction, said that he was very glad to receive this mark of esteem and attention from the King of England, and he hoped that peace and friendship should always subsist between them. He then delivered to me a present for His Majesty consisting of a kind of sceptre such as the Emperor has contantly upon his Throne, and made of a transparent stone accounted precious and of high value here, such Sceptre being emblematic of Prosperity and peace. He did me the honor also, as His Majesty's Representative, of a present of a handsome piece of green agat, and gave or sent some mark of attention to every Person in my suite. [Macartney gave to the Emperor as a personal gift a pair of enamelled watches set with diamonds.] I then retired from the Throne to a table covered with viands and fruits in vast variety.[78]

After Macartney had presented his credentials, Sir George Leonard Staunton came forward and was introduced as the Minister Plenipotentiary, and, after "kneeling upon one knee" as the Ambassador had done, he presented to the Emperor two elegant air-guns and received from the Emperor a greenish stone similar to the one which had been given to Macartney. The Emperor inquired whether any of the English spoke Chinese, whereupon young George Staunton, a boy of thirteen, came forward and spoke to the Emperor, who was so pleased that the took a purse from his girdle and presented it to the boy. Presents were later sent to every member of the suite.[79]

On the day following the reception the Ambassador was conducted over the western Imperial gardens by Ho Shen, Fu Ch'ang-an, Fu K'ang-an, and Sung Yün (called Sun-ta-gin by Macartney), a young Mongol, who had recently been employed upon the Russian frontier

---

[78] IOCM, XCII, 74-78.
[79] *Macartney's Journal*, pp. 303-07; Staunton, *Embassy* (1797), II, 224-39; Hüttner, *op. cit.*, pp. 77-91.

and who was a member of the Council of State. With this latter person Macartney had considerable conversation about Russia. The attitude of both Ho Shen and Fu Ch'ang-an was gracious and friendly, but that of Fu K'ang-an, Viceroy of Canton and general recently returned from Tibet, was blatantly unfriendly. When the arrival of the *Lion* at Chusan was mentioned, Macartney requested permission for Captain Mackintosh to go at once to join the *Hindostan* at Chusan, but the Viceroy at once opposed the idea, saying that it was improper for a foreigner thus to travel through China. Not wishing to press the subject, Macartney requested an opportunity to confer with Ho Shen on one of the days following, but the latter excused himself because of other matters.[80]

On September 16 various of the gentlemen of the suite went upon a short excursion into the country, but they were watched throughout, although not molested, by soldiers. Dr. Gillan was also requested to wait upon Ho Shen to give him advice about the rupture from which this Chinese official suffered, and a young Tartar named "Poo" visited the Ambassador and discoursed at great length about geography, history, and the lineage of the Emperor. September 17 being the Emperor's birthday, the Embassy went again to the Imperial Court. The Emperor did not show himself, but slow, solemn music was played, followed by a sudden silence. "At length the great band struck up with all their powers of harmony. . . . And then all the dwellers upon China earth there present, except ourselves, bowed down their heads, and prostrated themselves upon the ground at every renewal of the chorus." [81]

All the English documents agree that, on this occasion and at the Imperial audience on the 14th, the Ambassador and his suite knelt upon one knee and made profound bows. Most of the Chinese documents or works which mention the Embassy are either silent on the subject of the ceremony performed or make equivocal statements to the effect that the English performed the ceremony of congratulation, that they brought tribute, that they rendered homage, or that they had an audience. Some non-British writers say or imply that the *kotow* was performed. At the time of the Amherst Embassy in 1816 the Chinese insisted that at least on the Emperor's birthday Macartney had *kotowed*,

---

[80] *Macartney's Journal*, pp. 308-31; IOCM, XCII, 78-82; Staunton, *Embassy* (1797), II, 240-48; Giles, *Biographical Dictionary*, Nos. 590, 1843.
[81] *Macartney's Journal*, pp. 312-14; Staunton, *Embassy* (1797), II, 256; Hüttner *op. cit.*, pp. 98-100; IOCM, XCII, 83-86.

and Ch'en K'ang-ch'i, writing over a century after the event, asserts upon the authority of Kuan Shih-ming, a censor of the Ch'ien Lung period, that although Macartney refused to *kotow*, he was overcome by the presence of the Emperor and fell on both knees and prostrated himself. After a careful consideration of all the available evidence there seems to be no reason for departing from the English accounts. The *kotow* was not performed.[82]

After the ceremony on September 17 Macartney was conducted about the eastern gardens by the same four mandarins who had conducted him on the 15th. During this excursion Macartney repeatedly tried to turn the conversation to the subject of his mission; but Ho Shen was equally clever in parrying all the Ambassador's attempts, saying that they could discuss business after the return of the Embassy to Peking. The Ambassador, however, learned that the King's letter had been taken into consideration, that Fu K'ang-an had been consulted, and that even a deposed and imprisoned Hoppo had been sent for to give his testimony and advice. In Macartney's opinion, "Such counsellors must have been chosen to strengthen the Colao against the inclinations of the Emperor."[83]

On September 18 the Embassy went to the Imperial Court to attend a play and other diversion provided by the Emperor. During the performance the Emperor conversed for a time with the Ambassador, who endeavoured without success to turn the conversation toward the subject of the Embassy. The Emperor gave him a box containing "a little book with slight drawings and a few Chinese verses by his own hand," together with several agates considered especially valuable by the Chinese, which the Ambassador was to deliver to the King in token

---

[82] Yü, *op. cit.*, Ch. 23, pp. 3-6; Wang, *op. cit.*, Ch. 6, pp. 3-4; *Tung Hua Lu*, Ch. 118, p. 3; Wang Wên-t'ai, *Hung Mao Fan Ying Chi Li K'ao Lüeh*, p. 10; *Kuantung T'ung Chih*, Ch. 170, p. 42; *Ch'ing Shih Kao*, Ch. 160, Pang Chiao Chi II, England, p. 1; Ch'en K'ang-ch'i, *Liang Ch'ien Chi Wen* (1910), Ch. 5, p. 11; J. P. Abel-Rémusat, *Melanges Asiatiques* (Paris, 1825-26), I, 440-41; W. W. Rockhill, "Diplomatic Missions at the Court of Peking," *American Historical Review*, II (July, 1897), 632-33; Henry Ellis, *Journal . . . of the Late Embassy to China* (London, 1817), pp. 72, 92-95, 108, 110, 118, 123, 139-40, 147-48, 154, 169-70; G. T. Staunton, *The British Embassy to Peking in 1816* (London, 1824), pp. 22-24, 44-51, 53-54, 59-62, 94-96, 107-09; E. H. Pritchard, "Letters from Missionaries at Peking Relating to the Macartney Embassy," *T'oung Pao*, XXXI (1934), 35, 37-38, 56; the writer is at present preparing a detailed paper on "The question of the *Kotow* in the Macartney Embassy to China in 1793," which he hopes to be able to publish soon in some American historical or Oriental journal.

[83] *Macartney's Journal*, pp. 315-18; IOCM, XCII, 85-87; Staunton, *Embassy* (1797), II, 248-58; Hüttner, *op cit.*, p. 99.

of the Emperor's friendship. During the course of this day the Ambassador was also able to get a letter to Ho Shen translated into the proper Chinese with the aid of a Chinese secretary. It was copied by young Staunton to avoid endangering the translator, and was carried on the 19th by Jacob Ly to Ho Shen's yamen and delivered to one of the Minister's secretaries.[84]

The letter, dated September 18, requested permission for Captain Mackintosh to set out at once for Chusan and to take with him one of the missionaries from Peking to act as interpreter. It further asked permission for the *Hindostan* to trade at Chusan, and suggested that, if the Minister desired, Pères Hanna and Lamiot, who had been forced to go to Chusan, might return to Peking with the missionary who accompanied Captain Mackintosh. Finally, it requested that letters and communications be forwarded freely and quickly between Canton and the Embassy.[85] Late in the evening of the 19th the Legate came with Van and Chou and read, in answer to these requests, a paper which he would not give to the Ambassador. It stated that Captain Mackintosh could not return to Chusan except with the Embassy, gave the *Hindostan* permission to trade without being required to pay the Imperial duties, and extended to the two missionaries the privilege of coming to Peking and entering the Emperor's service; but it said nothing about the forwarding of correspondence.[86]

On September 11 Grammont had written again to Macartney, requesting him to obtain from the Emperor permission for the missionary to be second interpreter. He suggested that Macartney propose this while he was at the Emperor's table, and that he request the Emperor to give Grammont a blue button, which would make him free to help the Embassy. Because this was obviously a scheme of Grammont's for obtaining promotion, the Ambassador did not trouble to carry out the suggestion. His mind was already too much beset with troubles and doubts as to the outcome of his mission to wish to incur ill-will by promoting Grammont's private schemes, even though the Frenchman might have been of help to the mission. On September 20 the Emperor's presents to the King—consisting of lanthorns, silks, porcelains,

[84] IOCM, XCII, 88-91; *Macartney's Journal*, pp. 318-322; Staunton, *Embassy* (1797), II, 253-55.

[85] IOCM, XCII, 217-19.

[86] IOCM, XCII, 82-88; *Macartney's Journal*, p. 322; Staunton, *Embassy* (1797), II, 272-74.

teas, and drawings—were packed under the eyes of the mandarins, and on the 21st the Embassy set out for Peking.[87]

While these events were taking place, matters of importance were transpiring at Canton. On June 28 news was received at Canton from Bombay that war was impending between France and England. Consequently, Eyles Irwin availed himself of some missionaries who were traveling to Peking to send a private letter to Lord Macartney (dated July 2) summarizing the news from Europe up to January 10, 1793. The most important part of the letter was the statement that war fever was high in England when Parliament met, and that the King's speech hinted at an approaching rupture with France. On September 8 the supercargoes received from England dispatches for Macartney, together with positive news of the war between England and France. Besides, they received in a private letter from Bengal an account of recent events in Nepal. Captain Kirkpatrick had been sent to mediate between the Chinese and Nepalese forces—with the result that the Chinese general addressed a very friendly letter to Cornwallis promising to recommend his lordship very favorably to the Emperor.[88]

The Commissioners were already worried about the fate of the Embassy, inasmuch as none of the brigs had returned from the north; and the receipt of the dispatches and this important news made them feel that they must send it on to the Ambassador at once. The supercargoes, because of being unable to forward the dispatches through the Chinese without disclosing their contents and because of having no dispatch-boat, determined to buy a small vessel from the Portuguese which was offered to them for $10,500. She was renamed the *Iphigenia*, placed under the command of Lieutenant Inverarity, and dispatched on September 28 with orders to proceed to Tientsin. After arriving at Tientsin, Lieutenant Inverarity was to deliver the packet to whoever was in command of the squadron and then await dispatches from Macartney at Peking. If none of the squadron of the Embassy was at Tientsin, he was to address a letter to Macartney and await the Ambassador's orders before forwarding the dispatches. The *Iphigenia* sailed from Macao on October 5.[89]

[87] CMC, No. 215; Pritchard, *T'oung Pao*, XXXI (1934), 23-24; *Macartney's Journal*, p. 323; Anderson, *op. cit.*, p. 166.

[88] CMC, No. 259; IOCM, XCIII, 245-63; Morse, *Chronicle*, II, 222-23.

[89] IOCM, XCIII, 264-325.

6. *Attempts at Negotiations in Peking and the Dismissal of the Embassy (September 26—October 7, 1793).*

In the meantime, at the capital the last scene of this comic tragedy was being performed. The Embassy left Jehol on the 21st of September and reached Peking at about noon on the 26th. Van and Chou continued to be very friendly, but the Legate preserved the "same vinegar aspect without relaxation." The Chinese hurried the English in the arranging of the presents at Peking and dropped broad hints to the effect that the Embassy would be expected to depart soon. On September 28 the Legate came to inform Macartney, who was much indisposed with the gout and rheumatism, that the Emperor would be returning on the 30th, and that it was the custom for Ambassadors and great mandarins to go out about twelve miles to meet the Emperor.[90]

In the meantime the mandarins at Jehol had completed the consideration of their reply to the King's letter, and on September 23 an edict in answer was drawn up. It is not evident whether this edict was issued at once or retained until later. Nor can one be sure that the Emperor's letter to the King, which was delivered to the Ambassador on October 3, was identical with the edict of the 23rd of September, although their general content is the same.[91]

The reply, after dwelling upon the graciousness of the Emperor and the noble way in which he had received the Ambassador, refused the King's request for a resident minister at Peking, because it was "not consistent with the Customs of this our Empire." It went on to say that if foreigners wished to enter the Emperor's service they might come to Peking, but that they must adopt the Chinese dress and ways and remain there in "Perpetuity." It pointed out that the Emperor offered adequate protection to foreigners who traded at Canton, that a minister at Peking would be of no service to them, and that such a representative could not study Chinese institutions and practices to any advantage. The aim of the Chinese government, it said, was to preserve peace and tranquillity, and it did not place value on things from without. The Ambassador, having delivered his presents, was now dismissed, charged with valuable presents from the Emperor to his King,

[90] *Macartney's Journal*, pp. 323-26; Anderson, *op. cit.*, pp. 168-71.
[91] *Kuo Ch'ao Jou Yüan Chi*, Ch. 6, pp. 4-8; *Kao Ch'un Huang-ti Sheng Hsün*, Ch. 276, pp. 21-24; an English translation appears in Backhouse and Bland, *Annals & Memoirs of the Court of Peking*, pp. 322-25; IOCM, XCII, 243-55; *Yüeh Hai Kuan Chih*, Ch. 23, pp. 4-7; Bannister, *op. cit.*, pp. 239 ff.

which the latter should accept "and Act at the same time conformably to the Affection and Benevolence" which he had shown for the Emperor, by making

your Intentions correspond with mine. Adhere to Truth and Equity, Act with all Prudence and Benignity, Study the public Good, avert misfortunes from your Kingdom, and conduct yourself in such Wise, that we may reciprocally enjoy the Blessings of Peace and Tranquillity.

On the 30th of September the Ambassador repaired at 4 A.M. to the place where the Emperor's loyal subjects were to watch him pass. The Chinese fell upon their faces as the Emperor came by, but the English "bent one knee only to the ground." The Emperor in a message advised Macartney, because of being unwell, to return at once to Peking. The remainder of the presents (officially delivered on the 30th) were viewed by the Emperor on October 1, and on the same day Macartney sent a note to Ho Shen. This communication aimed to obviate the immediate dismissal of the Embassy, which Father Romaldo Kazielski, the only missionary allowed to visit the Embassy after its return, had intimated was intended. The note thanked the minister for the permission that had been granted to the *Hindostan* to trade at Chusan, requested that Captain Mackintosh be permitted to go to his ship at once in order to conduct the trade, and proposed to ask the Emperor's leave to depart for Canton soon after the new year (which fell early in February).[92]

Ho Shen's reply was a request to see Macartney the next day at the Yüanmingyüan. Macartney was much indisposed but complied with the request, and besides Ho Shen, found Fu Ch'ang-an and Fu K'ang-an awaiting him at the Palace. Some letters were delivered to him from the ships at Chusan, one being from Captain Gower, dated September 16. Ho Shen, who wished to know their contents, was readily informed that they explained that the *Lion* was preparing for a speedy departure, but that the *Hindostan* would not depart until her commander arrived.[93] Ho Shen then suggested that because the climate did not agree with the English, it would be advisable for them to depart as soon as possible. Macartney replied

that it was inconsistent with my duty to quit at once a Court to which I had barely opened my commission, and before any part of it's object could be accomplished; that my Sovereign's intentions were that I should continue

---

[92] CMC, No. 353; IOCM, XCII, 89-92, 225-27; *Macartney's Journal,* pp. 326-29; Barrow, *China,* pp. 119-21.

[93] CMC, Nos. 271, 272; *Macartney's Journal,* pp. 329-30.

long enough, and at his charge, to have frequent opportunities, of which a very few, indeed, had hitherto occurred, of paying my respects to His Imperial Majesty, for the purpose of cultivating and cementing a friendship so happily begun; with which view likewise, the King had instructed me to request that the Emperor would be pleased to send one or more of his Subjects as Embassadors to England, whom we should take and send back to China in our own Ships; that the Calao had, when at Geho, been so good as to flatter me with the hope of many meetings with him at Yuen-min-yuen, or Pekin, which however I anxiously wished for, my sudden departure must necessarily prevent. I then endeavoured to explain in general terms, what I should be most desirous of introducing into conversation at such meetings, ... The Calao preserved a perfect command over all his Sentiments: he did not enter into any earnest discussion of the topics I touched upon, but concluded by saying that the Emperor was actuated in his proposal for our going only by his anxiety for our welfare; but that our stay would be very agreeable to him. The Calao suffered me to take leave, without giving me the least intimation of the Emperor's answer to His Majesty's letter being actually prepared, and intended to be delivered to me the next day, of which, however, I had notice immediately afterwards, from a private hand [the missionaries], and which delivery is always meant as a signal for departure.[94]

Later in the day Van and Chou came to inform the Ambassador that he would probably be summoned to meet the minister again the next day, and that the Emperor's letter would probably be delivered on that occasion; they advised him, if he was given the Imperial letter, to request permission to leave without delay. Early on October 3 the Legate came and requested the Ambassador to attend a ceremony at the Palace. The latter was ill in bed, but arose and proceeded to the Palace, where the Emperor's letter to the King (the contents of which have already been described) and the remainder of the presents to the King were resting in state. The Ministers displayed a special stiffness and ill humor and refused to accept presents from Macartney. By the time the ceremonies were finished Macartney was so nearly exhausted that he requested leave to retire, but he first called attention to the points he had mentioned the day before which his sovereign wished him to submit, and requested that Staunton be allowed to continue the subject. Ho Shen declined, but said that a note containing the requests might be sent to him.[95]

Because Macartney realized that he would be forced to go very soon, he lost no time in drawing up his requests and forwarded them to

---

[94] IOCM, XCII, 90-96.
[95] IOCM, XCII, 94-96; *Macartney's Journal*, pp. 331-32; Staunton, *Embassy*, II, 320-36; for a list of the Imperial presents see IOCM, XCII, 317-48.

Ho Shen on the same day. These requests, solicited in the name of the King of Great Britain, were:[96]

(1) The right to trade at Chusan, Ningpo, and Tientsin, the English submitting themselves to the laws and customs of China.

(2) Permission to establish a warehouse at Peking under the same conditions formerly allowed the Russians.

(3) Permission to occupy some small unfortified place near Chusan to be used as a trade depôt and place of residence for English merchants.

(4) Permission to occupy a similar place near Canton, or at least the right to reside at Canton the year round, with freedom to ride and take exercise.

(5) The abolition of the transit charges between Macao and Canton, or at least their reduction to the level of the year 1782.

(6) Freedom from duties and fees beyond those established by the Emperor, a diploma of which should be given the English.

By this time Macartney was convinced that further attempts to delay his departure would accomplish no good purpose. He was strengthened in this opinion by a communication from Père Amiot, who told him that the Chinese expected embassies to depart soon after the Imperial audience; that delay might detract from the favorable impression thus far made; that the gains already made could be followed up by letters; that it might shortly be arranged to have a Consul at Canton, who could negotiate with the Viceroy and who might occasionally proceed to Peking upon ceremonial occasions and negotiate with authorities there; and that he considered it to the Ambassador's best interest to go at once. The receipt of Irwin's letter saying that war was imminent in Europe also served to strengthen Macartney's determination to leave, inasmuch as the *Lion* could be used to convoy the Indiamen home.[97]

Macartney, therefore, wrote to Ho Shen on October 4 that he would depart as soon as he had received a reply to his requests. He also signified his desire to go to Chusan to embark on the *Lion*, and he asked the Minister to forward a note to Captain Gower with all dispatch that it might reach the *Lion* before she sailed. He said further that, if the *Lion* had gone, it would be necessary for him to travel overland all the way to Canton. Later on the same day the Legate came to announce that the letter had been dispatched to Captain Gower, that the Ambassador's request to depart had been granted and the 7th fixed as the day

---

[96] IOCM, XCII, 259-61; *Macartney's Journal*, pp. 333.
[97] *Macartney's Journal*, pp. 333-35; IOCM, XCII, 97-100.

of leaving, and that the reply to his requests would be delivered on the day of his departure.[98]

The Chinese immediately drafted a reply to Macartney's request. It was completed either on the 4th or the 5th of October, and Pères Poirot and Raux were summoned to translate it into Latin. Among its various articles was one forbidding the English to send missionaries to Peking, to which these good fathers objected, saying that the English made no such request. Nevertheless, they were forced to translate it, but throughout the edict they softened the language as much as they safely could.[99]

On October 5 a secret edict was issued and sent to all the provinces. It stated that the English might stir up trouble, because their requests had been refused, and expressed apprehension that the envoys, upon returning to Canton, would make false statements and incite the barbarian merchants of other countries to use tricky methods. For this reason the officials were to be on the alert, the troops were to be put in order, and the coastal defenses strengthened so that if the English returned and attempted to trade at new ports contrary to the Imperial order they could be repelled. The troops were to be marshalled in the provinces as the Ambassador passed, in order to intimidate the English. Altogether, it expressed a fear that the English might retaliate, and directed that this information should be kept secret in order not to cause the people to become suspicious or frightened.[100]

On the same day Van and Chou informed the Ambassador that the young Mongol Colao, Sung Yün, would accompany the Embassy as chief conductor and that the Legate would go no farther than Tientsin. They were not sure whether or not they would attend the Embassy. Preparations for the departure of the Embassy were hurried, and at noon on October 7 the Ambassador left his hotel and set out for Tungchow. On his way from the city he stopped at the Minister's pavilion, where he received the Emperor's reply and a list of the presents which the Emperor had bestowed upon the King, the Ambassador, and other members of the suite.[101]

The Imperial reply (as delivered to the English, it was dated October 7), filled with high-sounding phrases and addressed alternately

---

[98] *Macartney's Journal,* pp. 335-37; IOCM, XCII, 100-04, 263-65.
[99] CMC, No. 308; Pritchard, *op. cit.,* pp. 40-43.
[100] *Kao Tsung Shun Huang-ti Sheng Hsün,* Ch. 288, pp. 16-17; *Yüeh Hai Kuan Chih,* Ch. 23, pp. 12-13.
[101] *Macartney's Journal,* pp. 337-39; IOCM, XCII, 317-48.

to King and Ambassador, practically amounted to a reprimand to the Ambassador for having been so impertinent as to impose upon the Emperor's good will by making requests contrary to the customs of the country. The six requests were refused; the first four were rejected peremptorily, and, in regard to the charges between Canton and Macao and in regard to the duties on trade, it was said that these had already been fixed and would have to be conformed to, but that the English would be treated like all other nations and not discriminated against. A seventh clause was included to say that the English religion could not be propagated in China. This arose undoubtedly because of Macartney's connections with Lamiot and Hanna. In conclusion, the letter stated that as the requests militated against the laws and customs of the Empire they could not be granted, and a solemn warning was issued to the English King that if his ships came to Ningpo, Chusan, or Tientsin, they would be forced to leave. "Let us therefore live in Peace and Friendship, and do not make Light of my Words." [102]

---

[102] Morse, *Chronicle*, II, 245-52; *Yüeh Hai Kuan Chih*, Ch. 23, pp. 8-12; for translation from Chinese see Backhouse and Bland, *op. cit.*, pp. 325-31.

Chapter IX

THE RETURN OF THE EMBASSY TO ENGLAND AND AN ESTIMATE OF ITS ACHIEVEMENTS (1793-1800)

1. *The Favorable Assurances of Sung Yün during the Journey to Hangchow (October 7—November 14, 1793).*

As the confused and disheartened Embassy wended its way from Peking toward Tungchow on October 7, 1793, it was the first and only great failure in Macartney's long diplomatic and political career and one of the most complete failures known to the diplomatic history of Great Britain. The Ambassador, as is shown in the extract from his *Journal* to follow, was so thoroughly aware of this that he was filled with gloom, and his feelings were shared to a greater or lesser degree by everyone else from the servants and soldiers to the Secretary of the Embassy.[1] On October 4 Macartney made the following entry in his *Journal*:

Having been selected for this Commission to China, the first of its kind from Great Britain, of which considerable expectations of success had been formed by many, and by none more than by myself, I cannot help feeling the disappointment most severely. I cannot lose sight of my first prospects without infinite regret. The consciousness of doing all in a man's power to do in the exercise of public employments is an ultimate consolation against most evils that can happen; but it requires no ordinary strain of philosophy to reconcile him at once to the immediate failure of success in a favourite undertaking, be the remote consequences ever so flattering.[2]

During the voyage down the Peiho and along the Grand Canal, Macartney's spirits and hopes were somewhat revived by the attention paid the Embassy, by flattering reports of the Emperor's satisfaction with the Embassy and of his favorable sentiments toward the English, and by the friendly, congenial disposition of Sung Yün and his assurances that the abuses at Canton would be reformed. Being thus reassured, the Ambassador entered as soon as possible upon the attainment of the secondary aims of the mission—namely, the reform of abuses at Canton. The Embassy left Tungchow on the 8th of October, and on the 10th Sung Yün paid the Ambassador a friendly visit.

---

[1] Staunton, *Embassy,* II, 336-54; Anderson, *op. cit.,* pp. 178-82; Holmes, *op. cit.,* pp. 149-52; Hüttner, *Voyage à la Chine,* pp. 126-30.
[2] *Macartney's Journal,* pp. 334-35.

Sung indicated that he would conduct the Embassy to Chusan, and that, if the ships were not there, he would conduct it to Canton. Sung also informed the Ambassador that his letter to Gower, requesting the *Lion* to remain at Chusan, had not been forwarded. When Macartney explained the necessity of sending the letter at once, because the *Lion* was likely to leave, he promised to write the Court immediately and felt sure that the request would be complied with. He later informed the Ambassador, after a long discussion about Russia, that the Chinese never sent embassies to foreign countries, that embassies from abroad were only occasionally received, and that, according to the laws of the Empire, they were allowed to remain but forty days, a custom which could not be broken without inconvenience or perhaps mischief to the state.[3]

In later conversations with Van and Chou, Macartney learned that the Emperor allowed T. 5,000 per day for defraying the expenses of the Embassy as it passed through the provinces; that if such amount was insufficient, the difference was made up by the provinces, and that T. 1,500 per day had been allowed for the expenses of their residence in Peking. Macartney received these figures with considerable scepticism. Progress down the river was slow because of the shallowness of the water, and on October 12, the day before the flotilla reached Tientsin, Sung paid another friendly visit and conversed freely with the Ambassador.[4]

Macartney assured him of the good intentions of the English and of the desire of the English King that British subjects should be well protected in China. He remarked that recently new and heavy duties had been levied on trade; that they had been steadily augmented since 1782; and that, if this continued, the English commerce with China would have to be relinquished. To this, Sung replied that the Emperor had lately given fresh orders that the English and others at Canton should be treated with indulgence and liberality. He further admitted that recently new duties had been levied because of the wars in Tongking and Tibet, but said that, as peace now reigned, the duties would be diminished, although it was impossible to fix them absolutely, because they must necessarily vary according to the exigencies of the state or of the particular province in which they were levied. He further

---

[3] *Macartney's Journal*, pp. 341-42; Staunton, *Embassy* (1797), II, 354-55.
[4] *Macartney's Journal*, p. 343.

assured Macartney of his willingness to convey and explain the sentiments of the English to the ministers.[5]

In the meantime navigation from Chusan to Japan had become very difficult because of the setting in of the northeast monsoon, and the change in weather and the low situation of the hospital at Chusan caused the slowly recovering crew of the *Lion* to be seized with fevers and ague. Accordingly, Captain Gower determined to proceed to the Ladrones to procure medicine and see whether a change in atmosphere would help the men. The *Endeavour* and the *Jackall* sailed for Canton on October 13 with a letter asking for medical supplies, and on the 15th Captain Gower wrote to Macartney explaining the reasons for his proceeding southward. The *Hindostan* was to remain until her Captain arrived. The *Lion*, after obtaining passes from the mandarins, sailed for the south on October 17 with sixty sick on board.[6]

In Tientsin the Embassy was given an especially sumptuous entertainment as a special mark of favor from Sung. From Tientsin the mission turned up a river leading to the Grand Canal, which it entered on October 22. The favorable disposition and assurances of Sung continued, and on the day before entering the Grand Canal, Macartney had a long conference with him.[7] Macartney, being convinced of Sung's good will, entered into a long discussion with him about the two Imperial letters which had ignored or refused the requests made by the English King and his Ambassador.

I had the consolation of hearing in return that the Emperor, notwithstanding any surmises that had been made about us, he entertained himself the best regards for us, and our Nation, and that he was determined to protect our trade, about which we appeared to interest ourselves so warmly; that he had indeed refused particular requests, not so much perhaps that they really were in themselves improper, as that they were introductive of something new, which at the advanced period of his life he did not think it prudent to adopt, at least upon the sudden; that as to the business of Canton, the detail of matters in that distant province was left for the most part to the discretion or recommendation of the Vice-roy, who, consulted on the answer, would not readily dictate an abolition of the practises he had permitted; but that his Imperial Majesty had as a peculiar mark of his attention to our wishes on this head, made a change in the Government of that Province, and named to it a person [Ch'ang Lin] endued with uncom-

[5] *Macartney's Journal*, pp. 344-46.
[6] IOCM, XCII, 357-58; BM, *Additional Manuscript (Journal of the Lion)*, No. 21,106, pp. 91-92 (173-75).
[7] *Macartney's Journal*, pp. 346-50; Staunton, *Embassy* (1797), II, 355-58; Barrow, *China*, p. 502; Holmes, *op. cit.*, pp. 158-60.

mon sentiments of Justice, and benignity towards all Strangers; that his Imperial Majesty had written in the strongest terms to this new Vice-roy, who had not yet quitted his latè Government of Chekiang, in which Cheusan is situated, to examine and revise as soon as he shall get to Canton the regulations of that Port, and to put an effectual stop to the vexations of which we complain. . . .

In the course of conversation, I insinuated to my friend that however satisfactory the intentions thus expressed were to us; yet that they were not warranted by the Emperor's public letters to his Majesty by which the future would alone be judged in England; but that a third letter from the Emperor would solve all doubts, and seemed indeed to be called for on account of the evident difference of the latin from the originals in one instance, and perhaps in many others. My friend seemed conscious with me of the gratification at least that such a letter must produce, but that the real public advantages would not be increased by it and that he was fearful the etiquette, which is so strictly observed here, however embarrassing it may be sometimes, will prevent any letter being sent by an Embassador after his departure from Court. He then added . . . that as the Capital of Chekian, where the Vice-roy of Canton still resides, lay in our way to Cheusan, he should introduce me to him there, who would give me a full confirmation of the assurances, I now received.[8]

On October 25 Sung brought Macartney newly received assurances of the Emperor's good will and of his intentions to grant new indulgences to the English. On the 29th Sung brought news that the *Lion* and smaller vessels had sailed, but that the *Hindostan* remained to take the Embassy to Canton. Macartney indicated that she was not large enough to carry the whole Embassy. Sung then proposed that the heavy baggage be embarked on the *Hindostan* and that the rest of the Embassy should proceed overland to Canton. To this Macartney raised no objection. On October 31 Sung arrived with the news that the Emperor was thoroughly convinced that the Embassy had not been sent from "any improper views or mischievous curiosity, but solely to do him honor and solicit commercial privileges and protection." He added that the new Viceroy was fully acquainted with the Emperor's sentiments and would allow the supercargoes to see him freely. Macartney once again intimated his desire for the Emperor's written sentiments upon these matters, whereupon Sung informed him that he had mentioned the matter in his dispatches to Court.[9]

The Embassy crossed the Yellow River (which at this time did not empty into the Gulf of Chihli) on November 2, and on November 6 it crossed the Yangtze River. On the next day Sung showed the

---

[8] IOCM, XCII, 100-110.
[9] *Macartney's Journal*, pp. 351-53; IOCM, XCII, 109-12.

Ambassador a letter from the Emperor saying the Embassy would be put under the direction of the new Viceroy Ch'ang Lin, at Hangchow, that Captain Mackintosh should join the *Hindostan*, and that the rest of the Embassy should proceed to Canton by land. It was decided that the presents, Benson, Dinwiddi, Alexander, and part of the guard should be embarked on the *Hindostan*. On November 9 the Embassy reached Hangchow, where it was greeted by Ch'ang Lin, who assured Macartney of the Emperor's good wishes, said that he would remedy abuses at Canton, presented the Embassy with additional presents from the Emperor to the King, and indicated that as the conditions for trade at Chusan were very unfavorable, it would be advisable for the *Hindostan* to go to Canton. After some objection to this latter point, Macartney agreed.[10]

On the same day Macartney directed a long dispatch to Dundas explaining all events from the time the Embassy left Macao until that date, and with it went twenty enclosures including every important paper that he had delivered or received while in China. A letter was also sent to Captain Gower requesting him to remain at Macao until the Embassy arrived. On November 13 Sung paid a farewell visit to the Ambassador, and he "seemed to be quite melted at parting from" the Embassy. He carried northward with him a letter from Macartney to Ho Shen, dated November 9.[11]

After thanking the Emperor for his kindness toward the Embassy since its departure, and noting the Imperial assurances received through Sung that the abuses and hardships at Canton would be remedied through the medium of the new Viceroy, Ch'ang Lin, the note went on to point out that the British requests for the opening of new ports were dictated by the laudable desire of the English to increase the communication between the two nations. Further, it explained that the English had no desire to obtain exclusive commercial privileges to the detriment of other nations, expressed satisfaction that the Emperor in reality did not consider that the Ambassador had made requests not authorized by his King, and explained that the English had no desires to spread their religion in China but were interested in trade only. It concluded by saying that as the Ambassador would be at Canton for some time he could receive further communications from Peking.[12]

---

[10] *Macartney's Journal,* pp. 353-56; IOCM, XCII, 111-14; Anderson, *op. cit.,* pp. 205-08.

[11] IOCM, XCII, 31-116, 357-66; *Macartney's Journal,* pp. 356-57.

[12] IOCM, XCII, 349-55.

2. *Discussions with the New Viceroy from Hangchow to Canton (November 14—December 19, 1793).*

The Embassy departed from Hangchow on November 14 under the direction of Ch'ang Lin. On the 16th the Viceroy visited the Ambassador and opened the subject of the Canton trade. He admitted little knowledge of the matter and requested a written statement of the principal points on which the English wanted assistance. He indicated his determination to see that justice was done and to grant what was reasonable and proper, but said that many difficulties would be placed in the way of his success by others at Canton. He also expressed concern that Macartney entertained doubts as to the friendliness of the Chinese administration toward England. If these doubts should be the cause of retaliation on the part of England, he would be held criminally responsible for any favors which he might grant the English. He therefore wished for a frank statement of the Ambassador's sentiments. Macartney indicated that he had felt this way when he left Peking, but that because of his favorable treatment and the Imperial assurances since received, he had not sent an adverse report to his Court.[13]

On November 19 the Viceroy informed the Ambassador that word had been received of the arrival of the *Lion* at Macao; and on the 20th, as the land portage over the mountains between Chekiang and Kiangsi provinces began, Ch'ang came again to talk with the Ambassador. He was still apprehensive that Macartney would send adverse accounts of his treatment to his superiors in England, but was pleased when Macartney once again indicated that his earlier unfavorable view had been materially changed.[14]

The Viceroy then asked if I could authorize him to assure the Emperor that the King would give a proof of the continuance of his good disposition by writing again soon to His Imperial Majesty, and by sending a Minister to China if the Emperor were disposed to allow of such, not with the parade and expence of the present Embassy, but simply as a testimony of the subsisting friendship of His Britannic Majesty. I ventured to say that the King would have no difficulty in writing to the Emperor to acknowledge the presents sent by the latter to him, and to thank him for the honorable reception of the Embassy; a circumstance distinct from the objects of it, which, I still hoped, might be brought about in time, and also that his Majesty had from the beginning intended to have, if not constantly, at least occasionally a Minister resident in China.[15]

---

[13] *Macartney's Journal,* pp. 359-61; IOCM, XCII, 395-400; Staunton, *Embassy* (1797), II, 470-71.

[14] *Macartney's Journal,* pp. 362-64; Staunton, *Embassy* (1797), II, 483-87.

[15] IOCM, XCII, 398-402.

At the conclusion of this discussion, Macartney gave to the Viceroy a paper containing "a General Idea of what the Ambassador wish[ed] to obtain for the English at Canton." The points were contained under eleven articles as follows:[16]

(1) That the English be subject to no duties or fees except those levied by the Emperor, and to insure this that they be given a list of such duties, showing what each ship and each article should pay.

(2) That no fees be charged on English persons, vessels, or goods in transit between Macao and Canton unless imposed by the Emperor, a list of such Imperial duties to be given to the English.

(3) That goods on which duties have once been paid shall not be subject to duties again.

(4) That, as a measure necessary to their health, the English be allowed freedom to ride and exercise in the neighborhood of Canton and not be confined to the factories.

(5) That a place be set aside for the use of English sailors, where a hospital might be erected for their use.

(6) That the English merchants be permitted to remain at Canton as long as necessary after their ships had departed.

(7) That the English be allowed to trade with any merchants, and not be confined to the Hong merchants.

(8) That the security merchant system be abolished, and the English allowed to pay the Imperial duties and charges directly to the officials.

(9) That a Chinese be allowed to instruct the English in the language of the country.

(10) That in criminal cases persons of the same nation not guilty of the offense should not be held responsible or made to suffer.

(11) That the English be not identified with the Americans, who spoke a similar language.

On November 23 a note of compliment, written in Chinese and copied by young Staunton, was given to Ch'ang. It laid emphasis upon the desire of England to cement a friendship with China, indicated England's desire to keep up a correspondence, called attention to the favorable promises of the Emperor conveyed through Sung and Ch'ang, and hoped that they would be signified by a letter or by specific orders to the Viceroy to treat the English properly."[17] On November 30 another conversation took place, in which the Viceroy asked many questions about British trade and indicated that he suspected great peculation

[16] IOCM, XCII, 411-14; Morse, *Chronicle*, II, 252-53; *Macartney's Journal*, p. 364.

[17] IOCM, XCII, 421-23.

among the officials at Canton, whereby the Imperial revenue was defrauded. Macartney did not express an opinion on this, but promised to
collect information on all matters after he arrived at Canton and to
transfer it to the Viceroy.[18]

In the meantime Ch'ang's report had reached Peking, and as a
result an edict was issued on December 1. It reached Ch'ang on
December 9 and was shown to Macartney, who was told that he was
to have a copy, and its general meaning was conveyed to him.[19] A copy
of the English translation as made at that time from the edict given
to Macartney differs considerably in language, although not in content,
from a literal translation from the Chinese, extracts of which will be
quoted below. The edict noted Ch'ang's report as to the "submissive
and respectfully obedient" attitude of the English, and stated that the
"improper requests" which the English had made at Peking were
refused because they were contrary to Chinese law and custom. It
then went on:

Now according to your petition you still desire to send a letter and to pay
tribute again. The Great Emperor, seeing the respectful attitude of your
Country's King, graciously gives his permission. But because of the un-
certainty of the conditions of the ocean it is not necessary to fix a definite
year; that is left entirely to the convenience of your country. As to the
arrival of the tribute goods at Canton, according to the rule of the Heavenly
Dynasty, all cases of barbarians sending letters and tribute are without
exception reported by the Governor-Generals and Governors. As soon as
the letter and tribute arrives they will report the whole cicumstance. The
Great Emperor will as a matter of course issue an edict giving his permission, and will send presents to make manifest the principle of giving more
than is received.[20]

On December 11 the Viceroy left the Embassy and hurried on to
Canton. The mission reached the outskirts on the 18th, where it was
met by the Commissioners and found that Macartney's message had
reached the *Lion*, and that she was now near Macao. On the 19th the
Embassy entered Canton in state, was received and feasted by the
Viceroy, Governor, and Hoppo, and then proceeded to its quarters
across the river from the factories.[21]

---

[18] *Macartney's Journal*, pp. 365-66.

[19] *Ibid.*, p. 368.

[20] *Kao Tsung Shun Huang-ti Shêng Hsün*, Ch. 276, pp. 33-34; IOCM, XCII,
431-36.

[21] *Macartney's Journal*, pp. 370-78.

3. *Final Discussions at Canton and the Return to England (December 19, 1793—September 4, 1794).*

Macartney was no sooner settled at Canton than he directed a letter to the Commissioners indicating that the Viceroy had promised to remedy abuses and desired information. Accordingly, he requested the Commissioners to give him full information about all the complaints and to supply "such elucidations as will prevent the Extortioners from evading the charges." [22] During the three days December 21, 22, and 23 the greater part of Macartney's time was taken up in receiving visits from the Viceroy, the Governor, the Hoppo, and other mandarins, some of whom came a considerable distance to see him.

In these visits I explained at length the different grievances of our trade. The Hou-pou was averse to any alterations, and wished everything to remain as he found it. The Viceroy thought every reasonable alteration should be made, and they debated together with great earnestness for a considerable time. The subject was renewed again and again, and I should hope, from the Viceroy's professions and assurances, that we have got the better of the Hou-pou.[23]

On December 23 Macartney addressed a long letter[24] to the Chairs explaining what had happened and expressing the view that substantial gains had been made, which would be followed by definite benefits to the Company when the favorable disposition of the Viceroy had had time to make its effect felt. He indicated the favorable effect which he thought the Embassy would have upon the attitude of the Chinese toward the British character. He said that the specimen goods brought along had been distributed at various judicious places, and believed they would help to stimulate the already strong taste for such British goods as woollens and watches. He then went on to indicate that the woollen cloth called fleecy hosiery, Irish linens, glass in all forms, hardware, and stationery were new articles which could be introduced into China, and that the sale of woollens, tin, and copper could be increased. He believed that a type of scarlet nankeen might be exported with success, and he said that there was no political prejudice against the exportation of bullion in return for acceptable imports.

Once the English sailors had been brought properly under control so as not to offend the Chinese, and some form of connection had been established with the superior mandarins

---

[22] CMC, No. 288.
[23] *Macartney's Journal*, p. 379.
[24] IOCM, XCII, 369-92.

I am inclined to believe that it is within our Power so to gain gradually upon them as successively to obtain from them most of the advantages they have hitherto refused us. I do not find that there is in fact any fundamental regulation of the Empire prohibitory of foreign commerce with northern Ports. Such a reason is put forward only to conceal the real motive, which they do not chuse avowing, and which is their apprehension lest too great a communication with Strangers should interfere with that profound tranquillity and that awful submission among all Classes of Mén the maintenance of which is in truth the ever-present and only inalterable maxim of this Government.[25]

Macartney further indicated that he had obtained some specimens of the tea plant and some of the flowers which were sometimes mixed with it, which he intended to send to Sir John Shore (Governor-General of Bengal). He had also obtained specimens of the mulberry tree together with silk-worm eggs and all the information about the manufacture of silk which the Company had requested. He had not yet secured information about porcelain, but the Viceroy had sent a special messenger to get specimens of the various materials used in making it. He had "undeceived" the Chinese as to the difference between Englishmen and Americans. In general he had lost nothing the Company already possessed, had obtained most of the information they desired, and had sufficient assurances to make him believe that existing abuses and charges would be decreased and that in time more extensive privileges might be gained.

In a dispatch to Dundas on the same date he described events from the time he left Hangchow until that date, indicated that he had decided to give up going to Japan and other Eastern Islands, both because it seemed unlikely that he would be successful there and because the existence of war made it advisable that the *Lion* should serve as convoy to the fleet of Indiamen which would soon be ready to sail. He emphasized the hostility of Fu K'ang-an, former Viceroy and Tibetan general, who had disseminated falsehoods about the English activity in Tibet. Macartney explained that he had satisfied Ch'ang Lin upon this point, and that Ch'ang had suggested that an explanation of the real state of England's connections with Tibetan affairs might be the subject of another letter from the King or the work of a later envoy. He concluded with a belief that the new Viceroy, who had already begun an examination into the state of affairs at Canton, would remedy abuses and punish those who were guilty of them.[26]

---

[25] IOCM, XCII, 379-81.
[26] IOCM, XCII, 393-406.

But on the same day Macartney records in his *Journal*:

After maturely considering all the circumstances before me, I have now, however painful to me, been obliged to dismiss from my mind many flattering ideas which I had entertained at the commencement of my Embassy, of distinguishing it by some happy discovery, some signal and brilliant success, in the prosecution of our political and commercial interests in these distant parts of the world. I have given up my projected visit to Japan, which (though now less alluring in prospect) had been always with me a favourite adventure as the possible opening of a new mine for the exercise of our industry and the purchase of our manufactures.[27]

On Christmas day the Embassy dined at the English factory, and on December 26 and 27 Macartney discussed commercial matters with Puankhequa and Chunqua in the presence of Irwin and Jackson. Chunqua expressed his willingness to try experiments in new articles of trade but Puankhequa was much more reserved.[28] In the meantime the Commissioners had been collecting the information which Macartney desired. They were unsuccessful in getting data definite enough to serve as a basis for complaints. Geowqua, who had recently been subjected to extortion, was interviewed, but, fearful of the wrath of the mandarins, would not give sufficient positive information to be of value.

The linguist Ngoqua gave considerable information about the fees paid by the ship compradores to the government, which amounted to $420 per ship in 1788 and had risen to $690 in 1792. He also testified that the linguist fee charged on every ship by the officials was T. 68, and from other sources the Commissioners found that the fees paid by the factory compradores amounted to $195. Munqua testified that $9,000 had recently been extorted from Geowqua, and he indicated that prior to 1786 the charges on the Consoo fund for presents said to be sent to the Emperor amounted to about $60,000 annually, but that it had now risen to three or four times that amount. If the Europeans could pay the duties directly, he intimated that the merchants would be able to reduce prices by about 11 per cent. Munqua also stated that during one month when the Governor had acted as Hoppo he had extorted $12,000, and that the Hoppo then at Canton had extorted ten times that amount.[29]

---

[27] *Macartney's Journal*, p. 380.
[28] *Ibid.*, pp. 380-81.
[29] CMC, No. 321.

Armed with this information, Macartney drew up a new and more detailed statement of the grievances of the English and the reforms which they desired. It was delivered to the Viceroy on January 1, 1794, when this official came to convey the contents of a new Imperial edict expressing satisfaction with the Embassy and giving promises of future favors and protection. The Viceroy was particularly "courteous and caressing" and said that he had issued two edicts announcing the severest punishments to anyone who should injure the Europeans or practice extortion in dealing with them.[20] Macartney's representation to the Viceroy was a long document stating in detail the various complaints and ending with a list of sixteen requests which the English desired the Viceroy to grant. Excluding those mentioned in the previous representation to the Viceroy, the points were as follows:[21]

(1) That in coming and going from Macao the English should be exempt from paying duties on clothes, furniture, wine, food, and personal articles, or at least that they should not have to pay duty on the same article more than once.

(2) That pilots be placed at Lintin so that the ships could come into the Bogue at once and not be forced to lie in an exposed condition at Macao.

(3) That the 1950 taels *cumshaw* charge on each ship be abolished.

(4) That no extortions be levied on ship compradores, and that the English ships be permitted to employ and purchase from whomever they chose.

(5) That ships be permitted to transfer naval stores from one to the other without paying duties.

(6) That the English be permitted to erect a hospital on Danes Island.

(7) That the security merchants be abolished and in lieu thereof the English should pay a deposit to the Hoppo equal to what the duties would amount to.

(8) That standard weights be fixed to avoid difficulties over duties.

(9) That the English be permitted to purchase the ground on which their present factory stood and such adjoining ground as was necessary to their trade.

(10) That the English supercargoes be permitted to hire porters and boatmen without the necessity of taking out special licenses.

(11) That the English be allowed to present petitions at any time to the Viceroy.

The Viceroy's reply to these requests, sent to Macartney, admitted the existence of "Secret Frauds, unfounded Calumnies, public injuries,

[20] *Macartney's Journal*, pp. 381-82.
[21] IOCM, XCII, 451-60.

and heavy oppressions," and promised to use the "utmost Care and Speed in the Prohibition of those Grievances" and to punish those who transgressed.

As to the Residue of what you have requested, you may rest secure that your Tranquillity and Safety shall be duely consulted, and that so far as the Laws of China will permit, we shall be peculiarly desirous and ready to settle every thing to your entire Satisfaction.[32]

On January 2 an edict was issued by the Viceroy threatening dire punishment to anyone who molested, plundered, annoyed, abused, or defrauded the English. It was directed especially against several "wicked men" who maintained night boats near the factories and by means of "Liquor, loose Women, and other Irregularities" inveigled the foreigners into all sorts of iniquities.[33] A second edict was issued on January 5, prohibiting extortion from the Europeans by the magistrates, military, and other persons, and threatening with dire punishment anyone apprehended in such practices.[34] The edicts represented the high water mark of Macartney's achievements.

During the first week in January Macartney visited the city of Canton, wrote letters to the Chairs and to Dundas, and indulged in speculation. After his visit to Canton Macartney penned the following words in his *Journal*:

Now, I am very much mistaken if, by a proper management, we might not gradually and in some few years be able to mould the China trade (as we seem to have done the trade everywhere else) to the shape that will best suit us. But it would certainly require in us great skill, caution, temper, and perseverance, much greater, perhaps, than is reasonable to expect.[35]

Again, he observed that Macao might be purchased or easily taken if the Portuguese objected, or "the Bocca Tigris might be demolished by half a dozen broadsides," and the mouth of the river seized and a British settlement established. Such an act might bring the Empire of China, "an old, crazy, first-rate Man of War" which had fortunately been held together by strong rulers, to the ground. Still such an act might lead to European complications; Russia might attack China from the north, so that the present valuable trade in tea and woollens would be interrupted. He finally rejected force for the process of peacefully following up the good beginning he had made. His conclusion was

[32] IOCM, XCII, 467-68.
[33] IOCM, XCII, 475-78.
[34] IOCM, XCII, 483-86.
[35] *Macartney's Journal*, pp. 382-88.

that a King's Minister should be placed at Canton with power to keep British subjects in order, to supervise trade, to command respect from the mandarins, to carry on negotiations with them, and at the proper times and when necessary to communicate with Peking.

On January 7 Macartney sent a very sanguine letter to Dundas pointing out the Viceroy's favorable promises and edicts. He further indicated that the Viceroy had already sent proper persons to inspect the island where the English wished to establish a hospital, and that this official had promised that in the future English ships would not be forced to wait for pilots at Macao: "There is indeed a likelihood of a permanent as well as a complete redress of every grievance, whenever a familiar access to the Viceroy shall be established, and the difficulty overcome of communicating freely with him in the Chinese language." [36]

On the following day, when Macartney met the Viceroy and other officials at the English factory for breakfast and introduced them to the supercargoes, he received a promise that in the future the Commissioners would have free access to the Viceroy upon all occasions. It was, therefore, with a considerably lighter heart that the Ambassador left the factory to embark on the *Lion.* Van and Chou, the two friendly conductors, had dinner with him on the *Lion,* and then with tears in their eyes bade him a farewell which "could proceed from none but sincere and uncorrupted hearts." The next day he received presents from them, to whom he had also given liberally, and on January 10 the *Lion* fell down below the first bar, and on the 13th anchored in Macao Roads. [37]

The Ambassador went ashore on the 15th, was greeted by the Governor of Macao, Don Manuel Pinto, and proceeded to the house of one of the supercargoes, where he remained until March 8. On that day he embarked on the *Lion,* and on March 17 the fleet of Indiamen sailed under convoy of the *Lion.* [38] While at Macao, Macartney had Lieutenant Parish study the military defenses of Macao, and also directed him to explore the region about Hongkong and Kowloon with a view to finding a satisfactory harbor and place for a future establishment. [39]

---

[36] IOCM, XCII, 443-46.
[37] *Macartney's Journal,* pp. 389-91; CMC, No. 290, unpublished part of *Macartney's Journal,* from Jan. 1 to March 16, 1794.
[38] CMC, No. 290.
[39] CMC, No. 371.

On December 28 Macartney had given to the Commissioners a list of twenty-two articles which he thought could be introduced with advantage at Peking. After consulting with the merchants, the Commissioners concluded on February 3, that the articles were better suited to Private trade than "adapted to the extensive scale of the Company's Investments," although they agreed to recommend that specimens be sent out since "his Excellency wishes an experiment should be tried." [40] Staunton also carried on a correspondence with Père Hanna, and through him seems to have sent a letter to Raux indicating that another Embassy might be sent and soliciting his good support. [41] The fleet reached St. Helena on June 10, 1794, and on September 4 Macartney announced his arrival at Portsmouth to Dundas and the Chairs. [42]

4. *The Achievements of the Embassy in the Light of Subsequent Events (1794-1800)*.

The two primary aims of the Embassy had been: (1) to put Anglo-Chinese relations upon a treaty basis by the negotiation of a commercial treaty which would provide for the opening of Ningpo, Chusan, Tientsin, and other ports to trade, the clear statement of all duties and charges to be levied on trade, the cession of trade depots to England at Chusan and Canton where English law could be administered, and the establishment of a resident Minister at Peking; (2) the opening of Japan, Cochin China, and the Eastern Islands as a market for British manufactures by the negotiation of commercial treaties. Its secondary objects were: (1) the collection of commercial and cultural information about China and the Far East; (2) the remedy of existing abuses at Canton if the fundamental objects of the mission were not attained; and (3) the development of a friendly respect for the English by the Chinese.

When Macartney and Staunton sailed from Canton, they were under no illusions as to the temporary failure of their primary objects. They both believed, however, that the Chinese had been much impressed by the mission, that a breach had been opened in the wall of Chinese exclusiveness, which could be followed up to advantage by letters and a later less ostentatious mission under Staunton, and that by careful

---

[40] CMC, No. 322.

[41] CMC, Nos. 292, 293, 310.

[42] CMC, No. 296; IOCM, XCIII, Macartney to Dundas, Sept. 4, 1794; IOCM, XCII, 487-89.

management in time a regular friendly intercourse could be established, new ports opened, and the consumption of British manufactures in China greatly increased.

As to the secondary objects of the mission, they felt that these had been or would be shortly achieved. They had collected considerable information about Chinese government, institutions, customs, manners, trade, relations with other nations, religions, agricultural methods and products, commercial and industrial methods, and the possible openings for British manufactures. They had also done all in their power to impress the Chinese with a favorable idea of the English character and England's good intentions, and believed they had laid the basis for a much freer intercourse and a better treatment of the English at Canton. Finally, they believed that the major abuses at Canton would be speedily reformed under the direction of the friendly Ch'ang supported by the Imperial will. In support of this belief they had received the following:

(1) Often repeated favorable promises that justice would be done and that their requests not contrary to law and usage would be granted.

(2) Two edicts from the Viceroy prohibiting the abusive and illegal treatment of foreigners and forbidding extortion.

(3) A promise from Ch'ang that their ships would not have to wait at Macao for pilots.

(4) An actual reduction in transit duties between Macao and Canton from $4,935 to $2,926 (really effected by the Commissioners).

(5) A promise from the Viceroy that natives would be allowed to teach Chinese to the English.[48]

(6) A favorable consideration of the project for establishing a hospital.

(7) A promise from Ch'ang that the supercargoes should have free access to him.

They had, however, failed to realize that the Imperial permission to send another mission had been granted in conformity to Chinese custom and under the assumption that the English were humbly requesting to be allowed again to send tribute and render homage; that favorable and well-sounding edicts to the effect that justice was to be done in conformity with Chinese law and custom, without specific grants, meant that nothing was to be done, and that favorable promises and flattery were only devices for getting a troublesome nuisance out of the way. Subsequent events show that not one of the promises was ever carried out, that not one of Macartney's requests was granted, that

---

[48] Staunton, *Embassy*, (1797), II, 581.

later letters from the King were accepted as marks of homage, and that the English were still considered as outer barbarians.

The favorable promises and good intentions of Ch'ang had, however, created a difficult situation at Canton. He was presented with the united opposition of all the other officials at Canton, whose emoluments would have been greatly reduced had he carried out his promises. Had he tried to reform the abuses he might have found himself responsible for a reduction of the Imperial revenue and presents sent to Peking, which would have meant his ruin. Under these circumstances his good intentions gave way before the opposition of the other mandarins, who found reasons aplenty why it would be dangerous to allow the Europeans any privileges or relief from existing charges, which, once established, had taken their place among those immutable laws and usages of the Empire. He retired from Canton to Chinking, where he would be difficult to reach if the foreigners made complaints. But the situation was still very awkward; and within six months he was recalled to undertake other business, and a successor, Chu Kuei, not bound by troublesome promises, was sent to Canton.[44]

Macartney had looked toward an increased sale of British woollens and had hoped that the Viceroy would lower duties and reduce the charges on the merchants, an improvement in prices thus being accomplished. But in 1794 the market for woollens was overcrowded and the price paid for worsters was reduced from T. 1 per yard to T. 0.9, that of supers from T. 1.5 per yard to T. 1.4, that of ordinary long ells from T. 7.5 per piece to T. 6.7, that of superior long ells from T. 9 to T. 6.7 per piece, and camlets from T. 39 to T. 27 per piece. The sales price of lead, tin, and cotton also fell, and the cost price of tea and nankeens increased.[45]

So far as the introduction of new products was concerned, Macartney's hopes were no more successful. As already noted, neither the Chinese merchants nor the supercargoes approved of the articles he suggested. In 1794 a shipment of Irish linens invoiced at £845 was not suitable to the market, but Mowqua took them at invoiced cost and sent them to Manila. The Commissioners indicated to the Court that they did not think Macartney's ideas would be successful, but in 1795 Irish linens invoiced at £589, stationery at £276, and a case of swordblades at £248 were sent out because of Macartneys' suggestions.

[44] *Yüeh Hai Kuan Chih*, Ch. 7, see under Ch'ang Lin.
[45] IOCCD, CIX, price list; Morse, *Chronicle*, II, 257.

Mowqua again sent the linens to Manila but at two-thirds prime cost; the stationery, all merchants declared, could be used only as presents, but Puankhequa agreed to send one case to Peking. No one would touch the sword blades. Again in 1796 a consignment of linen and shawls invoiced at T. 2,339 was taken over by five merchants collectively, but they urgently requested that no more be sent.[46]

The Chairman of the Company wrote to Macartney about the supercargoes' belief that the articles which he had mentioned were not suitable, and Macartney's answer is significant. He indicated that a taste for the articles could be introduced only in the course of time and at an initial loss of money, as had been true with woollens, but felt that as the Company engaged the exclusive privilege of trade it should undertake the responsibility for the benefit of the nation. The Hongists, he said, would object at first, but in the course of time markets could be built up, but "I cannot . . . be sanguine in proposing the experiment to be made, until your Agents shall be brought to think as favorably of the prospect as I do." [47]

In the all-important problem of freedom of access to officials, Macartney's hopes were no better realized. Before he had even sailed from Macao, the favorably disposed Ch'ang refused to receive the Commissioners when they came to give him a complimentary letter from Macartney, giving as a reason the fact that he had already reported to Peking that the Ambassador had departed. The supercargoes apparently never tried to see him again, but in February, 1795, the Governor returned unopened a remonstrance sent to him by the Select Committee. In January, 1796, the Governor received Henry Browne and Samuel Peach when they had a letter from the King to the Emperor to deliver, but he forced Browne to go upon both knees when the Imperial reply was delivered. The officials showed no greater readiness to hear complaints or grant redress than before, and, so far as the records show, another audience was not granted until January, 1805, when another letter from the King to the Emperor was to be delivered.[48]

In difficulties with the Hoppo, the result was similar. In 1794 the *Indispensable*, a ship from New South Wales which wished to anchor outside the Bogue, was forced to proceed to Whampoa and pay port charges, and the Hoppo refused to issue the grand chop to the *Jenny*,

[46] Morse, *Chronicle*, II, 256, 266, 283.
[47] IOCM, XCII, 529-32.
[48] Morse, *Chronicle*, II, 269, 275, 431; CMC, No. 323.

a small vessel from the Northwest Coast, until the supercargoes had loaded her or rather pretended to load her with some tea so that she would have export duties to pay. In 1795 the Hoppo had in contemplation a measure which would have forced the Hong merchants to form a still more monopolistic organization than the existing Co-hong. It was opposèd by the supercargoes and by some of the Hongists, the latter of whom finally prevented it by large gifts to the officials.[49]

In 1796 the *Indispensable* arrived again, and the Hoppo refused to let her have a pilot to bring her up to Whampoa because she carried no cargo. The *Crescent* also arrived in ballast and was refused a pilot. The supercargoes finally obtained permission for them to enter after giving a promise in writing that in the future vessels without cargoes would not apply for permission to enter the river. Two more ships shortly arrived in ballast, and the Hoppo "in a towering rage" ordered them to leave the coast. After the regular ships of the season had arrived and the Hong merchants had made suitable arrangements, these last two ships were, however, allowed to come to Whampoa. In 1797 several of the departing Indiamen were disabled in a typhoon and returned to refit, but the Hoppo would not permit them to return to Whampoa.[50]

If one turns to the subject of duties and extortion, the same sad story appears. The decrease in the charge on the annual migration to and from Macao was the one tangible achievement which could be attributed even indirectly to the Embassy, and the officials soon began to increase it again despite the protests of the English. The charges levied on the Consoo fund showed no decrease. In 1793 the total levy was T. 272,500, of which T. 155,000 was for presents to the Emperor and officials; but in 1805 the total had risen to T. 357,900, of which T. 210,000 was used for presents. This gives an adequate idea of the extortion practices when one realizes that only T. 55,000 was the amount officially required to be set aside for the purchase of Imperial presents. The Hoppo Su Seng-o, who was in office for six months in 1794, was said to have extorted $240,000. A new Hoppo who arrived in 1796 demanded a huge assortment of toys, jewellery, etc., from the merchants, but, because those supplied were not elegant enough, sent them back with demands for more costly ones.[51]

---

[49] Morse, *Chronicle*, II, 259, 268-69.
[50] *Ibid.*, II, 288-296.
[51] *Ibid.*, II, 264, 287, 330, 356 and III, 62.

The extortions of the mandarins and mismanagement on the part of the merchants caused the bankruptcy of several of the latter shortly after the Embassy. Shy Kinqua went bankrupt in the spring of 1795. His goods and properties were seized by the officials to pay the arrears in the Imperial duties, and what then remained was used to meet his debts to the Company and private individuals. After this, debts to the amount of T. 586,992 remained, which were to be paid in six annual instalments by the remainder of the Hongists. Shy Kinqua's brother was sent into exile, and Shy Kinqua died in prison in February, 1796, of a fever brought on by the bastinado. In April, 1796, Munqua committed suicide to escape a similar fate. His property was seized to meet the Imperial duties, and Mowqua, his old associate, was forced to assume his debts. Geowqua was declared bankrupt in the spring of 1798, and Puiqua assumed his debts due to the Company. Early in 1797 Conseequa, an associate of Puankhequa, was imprisoned for trading with the foreigners without a Hongist chop and obtained his release only after the payment of a large sum of money.[52]

In 1796 the Select Committee, finding that Macartney's requisitions had produced no effect, drew up a list of requests which, together with the Governor's replies, were as follows:[53]

(1) A correct statement of all duties—refused because it was impracticable and because it had been refused to the tribute ships.

(2) A reduction in charges between Canton and Macao—refused in a general way.

(3) A place to ride and exercise—allowed to go twice a month to Honam temple.

(4) Permission to erect a hospital—refused because it would afford a pretext to foreigners for remaining the year round at Canton.

(5) Permission to remain at Canton after ships departed—twenty days allowed.

(6) Permission to trade freely with outside shopmen—refused.

(7) Permission to pay duties directly to officials—refused because impracticable and likely to subject foreigners to extortion.

(8) Permission to have a Chinese teacher—foreigners were permitted to learn from linguists and compradores, but no others.

(9) Limitation of criminal responsibility to the particular ship to which the offender belonged, other persons not being held responsible—chief of the factory required to deliver up the offender.

---

[52] *Ibid.*, II, 261-64, 270-73, 283-84, 298-301.
[53] Morrison, *Commercial Guide* (1834), p. 48.

Let this account of the adversities following upon the heels of the Embassy be concluded by references to four events in the years 1799 and 1800. The arrival of numerous H.M. ships to serve as convoys during the European war had occasioned several disorders. In 1799 the Governor and Hoppo issued orders forbidding men-of-war to come within sight of the Bogue forts and providing that they might be supplied with provisions at Lintin or at a distance from the Bogue. The following year a schooner, the *Providence*, attached to H.M. *Madras* was sent to Whampoa. Some Chinese boats were seen hovering about one evening, and, in the belief that they were trying to cut her cable, the boats were fired at, with the result that one Chinese was injured and another jumped overboard and drowned. A long controversy followed, in which the Chinese demanded without success the surrender of the person who had fired the shot and held the Select Committee responsible for the actions of all English at Canton. The affair was finally settled without disaster, because the injured person recovered and the English were relieved of responsibility for the man who, by jumping into the river, drowned himself.[54]

On December 2, 1799, an edict was issued by the Hoppo prohibiting the importation of opium and threatening the Hong merchants with severe punishment if they became security for ships bearing opium. In this same year the Select Committee drew up a special report for the information of the Directors to show what restrictions had been relieved and what new ones had been added since the Embassy. The findings represented in this report showed very conclusively that the great hopes of Macartney and Staunton as to the reform of abuses had not been achieved.[55]

Against this array of disasters and difficulties, one may set the special attention paid to the English in their passage from Macao to Canton in 1796, but one discovers that it was dictated by a desire to have the English load some ships quickly in order that the Imperial revenue should not fall below the usual amount. Again in the spring of 1798 the Viceroy paid the supercargoes a visit in their factories, but here too one learns that his main object was to be able to report to the Emperor that he had found everything "very proper" in the factories. At the time of the *Providence* affair the Viceroy was very friendly and desirous of settling the affair without appeal to drastic measures,

[54] Morse, *Chronicle*, II, 331-43.
[55] Auber, *op. cit.*, pp. 202-203; Morse, *Chronicle*, II, 325-27, 344-46.

but this was more the result of personal inclination than any change in government policy, for the Hoppo was as determined as ever that someone should be surrendered for trial.[66] It is perhaps true that in the years following the Embassy less difficult controversies arose with the officials than during the years which preceded it, but this seems to be the result of chance rather than of any essential modification in the attitude of the Chinese.

Macartney and Staunton's project of building up through letters and a second mission a permanent communication between the two Courts was also doomed to failure. These gentlemen had no sooner arrived in England than they began preparations to put this idea into effect. Nor was Dundas loath to support it, although his energies were at the time chiefly occupied in prosecuting the war with France and repressing liberalism in England. As early as December, 1794, Macartney suggested that the intercourse with China should be continued by a resident or occasional Minister, who could support the English claims and "guard the Vice-Roy against the deceits and impositions" which would be "practised on Him." One of his immediate tasks would be to explain away all mis-impressions which might have arisen at Peking over the Nepaulese affair. On February 22, 1795, Macartney wrote to Dundas suggesting that Staunton be sent as the King's Minister to China and at the same time be made chief of the British supercargoes at Canton. Staunton also drew up a paper showing what arguments might be used to convince the Chinese of the desirability of carrying on an extensive intercourse with England.[67]

The idea was more fully developed and plans were made to send Staunton, but he was attacked by paralysis before the measure was put into effect. Consequently, the plan was temporarily abandoned, and a number of letters and some presents were sent out in the *Cirencester* in the spring of 1795. The ship reached Whampoa on December 28 with a letter from the King to the Emperor, one from Dundas to the Viceroy, one from Lord Macartney to the Viceroy, one from Sir George to the Viceroy, and one from the Chairman of the Company to the Hoppo, together with ten cases of presents from the King to the Emperor as well as presents to the other officials. The King's letter expressed satisfaction at the treatment of the Macartney Embassy and pointed out that the English had served as mediators between the

---

[66] Morse, *Chronicle*, II, 286-87, 302, 336-41.
[67] CMC, Nos. 313, 314, 444.

Goorkhas and Chinese. Staunton's letter to the Viceroy indicated that his illness prevented his coming out in 1795, but stated that he hoped to come the next year.[58]

The officials were notified of the arrival of the letter by Browne, but they demanded a copy of it, as a new Imperial order had come to the effect that if letters to the Emperor requested extension of privileges or other innovations they were not to be accepted. Browne had no copy of the letter and refused to open the original, and after considerable trouble an audience was arranged for January 8, 1796, with the Governor, Chu Kuei, who was then acting-Viceroy. The Governor and Hoppo remained standing during the entire audience to avoid dispute over the matter of etiquette, and as soon as the letter was presented opened it and read the accompanying Chinese translation. The Governor refused to accept the letters or presents for the former Viceroy, Ch'ang Lin, and the Hoppo also refused his letters and presents.[59]

The King's letter was forwarded to Peking on January 10, and on March 13 the Imperial reply, together with 140 pieces of silk as presents from the Emperor to the King, were presented to Browne. He was forced to receive the Emperor's letter on his knees, and at the same time the King's presents to the Emperor were officially delivered to be forwarded to Peking. The Emperor's reply, dated February 7, 1796, the last day but one of the reign of Ch'ien Lung, was written as usual in the style of a superior to an inferior. It accepted the tribute and the King's proffers of friendship, indicated that the Emperor's general had conquered the refractory tribes in Nepaul without the help of the English, said that the English had been misinformed on the matter, indicated that he (Ch'ien Lung) was shortly resigning his throne, and said that his successor would continue to treat foreigners with the same kindness and consideration as always.[60]

This reply reached England in December, 1796. News of the coming accession of a new Emperor had already reached England, and there was talk of sending another Embassy for this occasion, as is shown in a letter from Staunton to his son. But Staunton was busy writing his account of the Embassy at the time, nor did his health

---

[58] G. T. Staunton, *Memoir of G. L. Staunton*, pp. 45-48, 356-57; Morse, *Chronicle*, II, pp. 273-74.

[59] Morse, *Chronicle*, II, 275.

[60] CMC, No. 334; *Yüeh Hai Kuan Chih*, Ch. 23, pp. 12-13; *Kuo Ch'ao Jou Yüan Chi*, Ch. 6, pp. 9; Morse, *Chronicle*, II, 276.

ever sufficiently improve to permit him to undertake the expedition. As is shown in their correspondence, Staunton and Macartney continued to have vague ideas of an Embassy, which were revived by the *Providence* affair in 1800. But Staunton's death in 1801, the inability to find any other satisfactory person to undertake the mission, England's engagements in Europe, and doubts of material benefits resulting prevented these ideas from ever being put into effect.[61]

A resident Minister at Canton might have helped at that time, for the experience of the mission showed that a King's representative would be listened to and treated with respect by the Canton officials, although by 1834, when Lord Napier was sent out, this was no longer true. It is unlikely, however, that such a Minister would have been able even then to effect any substantial reforms at Canton, and it is certain that he could never have established a satisfactory communication with Peking. From these events one is inevitably forced to the conclusion that not one solitary benefit which Macartney and Staunton believed would follow from their final discussion before leaving China ever materialized, unless it be that the English at Canton were treated with a little more personal consideration.

5. *Various Attitudes toward the Embassy (1794-1926).*

Before the Embassy ever reached China it was the subject of ridicule from the pen of the eighteenth century satirical poet Peter Pindar (John Wolcott). In 1792 he published *A Pair of Lyric Epistles to Lord Macartney* and *Odes to Kien Long*, in which he scoffed at the Embassy with its commercial motive hidden beneath the pretense of presents and congratulations and predicted its failure and the punishment of the Ambassador. One of the first published adverse comments appeared in a work on China in 1795 by William Winterbotham. His wrath was directed mainly against the "Ministers[,] with their accustomed sagacity," and against Henry Dundas in particular, whom he quite rightly charged with hoping to improve his personal advantage by a successful Embassy. Further, he caustically contended that the character of the Embassy was "better calculated to succeed with a nation of Indians or with a petty African Prince, than with the Government of China; for if the Court of Peking was to be swayed by splendour, much more ought to have been done."[62] This and other

---

[61] G. T. Staunton, *Memoir of G. L. Staunton*, pp. 359-65, 382.
[62] Winterbotham, *op. cit.*, pp. 1-2 of "Narrative of the Embassy," in the back of the volume.

comments reveal a rather juvenile conception of the whole problem of the Embassy and can be dismissed with no further comment.

Francis Baring, under whose Chairmanship the East India Company conducted the preparations for the Embassy and who wrote the Company's instructions to the Ambassador, expressed his gratification after reading over the information which Macartney had collected. He said further in a letter to Macartney:

I was always of opinion that the information alone to be acquired from the Embassy would far more than compensate for the expence, & which I am happy to perceive is confirmed; as the Country & every circumstance belonging to it, appears in a light totally different from the general opinion & expectation, furnishing a wide field for speculation on one hand, & regulation on the other.[63]

Macartney wrote his official apology for the Embassy in December, 1794.[64] After indicating the initial jealousy with which it was received and the various intrigues against it by the natives, the Portuguese missionaries, and the other Europeans, he stated that the exemplary conduct of the Embassy caused an abatement of this jealousy and raised the estimation of the British character in the minds of the Chinese; that his conversations with officials on the way to Canton resulted in positive achievements, and that before the Embassy had left China he had received a request from the Emperor that another mission should be sent. In conclusion he said:

Thus it appears that the Embassy has already added considerably to our trade in woollens to China, with a prospect of its annual increase, that it has occasioned a demand for other of Our Manufactures, and introduced a taste for many more, that it has removed many of the prejudices entertained in China against the English, which affected their Credit, and injured their Trade in that Country, that it withdrew them from the Tyranny of an inimical and rapacious, and placed them under the protection of an upright and friendly Vice-Roy; that it procured Ordinances of Government for the punishment of offences against them, with assurances of being indulged in any reasonable desire; and above all, that it has laid a foundation of Amity, good offices and immediate intercourse with the Imperial Court, not only protective of Our present trade to that Country, but likely also to procure the extension of it, to a magnitude of which no adequate Idea can be formed, but by reflecting on the amazing population as well as fertility and Opulance of China.

Staunton's views, as expressed in his account of the Embassy, were similar to those of his chief, although he placed more emphasis upon

[63] CMC, No. 311.
[64] CMC, No. 313.

the value and possibilities of the Imperial request (permission) that another mission should be sent.[65] What the opinions of the British Ministers were is uncertain, although Dundas and Pitt, who had hoped for great things, must have been keenly disappointed.[66] No blame, however, was placed upon Lord Macartney, for they realized that he had done his best. If he received no censure, neither did he receive honor. The Irish Earldom which awaited him when he returned had been conferred in accordance with previous arrangements. His abilities, however, were fully recognized, and in the summer of 1795 he was sent on a confidential mission to Louis XVIII at Verona. He returned to London in 1796, and as a reward for his work on this mission was granted an English Peerage as Baron Macartney of Parkhurst in Surrey, thus attaining his great ambition. He immediately afterwards became Governor of the Cape of Good Hope.[67]

If Staunton and Macartney, whose apologies were written before events at Canton proved the vainness of their hopes, may be forgiven for forming a too favorable judgment of their undertakings, no such indulgence can be granted to Barrow. In 1804 he was so ill-advised as to state that the Embassy opened an "amicable correspondence" between the King and the Emperor which might ultimately produce the desired advantages, and that by it "the British Character became better known to the Chinese, and protection and respect were obtained for the British subjects resident at Canton." He does, however, indicate some substantial achievements: namely, the acquisition of a limited knowledge of Chinese by young George T. Staunton, the attainment of some nautical knowledge about the Yellow Sea, and the collection of considerable information about the country, its government, and its institutions.[68]

De Guignes, writing in 1808, was far nearer the truth when he said

Le Lord Macartney tremina son Ambassade à Peking sans aucun succès; ses demandes furent refusées, et les présens considérables de la cour de Londres ne produisirent d'autre résultat que celui d'avoir procuré à un petit nombre d'Anglois l'entrée de la Chine. . . . Les Chinois furent très-énorgueillis de voir des Européens venir des extrémités du monde pour rendre hommage à leur empereur; mais l'encens offert à leur vanité ne suspendit point la crainte et la méfiance ordinaire du Gouvernement, qui, constant dans sa

[65] Staunton, *Embassy*, II, 581-82.
[66] CMC, No. 254.
[67] Robbins, *op. cit.*, pp. 413-14, 438, 441-42; Morse, *Chronicle*, II, 231.
[68] Barrow, *China*, pp. 352-56, especially p. 354.

sombre politique, conserva tous ses soupçons, que des causes particulières augmentèrent encore.[69]

In 1818, following the Amherst Embassy, an unsigned pamphlet cast a number of insinuations as to the dishonorable conduct of the Embassy, which need hardly be considered.[70] Sir George Thomas Staunton's view was always that the Embassy had produced a favorable opening which, if followed up shortly by a second mission under a competent person, would have produced more substantial results.[71] Sir John Davis in 1836 expressed the well-founded view that "one of the principal effects of the mission was to draw a much greater share of the public attention toward China, and to lead gradually to the study of the language, literature, institutions, and manners of that vast and singular empire."[72] He and G. T. Staunton also were of the opinion that subsequent to the Embassy there were less trifling interferences with trade and an improved conduct of the mandarins toward the supercargoes. These latter beliefs cannot be supported by the facts.

In 1859 Saxe Bannister was guilty of making some absurd and nonsensical statements about the Embassy, such as: "Lord Macartney succeeded completely in his Embassy to China," and dispelled the illusion that the Chinese officials were at that time averse to intercourse with official representatives of foreign countries.[73] In 1908 Helen M. Robbins, a distant relative of Macartney, yielding perhaps to family ties, drew the untrue conclusion that the "mission was followed by a longer interval of commercial tranquillity, and freedom from annoyance, than had ever been before experienced."[74]

A year later another Englishman in a book surveying in a general way the whole history of Anglo-Chinese relations prior to 1842 concluded more correctly:

that the embassy was treated with such unusual courtesy by the Chinese was only policy, they hoped by this means to encourage a repetition of such pleasing visitations. How little the position and influence of England were appreciated was shown by the contumely that continued to be heaped on the English and Foreigners in general at Canton. The only permanent effect

---

[69] De Guignes, *op. cit.*, I, 253-54.
[70] *A Delicate Inquiry into the Embassies to China, and a Legitimate Conclusion from the Premises* (London, 1818).
[71] G. T. Staunton, *Memoir of G. L. Staunton*, pp. 45-48.
[72] Davis, *The Chinese* (1836), I, 69, 74.
[73] Bannister, *op. cit.*, pp. lxxviii-ix.
[74] Robbins, *op. cit.*, p. 461.

left upon the Chinese was that England was promptly enrolled on the list of tribute bearing nations.[15]

This array of opinions upon the achievement of the Embassy may be ended by the simple but true statement of the greatest authority upon the subject, Dr. H. B. Morse, that "the Embassy failed in the business for which it had been dispatched to China, and the procedure under which the foreign trade was conducted became even more fixed and regularized." [16]

It is hard to find a basis upon which to judge the Embassy. If one judges it by the ill success of other embassies previously and later sent to China prior to 1842, and considers the engrained opposition which the Chinese had to foreign intercourse, it achieved a considerable measure of success. It was honorably received and well treated, the *kotow* was avoided, some friendships were established, a great deal of information collected, and some few temporary reductions of charges obtained. If, however, one judges it in the light of what it hoped to attain, or even the minimum of what it hoped to attain, it was almost a complete failure. Neither of its two major aims was achieved, nor did it accomplish any permanent reform of conditions at Canton, so far as the Chinese regulations and abuses were concerned.

The Embassy did, however, indirectly cause a complete reformation in the East India Company administration at Canton, through the establishment of the Secret and Superintending Committee and the abolition of private commission. The reduction of transit duties between Macao and Canton was actually achieved by the Secret and Superintending Committee, though their success may perhaps be attributed to the coming of the Embassy. It also carried through a number of vital reforms directed toward efficiency and economy. It further conducted a thorough examination into commercial methods and a careful survey of the possibilities of increasing the sale of imports and lessening the expenses of exports." When the Committee disbanded in the spring of 1794, it left the conduct of affairs in the hands of a small Select Committee of three persons, which carried on the wise policy the Commissioners had begun. The improvement of conditions at Canton after 1794 must be attributed to a more intelligent and efficient management

---

[15] Eames, *op. cit.*, p. 127.

[16] Morse, *Chronicle*, II, 230.

[17] IO, *China: Superintending Committee's Consultations, 1792-94,* CCLXIV, *passim*; CMC, No. 320; Morse, *Chronicle*, II, 194-98, 206-11.

of the Company's affairs rather than to a changed policy of the Chinese officials.

This improvement in the administration of the Company's affairs was one of the two major achievements of the Embassy. The other was cultural—the collection of first-hand information and the publication of a number of books about China which stimulated interest in and study of China in England. By-products of value and worth, although purchased at enormous expense, were the acquisition of nautical knowledge about the Yellow Sea and the training of Sir George Thomas Staunton, who became the first English scholar of Chinese and was later of enormous commercial benefit to the Company as a supercargo. One can do no better than to conclude these remarks with the terse statement of Beckles Willson in *The Ledger and Sword*: "The Ambassador was received with the utmost politeness, treated with the utmost hospitality, watched with the utmost vigilance, and dismissed with the utmost civility." [78]

6. *Causes for the Failure of the Embassy: a Final Estimate.*

The Embassy had hardly left Peking before Père Grammont wrote to Señor Agoté at Canton, giving his explanation as to the cause of its failure: [79]

Ces Messieurs comme sont tous les étrangers qui ne connaissent la Chine que par les livres, ignoraient le train, les usages & l'étiquette de cette Cour & pour surcroît de malheur, ils avaient amené, avec eux, un interprète Chinois encore moins instruit, lequel a été cause, en grande partie, qu'ils n'ont jamais pû obtenir d'avoir auprès d'eux un Missionnaire Européen qui pourrait les instruire & les diriger. De là il est arrivé 1.° qu'ils sont venus ici sans apporter aucun présent, ni pour les Ministres d'État, ni pour les Fils de l'Empereur; 2.° qu'ils ont manqué au cérémonial du pays dans leur salut fait à l'Empereur, sans pouvoir en expliquer la raison d'une manière satisfaisante; 3.° qu'ils se sont présentés sous des habits trop simple & trop ordinaires; 4.° qu'ils n'ont pas eu soin de graisser la patte aux différentes personnes qui avaient soin de leurs affairs; 5.° qu'il manquait à leur demande le style & le ton du pays. Une autre raison de leur mauvais succès, &, selon moi, la principale, ce sont les intrigues d'un certain Missionnaire [Bernard d'Almeida] qui, s'étant imaginé que cette Ambassade nuirait au commerce de son

---

[78] Quoted in Robbins, *op. cit.*, p. 461 note, and in Auber, *op. cit.*, p. 200.
[79] André Everand van Braam Houckgeest, *Voyage de l'ambassade de la compagnie des Indes orientales hollandaises vers l'empereur de la Chine* (Philadelphia, 1797), II, 415-18; CMC, Nos. 292, 293; MSS. *Ministre des affaires étrangères. Mémoires et documents: Chine, 1793-1855*, XVII; BM, *Stowe Manuscripts*, No. 307, pp. 256-57; Pritchard, *T'oung Pao*, XXXI (1934), 34-35.

pays, n'a pas manqué, en conséquence, de semer bien des propos défavorables à la nation Anglaise.

Ajoutez à tout cela que l'Empereur est vieux & qu'il y a des cabales partielles & des artificieux dans tous les pays. D'ailleurs tous les Grands & les Favoris de l'Empereur sont avides de présens & des richesses.

Most of what Père Grammont says is either untrue or is sheer nonsense. The Embassy provided presents for the Ministers of State and the sons of the Emperor, but the presents to the Ministers were refused, and no opportunity was afforded of offering presents to the Emperor's sons. Nor were the gentlemen of the Embassy attired in common and simple dress; Macartney and Staunton were most gorgeously attired, and the other gentlemen and members of the suite were dressed as lavishly as possible, although Anderson does complain that the servants were not elegantly enough dressed.[50] The communications which were addressed to the Ministers were written by Chinese acquainted with the proper style and should therefore have afforded no cause for umbrage. As to the influence of the refusal to *kotow* and of the intrigues of d'Almeida, more will be said later. None of the various points mentioned by Grammont were of any real importance, and they had nothing to do with the failure of the Embassy.

Macartney, Staunton, and other members of the Embassy after them laid emphasis upon: (1) opposition thrown in its way by Cheng Jui and distrust aroused by Fu K'ang-an's hostility and his misrepresentations of the Tibetan affair; (2) various intrigues of the mandarins who were likely to be punished or to lose advantage if the Embassy succeeded; (3) intrigues of the Dutch, Portuguese, and other foreigners at Canton; (4) the opposition of d'Almeida and other Portuguese missionaries; and (5) the desire of the Emperor and officialdom in general to keep out foreigners and foreign ideas in order to maintain their complete domination over the public and to hide the essential weakness of China.[51]

In this last point they were near the truth; and yet Macartney was wrong in assuming that there was no fundamental axiom of government which opposed a free intercourse with the outside world. As to the essential importance of the first four points, Macartney and the other gentlemen were wrong. Steeped in the traditions of European diplomacy, the Ambassador, when faced with ill success, had to find a

---

[50] Anderson, *op. cit.*, pp. 137-41.
[51] *Macartney's Journal*, pp. 335-36; Staunton, *Embassy*, II, 48-67, 131-35, 208-09, 279, 285-86; Barrow, *China*, pp. 7-24, 393-94.

reason for it in some special occurrence which caused the Chinese to be suspicious and jealous of the English. He found this in the Tibetan affair and the progress of British power in India—or in the slanders and intrigues of nations or persons likely to be injured by his success.

The principles of European diplomacy did not apply to China, and Macartney was wrong in using them to find a cause for his failure. So far as one is able to judge, the intrigues of foreign nations, with the exception of those of the Portuguese, were very few, and their influence certainly did not extend beyond Canton. Most of the missionaries at Peking were favorably disposed toward the Embassy. The Portuguese at Macao had no influence worth mentioning, and those at Peking had no fundamental influence upon the attitude or policy of the Chinese administration. D'Almeida may have possessed enough personal influence with Ho Shen to make him suspicious of the English, but this had no influence on the official policy which the government had already adopted toward all foreigners.

As to the influence of intrigues and cabals formed by the officials themselves, it is more difficult to decide. One thing is certain: whatever desire the Emperor or the few far-seeing officials, such as Sung and Ch'ang, may have had for limited reform at Canton was killed through the opposition and greed of mandarins both at Peking and at Canton. There may have been a few officials, mostly Chinese, who saw the advantages to be gained from a free intercourse, but they were overruled by the Manchus Ho Shen, Fu Ch'ang-an, Fu K'ang-an, Chen Jui, and Su Seng-o (Hoppo), who saw in any relaxation of the exclusion policy of the government a menace to Manchu dominion, and in any reform at Canton the elimination of a most fruitful source of personal gain, for the Manchus in the Imperial Administration received their share of the spoils from Canton.[82]

Nor does it seem that the most favorably disposed persons—not even Ch'ang—considered any fundamental departure from the main restrictive outlines of the Canton system. Such a thing would have been contrary to all tradition, and had all of the things which the Europeans considered as abuses been abolished, most of the Chinese officials would have been left penniless. A certain amount of "squeeze," just as Justice of the Peace fees in America, was considered as part of the normal recompense to officials, and, in spite of the objections of Europeans, was legal and in Chinese custom entirely justified.

---

[82] Morse, *Chronicle*, II, 225-26.

It has also been argued that had Macartney performed the *kotow* he would have been favored with more success. This again is nonsense. If one considers the ill success of the Dutch embassies in 1655 and 1668, and the one in 1795 which readily performed the ceremony, it be-becomes evident that submission produced no more satisfactory results than resistance.[83] On the other hand, there is no reason to assume that refusal to perform it raised the name or reputation of the people who refused in the estimation of the Chinese, as the English believed. Such offenders as Macartney were merely considered as rude barbarians. Nor is it of importance here to discuss whether the performance of the ceremony by an Ambassador reflected disrespect upon the sovereign whom he represented. One thing is certain: the ceremony did imply complete submission to the Emperor on the part of the performer, but it is also true that the sending of a mission and the delivery of presents enrolled the sender upon the list of tribute-sending nations as effectively as a performance of the *kotow*.

Be these matters as they may, the intrigues of the missionaries or of other Europeans, the failure to deliver sufficient presents, the Tibetan affair, the bad diplomatic form of written documents, the failure to *kotow*, and the maneuvering of avaricious officials were of no funda-mental importance in causing the failure of the Embassy to gain its major points. The intrigues of officials caused it to fail to achieve even a slight measure of reform at Canton, but the one fundamental cause of its failure was the well-established and consistently pursued policy of opposition to foreign intercourse pursued by the Manchus through-out the eighteenth and nineteenth centuries.

China had never known free and regular intercourse with outside nations like that known in Europe. She had always been the dominator of the Eastern world, and she considered all missions as tribute bearers to the great Middle Kingdom. Officialdom was satisfied with Chinese culture and ideas as they were, and desired no change. In outside influence they saw a cause of trouble, although it can hardly be believed that the China which reached its greatest power under Ch'ien Lung was really afraid of the outside world. During the reign of K'ang Hsi, however, the official world had observed in the activities of the mission-aries a source of irritation from outside influences, and from the begin-

---

[83] John Nieuhoff, *An Embassy from the East-India Company of the United Provinces, to the Grand Tartar Cham Emperor of China* (London, 1669); John Ogilby, *Atlas Chinensis* (London, 1671); Van Braam, *op. cit., passim.*

ning of Yung Cheng's reign (1723-1735) onward the already exclusive tendencies of the government steadily increased. No matter how much value the Chinese merchants might see in a free intercourse or how friendly the rank and file of the masses might be, the official view was bound to prevail. In the face of this policy of studied opposition to change and to a free intercourse with foreign nations, it was utterly hopeless for diplomatic missions from Europe to attempt to accomplish their desires.

The outbreak of the European war prevented Macartney from going to Japan and the Eastern Islands, but there is no reason to believe that he would have received a favorable reception in Japan at that date. Conditions had profoundly changed when Perry went there in 1853. The Japanese then had before them the example of what had happened to China as a result of the pursuit of an exclusive policy, and from this they could judge the advisability of opening a friendly intercourse. In 1794 no such example existed, and in all probability Macartney would have met the same defeat as in China. Nor can one believe that he would have found a ready market for British goods in the Eastern Islands, no matter how friendly their rulers might have been. Their populations were not great; their wants were few, and the East India Company was not prepared to carry on the barter trade in nick-nacks which would have been necessary.

In conclusion one can say that the Embassy was an ill-conceived but well-executed measure. Its failure was certain before it left England, and no human power could have made it a success. The fault lay with those who conceived the idea—with Dundas and Pitt—although Macartney must bear a share of the blame, for he undertook it in defiance of the experience of other embassies, and in the belief, despite almost complete evidence to the contrary, that the Chinese government was not fundamentally opposed to foreign intercourse. In his plan for the Embassy and in his method of conducting it, Macartney showed exceptional knowledge and careful attention to detail. He did all that could be done to make it a success; he used great skill and every device possible in trying to accomplish its ends, and no censure can be given to his procedure in China. The fault lay with the premise upon which the Embassy was undertaken, against the will and better judgment of the Company. It may be argued that the experiment was worth while and that from it grew a more perfect knowledge of the realities of the situation. This may be true, but it is doubtful that the reform of the Company's China administration and the cultural knowledge gained— its two achievements— were worth the price of eighty thousand odd pounds which the Company had to pay.

CHAPTER X

CONCLUSION

There are six dates of major importance in the history of Anglo-Chinese relations prior to the Opium War. The first is 1600, the year in which the East India Company came into existence; the second is 1699, the year the *Macclesfield* galley successfully opened trade at Canton; the third covers a period of years from 1755 to 1761, in which the main outlines of the Canton system were rigidly fixed; the fourth is 1784, the date of the Commutation Act; the fifth is 1793, the year in which the Macartney Embassy visited Peking; and the sixth is 1833, the time when the East India Company's monopoly of the China trade ceased, British officials thus being brought face to face with Chinese contempt for foreigners. Three of these dates—1755-61, 1784, and 1793—definitely come within the scope of the present study.

The year 1755 saw, after a two-year struggle on the part of the supercargoes to have the security merchant system abolished, a series of provincial edicts which granted to the Hong merchants a monopoly of foreign trade, identified them with security merchants, and made them responsible to the government for the Imperial duties on trade and for the good behavior of the foreigners. Attempts of the English to break this monopoly by sending ships to Ningpo caused an Imperial edict and supplementary provincial edicts to be issued in 1757 effectively forbidding foreign trade at ports other than Canton. An appeal to the Emperor against this decision and against the method of trade at Canton produced an Imperial investigation which in 1760 led to an Imperial edict legalizing and solidifying the main outlines of the system of trade as it then stood. Later in the year the Hong merchants, with the consent of the officials, formed themselves into a corporation or Co-hong, in order more effectively to control foreign trade and meet the avaricious demands of the officials. In 1761 a special mission sent out by the Company to complain of abuses and request reform failed to accomplish anything substantial, the inability of commercial missions from the Company to the Canton officials to bring about any change in a system established by custom and enforced by Imperial edict thus being demonstrated.

The central government hoped by these edicts to free itself forever from the annoyances of the foreigners, secure to itself a substantial revenue from foreign trade, and free the Empire from the penetration of dangerous foreign ideas. The Canton officials hoped to end the constant controversy with the outside barbarians and ensure to themselves a monopoly of the bounty which could be drawn from the foreign trade. The effect was in the end bound to be the opposite to what officialdom wished, because the confinement of trade to Canton under troublesome and annoying rules by Imperial edict made its indefinite expansion impossible, and made foreign appeal to Peking in an attempt to free the trade from these limitations inevitable.

British trade with China expanded slowly between 1760 and 1784, but showed a tendency to decline between 1772 and 1783, as Continental European competition grew because of the high duties on tea in England. Such being the situation, the full force of the restricted system at Canton was not felt, and English trade got on as best it could under the supervision of the Company's supercargoes. The abolition of the Co-hong was accomplished after the payment of a large sum of money in 1771, but this so weakened the individual Hong merchants that they soon collapsed under the strain of the usurious debts they had contracted with Country traders and the increasing demands of the mandarins. Between 1771 and 1780 one of the eleven Hong merchants died and six went bankrupt.

The reduction of the number of merchants who could act as security for ships and who could transact business with the foreigners was a serious impediment to trade, but still greater adversity was to be visited upon trade as a consequence of these bankruptcies. The Country creditors, being unable to collect their debts and dissatisfied with the proposals made by the debtors, appealed to the Admiral commanding the Indian fleet. He accordingly sent a memorial to the Viceroy demanding that the debts be paid, with the result that the whole matter was referred to Peking. The Imperial reply in 1780 settled the debts of two of the bankrupt merchants in a manner unsatisfactory to the creditors, and also provided for the re-establishment of an association of merchants under official supervision. A Consoo fund, provided by a levy upon most articles of foreign trade, was established by the association to protect foreign traders against loss through the bankruptcy of Hong merchants and to protect themselves from the results of such bankruptcies and from the demands of the central and local government. The diversion of funds to this latter purpose was considered an abuse by the foreigners. The whole controversy led the private creditors to request the British government to send an Embassy to China and left the trade saddled with the Co-hong and the Consoo tax.

With but the addition of the new Consoo tax, the system of trade and life at Canton, as established by 1760, continued to stand uncontested until certain events in the year 1784 brought its dangers and defects so clearly to the attention of both the Company and the British government that an attempt to alter it was inevitable. The two crucial events in the year 1784 were the Commutation Act in England and the *Lady Hughes* affair in China. The first was important because it caused English trade with China to more than double in the course of a few years, and at the same time caused the trade of her Continental rivals to decline rapidly. As the trade expanded, the inadequacies of the restricted system at Canton became more evident. At the same time the progress of the Industrial Revolution created new cotton and metal interests in the north of England which demanded a wider market for their produce.

The *Lady Huges* affair, which led the whole British community to be held responsible for the acts of a single individual and which resulted in the execution of an innocent British subject by the Chinese, threatened to endanger the whole trade, and called attention in a most pointed manner to the insecure situation of the English in China and to the menace of the Chinese doctrine of responsibility. The conclusions resulting from the *Lady Hughes* affair were reinforced by reflection upon two previous executions of foreigners by the Chinese without a proper trial of the European sort, the unsatisfactory treatment of H.M. ships in Chinese waters, the increasing impositions upon trade, the increasing number of minor abuses, and the occurrence of a number of heated controversies between the officials and the supercargoes. The year 1784 also saw the beginning of American trade at Canton, which in a few years showed possible signs of replacing the European competition at which the Commutation Act was aimed.

The result of all these considerations was to impress upon the minds of government and Company the advisability of sending an Embassy to the Court of Peking, as suggested by the supercargoes after their first fright over the execution of the gunner in 1784. It was hoped that such an Embassy would put Anglo-Chinese relations upon a treaty basis, remove the existing restrictions and abuses, remove British subjects from the dangers of Chinese law and judicial procedure, and, by the opening of new ports to trade and the acquisition of a trade depôt near Chusan, lower the costs of teas, silks, and nankeens, and open the northern part of China as a market for British woollens and other products. Such commercial advantages would also complete the ruin of Continental competition and enable England to stifle possible American competition. An expanded trade also would help the government's revenue and improve the Company's financial situation in Europe, and an increased market for British goods in China would help to relieve the Company of the difficulties it was then encountering in obtaining ready cash at Canton to finance its growing export trade.

Henry Dundas, president of the Board of Control, which had been created in 1784 to supervise Indian affairs, was strongly in favor of the measure, and in consequence an Embassy was fitted out under the direction of Colonel Cathcart and dispatched to China in 1787. It died with the Ambassador, because no satisfactory arrangements had been made for a person to succeed him in case of his death. Plans to send a successor to this mission were abandoned for several years because of troubled conditions in India and Europe, the difficulty of finding a satisfactory person to send, and the lukewarm support of the Company.

The Company had begun to doubt the advisability of an Embassy, for it realized that its dominion over the China trade was secure because of the rapid decline of its foreign rivals. Furthermore, no more serious troubles with the officials had occurred in China, and the first adverse effects of the revival of the Co-hong and the imposition of the Consoo tax were being eliminated. In the attempt to acquire new privileges it saw a danger that the whole of its trade might be interdicted, and if too extensive privileges were gained its monopoly would be assailed with irresistible force by the new industrial and commercial interests in the north of England.

The idea of sending an Embassy upon a much more extensive scale, however, was revived by Henry Dundas and supported by Pitt, who hoped through it to open new markets and satisfy the growing demands of the industrialists. It was placed under the direction of Lord Macartney, probably the best qualified man in England for the task, and, besides achieving the aims of the Cathcart Embassy, it hoped to open Japan, Cochin China, and the Eastern Islands as a market for British manufactures. It arrived at Peking in the year 1793, but was doomed to failure before it was sent because of the aversion of the Chinese government to foreign intercourse. Its schemes of opening trade in Japan and elsewhere were abandoned because of the outbreak of the wars of the French Revolution. These wars, however, completed the ruin of England's Continental rivals in the China trade and left her master of that trade, except for the relatively unimportant American competition.

Although the Macartney Embassy failed to accomplish the purpose for which it was sent, it served some useful purposes. It showed definitely that China was not to be opened to foreign intercourse by ordinary diplomatic methods, and as the British were not yet ready to appeal to force, the trade was left to get on as best it could. It further led to a reformation in the management of the Company's affairs, which enabled its business to be conducted more efficiently and caused its representatives to offer a more effective resistance to new impositions and restraints on trade. Finally, the information which it collected about China and the books which were written in consequence of it stimulated England's intellectual interest in China. In this way it definitely marked the beginning of a new epoch in Anglo-Chinese relations. The commercial side of this new epoch began with the Commutation Act and the tremendous expansion of British trade with China, and the intellectual side began with the Macartney Embassy.

From this date onward, intellectual and cultural interest in China grew steadily, as did trade, and the government watched events in China more closely, hoping always for an opening which would enable it to put relations with China on a sounder basis. The first British missionary arrived in China in 1807, and the serious study of Chinese language, institutions, and culture was taken up. Reference to matters pertaining to China in papers and magazines became more common. But as British trade with and cultural interest in China grew, the decaying Manchu administration became more exclusive than ever, and the arrogance and abuses of the mandarins at Canton increased. Thus events marched on during the new period toward the inevitable trial of arms.

The era beginning with the decrees of 1755 to 1760, which crystalized the system at Canton, was closed by the failure of the Macartney Embassy, which tried to change the system established by those decrees. The gauntlet was clearly thrown down for the future. Either England would have to conform her commercial desires to the restraints of that system, or she would have to use more potent arguments than those conjured up by European diplomats to bring the exclusive, self-important, and superior-feeling Manchu administration to her terms.

Woollens Imported into China by the East India Company (1760-1800)[1]

Season	Broadcloth Sales value Tls.	Long Ells Sales value Tls.	Camlets Sales value Tls.	Total Sales value Tls.	Loss Tls.	Volume of Canton Diary
1760-61				110,000		
1761-62				179,444		
1762-63				?		
1763-64				?		
1764-65				227,793		
1765-66				141,600		
1766-67				?		
1767-68				?		
1768-69				378,570	23,690	
1769-70				?		
1770-71				400,000	50,000	
1771-72				?		
1772-73	228,505	135,539		364,044	54,120	
1773-74				?		
1774-75	93,058	63,280		156,338	23,899	
1775-76	167,367	180,880		348,247	47,804	58
1776-77	97,307	144,137	12,618	254,062	18,404	59
1777-78	150,172	203,502	13,644	367,613	24,341	62
1778-79	147,607	189,044	14,400	351,513	25,227	64
1779-80	23,647	37,513	5,760	66,920	3,165	67
1780-81	168,379	223,867	11,216	405,462	29,987	71
1781-82	68,920	93,247	4,266	166,433	14,893	74
1782-83	none	none	none	none	none	75
1783-84	234,150	429,394	45,085	708,629	35,920	78
1784-85	226,942	330,701	55,896	614,955	31,480	80
1785-86	226,229	311,791	39,348	577,368	14,589	81, 83
1786-87	282,336	447,648	12,168	742,152	28,725	85
1787-88	201,874	411,735	5,800	619,049	11,806	87
1788-89	292,420	800,948	-14,059	1,107,427	48,518	95
1789-90	234,793	701,092	25,447	965,398	27,780	97
1790-91	301,088	847,771	43,404	1,192,263	11,709	99
1791-92	416,765	963,715	70,655	1,451,795	14,464	100,102
1792-93	416,336	1,085,330	93,179	1,594,854	56,034	104
1793-94	462,066	1,334,746	154,894	1,952,970	48,168	107
1794-95	440,296	1,160,523	157,071	1,741,429	400,562	109
1795-96	390,764	1,105,936	129,754	1,635,358	74,657	111,115
1796-97	320,464	1,236,411	109,727	1,666,602	226,119	117
1797-98	196,531	829,453	162,958	1,193,826	164,975	120
1798-99	186,750	951,830	55,797	1,204,684	162,740	123
1799-00	449,752	1,480,590	151,279	2,081,626	329,267	130

[1]Based upon MSS. IO, China: Canton Diaries, volumes indicated in the right hand column, and Morse, Chronicle, V, 86, 100, 110-11, 124, 134, 145-46, 149, 157, 159, 166, 189 and II, 6, 28, 30, 40, 50, 83, 94, 111, 118, 135, 151, 173, 178, 184, 192, 205, 256, 265, 277, 294, 310, 321. The figures in the Diaries prior to 1775-76 are incomplete and Morse's careful summary of those given has been used. The Diaries give the invoice value of the cargo of each ship together with the sales value of that cargo. To the invoice value the Company added the supercargoes commission (5 per cent 1760 through 1785, 4 per cent in 1786, 3 per cent in 1787, 2¾ per cent in 1788 and about 2 per cent thereafter) and charges at 1 per cent to get the total cost value on the basis of which profits and losses were calculated. The invoice value itself was prime cost plus 10 per cent to cover insurance and interest on the money for two years. Woollens actually sold at a slight profit over prime cost. The total sales value column includes some miscellaneous woollens.

APPENDIX II

Metal Imported into China by the East India Company (1760-1800)[1]

Season	Lead Sales Value tls.	Tin Sales Value tls.	Copper Sales Value tls.	Total Sales Value tls.	Profit Loss – tls.
1760-61	15,000			15,000	
1761-62	14,114			14,114	
1762-63				?	
1763-64				?	
1764-65	65,656			65,656	
1765-66	77,970			77,970	11,222
1766-67				?	
1767-68				?	
1768-69	92,051			92,051	11,517
1769-70				?	
1770-71				?	
1771-72				?	
1772-73	90,948			90,948	51
1773-74				?	
1774-75	10,752			10,752	2,781
1775-76	21,592			21,592	5,767
1776-77	19,420			19,420	5,485
1777-78	27,022			27,022	7,942
1778-79	33,243			33,243	15,843
1779-80	10,000			10,000	4,906
1780-81	30,195			30,195	10,998
1781-82	32,370			32,370	11,184
1782-83	11,343			11,343	3,549
1783-84	60,652			60,652	4,501
1784-85	39,056			39,056	3,539
1785-86	84,479			84,479	- 415
1786-87	135,433			135,433	- 134
1787-88	115,557		7,217	122,774	1,487
1788-89	117,949		7,896	125,845	- 5,834
1789-90	98,752	14,332	54,392	167,476	-17,318
1790-91	133,338	218,076	75,524	426,938	60,582
1791-92	58,747	304,861	36,088	399,696	40,473
1792-93	64,401	242,428		306,829	28,444
1793-94	52,858	204,806		257,664	3,912
1794-95	112,646	295,603		408,249	- 9,681
1795-96	22,605	221,366		243,971	- 1,645
1796-97	66,776	297,113		363,889	10,750
1797-98	51,576	287,842		339,418	12,493
1798-99	16,761	302,601		319,362	- 444
1799-00	103,738	198,044		301,782	27,705

[1]References exactly as in note to Appendix I.

APPENDIX III

Indian Goods Imported into China by the East India Company (1760-1800)[1]

Seasons	Raw Cotton Sales Value tls.	Pepper Sales Value tls.	Sandalwood, Redwood and Miscellaneous Sales Value tls.	Total Sales Value tls.	Profit Loss – tls.
1760-61				71,371	
1761-62				46,072	
1762-63				53,418	
1763-64				166,689	
1784-65				292,575	
1765-66				241,197	
1766-67				115,397	
1767-68				83,376	
1768-69	97,225	29,658	11,341	158,204	25,774
1769-70	95,667		6,000	101,667	
1770-71	?	191,581	?	270,128	
1771-72	?	54,796	?	101,279	
1772-73	6,746	155,234	45,308	207,288	56,803
1773-74	8,956	82,608	44,465	136,029	
1774-75	8,982	19,161	45,526	73,669	28,721
1775-76		32,044	5,400	37,444	1,765
1776-77	24,724	94,998	26,717	146,439	54,169
1777-78	8,816	80,371		89,187	14,239
1778-79				none	
1779-80		134,490	1,086	135,576	17,388
1780-81	16,531		28,991	45,522	15,510
1781-82	38,989	56,203	774	95,966	8,671
1782-83			237,082	237,082	-47,095
1783-84	2,430	163,020	11,766	177,216	-16,212
1784-85	40,362			40,362	14,881
1785-86	5,954	19,478		25,432	- 7,408
1786-87	39,695	50,330		90,025	11,165
1787-88	91,825			91,825	10,980
1788-89	81,901	33,130		115,031	51,153
1789-90	90,552	74,373		164,925	58,254
1790-91	131,744	79,928		211,672	86,273
1791-92		87,207		87,207	28,174
1792-93	67,627	42,737	26,092	136,456	19,453
1793-94	65,830		22,228	88,058	4,083
1794-95			19,219	19,219	- 4,467
1795-96	61,597		27,745	89,342	9,805
1796-97	69,858			69,858	30,470
1797-98		65,220	67,825	133,045	24,290
1798-99				none	
1799-00		87,192	75,625	162,817	38,870

[1]References as in note to Appendix I except that from 1762 to 1771 Reports from the Committees of the House of Commons, 1715-1801, IV, 68-69 and VIII, 370-71 have been used to supplement Morse, Chronicle, V. The supercargoes commission in the case of Indian produce was calculated upon the sales value instead of the invoice cost.

APPENDIX IV

Total Goods Imported into China from England and India by the East India Company (1760-1800)

(1) Season	(2) Exported from England Prime Cost £	(3) Imported from England Sales Value tls.	(4) Total Goods Imported Sales Value tls.	(5) Losses on Miscellaneous Goods & Stores tls.	(6) Total Profits and Losses tls.
1760-61	60,019	125,000	196,371		
1761-62	81,335	193,558	239,630		
1762-63	59,218	302,540	355,958		
1763-64	72,729	184,998	351,687		
1764-65	70,281	287,154	579,729		
1765-66	73,842	219,570	542,022		
1766-67	54,718	396,825	510,222		
1767-68	136,384	232,999	316,375		
1768-69	154,467	470,621	608,825	2,000	11,601
1769-70	179,246	602,459	704,106		
1770-71	152,798	451,149	721,275		
1771-72	147,082	801,894	903,173		
1772-73	132,553	454,992	662,280	2,000	554
1773-74	80,051	448,146	584,175		
1774-75	92,810	187,090	240,759	2,500	5,103
1775-76	99,114	389,839	407,283	2,256	- 42,528
1776-77	107,848	273,482	419,921	1,836	37,414
1777-78	126,233	398,955	488,142	8,733	- 10,893
1778-79	92,745	390,876	390,876	7,347	- 16,731
1779-80	104,846	78,247	213,823	548	18,585
1780-81	182,066	433,657	479,179	4,092	- 6,371
1781-82	67,151	198,803	294,769	1,023	3,903
1782-83	106,126	11,343	248,425		- 43,549
1783-84	120,084	769,281	946,497	3,909	- 51,540
1784-85	177,480	654,011	694,373	5,178	- 18,238
1785-86	270,109	661,847	687,279	5,270	- 25,682
1786-87	245,529	877,585	967,610	2,883	- 14,577
1787-88	368,442	741,823	833,648	3,615	- 2,954
1788-89	401,199	1,233,272	1,348,305	3,153	- 6,349
1789-90	470,480	1,130,874	1,295,799	3,123	10,033
1790-91	541,174	1,621,201	1,832,873	2,746	132,400
1791-92	574,001	1,851,491	1,938,698	2,391	51,792
1792-93	680,219	1,901,683	2,058,139	2,484	- 10,621
1793-94	760,029	2,226,691	2,314,749	25,391	65,554
1794-95	744,140	2,152,225	2,171,444	4,011	-418,721
1795-96	632,310	1,881,107	1,970,449	10,235	- 76,132
1796-97	496,758	2,030,491	2,100,349	3,420	-188,319
1797-98	499,925	1,533,244	1,666,289	5,247	-145,459
1798-99	782,309	1,524,046	1,524,046	4,047	-167,231
1799-00	830,679	2,383,408	2,546,225	2,888	-265,376

(1) PP, Sessional Reports, Papers, etc., 1812-13, VIII, no. 152, pp. 399-404; Macgregor, Commercial Statistics, IV, 405-06; MSS. C, Macartney Correspondence, X, nos. 398-99, 415.
(2) From 1760 through 1774 based on Morse, Chronicle, V, pages cited in notes to Appendix I, and Reports from the Committees of the House of Commons, 1715-1801, IV, 68-69 and VIII, 370-71. From 1775 onwards the figures equal the sum of the metals and woollens imported as given in Appendix I and II plus miscellaneous goods imported amounting to T.4,320 in 1777-78, T.6,120 in 1778-79, T.1,327 in 1779-80, T.2,000 in 1790-91, T.16,057 in 1793-94, T.2,547 in 1794-95 and T.1,178 in 1795-96.
(3) Column 2 plus the Indian produce given in Appendix III.
(4) Factory stores as given in the Canton Diaries, volumes as in Appendix I, plus the losses on the miscellaneous goods imported.
(5) Profits and losses as given in Appendix I, II and III plus losses on miscellaneous goods and stores given in column 4.

APPENDIX V

Tea Exported from China and Sold by the East India Company in England (1760-1800)

Season	Exported from China (1) Piculs	Prime Cost Tls.	Sold at Company's Sales in England (2) lbs.	Total Cost £	Sales Value £	Profits £
1760-61	30,000	653,000	2,626,552		831,894	
1761-62	46,347	700,124	2,862,773		960,017	
1762-63	40,000	720,291	2,703,363		922,844	
1763-64	42,158	862,442	4,425,731		1,068,760	
1764-65	51,821	1,095,354	5,684,707		1,219,696	
1765-66	71,568	1,334,978	5,473,186		1,137,238	
1766-67	69,531	1,370,818	5,586,356		995,858	
1767-68	35,009	608,640	5,303,474		911,423	
1768-69	52,700	1,077,178	8,525,883		1,321,973	
1769-70	82,362	1,507,656	9,447,522		1,425,708	
1770-71	67,128	1,323,849	8,574,421		1,555,968	
1771-72	95,626	1,570,538	6,799,010		1,316,568	
1772-73	65,663	1,174,125	7,032,134		1,238,434	
1773-74	28,238	522,890	4,577,477		830,902	
1774-75	14,419	225,036	6,831,534		1,041,841	
1775-76	22,574	498,644	6,225,343		1,031,216	
1776-77	41,588	689,894	4,539,933	479,631	615,208	135,577
1777-78	45,900	904,739	5,545,752	725,804	974,885	249,081
1778-79	35,700	712,314	4,690,520	824,582	992,535	167,953
1779-80	23,620	524,604	6,603,202	756,174	958,698	202,524
1780-81	61,200	1,125,983	7,479,278	981,154	1,277,305	296,151
1781-82	58,279	1,144,633	4,913,419	864,957	963,457	98,500
1782-83	21,176	401,640	6,123,664	1,142,816	1,182,766	39,950
1783-84	69,000	1,498,024	5,617,883	706,066	1,047,342	341,276
1784-85	68,294	1,480,014	9,643,752	1,482,548	1,597,928	115,380
1785-86	103,865	2,564,701	14,721,114	1,052,470	2,198,988	1,146,518
1786-87	155,852	3,841,000	15,675,361	1,536,992	2,350,444	813,452
1787-88	161,303	4,315,879	15,833,962	1,954,720	2,337,269	382,549
1788-89	141,218	3,804,698	14,689,224	2,041,473	2,229,431	187,958
1789-90	129,847	3,770,049	16,013,564	1,934,276	2,338,813	404,537
1790-91	159,595	4,103,828	16,018,012	1,906,458	2,449,949	543,491
1791-92	94,754	3,010,926	16,293,795	2,022,440	2,422,858	400,418
1792-93	111,893	3,046,047	17,477,818	1,667,986	2,403,338	735,352
1793-94	148,250	3,480,986	16,335,978	1,615,891	2,325,191	709,300
1794-95	167,672	4,235,256	18,350,284	1,752,245	2,733,668	981,423
1795-96	112,840	3,126,198	19,416,200	2,114,389	2,821,842	707,453
1796-97	212,422	5,890,729	17,532,758		2,550,058	
1797-98	184,653	5,188,050	17,543,625		2,460,868	
1798-99	93,771	2,590,029	20,500,788		3,368,608	
1799-00	157,526	2,545,624	23,327,776		3,665,321	

(1) MSS. IO, China: Canton Diaries, volumes indicated in Appendix 1; MSS. C, Macartney Correspondence, X, Nos. 433, 445; Morse, Chronicle, V, 124, 131, 188. The prime cost value of tea is the difference between the invoice value of goods exported from Canton and the sum of the chinaware and sago, nankeens, raw silk, and Canton charges given in Appendix VI.

(2) Prior to 1776 these figures include tea imported in Private trade and sold at the Company's sales. After that date they relate to the Company's tea only. Based on Wissett, Compendium, II, section on tea; Milburn, Oriental Commerce, II, 534; Macpherson, India, pp. 416. The sales value for the years 1776 through 1779 is from Reports from the Committees of the House of Commons, 1715-1801, VI, 180-82, and from 1793 onwards from PP, Sessional Reports, Papers, etc., 1812, VI, No. 148, pp. 80-81, 493. For other years sales value is obtained by subtracting estimated value of Private trade from total sales amount. Total cost includes prime cost plus Canton charges, freight, supercargoes commission, and charges at 5 per cent calculated as in Appendix VII.

APPENDIX VI

Goods and Stores Exported from China by the East India Company (1760-1800)[1]

Season	No. of Ships	Chinaware & Sago Prime Cost Tls.	Nankeens Prime Cost Tls.	Raw Silk Prime Cost Tls.	Canton Charges Tls.	Total Invoice Cost Tls.	Supplies to India Tls.	Total Value of Exports Tls.
1760-61	8	12,000			40,000	705,000	2,000	707,000
1761-62	9	13,500	1,020		45,000	759,644	2,000	761,644
1762-63	6	9,000			39,786	769,077	13,149	782,226
1763-64	11	16,500		18,748	49,235	946,923	2,226	949,149
1764-65	14	21,000			83,012	1,179,366	4,847	1,184,213
1765-66	15	22,500	6,120	200,674	70,572	1,634,844	3,153	1,637,997
1766-67	12	18,000		152,500	64,599	1,585,917	1,349	1,587,266
1767-68	8	12,000		673,400	43,171	1,337,211	2,958	1,340,169
1768-69	12	18,000	7,600	666,136	56,958	1,825,872	2,297	1,828,169
1769-70	17	25,500	11,400		66,090	1,610,646	2,246	1,612,892
1770-71	13	19,500			68,340	1,411,689	2,127	1,413,816
1771-72	20	30,000		436,000	94,734	2,131,272	2,226	2,133,498
1772-73	13	19,500	4,750	385,520	71,553	1,655,448	3,480	1,658,928
1773-74	11	17,780		617,345	62,259	1,220,274	25,368	1,245,642
1774-75	4	7,429		552,543	36,765	621,573	3,684	625,257
1775-76	5	21,675	5,916	479,184	38,568	1,041,987	3,446	1,045,433
1776-77	8	29,368	9,766	430,535	53,205	1,212,768	5,430	1,218,198
1777-78	9	39,522	3,610	477,258	57,294	1,482,423	4,254	1,486,677
1778-79	7	20,957	8,000	464,675	50,250	1,256,196	3,777	1,259,973
1779-80	5	15,368	7,800	425,227	49,695	1,022,694	8,584	1,031,278
1780-81	12	39,903	8,000	772,456	74,964	2,021,310	4,732	2,026,042
1781-82	11	43,345	8,000	324,311	67,343	1,587,632	8,922	1,596,554
1782-83	4	9,498	8,800	327,404	43,701	791,043	5,328	796,371
1783-84	13	51,212	8,508	260,293	87,909	1,905,946	13,686	1,919,819
1784-85	13	41,886	9,360	200,355	86,230	1,817,845	7,162	1,825,061
1785-86	19	83,397	10,440	189,077	111,326	2,938,941	3,128	2,942,069
1786-87	29	95,661	20,000	849,914	152,186	4,958,761	3,387	4,962,148
1787-88	29	117,594	20,000	656,462	148,741	5,258,676	3,422	5,262,177
1788-89	26	86,577	22,425	503,526	149,427	4,566,653	12,196	4,578,849
1789-90	21	95,567	24,800	418,958	124,057	4,433,431	7,020	4,440,451
1790-91	25	43,219	24,800	355,273	141,016	4,688,136	1,675	4,689,811
1791-92	11	21,935	24,800	189,171	102,449	3,349,281	4,255	3,353,536
1792-93	16		35,800	340,120	113,439	3,535,406	5,419	3,540,825
1793-94	18		39,800	194,268	123,814	3,838,868	7,514	3,846,382
1794-95	21		47,700	293,471	128,061	4,704,488	10,418	4,714,906
1795-96	16		40,000	188,318	112,303	3,508,839	12,332	5,521,171
1796-97	23		68,260	149,686	140,265	6,248,940	44,817	6,293,757
1797-98	18		87,190	108,736	121,999	5,505,975	50,826	5,556,801
1798-99	16		82,840	131,730	106,652	2,911,251	54,228	2,965,479
1799-00	15		121,602	235,227	113,660	4,016,113	75,779	4,091,892

[1]From 1760 to 1775 based upon Reports from Committees of the House of Commons, 1715-1801, IV, 68-69 and VIII, 370-71, and Morse, Chronicle, V, 101, 108, 110, 112, 124, 130, 131, 157-38, 146, 156, 160, 165, 168, 176, 178, 186, 188. From 1775 onwards based upon the Canton Diaries, volumes indicated in Appendix 1; the Reports referred to above; MSS. C, Macartney Correspondence, X, Nos. 396, 410; Morse, Chronicle, IV, 387-88, and II, tables in the back for measurage charges; PP, Accounts and Papers, 1794, No. 786 (9), 1796-7, No. 871 (9), 1798-9, No. 948 (9), 1799-1800, No. 994 (2), 1812, VI, No. 148, p. 44 for the Canton charges from 1791 to 1800. Canton charges include factory expense and measurage charges. The invoice cost includes the prime cost value of chinaware and sago, Nankeens, silk, and tea (Appendix V) exported plus Canton charges. From 1760 to 1772 the value of chinaware has been estimated at T. 1,500 per ship.

APPENDIX VII

Value of and Profit on Goods Exported from China by the East India Company (1775-1815)

Season	Invoice Value (1) £	Duties (2) £	Freight (3) £	Super-cargoes Commission (4) £	Total Cost(5) £	Sales Value(6) £	Profit £
1776-77	530,217	172,866	108,537	47,699	719,153	953,975	234,822
1777-78	404,258	255,717	174,771	65,123	970,634	1,262,464	291,830
1778-79	436,102	268,248	187,517	64,365	1,035,799	1,287,304	251,505
1779-80	408,721	270,928	183,890	62,898	1,003,775	1,257,850	254,075
1780-81	543,484	368,370	129,050	77,140	1,212,444	1,542,801	330,357
1781-82	471,184	302,730	345,559	70,658	1,288,963	1,411,161	122,198
1782-83	529,211	359,234	318,595	72,852	1,377,962	1,456,646	78,684
1783-84	263,881	318,047	166,405	65,458	890,588	1,309,161	418,773
1784-85	635,315	317,423	635,111	94,755	1,697,450	1,895,061	197,611
1785-86	605,948	24,416	355,232	95,012	1,221,967	2,575,275	1,155,508
1786-87	979,647	27,910	749,550	74,673	1,996,019	2,489,126	493,107
1787-88	1,628,235	69,059	483,029	77,097	2,435,057	2,803,552	368,495
1788-89	1,514,881	58,505	419,221	65,368	2,254,686	2,554,702	300,016
1789-90	1,534,700	57,953	488,964	59,220	2,289,408	2,631,959	342,551
1790-91	1,438,311	49,260	463,041	53,752	2,178,289	2,687,571	509,282
1791-92	1,457,977	55,212	469,624	55,990	2,192,747	2,699,538	506,791
1792-93	1,487,339	42,415	477,348	61,603	2,262,005	2,737,918	475,913
1793-94	1,336,739	41,284	418,028	56,578	2,025,565	2,514,594	489,029
1794-95	1,595,493	27,322	372,346	64,582	2,263,729	2,861,422	597,693
1795-96	1,408,087	25,802	472,487	66,886	2,167,521	2,972,664	805,143
1796-97	1,285,765	20,341	521,074	55,366	2,046,306	2,668,346	622,040
1797-98	1,292,803	18,589	601,413	51,558	2,130,001	2,577,890	447,889
1798-99	1,601,606	43,727	763,404	73,046	2,714,607	3,652,283	937,676
1799-00	1,830,569	7,459	788,507	75,900	2,929,880	3,794,982	865,102
1800-01	1,783,254	7,534	697,474	72,328	2,808,014	3,616,381	808,367
1801-02	1,669,103	9,963	723,510	70,788	2,707,752	3,559,404	831,652
1802-03	1,741,007	6,822	719,660	75,006	2,517,208	3,753,252	236,044
1803-04	1,771,947	5,985	732,112	72,594	2,778,607	3,629,677	851,070
1804-05	1,559,286	7,962	615,720	66,150	2,433,314	3,307,495	874,151
1805-06	1,706,225	7,629	644,558	74,814	2,652,170	3,740,699	1,087,529
1806-07	1,677,652	7,484	659,497	74,182	2,646,044	3,709,046	1,063,002
1807-08	1,688,470	1,389	721,437	76,936	2,747,210	3,846,756	1,099,546
1808-09	1,722,000	7,951	746,822	79,766	2,817,315	3,988,267	1,170,952
1809-10	1,487,060	18,501	687,168	74,462	2,522,218	3,723,116	1,200,898
1810-11	1,564,915	3,085	851,161	80,504	2,734,224	4,015,207	1,280,983
1811-12	1,569,497	8,103	795,449	74,006	2,678,192	3,700,285	1,022,093
1812-13	1,889,075	5,000	915,000	80,102	3,095,689	4,005,112	909,423
1813-14	2,195,706	6,000	990,000	88,798	3,525,774	4,459,855	914,081
1814-15	2,082,171	5,528	915,050	96,456	3,365,851	4,822,792	1,456,941
1815-16	1,751,718	1,905	776,420	75,880	2,869,108	3,793,992	924,884

(1) For the years 1776 through 1779 PP, Reports from the Committees of the House of Commons, 1783, VI, 180-82; from 1780 through 1785 Appendix VI; from 1786 onward PP, Accounts and Papers, 1787, No. 403; ibid., 1792-93, No. 474, and Sessional Reports, Papers, etc., 1812-13, VIII, No. 104 pp. 242; ibid., 1812, VI, No. 148, pp. 82-83; Macgregor, Commercial Statistics, IV, 41, and V, 77-78.

(2) Reports referred to above, and PP, Sessional Reports, Papers, etc., 1806, VI, No. 209, pp. 1006, and ibid., 1812-13, VIII, No. 104, pp. 242, and as in Note 1.

(3) From 1780 through 1785 calculated upon the basis of the tonnage arrived each year from China (Macgregor, op. cit. V, 39) and the current freight rates (Wissett, Compendium, II, section on freight, and Macgregor, op. cit., IV, 362); for other years as in Note 1.

(4) Calculated from the sales value of Chinese goods, using the percentages allowed by the Company and given in the notes to Appendix 1.

(5) Total cost includes charges at 5 per cent upon the sales value, the value of supplies sent to India as given in Appendix VI, interest at 5 per cent upon the money taken up and invested at Canton and various extraordinary charges.

(6) As in Note 1.

APPENDIX VIII

Net Profit of the East India Company Upon Its Trade with China (1775-1815)

Season	Actual Capital Invested in Goods and Stores (1) £	Profits Losses - on Imports into China (2) £	Receipts from Freight(3) £	Profits on Exports from China (4) £	Duties collected on Private Trade (5) £	Net Profit above 4% Interest £
1775-76	348,478	- 14,176	15,000	234,822	6,000	241,646
1776-77	406,066	- 15,130		291,830	6,150	282,850
1777-78	495,559	- 12,247		251,505	7,590	246,848
1778-79	419,991	- 7,957		254,075	10,195	256,313
1779-80	343,759	6,194		330,357	7,836	344,389
1780-81	675,347	- 2,190		122,198	10,066	130,074
1781-82	532,185	1,301		78,684	11,406	91,391
1782-83	265,457	- 14,516		418,773	14,428	418,685
1783-84	939,949	- 17,470		197,611	31,765	211,906
1784-85	608,354	- 6,079	3,408	1,153,308	21,544	1,172,181
1785-86	980,690	- 8,561		493,107	22,168	506,714
1786-87	1,654,049	- 27,899		368,495	23,230	363,826
1787-88	1,754,059	- 22,511		300,016	26,128	303,833
1788-89	1,526,283	- 40,663	14,593	342,551	29,230	345,512
1789-90	1,480,150	- 16,950	31,043	509,282	29,578	553,954
1790-91	1,556,604	25,144		506,791	41,915	573,850
1791-92	1,117,845	14,611		475,913	27,048	517,572
1792-93	1,180,275	- 10,044		489,029	36,997	515,982
1793-94	1,282,127	- 21,851	5,814	597,693	29,960	611,614
1794-95	1,571,655	-159,574		805,143	50,158	715,727
1795-96	1,173,724	- 25,877		622,040	31,513	628,176
1796-97	2,097,919	- 64,968	9,205	447,889	37,856	429,980
1797-98	1,852,267	- 61,410	2,947	937,676	45,605	924,818
1798-99	988,493	- 71,031	29,882	865,102	28,576	852,528
1799-00	1,385,964	-105,247	9,999	808,367	38,386	753,505
1800-01	1,452,111	-244,439	1,865	831,652	44,583	633,662
1801-02	2,057,732	- 71,019		236,044	67,104	232,129
1802-03	2,001,034	-142,667	1,678	851,070	52,315	762,396
1803-04	1,802,668	-173,562	6,074	874,181	50,397	757,090
1804-05	2,097,687	-165,120	8,054	1,087,529	47,296	977,759
1805-06	1,740,618	-132,983	6,283	1,063,002	38,215	974,517
1806-07	1,845,654	- 63,103	16,368	1,099,546	34,017	1,086,827
1807-08	1,285,597	8,906		1,170,952	68,089	1,247,947
1808-09	1,372,559	11,149		1,200,898	50,488	1,262,535
1809-10	1,296,155	- 27,161	23,333	1,280,983	41,230	1,318,386
1810-11	1,427,605	36,100		1,022,093	54,285	1,112,476
1811-12	1,836,667	- 29,164		909,425	61,349	941,608
1812-13	2,141,869	- 23,949		914,081	62,077	952,209
1813-14	1,880,463	- 44,842		1,456,941	83,873	1,495,972
1814-15	1,977,196	- 25,342		924,884	95,405	994,947

(1) Total money invested in goods and stores in China as given in Appendix V reduced to pounds. This represents the total capital employed in both imports and exports for a two year period. Net profits, therefore, are upon a two year investment.
(2) Appendix IV and IX.
(3) Morse, Chronicle, II, 5, 94, 152, 172, 205, 278, 294, 310, 322, 388, 401, 416, and III, 1, 27, 101.
(4) Appendix VI.
(5) Calculated upon the basis of figures in Milburn, Oriental Commerce, II, 480; Macgregor, Commercial Statistics, V, 79-81; PP, Sessional Reports, Papers, etc. 1812, VI, No. 148, p. 102, considering the duties as 12½ per cent, upon the sales value of Private Trade goods from 1776 through 1782 and from thence onward as 14½ per cent.

APPENDIX IX

Silver Imported into China from England and India by the East India Company (1760-1800)

Season	Exported from England (1) £	Realised on England Tls.	Silver imported at Canton(2) India Tls.	Total Tls.	Cost of Silver Imported (3) Tls.	Losses Tls.
1760-61	55,081	368,694	396,720	765,414		
1761-62	25,154	158,000	58,000	216,000		
1762-63	28,126	75,384	247,026	322,410		
1763-64		93,000	435,609	528,609		
1764-65	307,410		338,781	338,781		
1765-66	294,526	1,098,255	673,479	1,690,479		
1766-67	946	789,807	1,140,786	1,930,593		
1767-68			620,040	620,040		
1768-69	168,137		521,427	521,427		
1769-70	233,045	489,186		489,186		
1770-71	293,210	669,762	152,286	822,044		
1771-72	199,615	879,650		879,650		
1772-73		505,298	69,574	574,872		
1773-74			81,452	81,452		
1774-75				None		
1775-76				None		
1776-77	68,574		394,016	394,016	476,820	82,804
1777-78		160,148	70,252	230,400	256,249	25,849
1778-79		69,120	21,600	90,720	99,861	7,141
1779-80				None		
1780-81				None		
1781-82				None		
1782-83				None		
1783-84			8,640	8,640	9,511	871
1784-85				None		
1785-86	704,254			None		
1786-87	694,962	2,062,080		2,062,080	2,131,200	69,120
1787-88	626,897	1,912,320		1,912,320	1,976,298	63,978
1788-89	469,408	1,992,638	102,240	2,094,878	2,210,515	115,637
1789-90	714,233	1,321,920		1,321,920	1,382,802	60,882
1790-91		2,106,041		2,106,041	2,163,009	59,968
1791-92	377,685	172,800		172,800	180,759	7,959
1792-93		518,400		518,400	537,921	19,521
1793-94				None		
1794-95				None		
1795-96	58,150			None		
1796-97	200,656	120,960		120,960	127,545	6,585
1797-98	411,466	626,965		626,965	667,755	40,790
1798-99	498,493	1,326,850		1,326,850	1,372,692	45,862
1799-00	140,308	1,623,171		1,623,171	1,673,555	50,384

(1) PP, Sessional Reports, Papers, etc., 1812-13, VIII, No. 152, pp. 399-403; Milburn, Oriental Commerce, II, 475; Macgregor, Commercial Statistics, IV, 404-6 and V, 76, Wissett, Compendium, II, 22-23.

(2) From 1760 to 1775 worked out upon the basis of figures in Reports from Committees of the House of Commons, 1715-1801, IV, 68-69 and VIII, 370-71, and Morse, Chronicle, V, 86, 100, 107, 111-12, 123-24, 130-31, 134, 144-46, 149, 156-57, 166, 176-77. From 1775 onwards Canton Diaries, volumes given in Appendix I; PP, Accounts and Papers, 1792-95, XXXVIII, No. 773(9); Morse, Chronicle, IV, 387.

(3) Includes interest and insurance at 10 per cent and charges at 1 per cent on the prime cost of silver from England, and charges, as recorded in the Diaries, on silver from India. The prime cost is given in the Canton Diaries, volumes indicated in Appendix I.

APPENDIX X

Money Realized at Canton through Bills, Certificates, Bonds, Freight, etc. (1760–1800)[1]

Season	Bills on London Tls.	Bills on India Tls.	Indian Engagements Tls.	Certificates $	Bonds and Freight Tls.	Total Receipts Tls.	Bills and Bonds Paid Tls.
1760-61	None					None	
1761-62	44,775					44,775	
1762-63	6,075		3,888			9,963	7,590
1763-64	29,769		1,438		51,790	82,998	10,386
1764-65	51,121	60,117	11,522		118,499	241,259	8,706
1765-66	175,635	22,482				198,117	11,190
1766-67			8,709			8,709	
1767-68						None	5,430
1768-69					7,560	7,560	4,245
1769-70	125,229					125,229	600
1770-71	256,566		37,800			294,366	6,897
1771-72	360,000		124,272		3,406	487,680	91,422
1772-73	620,860		75,600			696,460	9,099
1773-74	117,695		75,163	46,426		226,285	500
1774-75			160,346	71,285	2,475*	214,029	4,958
1775-76	393,519				45,001*	438,520	51,085
1776-77	692,829					692,829	10,254
1777-78	722,745		$		11,216*	733,961	
1778-79	497,722		315,555		46,080	767,922	624
1779-80	1,537,996					1,537,996	50,349
1780-81	1,585,977			185,295		1,517,949	
1781-82	1,107,418			11,924		1,115,461	
1782-83	748,986			436		697,320	231,670
1783-84	696,993			105,256	100,101	876,056	21,606
1784-85	525,242			56,842	10,225:	576,393	42,651
1785-86	2,002,140	$		223,784		1,802,665	11,654
1786-87	1,771,856	340,271		149,868		1,684,344	10,735
1787-88	4,026,292				13,529	2,889,452	
1788-89	2,182,564		1,030,561	109,664	43,178*	2,498,464	58,859
1789-90	1,610,452		502,690	195,136	96,150*	1,745,470	
1790-91	1,975,985		608,890	303,484		2,076,140	
1791-92	1,465,564		874,090	218,648		1,835,982	
1792-93	1,660,582		723,108	176,254		1,843,160	
1793-94	1,613,267			287,984	17,422*	1,386,343	31,050
1794-95	1,565,035		127,499	281,319		1,419,358	
1795-96	1,907,876		42,160	21,637	186,322	1,601,373	
1796-97	1,836,966	115,446		300,000	27,609*	1,649,346	9,852
1797-98	2,613,499	756,483	99,000	300,000	8,840*	2,710,189	176,470
1798-99	2,265,279	600,000	194,966	300,000	89,647:	2,497,576	
1799-00	1,575,302	938,314	529,828	115,127	29,996:	2,297,424	

[1]From 1760 through 1774 based on PP, Reports from the Committees of the House of Commons, 1715-1801, IV, 68-69, and VIII, 370-71, and Morse, Chronicle, V, 102, 107-08,110-12, 122-23, 145-46, 149-50, 157, 167, 177, 189-90; from 1775 onward based on the lists of bills given in the Canton Diaries, volumes given in Appendix I; Morse, Chronicle, II, 5-7, 9-10, 26, 31, 40, 50, 62, 74, 85, 94, 111, 119, 121, 135, 141, 150, 172, 179, 184, 192, 205, 256, 266, 277, 294, 310, 321, 347, 352; MSS. C, Macartney Correspondence, I, No. 392; PP, Accounts and Papers, 1792-93, XXXVIII, No. 775; the Reports referred to above. * in the column on bonds and freight means freight.

APPENDIX XI

Private Trade at Canton (1764-1800)[1]

Season	English Goods Tls.	Furs Tls.	Ginseng Tls.	Cotton Tls	Tin Tls.	Pepper Tls.	Total Imports Tls.	Exports Total Tls
1764-65							432,180	550,800
1765-66							462,050	584,000
1766-67							370,440	556,000
1767-68							246,960	208,000
1768-69	?			54,164	19,140	?	570,440	504,000
1769-70							524,790	520,000
1770-71							401,310	400,000
1771-72	60,000	21,389		330,000	85,076	72,928	617,400	600,000
1772-73	30,000	8,484		178,548	178,548	22,692	401,310	240,000
1773-74							359,570	299,570
1774-75	25,000			47,587	40,944	1,596	123,480	69,480
1775-76	41,756	8,252	13,600	20,000	2,000	1,584	115,204	113,260
1776-77	55,003	13,911	2,000	40,425	71,204	7,500	251,120	225,000
1777-78	120,964	10,509	31,200	45,325	144,466	12,051	391,315	340,000
1778-79	105,126	11,226	9,570	50,600	76,622	56,526	332,680	300,000
1779-80	23,125	9,940	66,000	14,179			193,260	175,000
1780-81	170,747	11,203	1,800	60,898	32,994	28,310	410,520	278,560
1781-82	107,891	11,793	12,000	55,180		7,095	260,840	253,030
1782-83	18,356	1,140	23,184	20,120			91,350	85,650
1783-84	28,427	31,200	22,000	52,728	3,465	24,520	267,420	191,820
1784-85	79,992	23,389	26,578	65,240	70,410	22,920	417,945	377,625
1785-86	86,546	39,336	92,620	74,012	32,976	4,210	426,725	515,510
1786-87	69,442	46,018	62,590	145,744	55,310	5,600	601,300	494,020
1787-88	74,206	55,267	41,800	140,460	64,496	3,102	431,930	410,930
1788-89	93,858	185,127	58,050	130,948	134,844	9,422	640,445	561,965
1789-90	72,891	211,949	9,440	105,496	78,255	23,534	516,570	576,120
1790-91	64,526	395,998	6,600	125,520	119,520	77,120	804,265	586,105
1791-92	24,747	396,168	5,054	55,548	92,864	62,528	636,560	479,400
1792-93	67,055	494,065	3,750	80,827	61,485	116,752	971,650	843,950
1793-94	115,130	474,964	3,000	80,273	119,235	13,118	984,255	776,895
1794-95	81,650	323,315	6,350	105,934	25,942	13,884	663,475	461,155
1795-96	110,620	110,908	1,305	125,435			375,960	558,840
1796-97	66,889	39,909	1,125	115,592	79,828	8,606	365,742	550,742
1797-98	111,460	46,991	8,250	90,540	187,502	22,140	700,598	690,598
1798-99	46,875	118,009	4,080	80,932	258,735		555,806	545,806
1799-00	89,060	113,716	6,280	75,508			557,622	454,822

[1]Based on the Canton Diaries, volumes indicated in Appendix I. Only the quantities of Articles imported or exported are given in the Diaries. The values have been obtained by multiplying the quantities imported or exported by the current prices given in the Diaries. The values thus obtained are only approximately accurate, but serve to show the general value of the trade. For the seasons 1764-65 to 1767-68, 1769-70, 1770-71, and 1773-74, the figures have been destroyed. The total values given for these years are estimated based on the number of ships.

APPENDIX XII

Country Trade at Canton (1764-1800)[1]

Season	Metals Tls.	Pepper Tls.	Imports Woods Tls	Cotton Tls.	Total Tls.	Raw Silk Tls.	Exports Sugar & Candy Tls.	Total Tls.
1764-65					189,600			162,900
1765-66					316,000			271,500
1766-67					252,000			217,200
1767-68					316,000			271,500
1768-69	39,720	?	?	66,430	189,600	?	?	162,900
1769-70					316,000			271,500
1770-71					379,200			325,800
1771-72	19,164	2,976	560	50,732	126,400	2,700	?	108,600
1772-73	52,308		80	138,198	252,000	28,550	?	217,200
1773-74					632,000			543,000
1774-75	234,584	76,092	67,840	397,176	948,000	62,730	?	714,500
1775-76	231,944	12,576	23,310	184,840	624,091	239,200	130,878	528,020
1776-77	152,102	7,524	26,858	484,536	754,114	150,900	166,164	462,413
1777-78	151,438	52,325	8,460	245,375	577,883	296,920	106,760	592,367
1778-79	149,926	71,722	22,020	250,440	649,225	53,840	45,605	359,250
1779-80	164,945	124,264	11,415	92,411	428,440	527,020	25,248	707,004
1780-81	189,956	94,030	21,765	269,609	727,880	149,620	22,868	292,212
1781-82	40,740	41,800	7,308	130,382	537,100	81,740	24,435	188,080
1782-83	?	?	?	164,440	487,405	?	?	54,300
1783-84	23,971	4,060	4,434	42,302	213,140	31,160	33,072	158,950
1784-85	49,870	29,250	18,675	206,180	433,010	43,710	42,614	392,900
1785-86	58,368	114,910	40,456	564,150	1,284,873	68,540	98,834	628,067
1786-87	208,028	82,170	30,700	933,560	1,524,630	68,790	124,685	303,484
1787-88	75,808	77,440	10,926	1,927,932	2,412,200	200,100	45,410	426,801
1788-89	194,599	15,512		1,828,352	2,272,275	239,920	113,526	793,245
1789-90	185,265	58,520	81	2,329,424	2,820,230	577,600	140,725	961,784
1790-91	91,680	39,520	1,456	1,975,254	2,550,755	304,000	402,065	1,245,510
1791-92	199,952	144,304	11,253	329,060	935,755	343,440	368,324	955,062
1792-93	78,915	25,832	140,700	2,000,724	2,548,100	519,200	245,800	1,291,544
1793-94	102,240	125,902	48,195	1,836,730	2,426,550	304,790	566,760	1,260,050
1794-95	72,884	62,751	85,640	1,562,557	2,221,385	263,520	617,220	1,193,480
1795-96	28,410	54,236	24,150	1,375,325	2,244,996	303 548	303 548	863,387
1796-97	29,134	121,745	6,305	1,781,016	2,822,112	326,180	222,004	931,770
1797-98	99,424	170,244	15,782	2,330,444	3,375,207	339,600	465,274	1,001,401
1798-99	40,590	60,962	74,004	1,814,072	3,342,084	257,850	247,700	1,012,844
1799-00	71,196	105,220	63,975	1,458,464	2,740,390	29,970	519,825	1,002,768

[1]Reference as in notes to Appendix XI. Metals include mainly tin, but contain a little lead.
Woods include sandalwood, redwood, and blackwood or ebony. Although opium was probably the second
most important article imported in the Country trade, no even approximately accurate figures are
available.

BIBLIOGRAPHY

1. Handbooks, Manuals, and Bibliographical Aids.

The materials for a study of Anglo-Chinese relations during the late eighteenth and early nineteenth centuries are very extensive and complete. They consist in the main of several large collections of manuscripts, a considerable number of published documents, a large number of Parliamentary and State Papers giving statistical and documentary information, numerous published works by contemporary observers, several periodicals and a few newspapers, and a host of secondary works published throughout the nineteenth and early twentieth centuries. Before a survey of the manuscript sources is given, it seems advisable to list the best bibliographies, handbooks, and manuals. Bibliographical sources are discussed at length in the introduction to Cordier, *Bibliotheca sinica,* and works referred to there will generally not be mentioned.

Andreae, V., and Geiger, John. *Bibliotheca sinologica.* Frankfurt a.M., 1864. A selection of European publications prior to 1863.

Birdwood, Sir George. *Report on the Miscellaneous Old Records of the India Office.* London: Eyre and Spottiswoode, 1879 and 1890. Contains valuable information about the miscellaneous manuscripts in the India Office.

British Museum. *A Guide to the Chinese and Japanese Illustrated Books Exhibited in the King's Library.* London, 1887.

Catalogue of Chinese Government Publications in the Metropolitan Library, Pei-Hai Park, Peking. Peiping, 1928.

Catalogue of the Library of the North China Branch Royal Asiatic Society (contained in the Society's building, No. 5. Museum Road, Shanghai). 1st ed., by Henry Cordier. Shanghai, 1782. 5th ed. Shanghai, 1921.

Catalogue of the Library of the East India Company. London, 1845. Supplement in 1851.

Catalogue of the Library of the British Factory at Canton. Canton, 1832.

Cordier, Henri. "Manuscrits relatifs à la Chine. Notes bibliographiques." *Revue de l'Extrême-Orient,* Jan. 1882 to Dec. 1884. Paris, 1882-84. Contains a description of manuscripts on China in the British Museum, the India Office, the Bibliothèque Palatine in Vienna, and the Library of the Royal Asiatic Society in London.

Cordier, Henri. *Bibliotheca sinica; dictionnaire bibliographique des ouvrages relatifs à l'empire chinois.* 2nd ed. 4 vols. Paris: Librairie Orientale et Américaine, 1904-08. *Supplément.* Vol. 1. Paris: Librairie Orientaliste Paul Geuthner, 1922-24. This work includes practically all other bibliographies mentioned in this list and is the most complete and reliable bibliography of works in European languages extant.

Courant, Maurice. *Bibliothèque Nationale, Départment des Manuscrits: Catalogue des livres chinois, coréens, japonais, etc.* 3 vols. Paris: Ernest Leroux, 1902-12. Contains 9,080 numbers.

Douglas, Robert Kennaway. *Catalogue of Chinese Printed Books, Manuscripts and Drawings in the Library of the British Museum.* London: Longmans, 1877. *Supplement*—London: Longmans, 1903.

Dudgeon, J. "List of Russian Works on China." *The Chinese Recorder,* IV, 207. Shanghai, 1878.

Edkins, Joseph. *A Catalogue of Chinese Works in the Bodlean Library.* Oxford: Clarendon Press, 1876. Continued in Professor Legge's manuscript, *Catalogue of Bodlean Chinese Books Not in Edkin's Catalogue.* Bodlean works are not catalogued to date.

Foster, Sir William. *A Guide to the India Office Records, 1600-1858.* London: Eyre and Spottiswoode, 1919. An invaluable guide to the 48,000 volumes of East India Company manuscripts in the India Office.

Giles, Herbert Allen. *A Chinese Biographical Dictionary.* London: Bernard Quaritch, 1897-98. Very useful and valuable for identifying persons, although it contains many errors.

Griffin, Appleton Prentiss Clark. *Select List of Books (with References to Periodicals) Relating to the Far East.* Washington: Gov. Printing Office, 1904.

Hoang, Père Pierre. *Concordance des chronologies néoméniques chinoise et européenne.* Chang-Hai: Imprimerie de la Mission Catholique, 1910. An absolutely essential work for translating Chinese dates into European.

Hoang, Père Pierre. *Mélanges sur l'administration.* Chang-Hai: Imprimere de la Mission Catholique, 1902. An extremely valuable handbook dealing with the names of offices and institutions of government during the Ch'ing Dynasty.

Holt, Henry F. "A Catalogue of the Chinese Manuscripts in the Library of the Royal Asiatic Society." *Journal of the Royal Asiatic Society,* Jan., 1890. London, 1890.

India Office. *List of Factory Records of the East India Company, preserved in the Record Department of the India Office.* London, 1897.

India Office. *List of General Records, 1599-1879, preserved in the Record Department of the India Office.* London: Eyre and Spottiswoode, 1902.

India Office. *List of Marine Records of the Late East India Company 1605-1856.* London, 1896. The last three works are invaluable, although now to some extent incomplete, guides to the early factory records, the marine records, and the general records of the East India Company.

Library of Congress, Division of Chinese Literature. *Orientalia.* Washington: Government Printing Office, 1920-35. Catalogue of Chinese works in the Library of Congress.

Maspero, Henri. "La Chine et l'Asie centrale." *Histoire et historiens depuis cinquante ans,* II, 517-59. Paris, 1928. Excellent survey of Western historians dealing with China and their work.

Mayers, William Frederick. "Bibliography of the Chinese Imperial Collection of Literature." *The China Review,* VI. Hongkong, 1778.

Mayers, William Frederick. *The Chinese Government. A Manual of Chinese Titles, Categorically Arranged and Explained.* Shanghai: Mission Press, 1878. 2nd ed. Shanghai: Kelly and Walsh, 1886.

Mayers, William Frederick. *The Chinese Reader's Manual. A Handbook of Biographical, Historical, Mythological and General Literary References.* Shanghai: Mission Press, 1874. The immense value of the last two works need hardly be mentioned.

Morrison, Dr. G. E. *Catalogue of the Asiatic Library of . . .* 2 vols. Tokyo: Oriental Library, 1924. Vol. I deals with English works and Vol. II with works in other European languages. The Morrison collection in Tokyo is the largest single collection of works in European languages dealing with China in the world.

Möllendorff, P. G. von. *Manual of Chinese Bibliography, Being a List of Works and Essays Relating to China.* Shanghai, 1876. A very handy bibliography of European works on China, but it is incomplete, as well as erroneous in places.

Nanjio, Bunyiu. *A Catalogue of Japanese and Chinese Books and Manuscripts Lately Added to the Bodlean Library (1876-81).* Oxford: Clarendon Press, 1881.

Nankai University, Pa Li Tai Library. *Library Catalog.* Tientsin and Peiping: Kuang Hua Press, 1926.

Peake, Cyrus H. "Documents Available for Research on the Modern History of China." *The American Historical Review,* XXXVIII (October, 1932), 61-70. New York: Macmillan, 1932. An account of documents contained in the Historical Museum, the Sinological Research Institute of the Peiping National University, the Palace Museum, and the Imperial Rain-Temple at Peiping. They include the records of the Grand Secretariat and the Council of State during the Ch'ing dynasty.

Powell, J. B. and Rawlinson, Frank. *Annotated Bibliography of English Books on China.* Shanghai: Christian Literature Society, 1928. Limited in scope.

Summers, James. *Descriptive Catalogue of the Chinese, Japanese, and Manchu Books in the Library of the India Office.* London, 1872.

Taylor, Louise Marion. *Catalogue of Books on China in the Essex Institute.* Salem, Mass.: The Essex Institute, 1926. Valuable only for determining what books are in the Essex institute.

Tsing Hua University Library. *Classified Catalog of the Tsing Hua Library.* Peiping: Tsing Hua College, 1927.

Wylie, A. *Notes on Chinese Literature.* Shanghai, 1867. Reprint. Shanghai: Presbyterian Mission Press, 1922.

2. Manuscript Sources.

Manuscripts relating to Anglo-Chinese relations are to be found in a number of repositories, but the two most important collections are the records of the East India Company in the India Office and the Macartney Papers in the Wason Collection in the Cornell University Library, Ithaca, New York. There are 44 volumes of manuscripts at Cornell dealing with China, and there are 364 volumes in the India Office relating to the China factory. Many of the other collections in the India Office also have material which relates directly or indirectly to China. Some valuable manuscripts relating to the period covered by this study are also to be found in the Public Record Office, the British Museum, the Bodlean Library, the American State Department, the Library of Congress, and *Ministère des affairs étrangères.* The author has collected several manuscripts of value, which are now deposited in the Library of the State College of Washington.

India Office

China Factory Records [old collection], 1596-1840. 292 vols. These records consist of the supercargoes' *Diaries,* which deal with routine commercial matters and are a mine of statistical material, and the *Consultations,* which deal with correspondence and consultations and in general give a narrative of all important events from day to day. A complete inventory of this collection is to be found in the published *List of Factory Records.* All of the material in this collection, except volumes 258 to 263, has been summarized by Doctor H. B. Morse in *Chronicles of the East India Company Trading to China,* although he has omitted most of the material relating to the several embassies. Sir William Foster has summarized these records under the following headings:

1-10. *Materials for a History of Relations with China and Japan, 1596-1725* (the 1705-11 volume is missing).

11, 12. *Memoir on Intercourse with China, 1518-1832* (in duplicate). Published with additions by Auber under title of *China* (1834).

13. *Early Papers on China, Japan, etc. 1623-99.*

14. *Attempts to Trade at Chusan, 1699-1759.*

15. *Letters from Richard Wickham in Japan, 1614-16.*

16. *Consultations, Letters, etc., China and Japan, 1614-1703* (including Weddell's China voyage of 1637).

17. *Tonquin and Cochin China, 1672-97.*

18. *China and Cochin China: Miscellaneous Papers, 1753-78.*

19. *Miscellaneous Correspondence, 1768-97.*

20. *Miscellaneous Documents, 1782-1815.* This volume has considerable material relating to the Macartney Embassy.

21-55. *China Supercargoes' Ship Diaries, 1721-42; 1745-47; 1749-51.* Most of the missing years shown here and in the next entry are made up in *Factory Records China II*, to be noted later.

56-89. *Canton Diaries and Consultations, 1751; 1753; 1775-88* (including Letterbooks for 1776-78 and 1779).

90. *Col. Cathcart's Embassy to China, 1787-89.*

91-93. *Lord Macartney's Embassy, 1787-1810.*

94-194. *Canton Diaries and Consultations, 1788-1815.*

195. *China and Japan: Miscellaneous, 1710-1814.*

196-98. *Lord Amherst's Embassy, 1815-17.*

199-257. *Canton Diaries and Consultations, 1815-34* (including Commercial Consultations for 1832-34 and Financial for 1834).

258-263. *Canton Agency Consultations, 1834-40.* Not summarized by Morse.

264. *Superintending Committee's Consultations, 1792-94.*

265-277. *China Secret Committee's Consultations, 1793; 1796-1832.*

277A. *Abstract of China Public Consultations, 1831-33, and of Factory Consultations, 1833-35.*

278-283. *Letters Received from China, 1823-34.*

284-287. *Secret Letters Received from China, 1821-27; 1830-32.*

288-290. *Despatches to China, 1829-32.* This set of letters is completed back to 1784 by *Court Letters to China*, to be noted later.

291. *Secret Commercial Drafts to China, 1813-32.*

Between 1928 and 1931, through the agency of the Foreign Office, seventy-two more volumes relating to the East India Company's affairs in China were obtained from Peking and added to the India Office collection. These latter volumes are not mentioned in Foster or the *List of Factory Records.* These new records are as follows:

Factory Records China II, 1623-1803. 21 vols. Volumes 3 to 7 are summarized in Morse's *Chronicle*, V. The remaining volumes duplicate material already in the India Office.

1. *Trade Extracts with China, Japan, Siam, etc. 1623-1683.*

2-5. *Diaries and Consultations, 1727-69.*

6-8. *Letter Books, 1763-79.*

9. *Diaries, 1771-77.*

10-20. *Consultations, 1779-1792.*

21. *Consultation Index, 1785-1803.*

Secret Consultations, 1796-1834. 11 vols. With the exception of Volumes 9, 10, and 11, this set is duplicated in the earlier collection.

Court Letters, 1784-1833. 34 vols. Practically none of this collection is duplicated and none of it has been summarized by Morse.

1-30. *Court Letters to China, 1784-1833.*

31-34. *Secret Letters to the Court, 1810-27.*

Miscellaneous, 1771-1841. 6 vols. These volumes have not been summarized by Morse.

1. *Miscellaneous: Covenants, Instructions, Debts, etc., 1771-92.*
2. *Secret Consultations of Supercargoes, 1818-26.*
2A. *Duplicate Letters to Supercargoes, 1816-1831.*
3. *Mr. Lindsay's Journal of the Lord Amherst's Journey, 1832.*
4-5. *Letters to the Foreign Office, 1840-41.*

Besides the records relating to the China factory, there are many others in the India Office which have a certain amount of material relating to China affairs. It will be advisable to mention these as briefly as possible.

Court Minutes or Court Book, 1599-1858. 191 vols. Until 1833 this series includes not only the minutes of the Court of Directors, but also the proceedings of the Court of Proprietors. All of the important material in this series down to 1673 has been summarized in the published works, *Calendars of State Papers, Colonial: East Indies, 1513-1634, Court Minutes, 1635-73,* and *Dawn of British Trade to the East Indies, 1599-1603.* The material relating to the period covered in this study begins with Vol. 83 and extends through Vol. 133. Most of the volumes are indexed, but the indexes are very unsatisfactory, and, as there is very little material of importance in them relating to China, they are hardly worth referring to unless specific information is wanted about action taken by the Court on or near a known date.
Committee of Secrecy: Minutes, 1778-1858. 6 vols. These are preserved in the Political Department of the India Office and are of no particular use unless the approximate date wanted is known.
Committee of Correspondence: References, 1704-1833. 13 vols., two of which are indexed. They contain lists of papers submitted to the Committee and are of little use except in specific instances. There are gaps from 1705-15, 1749-54, and 1757-83.
Committee of Correspondence: Minutes, 1784-1834. 17 vols. All except the first three volumes have indexes and are of value in discovering the activity of the Committee on or near known dates.
Committee of Correspondence: Reports, 1719-1834. 6 vols. There are gaps from 1820-21 and 1823-25. Most of the volumes have indexes and contain considerable valuable information about the appointment of supercargoes, the commissions allowed to them, and reports made by the Committee to the Court in response to matters referred to it.
Committee of Correspondence: Memoranda, 1700-1858. 58 vols. These include draft minutes, papers, etc. relating to matters considered by the Committee. They are unindexed, and although some information of value is to be found in them, it requires enormous work with little compensation.
Correspondence: Home Letters Received, 1701-1858. 195 vols. indexed until 1827. An occasional bit of valuable information can be found in these volumes, but they are of little importance.
Despatches to Bengal, 1753-1833. 124 vols. There is a modern index of 13 vols. to these dispatches, and reference to China matter can easily be found. There is considerable information of value in these dispatches. The corrections in red ink were made by the Board of Control.
Despatches to Madras, 1753-1858. 131 vols. There is a separate modern index, and Chinese matters can be discovered easily.
Despatches to Bombay, 1753-1858. 117 vols. A modern index is being compiled.
Despatches from the Secret Committee to all Presidencies, 1778-1858. 24 vols., without index. Of value if the approximate date of dispatch is known, but not of sufficient value to warrant a laborious searching through each volume.
Bengal: Commercial Reports (External). Range 174. Vols. 13 to 27 deal with the Private trade in India from 1795 onward. These volumes have a complete account of the Country trade between Bengal and China and are therefore of great value. Full details of ships arriving from and clearing for China are given, including tonnage, cargoes, etc. These volumes are of great statistical value.

Marine Records: Logs; Ledger and Receipt Books, 1605-1856. Several thousand vols. A complete account of these records is to be found in the *List of Marine Records.* The logs are of little use unless the movements of a particular ship are desired, in which case they become of enormous value, because the log of practically every ship which sailed from London to the East is contained in this series.

Marine Records: Miscellaneous, 1600-1866. 900 vols. Several volumes in this collection are of interest and value in studying the shipping policy of the Company, freight rates, ships sent out, and value of cargoes sent on them. The following volumes may be noted:

  1. *Historical Sketch of the Company's Shipping Concerns and other Papers, 1600-1796.*
  6. *Accounts of Richard Cocks in the Eighth Voyage, 1611-13.*
  17. *Letters and Consultations in the Voyage of the Loyal Adventure to the Philippines and China, 1684-86.*
  504A. *Lists of Ships Sent Out Each Season, 1673-1711; 1791-1827.*
  505. *Lists of the Company's Own Ships Sent Out, 1772-1810.*
  506-8. *Lists of Ships in the Service, etc. 1773-1832.*
  530-39. *Freighting and Hiring of Ships, 1780-1830.*
  644-8. *Company's Own Ships: Regulations, Lists of Officers, etc. 1736-1833.*
  649. *List of Officers in the Company's Service, 1796-1828.*
  651. *Register of Commanders, 1737-1832.*
  676-8. *Free Mariners, 1791-1832.*

General Journals and Ledgers (1644 onward). Contains an account of the cargoes of every ship sent out, together with other commercial and financial information. With a good deal of work the statistics of the China ships could be separated from the others and tabulated.

Private Trade and other Journals and Ledgers (1671 onward). With a good deal of effort some statistics of Private trade to China from London and from China to London could be collected from these volumes.

Home Miscellaneous, 1631-1881. About 800 vols. This is a heterogeneous series ranging over the whole history of the Company, and contains many papers originating in the East. A detailed list of the volumes begins on page 92 of the *List of General Records,* and there are several volumes in the series which are of value. The most important are the following:

  61. *Correspondence, etc. Regarding Customs Duties at Home, 1696-1814.*
  64-65. *Parliament and the Company; Bills and Miscellaneous Papers, 1702-1815.*
  434. *Letters from Mr. George Smith to Mr. Dundas, 1781-1791.*
  689. *Correspondence Regarding the Defence of Portuguese Possessions in India and China against the French, 1801.*

The Wason Collection at Cornell

The most important manuscripts in the Wason Collection consist of private papers of the Earl of Macartney relating to his Embassy to China and to the East India Company's trade with China for a century before the Embassy. The Macartney papers, together with a few other manuscripts, may be summarized as follows:

Macartney Correspondence, 1791-1795. 10 vols. There are a few papers which fall outside the dates indicated, but the collection in the main consists of documents and correspondence relating to the Embassy. There are 448 documents arranged chronologically and numbered, a list of which, classified under the names of the writers, is given in Vol. 1. It includes a full account of the correspondence between Macartney, Dundas, and Baring, together with letters and notes delivered and received by the Ambassador while in China. Vol. 10

consists mostly of statistics and of instructions sent by the Court of Directors to the Superintending Committee in China. The collection was purchased by Mr. Wason from Mr. C. G. Macartney in 1915. A large percentage of this material is not duplicated in the India Office.

Macartney Documents Relating to the East India Company's Affairs in China, 1622-1791. 21 vols. This collection is the book-packet delivered to Lord Macartney by the East India Company on September 8, 1792, before he sailed to China. It consists of detailed extracts from the Company's China records ranging over the whole history of its relations with China. Some of the material fills in gaps still remaining in the India Office China records. These documents passed into Sir Thomas Phillipp's collection of manuscripts early in the 19th century, and were purchased for the Wason Collection in September, 1913. The various volumes are as follows:

1. *Queries put by the Court of Directors to Persons now in England who have served the Company in China with the Answers thereto* [October, 1791-January, 1792].
2. *Extracts Respecting the Trade with China, Tywan, Borneo, Japan, Mindanao, Manilha, Cambodia, Tonquin and Siam, 1622-1686.*
3. *Extract of the Company's Instructions to the Supercargoes at Canton, 1777-1791.*
4. *Fort Saint George Proceedings Relative to the Chinese Debts, 1778-82.*
5. *Extract of China Diaries and Consultations, 1757-1785.*
6. *China Diaries and Consultations Relative to the Chinese Debts, 1779-1781.*
7. *Proceedings* [in England] *Relative to the Chinese Debts, 1771-87.*
8. *Extracts of China Diaries and Consultations, 1727-1740.*
9. *Papers Relative to Seizing Unlicensed Persons in China, 1770-82.*
10. *Extracts Canton Diaries and Consultations, 1741-55.*
11. *Edicts, etc. Communicated by Thomas Fitzhugh, Esq., 1756-1785.* Deal mainly with Flint's expedition to Tientsin in 1759-60.
12. *Extracts and Copies of Letters to Canton, 1790-1791.*
13. *Extracts of Capt. Math*w*. Court's Journal, in the Ship Earl Holderness from the 12 April to 17th May, and 1st June to 18th July, 1755 and from 30th Jan. to 10th Feb., 1756.*
14. *Intercourse with the Chinese, 1778-1792.*
15. *Edicts, Chops, etc. from 1755 to 1777.*
16. *Copies of Letters from Canton, 1791-1792.*
17-19. *First, Second, and Third Reports of the Select Committee Appointed to Take into Consideration the Export Trade from Great Britain to the East Indies, 1791-92* (India, China, Japan and Persia).
20-21. *Embassies to China.* [By James Cobb]. Duplicate copies.

*Catalogue of the Books of the Right Hon*ble *Lord Macartney, 1786.*
Commonplace Book Kept by Lord Macartney during His Embassy in China, 1793-4. Of little value or interest.
A Collection of 69 Original Manuscript Orders Drawn on Messrs. Coutts of London [by Lord Macartney] *to Defray the Various Expenses of the Embassy to China May 17 to Aug. 30, 1792.*
A Journal of the Proceedings of His Majesty's Ship Lion, Commanded by Sir Erasmus Gower, Knt., Aug. 5, 1793 to Jan. 9, 1794. Duplicated in the British Museum.
Original Autograph Letters Relating to China . . . together with the Frst Chinese Proclamation Printed in English, a Manuscript Map of the Opium War, Original Checks of the Earl of Macartney, Early Customs Receipts, etc.
Collections of Monsieur Isaac Titsingh, Governor of Batavia, 1792-1796. Includes various letters and official documents in Dutch and English relating to the Macartney and Dutch Embassies. The Dutch documents have been translated into English, and the translations form an additional volume.
Robinson, George. *Journal of My Proceedings on Board the Ship Inglis from England to Bombay and China, Jan. 1, 1815 to May 15, 1816.*

A Narrative of the Occurrences in a Voyage to the Kingdom of Cochin China, 1778. Prepared by Chapman. Account of an expedition sent to Cochin China by the East India Company.

Original Manuscript Log Book Recording the Voyage of the Ship Alfred from England towards China, and the Return Voyage to England, May 2, 1794 to July 22, 1795.

Warden, Henry. *Original Manuscript Journal of Voyages to China, 1807-1820.* 3 vols. Authenticity questionable.

Gibson, John. *Observations on the Manner of Trading at Canton, 1807.* Valuable account of the system and methods of trade at Canton.

British Museum

Most of the manuscripts in the British Museum relating to China are in the *Additional* collection, and are of no great importance so far as the period under discussion is concerned. The following should be noted:

Additional Manuscripts.

13,818. *Statements Relative to the Trade between Europe, India, and China in General, and the English East India Company's in Particular, 1792.* [By James Cobb of the India House.]

13,822. *Papers Relative to the Opium Trade, 1801.*

13,823. *Reports of Sales of Opium and Salt at Calcutta, 1798-1805.*

13,875. *Report on European Relations with, and History of China, Relative to a Projected Embassy to That Country,* [1792]. [By James Cobb.] See *Macartney Documents,* Vols. 20 and 21.

13,882. *Journal Kept on Board the Ship Frederick in the China Sea, Aug.-Oct. 1803.*

16,363-65. *Charts of the Coast of China Drawn by European Hands.* Some were done by J. R. Morrison, Jr., and 16,363 and 16,365 relate to Canton.

17,641A. *Plano del Rio por el qual se navega con Embarcaciones menores entre Macao y Canton levantado Par Manuel de Agate primer Sobrecargo de la Rl Compa. de Filipinas.* 1792.

19,822. *Maps, Plans, and Sketches of Places and Scenes in China, by H. W. Parish, 1792-94.*

21,106. *A Journal of His Majesty's Ship Lion Beginning the 1st of October 1792 and Ending the 7th September, 1794.* Similar to the one in the Wason Collection.

26,605. *Notes and Collections on China, by W. Erskine, 1796-1810.*

28,940. *Proposals for Establishment of a China and Japan Company, 1695.*

29,198. *Voyage to and from China, 1774-75.*

29,200. *Proposals for the Establishment of a Colony of Chinese at Calcutta, 1783.*

29,210. *China. Debts Due from Chinese Merchants to Englishmen, 1780.*

29,861. *Voyage to China, by Capt. Johnson, 1814-17.*

31,348-50. *Various Maps, Charts, Views, etc. of Canton, Macao, and Vicinity, 19th Century.*

32,165. *Journal of a Mission to India and China by an Agent of the Austrian Government in Connexion with the Company Trading in the East, 1782-85.* In French.

33,411. *Various Notes, Papers, Memorandums, etc. Relating to China and Cochin China, 1811-23.* Relates especially to John Crawfurd's Embassy to Cochin China, 1811.

33,931. *Drawings Made on Lord Macartney's Embassy, by Barrow, Alexander, Daniell, and Parish.* Daniell was not a member of the Embassy, but was at Canton in 1785.

34,444. *Letters from Henry Dundas to Lord Macartney, 1792.* One letter relates to the Dutch Memorial of 1792. Folios 233, 238.

34,444. *Letter from the Dutch East India Company to Lord Auckland, 1792.* Relating to the Macartney Embassy. Folio 170.

34,451. *Reply of Dutch East India Company to Lord Grenville's Inquiries on the State of the Company, 1793.*

34,468. *Statement on the Monopoly of Salt, Opium and Saltpetre, 1786.* (Auckland Papers).

35,300. *Barrow Bequest,* Vol. I—*Original Drawings by William Alexander and Samuel Daniell on the Macartney Embassy, 1792-3.*

35,302. *Barrow Bequest,* Vol. III—*An Autobiographical Memoir of Sir John Barrow, Bart., 1847.* Published.

35,348. *Logs of the Ships Triton and Exeter to India and China, 1792-4.*

38,330, 38,332, 38,335, 38,337, 38,397, 38,407, 38,761. *Liverpool Papers Relating to the Tea Trade, 1717-1821.*

38,352, 38,356, 38,409, 38,410. *Liverpool Papers, 1792-1818.* Papers relating to British trade with China.

Harleian Manuscripts.

306. *Elizabeth's Charter to the East India Company (Dec. 31, 1600).* Early 17th century copy.

Stowe Manuscripts.

307. *Translated Extract of a Letter from a Missionary at Pekin in China Relating to the English Embassy There of Lord Macartney and Sir George Staunton.* The writer of the letter was Père Grammont.

Public Record Office

Colonial Office Papers: East Indies (C.O. 77).

23-29. *Original Correspondence of the Secretary of State, 1775-1828.* Vol. 29 deals with the Macartney Embassy, but all the papers in it are duplicated in the India Office. Vol. 26 also has a few letters of interest.

Board of Trade Papers: Miscellanea (B.T. 6). There are some valuable statistics on the China trade in these volumes.

42. *East Indies: Reports on the Export Trade from Great Britain, 1791-2.*

93, 95. *South and Greenland Whale Fisheries, 1786-92.*

185. *Tables of Trade and Navigation, 1697-1802.*

227. *East Indies: Trade Statistics, 1778-1793.*

Foreign Office Papers: China (F.O. 17). These volumes all relate to the Amherst Embassy and the events immediately following it.

-. *British Mission to China. Notes, 1816* (F.O. 97/95).

1. *Memoir, Part 1, 1815-18*

2. *Memoir, Part 2, 1819-32.*

3. *Lord Amherst, Henry Ellis and Various, 1815-17.*

Treasury Papers: Miscellanea—East India (T. 49).

34. *Canton, 1779-80.* Transcripts relating to the Chinese debts prepared for the use of Lord North.

Bodlean Library

There is practically no material in the Bodlean dealing specifically with the period covered in this work, but there are several volumes relating to earlier periods which should be noted. These are to be found in the Rawlinson Collection as follows:

Rawlinson Manuscripts.

A.299. *Journal of Weddell's Expedition to Canton, 1636-37.* Published in *Travels of Peter Mundy.*

A.303. *Various Papers Relating to the Early China Trade and William Cocley, Supercargo.* N.d.

A.315. *Itinerarium Mundii, 1611-1639.* An account of the travels of Peter Mundy, including his voyage to China with the Weddell Expedition. Published.

A.334. *Description of the Chief Ports and Commercial Cities in Arabia, East Indies, Sumatra, Malacca, Siam and China.* N.d.

D.391. *Long Letter from Francis Terne, Engaged in the Trade with China . . . Giving a Full Account of the Island of Amoy, the Manners of the Chinese, etc., April 25, 1703.*

D.592. *Au nom de Dieu sait bien commance de la travercé de la Chine pour a Ler [i.e. aller] en France et autre part, dans le vaisau La rainne Despange, commandé par monsieur Brunet, Nov. 1713-Jan. 1714.*

Poet. 64. A petition in Chinese from an English merchant asking to be allowed to enter and trade in the port of Amoy, Aug. 31, 1713 (11th day, 7th moon, 52nd year of K'ang Hsi).

Archives of the American State Department

Very little material relating to the period discussed in this work is to be found in the American State Department. All the material for this early period of American relations with China has been used by Tyler Dennett in his excellent work on *Americans in Eastern Asia.* The following collections are, however, worth noting, because they touch upon the period dealt with in this study and occasionally give material illustrating English relations with China.

Canton Consular Letters, 1792-1849. 3 vols. Contains letters received from Consuls at Canton.

Despatches to Consuls, 1800-1835. 6 vols. A few letters sent to Consuls in China are included in this series.

Library of Congress

The only manuscript in the Library of Congress of interest in connection with the present study is:

Journals and Diaries, No. 1. "Relation du voyage fait à la Chine sur le vaisseau *L'Amphitrite,* en l'année 1698," by Giovanni Gherardini. February, 20, 1699. This has long since been published.

Ministère des affaires étrangères

Among the documents in the French Foreign Office, the following series contains two volumes of interest:

Mémoires et documents: Chine, 1720-1888. 24 vols.
   16. *Organisation diplomatique et consulaire. Cérémonial. Concessions. Jurisdiction consulaire, 1794-1880.*
   17. *Mémoires et notes divers sur la Chine, 1793-1855.* Contains some letters from Grammont and De Guignes relative to the Macartney Embassy. Also a plan for a projected French expedition to China, 1793.

State College of Washington Library

Pritchard Collection of Macartney Documents on China. 1 vol.
   Collected by Earl H. Pritchard in England and given to the Library in 1936. The volume contains twenty-four original manuscripts relating to the Macart-

ney Embassy, which were delivered to the Ambassador on September 10, 1792, by the East India Company. The most important documents are as follows:

1. "Instructions from the East India Company to Lord Macartney," September 8, 1792. This is the original document and is not in the India Office. A copy is at Cornell.
9. "Covenant between Lord Macartney and the East India Company," August 29, 1792.
10. "Copy of Covenant between Sir George Leonard Staunton and the East India Company."
16. "Copy of the Instructions from the Secret Committee to Captain Mackintosh," September 8, 1792.
17. "Copy of the Court's Instructions to Captain William Mackintosh," August 15, 1792.
20. "Copy of the Hindostan's Charter-party," June 13, 1792.
24. "Copy of Colonel Cathcart's Instructions," November 30, 1787.
26. "Copy of a Letter from the Chairman and Deputy Chairman to the Secret and Superintending Committee at Canton," April 25, 1792.

3. Published Contemporary Sources.

Absolute Necessity of Laying Open the Trade to the East Indies. London, 1767. Attack upon the Company's monopoly.

A Collection of Letters Relating to the East India Company, and to a Free Trade. London, 1754.

A Demonstration of the Necessity and Advantages of a Free Trade to the East Indies, and of the Termination to the Present Monopoly of the East India Company. London, 1807.

A Free Trade between Ireland and the East Indies. [London, 1791.]

A Hint to the British Nation on the Violation of their Constitutional Rights. London, 1787. An attack upon the Company. There are a large number of pamphlets attacking the Company's monopoly, but it has been possible to give only a few of them.

Alexander, William. *The Customs of China* (illustrated in 48 colored engravings). London: William Miller, 1805. Produced by the artist accompanying the Macartney Embassy and relates to scenes and personalities in 1793-94.

A List of Plants and Seeds Wanted from China and Japan, with Directions for Bringing Them to Europe. London, 1789.

Allom, Thomas. *China, in a Series of Views, Displaying the Scenery, Architecture, and Social Habits, of that Ancient Empire.* London: Fisher Sons & Co., 1843-45. Original sketches.

An Account of the Monies, Weights and Measures in General Use in Persia . . . China, etc. [London], 1789.

An Account of a Voyage to India, China, etc., in His Majesty's Ship Caroline Performed in the Years 1803-04-05. London: Richard Phillips, 1806. Some account of conditions at Canton.

Anderson, Adam. *An Historical and Chronological Deduction of the Origin of Commerce.* 4 vols. London: J. Walter, 1787-89. A standard work for all phases of British economic development. Has valuable statistics.

Anderson, Aeneas. *A Narrative of the British Embassy to China, in the Years 1792, 1793, and 1794.* London: J. Debrett, 1795. Several later editions. Anderson was merely a personal servant of the Ambassador, and although the book contains interesting descriptive material, it has little official information of importance. Dates are often wrong. An abridged edition was edited by some other attendant of the Embassy (possibly Dr. Dinwiddi) in 1795 and was published by Vernor and Hood.

Anderson, George. *General View of the Variations in the Affairs of the East India Company from 1784-1791.* London, 1792. Valuable for studying home difficulties of the Company.

Après de Mannevillette, Jean Baptiste Nicolas Denis d'. *Le Neptune Oriental.* 2nd ed. Paris: Demonville, 1775. First edition was in 1745, and it was the best guide to the Eastern seas prior to Dalrymple and Horsburgh's works.

Backhoff, Feodor Jskowitz. "The Travels of Feodor Jskowitz Backhoff from Muscow into China (1654-56)," in Churchill's *Collection of Voyages and Travels,* II, 469-73. London: Henry Lintot and John Osborn, 1752. Account of an early Russia mission to China.

Backhouse, E. and Bland, J. O. P. *Annals & Memoirs of the Court of Peking* (From the 16th to the 20th Centuries). London: William Heinemann, 1914. Contains many edicts in translation and other illustrative material.

Baddely, John F. *Russia, Mongolia, China, 1602-1676.* 2 vols. London: Macmillan, 1919. An extremely valuable work containing many documents in Russian with English translations.

Bannister, Saxe. *A Journal of the First French Embassy to China, 1698-1700.* London: Thomas Cautley Newby, 1859. Translation from a French manuscript by François Froger, who accompanied the ship *L'Amphitrite.* Also contains an introduction filled with many untrue remarks, and an appendix with some valuable documents relating to the Cathcart and Macartney Embassies.

Barrow, John. *A Voyage to Cochinchina, in the Years 1792 and 1793.* London: T. Cadell, 1806. Barrow's account of the Macartney Embassy from England to Cochin China with many additional remarks about the places visited. Must be used with caution.

Barrow, John. *Travels in China.* London: T. Cadell, 1804. Barrow was Comptroller of the Macartney Embassy, and his account should be valuable, but it is absolutely unreliable. For devastating criticism of it see Proudfoot.

Barrow, John. *Some Account of the Public Life and a Selection from the Unpublished Writings of the Earl of Macartney.* 2 vols. London: T. Cadell, 1807. Vol. II contains Macartney's *Journal* of the China Embassy, but a comparison of this with Robbins' account indicates that Barrow has altered the language on occasions to suit his interest.

Barrow, John. *An Auto-biographical Memoir of Sir John Barrow.* London: John Murray, 1848. Sings the praises of a man who rose from poverty to fame. Has numerous references to the China Embassy.

Bell, John of Antermony. *Travels form St. Petersburg in Russia to Diverse Parts of Asia, in 1716, 1719, 1722.* 2 vols. Glasgow: Robert and A. Foulis, 1763. Several later editions. Account of the Russian Embassy to China in 1719-21 by an Englishman who attended it.

Birdwood, Sir George C.M. *Papers of the East India Company.* Apparently published for the *Journal of Indian Art.* N.d. or place, but it was published after 1860. Contains pictures and facsimile copies of charters and papers of the East India Company.

Birdwood, Sir George C.M. and Foster, Sir William. *Register of Letters, etc. of the Governor and Company of Merchants of London Trading into the East Indies, 1600-1619.* London, 1893. This is the first letter book of the East India Company.

Blancard, Pierre. *Manuel du commerce des Indes orientales et de la Chine.* Paris, 1806. Valuable description of articles of commerce and commercial methods.

Bougainville, M. Le Baron de. *Journal de la navigation autour du Globe de la frégate la Thetis et de la corvette l'Espérance pendant les années 1824, 1825 et 1826.* 2 vols. Paris: Arthur Bertrand, 1837. Chap. 7 of Vol. 1 has a description of British trade at Canton in 1825.

Brand, Adam. *Beschreibung der Chinesischen Reise, welche vermittelst einer Zaaris Gesandschaft durch Dero Ambassadeur Isbrand. Ao. 1693, 94 und 96 von Moscau . . . durch die Mongolische Tartarey verrichtet worden.* Hamburg, 1698. English ed. London: D. Brown, 1698. Account of Ides' Embassy to China by its Secretary.

Breton, M. *China: its Costume, Arts, Manufactures, etc.* 4 vols. 2nd ed. London: J. J. Stockdale, 1812-13. Pictures and views taken from the originals in the collection of M. Breton.

Brooks, Thomas. *An Authentick Account of all the Different Coins (both Real and Imaginary) by which Accounts in the East Indies are kept.* London, 1766. Has valuable account of the duties and charges at Canton.

Brunel, M. "Memoir on the China trade," in Abbé Rochon's *Voyage to Madagascar and the East Indies.* London: Edward Jeffery, 1793. Principally an account of the articles of trade.

Calendar of Court Minutes and *Calendar of State Papers.* See Sainsbury.

Careri, Dr. John Francis Gemelli. "A Voyage Round the World." In Churchill's *Voyages,* IV. London: Henry Lintot and John Osborn, 1752. Account of travels and experiences of an Italian who was in China in 1695.

Charpentier-Cossigny de Palma, Joseph François. *Voyage à Canton . . . suive d'observations sur le voyage à la Chine, de Lord Macartney et du Citoyen Van-Braam.* Paris: André, 1799. Voyage was made sometime between 1783 and 1793. Contains valuable description of conditions at Canton at that time, but the comments on the Macartney Embassy are of no consequence.

Charters Granted to the East India Company from 1601. London, about 1774.

Chinese Official Account of Portuguese and English Embassies translated from the Li-pu-tse-li. Canton, 1844. From the *Chinese Repository.*

Cobbett, William. *Parliamentary History* (1600-1803). London: Longmans and T. C. Hansard, various dates. Record of the Parliamentary debates.

Cocks, Richard. *Diary of* (1615-22). 2 vols. London: Hakluyt, 1883. Valuable account of early British trade in Japan and plans to open trade with China.

Collection of Statutes Concerning . . . the East India Company. London, 1786. Contained only in the India Office under Charters; see *List of General Records,* p. 76.

Collection of Charters and Statutes relating to the East India Company. London, 1817.

Complete View of the Chinese Empire. London: G. Cawthorn, 1798. An abridged account of the Macartney Embassy based upon other works.

Comparative View of the Dutch, French, and English East India Companies. London, 1770.

Considerations on the Dangers and Impolicy of Laying Open the Trade with India and China. London, 1812. A well-written defense of the Company's monopoly.

Cordier, Henri. *La France en Chine au dix-huitième siècle.* Documents inédits publiés sur les manuscrits conservés au depot des affaires étrangères avec une introduction et des notes par Henri Cordier. Paris, 1883. Relate in the main to the records of the French Consulate at Canton from 1776 to 1783.

Cordier, Henri. *Mélanges d'histoire et de géographie orientales.* 4 vols. Paris: Jean Maisonneuve et Fils, 1914-23. Contains the following articles relating to China formerly published by Cordier in various magazines. (1) "Voyage de Montferran en Chine" (prior to 1615). (2) "Travaux historiques sur la Chine." (3) "Mémoire sur la Chine addressé à Napoléon 1er," par F. Renouard de Sainte-Croix. (4) "La mission de M. le Chevalier d'Entrecasteaux à Canton, en 1787, d'après les archives ministère des affaires étrangères." (5) "Voyages de Pierre Poivre de 1748 jusqu'a 1757." Includes one voyage to China.

Dalrymple, Alexander. *General Collection of Nautical Publications, by A. Dalrymple: being Plans, Charts, and Memoirs.* 9 vols. London, 1770-90. Contains charts and memoirs on China.

Dalrymple, Alexander. *A Collection of Charts and Memoirs.* London, 1771-72. Later editions with additions in 1786 and 1787. Contains several charts and memoirs relating to Canton and the China Sea.

Dalrymple, Alexander. *A Collection of Plans of Ports in the East Indies.* London, 1774-75. Later editions in 1782 and 1787.

Dalrymple, Alexander. *Memoir Concerning the Passages to and from China.* London: George Biggs, 1785. Relates to the Eastern passage and routes along the coast of the Philippines.

Dalrymple, Alexander. *Memoir Concerning the Passage, at a Late Season, from India to China.* London: George Biggs, 1788. Relates to the Eastern passages. For a complete list of his numerous nautical publications see *Catalogue of the British Museum.*

Daniell, Thomas and William. *A Picturesque Voyage to India; by the way of China.* London: Longmans, 1810. Views aind scenes in China drawn by the artists while at Canton in 1785.

Danvers, Frederick Charles. *Letters Received by the East India Company from its Servants in the East* (1602-1617). 6 vols. London, 1896-1902. Verbatim edition of letters received from the East.

Davis, John Francis. *Scenes in China, Exhibiting the Manners, Customs . . . and . . . Peculiarities of the Chinese.* London: E. Wallis and A. Wallis, [1820]. Also has an account of the Amherst Embassy which Davis accompanied as one of the interpreters.

Davis, John Francis. *Sketches of China; partly during an inland journey of four months, between Peking, Nanking, and Canton.* 2 vols. London: Charles Knight & Co. 1841. Davis's account of the Amherst Embassy.

De Guignes, Chrétien Louis Joseph de. *Voyages à Peking, Manille, et l'Ile de France, faite dans l'intervalle des années 1784 à 1801.* 3 vols. Paris: L'Imprimerie Imperiale, 1808. This work is especially valuable because De Guignes was French Consul at Canton from 1784 to 1796. The volumes deal with the Dutch Embassy to Peking in 1795, to which De Guignes served as interpreter, and gives an account of life, trade, and commercial institutions at Canton as well as a description of the commerce of all foreign nations trading there.

Debates at the India House on the Company's New Charter. London, 1793.

Downing, C. Toogood. *The Fan-qui in China in 1836-37.* 3 vols. London: Henry Colburn, 1838. Intensely interesting account of life, scenes, personalities, and commercial institutions at Canton prior to the Opium War. Written by a doctor who spent several years at Canton.

Dunn, Samuel. *A New Directory for the East Indies.* London, 1780. Really the 5th ed. of Herbert's *Directory,* revised and enlarged.

Eastwick, Robert William. *A Master Mariner. Being the Life and Adventures of Captain R. W. Eastwick.* London, 1890. Edited by H. Compton. Interesting and valuable memoirs of a man who travelled many times to the East and China during the latter 18th and early 19th centuries.

Ellis, Henry. *Journal of the Proceedings of the Late Embassy to China.* London: John Murray, 1817. There is a 2-vol. ed. in 1818. Ellis was third Commissioner of the Embassy, and his work is the official account of the mission.

Elmore, H. M. *The British Mariner's Directory and Guide to the Trade and Navigation of the India and China Seas.* London: Black and Parry, 1802. An extremely valuable account of the methods of trade between India and China and of the system of trade at Canton.

Facts Relative to the China Trade, Shewing Its Importance to This Country and the Inexpediency of Its Remaining Exclusively in the Hands of the East India Company. Edinburgh, 1813.

Foster, Sir William. *The English Factories in India* (1618-1673). 15 vols. Oxford: University Press, 1906-34. Continuation of Danvers' work, but an abstract only of the records of the factories in India. There are some matters relating to China, which can be found in the index. Still being published.

Froger, François. *Relation du premier voyage des Français à la Chine fait en 1698, 1699 et 1700 sur le vaisseau l'Amphitrite.* Edited by Ernst Arthur Voretzsch. Leipzig: Asia Major, 1926. Similar to Bannister's account but taken from a different manuscript and carefully edited in the French.

Gerbillon, Père Jean François. "Voyages en Tartarie (1688-98)." In Du Halde's *Description . . . de la Chine*, IV, 87-422. Paris: P. G. Lemercier, 1735. Contains a valuable account of the Chino-Russian negotiations in 1688-89, for which Gerbillon served as interpreter.

Ghirardini, Gio. *Relation du voyage fait à la Chine sur le vaisseau L'Amphitrite en 1698.* Paris: Peintre Italien, 1700. Ghirardini was an Italian painter who accompanied the French expedition.

Gilbert, Thomas. *A Voyage from New South Wales to Canton in the year 1788.* London: J. Debrett, 1789. Gilbert was commander of the Indiaman *Charlotte* which made the voyage.

Glasspoole, Captain R. *Captured by the Ladrones.* London: Kelvedon, 1902. An interesting account of Glasspoole's experiences and observations while held a captive by the Ladrone pirates about 1810.

Hardy, Charles. *A Register of Ships Employed in the Service of the Honorable . . . East India Company, from the Year 1760 to 1812.* London: Black, Parry & Co., 1813. An invaluable reference.

Hansard, T. C. *Parliamentary Debates* (1803-1843). London: Longmans and T. C. Hausard, various dates.

Hamilton, Capt. Alexander. *A New Account of the East Indies.* 2 vols. Edinburgh: John Mosman, 1727. Contains details of several voyages to Amoy and Canton with a description of trade.

Harris, John. *An Account of the Expedition of George Anson, Esq. in the Centurion . . . round the World.* London: T. Woodward, 1744. The *Centurion* obtained permission to re-fit at Whampoa after considerable difficulties with the Chinese in 1741-42.

Herbert, William. *A New Directory for the East Indies.* London, 1759. Largely a recapitulation of *Le Neptune Oriental.*

Hertslet, Godfrey E.P. *Treaties between Great Britain and China; and between China and Foreign Powers.* 2 vols. London: Harris and Sons, 1908.

Hickey, William. *Memoirs of.* Edited by Alfred Spencer. 3 vols. London: Hurst and Blackett, 1913-23. Vol. I has an interesting and valuable account of a season's residence at Canton in 1769-70.

Hillard, Catherine. *My Mother's Journal* (Miss Harriet Law). Boston, 1900. Interesting description of life at Macao during the pre-treaty days as experienced by an American woman.

Holmes, Samuel. *Journal of Mr. Samuel Holmes . . . as one of the Guard on Lord Macartney's Embassy.* London: W. Bulmer & Co. 1798. Of practically no value so far as the official business of the Embassy is concerned.

Horsburgh, James. *Directions for Sailing to and from the East Indies, China, etc.* 2 vols. London: Black, Parry, & Kingbury, 1809-11. Many later and enlarged editions. Invaluable guides to the navigation of the Eastern seas during the early 19th century.

Horsburgh, James. *Memoirs: Comprising the Navigation to and from China.* London: C. Mercier & Co., 1805.

Horsburgh, James. *Observations on the Navigation of the Eastern Seas.* London: W. Bennett, 1797. Both of the two latter works are valuable accounts of navigation in the China Seas.

Huddart, J. *A Survey of the Tigris from Canton to the Island of Lankeet.* London, 1786.

Hunter, W. C. *The Fan-kwae at Canton before Treaty Days, 1825-44.* London: Kegan, Paul, Trench & Co., 1882. An invaluable account of the Canton system before treaty days by an American who resided there almost continuously after 1825.

Hüttner, J. C. *Nachricht von der Brittischen Gesandtschaftsreise durch China und einen Theil der Tartarei.* Berlin: Vossischen Buckhandlung, 1797. French editions at Paris in 1799 and 1803. Hüttner attended the Macartney Embassy as tutor to young George Staunton, and, being the best Latin scholar, did most of the necessary Latin translating.

Ides, Everard Ysbrants. *Three Years Travel from Moscow over Land to China.* Translated from the Witzen Dutch edition. London: W. Freeman, 1706. Official account of the Ides' Embassy from Russia to China in 1693-95.

India Company and Their Trade to India and China. A Short History by a Proprietor. London, 1793.

Jefferys, Thomas. [*Maps of*] *the East Indies, with the Roads.* London, 1768.

"Journal of His Majesty's Ship *Lion* beginning the 1st of October 1792 and ending the 7th September 1794." *Revue de l'Extrême-Orient,* II (1884), 578 ff. Paris, 1884.

Journal of the House of Commons (1547-1872). 127 vols. London, various dates.

Journal of the House of Lords (1509-1872). 104 vols. London, various dates.

Klaproth, Heinrich Julius von. *Chrestomathie Mandchou.* Paris, 1828. Contains several treaties translated from the Chinese.

Kirkpatrick, Colonel W. *An Account of the Kingdom of Nepaul, Being the Substance of Observations Made during a Mission in That Country in 1793.* London, 1811. Account of Col. Kirkpatrick's mission to Nepal, an event which was the cause of difficulties at Peking during the Macartney Embassy.

Krusenstern, Adam Johann von. *Reise um die Welt in den Jahren 1803, 1804, 1805, und 1806 auf befehe seiner Kaiserlichen Majestät Alexander des ersten.* 3 vols., atlas. St. Petersburg and Berlin, 1810-11. English 2-vol. ed. in 1813. Krusenstern's ships came to Canton to trade in 1805. Only after a great deal of trouble were they allowed to trade, and the coming of Russian ships to Canton in the future was forbidden.

Lange, Laurence de. *Journal of the Residence of Mr. De Lange, Agent of His Imperial Majesty of All the Russians, Peter the First, at the Court of Peking, during the Years 1721 and 1722.* In Bell's *Travels,* II. Glasgow: Robert & A. Foulis, 1763. An account of Ismailoff's Embassy in 1721 and De Lange's unsuccessful attempt to reside there afterwards.

Lange, Laurence de. *Journey from Petersbourg to Peking (1717).* In *The Present State of Russia,* II. London, 1723. Account of a mission from Russia to China preliminary to Ismailoff's.

Lange, Laurence de. *Tagebuch Zwoer Reisen . . . in den Jahren 1727, 1728 und 1736, von Kjachta und Zuruchaitu durch die Mongoley nach Peking.* Leipzig: Johann Zacharias Logan, 1781. Further information about Russia's relations with China in the 1720's.

Le Comte, Père Louis. *Nouveaux memoires sur l'Etat present de la Chine.* 2 vols. Paris: Jean Anisson, 1696. This work went through many editions at various times, and was translated into English and first published by Benj. Tooke in 1697. A valuable account of China toward the end of the 17th century.

Leimbeckoven, Gottfried. *Reisebeschreibung von Wien nach China.* Vienna, 1740.

List of the Names of the Members of the United Company of Merchants of England, Trading to the East-Indies, Who Appear Qualified to Vote at Their General Court (Wednesday, April 8, 1795). London: East India House, 1794.

Lockyer, Charles. *An Account of the Trade in India.* London: Samuel Crouch, 1711. Has an invaluable chapter on trading conditions at Canton in 1704, including an account of prices, port charges, and duties.

Macartney, Lord George. *A Journal of an Embassy from the King of Great Britain to the Emperor of China, in the years 1792, 1793, and 1794: Appendix to the Journal.* See Barrow, *Life of . . . the Earl of Macartney,* II, and Robbins, *Our First Ambassador to China.* The appendix includes observations on Chinese law, government, institutions, religion, customs, and culture in general.

Macgregor, John. *Commercial Statistics.* 5 vols. London: Whittaker and Co., 1844-50. Vols. IV and V have valuable statistical tables relating to the China trade, but they must be used with care and caution as Macgregor has not used sufficient care in compiling them.

Macpherson, David. *Annals of Commerce, Manufactures, Fisheries, and Navigation.* 4 vols. London: Nichols & Sons, 1805. A standard reference work for all phases of England's commercial and industrial progress.

Madrolle, C. *Les premiere voyages français à la Chine. La Compagnie de la Chine, 1698-1719.* Paris: Librairie Challamel, 1901.

Mason, George Henry. *The Costume of China, Illustrated by Sixty Engravings: with Explanations in English and French.* London: W. Miller, 1800.

[Mason, George Henry]. *The Punishments of China, Illustrated by Twenty-two Engravings.* London: W. Miller, 1801. Interesting pictures.

Matheson, James. *The Present Position and Prospects of the British Trade with China.* London: Smith, Elder & Co., 1836. Has some valuable material for earlier period, and is an excellent account of things as they were about 1835.

McCulloch, John Ramsay. *Collection of Early English Tracts.* London: Lord Averstone, 1859. Contains a valuable collection of tracts attacking the East India Company and discussing economic problems of the 18th century.

Meares, John. *Voyages Made in the years 1788 and 1789, from China to the North West Coast of America.* London: J. Walter, 1790. Valuable account of the beginnings of the fur trade between the Northwest Coast and China, with an introduction describing the Canton system, and an appendix dealing with the seizure of his ships by the Spanish at Nootka in 1789.

Milburn, William. *Oriental Commerce.* 2 vols. London: Black, Parry & Co., 1813. An invaluable account of trade in India and China, illustrated with many statistics, by a person who had made numerous voyages to China and the East.

Montanus, Arnoldus. *The Embassy of John van Campen and Constantin Noble to Sing la Mong, Vice-Roy of Fo kyen* (1662-63). In Astley's *Voyages,* III, 431-40. London: Thomas Astley, 1746. An abridged account from the Dutch original.

Morrison, John Robert. *A Chinese Commercial Guide.* Canton: Albion Press, 1834. The most concise, complete, and reliable description of the system of trade just prior to the Opium War obtainable.

Morrison, Dr. Robert. *A Memoir of the Principal Occurrences during An Embassy from the British Government to the Court of China in the year 1816.* London: Hatchard & Son, 1820. Morrison served as chief interpreter during the Amherst Embassy. His account is, therefore, of especial value.

Morrison, Dr. Robert. *Memoirs of the Life and Labours of.* 2 vols. London: Longmans, 1839. Compiled by his widow. Is rather laborious reading.

[Morrison, Dr. Robert]. *Notices concerning China, and the Port of Canton. Also a Narrative of the Affair of the English Frigate Topaze, 1821-22, with Remarks on Homicides, and an Account of the Fire of Canton.* Malacca: Mission Press, 1823.

Mortimer, Lieut. George. *Observations and Remarks Made during a Voyage to . . . the North West Coast of America . . . and from Thence to Canton in the Brig Mercury Commanded by John Henry Cox.* London: T. Cadell, 1791. An interesting contribution to the early history of the fur trade with Canton.

Mortimer, Thomas, and Dickinson, William. *A General Commercial Dictionary.* 2nd ed. London: Longmans, 1819. 1st ed. in 1810. Valuable as a dictionary of articles of trade, places, and monies used in the East at that time.

Mundy, Peter. *The Travels of Peter Mundy.* 2 vols. London: Hakluyt, 1919. A valuable account of the Weddell expedition to China in 1637. It is amplified by other documents from the Bodlean Library and the India Office.

Nieuhoff, John. *An Embassy from the East-India Company of the United Provinces, to the Grand Tartar Cham Emperor of China* (1655). London: J. Macock, 1669. Translated from the Dutch by John Ogilby.

Morse, H. B. *Chronicles of the East India Company Trading to China* (1635-1834). 5 vols. Oxford: Clarendon Press, 1926-29. Masterly summary of about 200 volumes of the China factory records in the India Office.

Ogilby, John, and Montanus, Arnoldus. *Atlas Chinensis.* London: Thos. Johnson, 1671. Contains a summary of Goyer and Keyzer's Embassy in 1655, some account of Van Campen's mission to the Viceroy of Fukien in 1662, and a detailed account of Van Hoorn's Embassy to Peking in 1666-68. Translated from the Dutch.

Orange, James. *The Chater Collection.* London: Thornton Butterworth, 1924. A set of excellent pictures relating to China, Hongkong, Macao, Canton, etc. from 1655 to 1860, illustrated with historical notes.

Osbeck, Peter. *Reise nach Ostindien und China.* Rostock: Johann Christian Koppe, 1765. Osbeck went to China as chaplain of a Swedish Indiaman between the years 1750 and 1752. It is an interesting and valuable account of life and trade at Canton during the middle of the 18th century. English translation by Reinhold Forster. 2 vols. London: Benjamin White, 1771.

Papers Respecting the Negociation for a Renewal of the East India Company's Exclusive Trade. London, 1793. Correspondence between the Chairs and Henry Dundas and between the Chairs and various manufacturing and commercial interests.

Parliamentary Papers. These are classified under Bills, Reports, and Accounts and Papers. There are a number of Reports relating to China or the East India Company which are of great importance, and there are hundreds of Accounts and Papers giving commercial statistics, correspondence, etc. which in one way or another relate to China. Only a few of the more important of the latter will be mentioned.

Reports.
1773. "Third Report of the Committee of Secrecy Appointed to Enquire into the State of the East India Company, Feb. 9, 1773."
1782. "Sixth Report from the Committee of Secrecy on the Course of the War in the Carnatic, March 6, 1782."
1783. "Ninth Report of the Secret Committee on the Administration of Justice in India, June 25, 1783."
1783-84. Nos. 58-60. "First, Second, and Third Reports of the Committee . . . [on] the illicit practices used in Defrauding the Revenues, 24th December, 1783, 1st March, 1784, 23rd March, 1784."
1810. No. 255. "First Report of the Select Committee on the Affairs of the East India Company, May 11, 1810."
1810. No. 363. "Second Report . . ., May 11, 1810."
1811. No. 250. "Third Report . . ., June 21, 1811."
1812. No. 148. "Fourth Report . . ., China, St. Helena, Home Accounts, Private Trade, etc., April 10, 1812."
1812. Nos. 151, 182. "Supplement to Fourth Report, April 13th and 22nd, 1812."
1812. No. 377. "Fifth Report . . ., July 28, 1812."
1821. No. 535. "Second Report from the Select Committee appointed to consider the means of maintaining and improving the Foreign Trade of the Country (East Indies and China)."
1821. No. 746. "Third Report from the Select Committee . . . "
1830. No. 644. "First Report from the Select Committee appointed to inquire into the present state of the affairs of the East India Company, and into the Trade between Great Britain, the East Indies, and China."
1830. No. 655. "Second Report . . .: China Trade."
1830. No. 646. "Report from the Lord's Select Committee . . . ."
1831. Nos. 65, 320. "Third Report . . . and appendices."
1840. No. 359. "Report from the Select Committee appointed to inquire into the grievances complained of in the Petition of Merchants interested in the Trade with China" (opium).

Accounts and Papers. These may be summarized as follows:
"Annual East India Accounts." 1787, No. 406; 1788, No. 525; 1789, No. 593; 1790, Nos. 681-684; 1791, Nos. 718-22; 1792, Nos. 753-54; 1793, Nos. 773-

74; 1794, Nos. 786-87; 1795, Nos. 805-06; 1796, Nos. 836-38; 1797, Nos. 870-72; 1798, Nos. 948-49; 1799, No. 994. These accounts all contain figures on the China Trade.

"Accounts Relating to the Tea Trade and Duties Thereon." 1784, Nos. 50, 55, 60-63; 1785, No. 72; 1786, Nos. 154, 158-63; 1787, No. 374; 1788, Nos. 466-84; 1789, Nos. 581, 585; 1790, No. 680; 1807, No. 74; 1812-13, No. 101.

"Accounts Relating to the China Trade Generally." 1787, No. 403; 1788, Nos. 462-65; 1789, Nos. 587-88, 595; 1790, Nos. 685, 691; 1806, No. 209 (silk); 1807, Nos. 72, 73 (tonnage and manufactures exported, 1773-1808); 1810, Nos. 288-89; 1810-11, Nos. 92, 187; 1812, Nos. 204-06; 1812-13, Nos. 83, 78, 85, 104, 136, 152-54, 191-93, 225, 247, 248, 278. Most of the accounts for the years 1812-13 are of great value.

"Accounts Relating to the Opium Trade." 1786, No. 154; 1787, Nos. 334, 354, 372.

"Three Reports of the Select Committee of the Court of Directors upon the Export Trade from Great Britain to the East Indies (India, China, Japan, Persia)." 1792-93, No. 774b.

"Report of the Select Committee . . . upon the Subject of the Cotton Manufacture of this Country." 1792-93, No. 774e.

"Minutes of Evidence Taken before the Committee of the Whole House, March 30 to May 13, 1813." 1812-13, VII, No. 122. Many of the persons examined were former supercargoes or persons who had resided in China, and their testimony is valuable.

Parker, E. H. "Letters from the Emperor of China to King George the Third (translated from the *Tung-hwa-luh*), September, 1793." *Nineteenth Century*, XL (July, 1896), 44-55, and the *North China Daily News*, Sept. 4, 1896.

Paske-Smith, M. *Western Barbarians in Japan and Formosa in Tokugawa Days, 1630-1868*. Kobe: J. L. Thompson, 1930. Consists in the main of extracts from the records of the East India Company.

Pauthier, G. *Documents statistiques et officiels sur l'empire de la Chine, traduits du chinois*. Paris, 1841.

Pauthier, G. "Documents officiels chinois sur les Ambassades étrangères envoyées près de l'empereur de la Chine." *Revue de l'Orient*, II(1834), 1-22.

Perouse, Le Comte de la. *Voyagé autour du monde*. 3 vols. Paris, 1797. The ship *La Boussole*, commanded by Perouse, arrived at Canton on Jan. 5, 1787.

Philips, John. *An Authentic Journal of the Late Expedition under the Command of Commodore Anson*. London: J. Robinson, 1744. This account of Anson's voyage round the world was written by a midshipman and contains an account of the *Centurion* affair at Canton in 1741-42.

Pritchard, Earl H. "Letters from Missionaries at Peking relating to the Macartney Embassy, 1793-1803." *T'oung Pao*, XXXI (1934), 1-57. Edited letters which throw considerable light upon certain phases of the Embassy.

Proudfoot, William Jardine. *"Barrow's Travels in China." An Investigation into the Origin and Authenticity of the "Facts and Observations"* [*in it*]. London: George Philip & Son, 1861. A devastating study of Barrow's book. According to Proudfoot, hardly a fact in Barrow can be relied upon.

Purchas, Samuel. *Purchas His Pilgrimes*. London, 1625. Has considerable material relating to early English voyages to the East.

Register of Ships Employed in the Service of the Hon. The United East India Company. 2 vols. Vol. I (1707-60), Vol. II (1760-1812). London, 1800-12.

Reichard, John Peter. *Reisen nach China*. Onolzbach, 1755. Contains a description of Canton.

Reports from the Committees of the House of Commons, 1715-1801. 15 vols. London, 1803. A specially published series. The first three *Reports* referred to above under *Parliamentary Papers* are to be found in Vols. IV, 68-69; VIII, 370-71, and VI, 180-82 of this series. They contain valuable statistics.

Robbins, Helen M. *Our First Ambassador to China.* London: John Murray, 1908. A biography of Macartney containing the *Journal* of his Embassy to China.

Robertson, George. *A Short Account of a Passage from China, late in the Season, down the China Sea.* London: S. Couchman, 1802.

Ross, Daniel and Maughan, Philip. *Survey of Part of the South Coast of China.* Atlas in folio. London, 1807. Survey carried on by Lieutenants Ross and Maughan of the Bombay Marine under orders of the Court of Directors.

Russell, F. *A Collection of Statutes concerning the Incorporation, Trade, and Commerce of the East India Company.* London, 1794.

Die Russische Gesandtschaft nach China im Jahre 1805. St. Petersburg and Leipzig, 1809. Apparently the only published account of the Russian embassy of 1805, which was stopped at the border and not allowed to proceed to Peking.

Sainsbury, W. Noel. *Calendar of State Papers, Colonial Series: East Indies* (1513-1634). 5 vols. London: Eyre and Spottiswoode, 1862-92. Abstract of all early records in the Public Record Office and India Office relating to British affairs in the East. By the use of the index, matters relating to China can be found quickly.

Sainsbury, Ethel Bruce. *Calendar of the Court Minutes of the East India Company* (1635-73). 9 vols. Oxford: University Press, 1907-33. Continuation of the previous work, but a summary of the Court Minutes only. Chinese matters can be found by using the index.

Sainte-Croix, Felix Renouard de. "Mémoire sur la Chine addressé à Napoléon 1er." *T'oung Pao,* II (May, 1901), 139-45.

Sainte-Croix, Felix Renouard de. *Voyage commercial et politique aux Indes Orientales, aux Iles Philippines, à la Chine, avec des notions sur la Cochinchine et le Tonquin, pendant les années 1803, 1804, 1805, 1806 et 1807.* 3 vols. Paris: Clament frères, 1810. Valuable account of French activity in the Far East under Napoleon.

Satow, Ernest M. *The Voyage of Captain John Saris to Japan, 1613.* London: Hakluyt, 1900. Account of the voyage of the first British sent to Japan from manuscripts in the India Office.

Schnelles Steigen des chinesischen Handels der englisch ostindischen Compagnie seit 1784. N.p., 1794.

Scott, Edmund. *An Exact Discourse of the Subtilties, Fashions, Pollicies, Religion, and Ceremonies of the East Indians, as well Chyneses as Jauans, There Abyding and Dweling.* London: Walter Burre, 1606. First original book relating to China published by an Englishman, after a residence of three years in the East.

Shaw, J. *Charters Relating to the East India Company, 1600-1761.* Madras, 1887.

Shaw, Major Samuel. *The Journals of . . .* Edited by Josiah Quincy. Boston: Wm. Crosby & H.P. Nichols, 1847. Shaw's account of the voyage of the first American ship to China in 1784 and his second voyage there as American Consul, 1786-87. Contains extremely valuable observations upon the system of trade and the commerce of all nations trading at Canton.

Sonnerat, M. *Voyage aux Indes orientales et à la Chine, fait par ordre du Roi, depuis 1774 jusqu'en 1781.* 2 vols. Paris, 1782. Valuable account of French expeditions to China during the years mentioned.

Statutes at Large. Edited by George K. Richards. London: Eyre and Spottiswoode, various dates.

Staunton, Sir George Leonard. *An Authentic Account of an Embassy from the King of Great Britain to the Emperor of China.* 2 vols., with atlas in folio. London: G. Nicol, 1797. This work went through many editions, and an abridged account was also published in 1797 by John Stockdale, entitled *An Historical Account of the Embassy . . .* It is the official account of the Macartney Embassy, but, although well written and illustrated with details of Chinese culture, the amount of official information given is rather disappointing.

Staunton, Sir George Thomas. *Notes of Proceedings and Occurrences during the British Embassy to Peking in 1816.* London: Henry Skelton, 1824. Staunton's account of the Amherst Embassy of which he was second of the three Commissioners sent. Full of detailed and valuable information.
Staunton, Sir George Thomas. *Miscellaneous Notices Relating to China.* 2 vols. London: John Murray, 1822-50. Contains much valuable information relating to trade, edicts, etc.
Staunton, Sir George Thomas. *Memoir of the Life and Family of the Late Sir George Leonard Staunton, Bart.* London: Havant Press, 1823. Contains some valuable documents relating to the Macartney Embassy.
Staunton, Sir George Thomas. *Memoirs of the Chief Incidents of the Public Life of . . .* London: L. Booth, 1856. Autobiographical.
Staunton, Sir George Thomas. *Memoir of Sir John Barrow, Bart.* [London, about 1850.] Most of the material appeared in *The Times.*
Staunton, Sir George Thomas. *Ta Tsing Leu Lee; Being the Fundamental Laws, and a Selection from Supplementary Statutes of the Penal Code of China.* London: T. Cadell and W. Davies, 1810. An invaluable (English translation) work relating to the laws of China at the beginning of the 19th century.
Staunton, Sir George Thomas. *Translations from the Original Chinese with Notes.* Canton, 1815. Contains official documents, dispatches etc. from the years 1795 and 1805.
Staunton, Sir George Thomas. *Narrative of the Chinese Embassy to the Khan of the Tourgouth Tartars, in the Years 1712, 13, 14 and 15; by the Chinese Ambassador.* London: John Murray, 1821. This published volume also contains a number of other translations from the Chinese, one of which deals with the Macartney Embassy, and two of which deal with events in 1805.
Stevens, Henry. *The Dawn of British Trade to the East Indies as Recorded in the Court Minutes of the East India Company* (1599-1603). London: Henry Stevens, 1886. A verbatim reproduction of the first *Court Book.*
Stevens, Robert. *A Complete Guide to the East-India Trade.* London: R. Stevens, 1766. Stevens was a merchant of Bombay, but the work has little information of value in it beyond an account of the monies of the East.
[Thomas, Pascoe]. *An Authentic Account of Commodore Anson's Expedition . . . Taken from a Private Journal* (1740-44). London: M. Cooper, 1744.
Thornton, Thomas. *Oriental Commerce.* London: Kingsbury, Parbury, & Allen, 1825. A condensed and less valuable version of Milburn.
Toreen, Olof. *Eine Ostindische Reise nach Suratte, China, etc., von 1750 den 1 April bis 1752 den 26 Jun.* Rostock: Johann Christian Koppe, 1765. In Osbeck, also in Vol. II of Osbeck's English edition. Less valuable than Osbeck.
Turner, J. L. *Account of the Captivity of Mr. J. L. Turner amongst the Ladrones.* London, 1810. Interesting account of the Ladrones.
Twining, Richard. *Remarks on the Report of the East India Directors respecting the Sale and Price of Tea.* London: T. Cadell, 1784. Twining also published several other pamphlets in 1784 and 1785 to show that the Company had not lowered the price of tea in accordance with the Commutation Act as promised.
Unverzagt, Georg Johann. *Die Gesandschaft Ihro Käyserl. Majest. von Gross-Russland an den Sinesischen Käyser, wie solche anno 1719 aus St. Petersburg nach der Sinesischen Haupt-und Residentz-Stadt Pekin abgefertiget.* Lübeck, 1725. Official account of the Russian Embassy to China from 1719 to 1721.
Van-Braam Houckgeest, André Everard. *Voyage de l'Ambassade de la compagnie des Indes Orientales hollandaises, vers l'empereur de la Chine en 1794 et 1795.* 2 vols. Philadelphia, 1797. An edition minus the Appendices was published in Paris in 2 vols. in 1798, from which an English translation was made and published by R. Phillips in London in 1798. Van-Braam was second member of the Dutch Embassy in 1794-95, as well as chief Dutch supercargo at Canton.

Vivani, P. *The Legation of Charles Ambrose Mezzabarba . . . from the Pope to the Emperor Kang hi in 1720,* in Astley's *Voyages.* III, London: T. Astley, 1746.

Walter, Richard. *A Voyage Round the World in the Years 1740-44.* 2 vols. London: John & Paul Knapton, 1748. Another account of the voyage of George Anson around the world and to China in the *Centurion* by the ship's chaplain.

Wathen, James. *A Journal of a Voyage in 1810 and 1812 to Madras and China . . . in the H.C.S. The Hope.* London: J. Nichols, Son, & Bentley, 1814. Has a valuable chapter on Canton.

Williams, Samuel Wells. *A Chinese Commercial Guide.* Macao: S. W. Williams, 1844. A revised edition of Morrison's *Guide* to conform with the changes brought about through the Opium War. Morrison's work is entirely re-written.

Wilkinson, George. *Voyage to China and the Ladrones, 1811-12.* London, 1814. A superficial performance taken up with the writer's complaints while on ship board.

Wilkinson, George. *Sketches of Chinese Customs and Manners in 1811-12. Taken on the Spot.* Bath: J. Browne, 1814.

Wissett, Robert. *A Compendium of East India Affairs, Political and Commercial Collected and Arranged for the Use of the Court of Directors.* 2 vols. London: E. Cox and Sons, 1802. Has valuable statistical tables as well as information on laws, statutes, charters, by-laws, and committees of the East India Company.

4. *Chinese Materials.*

Chang Ku Ch'ung P'ien (A Series of Documents of the Ch'ing Dynasty). Series I. 10 vols. Peiping: Palace Museum, 1928-30. The collection consists of select documents from the archives of the Council of State. Vols. 1, 2, 3, 5, 6, 7, 8, 9 contain material relating to the Macartney Embassy. The series is continued in *Wen Hsien Ch'ung P'ien.*

Ch'en K'ang-ch'i. Lang Ch'ien Chi Wen. First series. Shao Yeh Shan Fang edition, 1910. Chüan 5, p. 11, has a brief note about the Macartney Embassy.

Chi Ying Chi Li Ch'iu Ao Shih Mo (Narrative of the English Attempts to get Macao). Has a little material relating to the period of this study.

Ch'ing Shih Kao (Draft History of the Ch'ing Dynasty). 131 vols. Peiping, Historiographical Board, 1928. Chüan 160 has a little material relating to Anglo-Chinese relations prior to 1842, but the whole section on foreign relations is incomplete and badly done. For reviews see *T'oung Pao,* XXVIII, 180; *Asia Major,* VI, 410; T. F. Tsiang (Chiang T'ing-fu), *Bulletin of the Metropolitan Library,* Peiping, June and July, 1929; A. W. Hummel, *Library of Congress Division of Chinese Literature* (1929-30), pp. 346-48.

Ch'ing Tai Wai Chiao Shih Liao (Documents on the Foreign Relations of the Ch'ing Dynasty, 1723-1735). Vols. 1-6 have appeared. Peiping: Palace Museum, 1932. Other volumes may have appeared, but the six volumes mentioned covered the period from 1796 to 1820. The documents are from the records of the Council of State in the Palace Museum.

Chung Hsi Chi Shih (Records of Chinese and Western Relations). 8 chüan. Published by Hsia Hsieh. Final contents, 1865. Has a little interesting material dealing with the period prior to 1800. Parts of it have been translated by E. H. Parker in *China's Intercourse with Europe.* Shanghai, Kelly & Walsh, [1888].

[Hsiao] Siao I-shan. *Ch'ing Tai T'ung Shih* (General History of the Manchu Dynasty). 3 vols. Shanghai: Commercial Press, 1928. The whole work relies heavily on Western sources, and Vol. 2 deals with the period of this study.

I Fei Wen Chi (News about Barbarian Pirates). 5 chüan. 1883. The work is in manuscript only, and deals in the main with the Opium War. Two copies are in Cornell University Library.

Kao Tsung Shun Huang-ti Shêng Hsün (Edicts of Ch'ien Lung). 100 vols. Peking, 1807. A number of edicts relating to the Macartney Embassy are in Chüan 276.
Kuangtung T'ung Chih (Gazetter of Kuangtung Province). Compiled by Yüan Yüan and others. Canton, 1822. Chüan 170 has some material of interest.
Liu Fu. *Ch'ien Lung Ying Shih Chin Chien Chi* (Diary of the English Embassy's Audience with the Emperor Ch'ien Lung). Shanghai: Chung Hua Book Co. 1930.
Ming Ch'ing Shih Liao (Historical Documents Relating to the Ming and Ch'ing Dynasties, 1567-1776). First series. 10 vols. Peiping: Academia Sinica, 1930-31. Documents taken from the archives of the Grand Secretariat (*Nei Ko*). Presumably more of these documents have been or will be published.
Shih Liao Ts'ung K'an Ch'u P'ien (Collection of Historical Documents). Ed. by Lo Chên-yü. 10 vols. Published by Tong Fang Hio Houei, 1924. Selected records from the archives of the Grand Secretariat.
Shih Liao Hsün K'an (Historical Material Relating to the Ch'ing Dynasty). 31 vols. Peiping. Palace Museum, 1930-32. The series contains documents from the records of the Council of State, and material was to have appeared every ten days until the period from 1660 to the Opium War had been covered. Although the series appears to be incomplete, it contains much valuable material relating to the commercial and semi-diplomatic relations between China and outside countries. Vols. 3, 4, 5, 6, 9, 10, 14, 16, 18, 20, 22, 24, 31 contain material relating to Anglo-Chinese relations, especially between the years 1753 and 1759.
Ta Chung Chi. Edited by Hsu Ti-shan. Peiping: Peking Union Book Store, about 1932. A collection of material relating to Sino-British trade about 1830, copied from MSS. Bodlean Library, Oxford, Chin. c23. Most of the letters and communications have to do with the merchant H. H. Lindsay.
Tsiang, T. F. [Chiang T'ing-fu]. *Ch'ing Tai Chung Kuo Wai Chiao Shih Liao Chi Yao* (Collection of Essential Sources of Modern Chinese Diplomatic History). Pt. 1. Shanghai, 1931.
Tuang Hua Lu (Records of the Eastern Gate). Compiled by Wang Hsien-ch'ien. Peking: Shan Ch'eng T'ang, 1890. The series is a summary of the edicts posted at the Eastern Gate of the Forbidden City in Peking, arranged according to reigns. Ch'ien Lung, Chüan 118, contains some edicts relating to the Macartney Embassy.
Wang Chih-ch'un. *Kuo Ch'ao Jou Yüan Chi* (Record of the Foreign Relations of the Ch'ing Dynasty). 6 vols. Canton: Kuang Ya Shu Chu, 1891. Has a little material relating to the period prior to 1800.
Wang Ch'ing-yün. *Shih Chü Yü Chi.* A memoir in 6 chüan found in *Pi Lin Lang Kuan Tsung-shu.* Ed. by Fang Kung-hui. Printed in 1884. Chüan 5, pp. 56-61, has a brief account of the Macartney Embassy.
Wang Wên-t'ai. *Hung Mao Fan Ying Chi Li K'ao Lüeh* (A Short Study of the Red-haired English Foreigners). Has a little material prior to 1800.
Wen Hsien Ch'ung P'ien (Series of Authentic Documents and Memoirs of the Ch'ing Dynasty). 5 vols. or more. Peiping: Palace Museum, 1930. A continuation of the *Chang Ku Ch'ung P'ien,* and contains documents from the archives of the Council of State.
Wei Yüan. *Hai Kuo T'u Chih* (Maps and Records of Seas and Nations). Introduction, 1852. Based on material taken from the old Canton archives, and has a brief resumé of China's foreign relations prior to 1834.
Ying I Shuo (Records of the English Barbarians). One of the sources of Wang Wen-t'ai's work.
Yü K'un. *Yüeh Hai Kuan Chih* (Annals of the Kuangtung Customs). 30 chüan. Canton, about 1838. An extremely valuable work. Ch. 1 deals with moral maxims of the Ch'ing dynasty; Ch. 2-4, with facts about earlier periods; Ch. 5-6, with ports; Ch. 7, with the mandarins; Ch. 8-13 with custom regulations; Ch. 14-15, with reports to the throne; Ch. 17-19, with prohibitory orders; Ch. 20, garrisons; Ch. 21-23, tribute ships; Ch. 24, merchant ships; Ch. 25, Hong merchants; Ch. 26-29, foreign merchants; Ch. 30, miscellaneous.

5. *Periodicals and Newspapers.*

Information relating to Chinese affairs is found to a greater or less degree in all of the select list of periodicals mentioned below.

Journal des savants. 111 vols. Paris, 1665-1816.

Lettres édifiantes et curieuses. 34 vols. Paris, 1717-1776.

The Monthly Review; or Literary Journal. 350 vols. London: R. Griffiths, 1749-1825. Reviews of published books in the main.

The Critical Review; or Annals of Literature. 114 vols. London, 1756-1817. Reviews of books on China may be found in it.

Annual Register. Annual volume until present time. London, 1758 until present. Contains general review of world affairs, and from 1795 onward references to Chinese matters are included.

Memoires concernant l'histoire, les sciences, les arts, les moeurs, les usages, etc. des chinois, par les missionaires de Pékin. 16 vols. Paris, 1776-1814. Considerable valuable information written by such men as Amiot, Bourgeois, Cibot, Ko, Poirot, Gaubil is to be found in these volumes.

The Times. London, 1786 to present.

Oriental Repertory. Ed. by Alexander Dalrymple. 2 vols. London: George Bigg. 1791-97. Each volume has considerable material relating to China.

The Asiatic Annual Register. 12 vols. London: J. Debrett, 1800-1812. Has annual summary of affairs relating to India, China, the East India Company, etc. A valuable publication.

Edinburgh Review. Edinburgh, 1803 to date. Reviews only during its early years.

Annales des voyages, de la geographie et de l'histoire. 24 vols. Paris: M. Malte-Brun, 1808-14. *Nouvelles annales . . .* 144 vols. Paris, 1819-54. Has various articles and information.

Asiatic Journal and Monthly Register. 72 vols. London: Black, Parbury & Allen, 1816-45. A monthly summary of India, China, and East India Company's affairs. Continuation of the *Asiatic Annual Register,* and a valuable work.

Journal Asiatique. 222 vols. Paris, 1822 until present.

Revues de deux mondes. Paris, 1831 until present.

Journal of the Royal Asiatic Society of Great Britain and Ireland. London, 1834 until present.

Chinese Repository. 20 vols. Ed. by E. C. Bridgman and S. Wells Williams. Canton, 1832-51. One of the richest source material in existence for the years it covers; also has articles and information which reach back to the Macartney Embassy.

Journal of the North China Branch of the Royal Asiatic Society. Shanghai, 1858 until present.

China Review or Notes and Queries on the Far East. 25 vols. Hongkong, 1872-1901.

Asiatic Quarterly Review. 10 vols. London, 1886-90. Ed. by D. C. Boulger.

T'oung Pao. Leiden, 1890 until present.

6. *Secondary Materials.*

The following list of secondary books does not pretend to be complete. Only the more important out of many hundreds have been selected.

Astley, Thomas. *A New General Collection of Voyages and Travels.* 4 vols. London: Thomas Astley, 1745-47. Numerous works of value in it have been entered separately.

Auber, Peter. *An Analysis of the Constitution of the East-India Company.* London, 1826-28. The most thorough existing treatise upon the internal organization and constitution of the East India Company.

Auber, Peter. *China, an Outline of its Government, Law and Policy: and of the British and Foreign Embassies to and Intercourse with that Empire.* London: Parbury, Allen Co., 1834. A chronological narrative of English intercourse with China by the secretary of the Court of Directors. It is based upon personal knowledge, and the author had access to the documents. It is one of the two most complete connected accounts obtainable. Is generally accurate.

Ball, Samuel. *History of the Culture and Trade in Tea.* Canton, 1835.

Bantysh-Kamenskii, N. *Diplomaticheskoe sobraine diel mezhdu Bossiiskim i Kitaishim gosudarstvami s 1619 po 1792 god.* Kazan, 1882. A history of the diplomatic relations between China and Russia from 1619 to 1792 based on documents in the Russian archives.

Bau, Mingchien Joshua. *Foreign Relations of China.* New York: Fleming H. Revell Co., 1921. A valuable work by an American-trained Chinese.

Biographical Memoir of Sir Erasmus Gower. London: W. Woodward, 1800-10.

Bruce, John. *Annals of the Honorable East India Company, 1600-1708.* 3 vols. London: Cox, Son, and Baylist, 1810. The best obtainable account of the East India Company from 1600 to 1708. It is written by the keeper of the King's State Papers and Historiographer of the Company. He had access to all of the documents and used them extensively.

Cahen, Gaston. *Histoire des relations de la Russie avec la Chine sous Pierre le Grand, 1689-1730.* Paris: F. Alcan, 1912. An excellent and detailed study.

Cawston, George and Keane, A. H. *Chartered Companies, 1296-1858.* London: Edward Arnold, 1896. A valuable treatment of early chartered companies with a good chapter on the East India Company.

Chang, T'ien-tsê. *Sino-Portuguese Trade from 1514 to 1644.* Leiden: E. J. Brill, 1934. An excellent study based upon Chinese and Portuguese sources.

Chatterton, E. Keble. *The Old East Indiamen.* London, n.d. The best account of the early ships and shipping of the East India Company.

Chinas Handel. Stockholm: Beckman, 1848.

Churchill, Awnsham and John. *A Collection of Voyages and Travels.* 8 vols. London: Thomas Osborne, 1752.

Cordier, Henri. *Histoire générale de la Chine et des ses relations avec les pays étrangères.* 4 vols. Paris, 1920-21.

Corner, Julian. *History of China and India.* London: Dean and Co., 1846. An ordinary brief discussion of the history of China and India.

Davis, John Francis. *The Chinese: A General Description of the Empire of China and Its Inhabitants.* 2 vols. London: Charles Knight, 1836.

Davis, John Francis. *China: A General Description of That Empire and Its Inhabitants.* 2 vols. London: John Murray, 1857. Written by a one-time supercargo and one of the Superintendents of British Trade after the abolition of the Company's monopoly. He defends the Company, but his facts are generally reliable.

Dennett, Tyler. *Americans in Eastern Asia.* New York: Macmillan, 1922. The standard work on Chino-American relations.

Douglas, Robert K. *Europe and the Far East.* Cambridge: University Press, 1904. A valuable account of relations between the Far East and Europe with excellent chapters on the period covered in this work.

Dutt, Romesh. *The Economic History of India under Early English Rule, 1757-1837.* London: Kegan Paul, Trench, Trübner, 1906. An excellent discussion of the economic forces in India which had their reaction upon the Indo-China trade.

Du Halde, Jean Baptiste. *Description geographique, historique, chronologique, politique, et physique de l'empire de la Chine et de la Tartarie chinoise.* 4 vols. Paris: Lemercier, 1735. English translation, 1736. Probably the most famous work on China during the 18th century.

Dulles, Foster Rhea. *The Old China Trade.* Boston: Houghton Mifflin Co., 1930. An extremely well written and interesting account of American trade with China prior to the Opium War. Nothing particularly original about it.

Eames, James Bromley. *The English in China, 1600-1843.* London: Pitman and Son, 1909. Based upon a study of the East India Company's records. Is probably a more valuable and complete account of the East India Company's relations with China than is Auber.

Foster, Sir William. *England's Quest for Eastern Trade.* London: Black, 1933. Has one excellent chapter on the beginning of the China trade.

Grant, Robert. *A Sketch of the History of the East India Company, 1600-1773.* London, 1813.

Gundry, R. S. *China and Her Neighbors.* London: Chapman and Hall, 1893. Has an illuminating chapter on the relations between Tibet and India, but otherwise is only of ordinary interest.

Gutzlaff, Rev. Charles. *A Sketch of Chinese History, Ancient and Modern; a Retrospect of the Foreign Intercourse and Trade with China.* 2 vols. London: Smith, Elder Co., 1834. One of the best early histories of China by a German missionary. Based upon personal experience and documentary evidence. Referred to in the footnotes as Gutzlaff, *Chinese History.*

Gutzlaff, Rev. Charles. *China Opened, or a Display . . . of the Chinese Empire.* 2 vols. London: Smith, Elder Co., 1838. A valuable work by a German missionary, but requires checking in many details. Personal observation and documentary evidence are blended. Referred to in footnotes as Gutzlaff, *China Opened.*

Harris, John. *Navigantium atque Intinerantium Bibliotheca, or a Complete Collection of Voyages and Travels.* 2 vols. 2nd ed. London: T. Woodward, 1744-48.

Hsieh, Pao Chao. *The Government of China, 1644-1911.* Baltimore: John Hopkins Press, 1925. By far the best account of the government of China during the Manchu period. The author has used both the Chinese and foreign sources and secondary works.

Hudson, G. F. *Europe and China.* London: Edward Arnold and Co., 1931.

Hunter, Sir William Wilson. *History of British India.* 2 vols. London: Longmans, 1899. A very complete and interesting account of the rise and expansion of English trade and power in the East by a competent and thorough student. A standard work.

Ilbert, Sir Courtenay. *The Government of India.* London: Humphrey Milford, 1915. Perhaps the best historical account of the development of British rule and government in India. Good summary of early charters of the Company.

Jernigan, T. R. *China in Law and Commerce.* New York: Macmillan, 1905. A clear compilation from the best secondary and a number of original sources.

Kaye, John William. *The Administration of the East India Company; a History of Indian Progress.* London: Richard Bentley, 1853. A good discussion of the Company's rule in India showing its relationship to policies pursued in China.

Keeton, G. W. *The Development of Extraterritoriality in China.* 2 vols. London: Longmans, 1928. An excellent and reliable study.

Krishna, Bal. *Commercial Relations between India and England, 1601-1757.* London: George Routledge, Sons, 1924. Has a good account of the development of English trade with India, and has invaluable trade figures based upon authentic documents. Figures are scattered throughout the book and the appendix is filled with tables.

Latourette, Kenneth Scott. *The Chinese: Their History and Culture.* 2 vols. New York: Macmillan, 1934. The standard work on Chinese history and culture.

Latourette, Kenneth Scott. *History of Early Relations between the United States and China, 1784-1844.* New Haven: Yale University, 1917. The best account of early Sino-American relations. It is based upon an extensive study of American documentary materials.

Latourette, Kenneth Scott. *A History of Christian Missions in China.* New York: Macmillan, 1929. The very latest and most reliable single volume on missionaries in China. It is a carefully compiled and documented work.

Macpherson, David. *History of European Commerce with India.* London: Longmans, 1812. The best connected account of the early relations of all nations with China, India, and the Spice Islands. It is based upon valuable original sources and has many statistics. Referred to in footnotes as Macpherson, *India.*

Martin, R. Montgomery. *China, Political, Commercial, and Social.* 2 vols. London: James Madden, 1847. Martin was in a position to get at the records and he gives a great mass of valuable material, but it is tinged with a bias against China and opium, and many of his dates are wrong. The volumes are filled with inaccuracies.

Morse, H. B. "Provision of Funds for the East India Company's Trade at Canton during the Eighteenth Century." *Journal of the Royal Asiatic Society,* April, 1922, pp. 238ff.

Morse, H. B. "Currency in China." *Journal of the North China Branch of the Royal Asiatic Society,* 1908.

Morse, H. B. *Trade and Administration of China.* New York: Longmans, Green and Co., 1921.

Morse, H. B. *The Gilds of China.* New York: Longmans, 1909. The standard work on the gilds of China, with an especially worthwhile chapter upon the Canton-Co-hong.

Morse, H. B. *International Relations of the Chinese Empire.* 3 vols. London: Longmans, 1910-18. This is the standard work on the trade and foreign relations of China. It represents a carefully compiled mass of information, and is better for the 19th century than for earlier dates.

Muto, Chozo. "A Brief Survey of the History of Anglo-Japanese Relations," in *Kaikoku Bunkwa (Foreign Intercourse with Japan).* Tokyo: Asaki Publishing Co., 1929. In Japanese with many English notes.

Owen, David. *British Opium Policy in China and India.* New Haven: Yale University Press, 1934. Early chapters deal with the opium problem prior to 1800.

Parker, Edward Harper. *China Past and Present.* London: Chapman and Hall, 1903, and

Parker, Edward Harper. *China, her History, Diplomacy and Commerce.* London: John Murray, 1917. Two excellent works by an English professor of Chinese who lived a great many years in China. Many facts are packed into a small space.

Pauthier, G. *Histoire des rélations politiques de la Chine, aves les puissances occidentales depuis les temps les plus anciens jusqu'a nos jours.* Paris, 1859.

Pinkerton, John. *A General Collection . . . of Voyages and Travels.* 17 vols. London, 1811-14.

Pitkin, Timothy. *Statistical View of the Commerce of the United States.* New Haven: Durrie and Peck, 1835. Has excellent statistical tables showing American trade with China.

Pritchard, Earl H. *Anglo-Chinese Relations during the Seventeenth and Eighteenth Centuries.* Urbana: University of Illinois Press, 1929.

Pritchard, Earl H. "The Struggle for Control of the China Trade during the Eighteenth Century." *Pacific Historical Review,* III, (Sept. 1934), 280-95.

Raynal, L'Abbé Thomas Guillaume, *Histoire philosophique et politique des etablissements et du commerce des Européens dans les deux Indies.* 5 vols. Geneva: Jean-Leonard Pellet, 1780.

Reichwein, A. *China and Europe.* New York: Knopf, 1925. A study of intellectual and artistic contacts during the 18th century.

Rockhill, William Woodville. "Diplomatic Missions to the Court of Peking: the Kotow Question." *American Historical Review,* II (April and July, 1897), 427-42 and 627-43. Also published separately in London: Luzac and Co., 1905.

Robinson, F. P. *The Trade of the East India Company from 1700-1813.* Cambridge, 1912. A reliable account of the trade of the East India Company, with an especially good chapter on China.

Sargent, Arthur John. *Anglo-Chinese Commerce and Diplomacy.* Oxford, 1907. The best short connected account covering the whole of Anglo-Chinese relations. It has only a few chapters dealing with relations before 1840.

See, Chong-su. *Foreign Trade of China.* New York, 1919. A fairly good work for the 19th century relations, but has little material of value prior to that time.

Soothill, William Edward. *China and the West, a Sketch of Their Intercourse.* Oxford: University Press, 1925.

Soothill, William Edward. *China and England.* Oxford: University Press, 1928. Excellent summary work, enriched by the knowledge gained through long residence in China.

Winterbotham, William. *An Historical, Geographical, and Philosophical View of the Chinese Empire.* London: J. Ridgway, 1795. It includes a short and critical account of the Macartney Embassy.

Wissett, Robert. *A View of the . . . State of the Tea Trade in Europe.* [London, 1801.]

Woodward, William Harrison. *A Short History of the Expansion of the British Empire, 1500-1870.* Cambridge: University Press, 1899.

Williamson, James A. *A Short History of British Expansion.* New York: Macmillan, 1922. The last two books both contain sound, well-written chapters dealing with the expansion of England into the Far East.

Williams, S. Wells. *The Middle Kingdom.* 2 vols. New York: Scribners, 1883. For many years the standard analysis of Chinese culture. Referred to in footnotes as Williams, *Middle Kingdom.*

INDEX AND GLOSSARY

Italicized page numbers indicate definitions or especially important material. A brief description of the less well-known articles of trade has been added to this index to serve as a glossary. The abbreviation *E.I.C.* refers to the British East India Company and *Ch.* is used for Chinese.

ERRATA

Page 225, line 27. **For** seasan **read** seaman.

Page 260, last line and 261, line 5. **For** Maderia **read** Madeira.

Page 318. **For** Rio de Janerio **read** Rio de Janeiro.

Page 345, footnote 91. **Insert** *Tsung* **after** *Kao* **and for** *Ch'un* **read** *Shun.*

Page 426, line 36. Canton **should not be italicized.**